Preface to the Second Edition

A first edition of a book is always something of an experiment. We wrote *Managing Your Mind* on the basis of many years of helping people with the ups and downs, the stresses and strains, of life. We wanted to make available the ideas and skills that had helped the clients whom we saw. But would we be able to get across these ideas and skills in print? We have been very pleased to find that the methods that worked well face-to-face have also been helpful to readers of this book.

This second edition has had the benefit of feedback from around the world. Many readers have taken the trouble to write and tell us how the book has helped them. They have also asked us questions, and answering these has shown us where it could be improved. So we have made changes throughout this second edition to clarify those points that had not been so well expressed. Most importantly we have added five completely new chapters. These chapters are *Anger in Relationships, Sexuality and Intimate Relationships*, and the three chapters that make up the new section on traumatic experience: *Loss and Bereavement, Dealing with the Past*, and *Recent Traumatic Events and Their Aftermath*.

One of the artificial divisions of modern life is that between work and personal time. It is widely held that there is a set of skills that we need for the one and a quite different set that we need for the other. But in *Managing Your Mind* we show that this is not true. The skills of problem solving, for example, are of great value in our personal lives, and overcoming stress and anxiety is a key skill in our work. Being fair to yourself and to others helps both personal and work relationships. Low mood is a major cause of unhappiness and also reduces effectiveness at work. In *Managing Your Mind* we explain how you can make use of effective strategies, for example giving yourself rewards (Chapter 7), or using the methods of cognitive therapy (Chapter 9). We also describe simple techniques, for example "Distant Elephants" (p. 40), or "Swatting the NATs" (p. 303).

We would like to acknowledge, with thanks, many people who have made the writing of this book possible. First and foremost are all those people whom we have seen with difficulties in their lives and who have taught us what methods and ideas they have found helpful. Comments made by some of them on the draft material for this second edition have helped us to make some complex ideas, such as those for dealing with past distressing experiences, readily usable. Indeed, reactions to individual chapters from our friends, relatives and colleagues have been most important. Then there are readers of the first edition who have given us such valuable feedback. We thank our teachers and colleagues from whom we have learned techniques and refined our use of them. We have also been helped by the writers of other books, some of which we have referenced in the section on Further Reading. It is the fact that we have found books so helpful, both for ourselves and for helping others, that gave us the impetus to write this book in the first place.

We thank the many colleagues who helped us develop our own methods and thoughts including Julie Chalmers, Nigel Eastman, Chris Fairburn, Melanie Fennell, Maria Gilbert, Helen Kennerley, Joan Kirk, Deborah Lee, Martina Mueller, Catherine Oppenheimer, John Sadler, and Alan Stein, and members of the Oxford Cognitive Therapy Centre.

We thank our agent, Caroline Dawnay at Peters Fraser and Dunlop, and all those who have given such support and encouragement at our publishers, Oxford University Press, both in Oxford and New York. These include Joan Bossert, Kate Martin, Angela Butterworth, Martin Baum, Alison Bowker, Kate Farquhar-Thomson, Ruth Mannes, and Marion Osmun. We would also like to thank Marie-Anne Martin for her witty and imaginative index.

Without the continual support and encouragement of our families, in particular from Christopher Butler and Sally Hope, we could never have written this book, nor found the time and energy needed for updating and revising it for this second edition.

This guide is intended to be practical. We hope that it achieves its aim of making available to the reader a wide variety of strategies and techniques for managing the mind.

Oxford, England   G.B.
September 2006   T.H.

Contents

Preface   v

INTRODUCTION   1
1. What to Expect from This Guide   3
2. The Scientific Background   8

PART ONE   TWO PRINCIPLES UNDERLYING MENTAL FITNESS   13

3. Valuing Yourself   15
4. Recognizing That You Can Change   20

PART TWO   THE SEVEN BASIC SKILLS   29

5. Managing Yourself and Your Time   31
6. Facing the Problem   45
7. Treating Yourself Right   52
8. Problem-Solving: A Strategy for Change   61
9. Keeping Things in Perspective: Help from Cognitive Therapy   71
10. Building Self-Confidence and Self-Esteem   89
11. Learning How to Relax   104

PART THREE   HOW TO IMPROVE YOUR RELATIONSHIPS   117

12. The Importance of Relationships   119
13. The First Key to Good Relationships:
Be Fair to Yourself and to Others   127
14. The Second Key to Good Relationships:
Recognizing Voices from the Past   144
15. The Third Key to Good Relationships:
Relationships as Systems   158

16. Anger in Relationships   170
17. Sexuality and Intimate Relationships   190

PART FOUR   THE TWIN ENEMIES OF GOOD MOOD   215

Anxiety
18. Getting the Better of Anxiety and Worry,
     or Defeating the Alarmist   217
19. Overcoming Fears and Phobias   235
20. Stress: How to Live with the Right Amount of It   254
21. Dealing with Panic: Controlling the Alarm System   270

Depression
22. Depression—The Common Cold of the Mind   283
23. Digging Yourself Out of Depression   294
24. How to Become Less Vulnerable to Depression   315

PART FIVE   TRAUMATIC EXPERIENCE   323

25. Loss and Bereavement   325
26. Dealing with the Past   342
27. Recent Traumatic Events and Their Aftermath   367

PART SIX   MIND AND BODY   387

28. Breaking Habits and Stopping Smoking   389
29. Averting Problems with Alcohol   406
30. Overcoming Sleep Problems   423
31. Good Eating Habits   434

PART SEVEN   THE WORKING MIND   447

32. The Fundamentals of Effective Study   449
33. Key Study Skills: Reading, Taking Notes,
     and Using the Material   457
34. How to Improve Your Memory: Part 1: The Palest Ink
     and Other External Memory Aids   470
35. How to Improve Your Memory: Part 2: Internal
     Memory Aids   477
36. Making Decisions   492
37. Thinking Straight   502

Notes   513

Further Reading   515

Index   519

INTRODUCTION

1

What to Expect from This Guide

"The past is a foreign country; they do things differently there."[1] The future, too, can be a different country. This book is both an invitation and a guide. It is an invitation to you to find more enjoyment in your life, and it is a guide for achieving such enjoyment. It is based on our accumulated forty years' experience of helping people through times of difficulty, and it is based on modern scientific research.

You can expect to find, in this guide, practical ways of improving many aspects of your life: your life as it affects your relationships, your mood, your health, and your work. These practical ways have been developed both through helping people with the stresses and strains of life and through helping to increase the effectiveness of managers we have worked with.

You can expect to find many ideas on how to improve your life by developing skills, understanding, and strategies to suit your circumstances and inclinations. Using this guide will help you to develop your mind and improve your psychological fitness. Specific ideas are presented in a step-by-step manner. Psychological skills, skills of the mind, just like physical skills, are usually best learned by adopting a clear step-by-step approach. You would expect a fitness book to give some precise guidelines about specific exercises. You would expect a cookbook to give precise recipes so that you know what you should be doing at each stage. This book is intended to be used in just the same way to make practical improvements in your day-to-day life.

Psychology and Management: The Two Bookshelves

Look around your local bookstore. On one shelf there are books on psychology—for example, "How to treat your anxiety." On another there are books on management skills—for example, "Effective time management." These two types of book seem to inhabit different worlds. The first is the world of your personal life, your feelings, and your home. The second is the world of work: the world of action and the office. We believe that these two worlds are not so different and that we need to integrate feelings and action, work and play. The skills and attitudes which help you to be more effective in your work also help you to find fulfillment in your personal life. The attitudes and skills which help in personal life are relevant to improving your effectiveness in your work.

It is time that we gave up the habits which separate feelings and action, home and work. They originate in old-fashioned and unhelpful stereotypes. It is time for the techniques of psychology and of management to be integrated so that we can develop our own strategies for personal growth. One purpose of this book is to bring about such an integration.

A Fitness Guide to the Mind

The relationship of physical fitness to health is now well known. Simple measures can improve physical health: for example, exercise and sensible diet. We no longer think about physical health only when we are ill; but do things regularly, as a matter of course, which will help us to keep fit and well. Such a fitness approach is also relevant to the mind. There are specific ways of improving mental as well as physical health, of stretching and strengthening the mind as well as the body, which will enable us to lead a fulfilling life and help to prevent us from becoming overwhelmed by the stresses and strains which none of us can entirely avoid. A second purpose, therefore, of this book is to provide you with specific methods and techniques needed for keeping the whole person, not just the body, in good working order.

The Inner Game of Life

How one plays a sport depends on the mind as much as on the body. Indeed, it is first and foremost the mind that is important. For the mind is the seat of motivation: it determines how well and usefully and frequently we practice, and it determines whether we want to do it, and whether we enjoy playing the game. It is also the mind that determines whether, like true champions, we rise to the challenge at key moments, or let ourselves down on the points that really matter. In short, even with physical activities, inner factors—mental factors—are of critical importance.

This book could be called the *inner game of life*. Whether you are concerned about managing your work or your personal life or your leisure, success and satisfaction will depend on your inner thoughts. Your inner thoughts will help to determine your outer life (just as the inner game of tennis determines how much and how well you practice); and your inner life will affect how you react to your experiences (just as the inner game determines whether you enjoy the tennis).

This book will help you with this "inner game" so that you can increase both enjoyment in life and success—however *you* would like to measure success. And this last point is important. This book is not designed to impose our way of living on you. How you want to live is up to you. What we want to show you is how you can develop your inner skills so that you can live life in the way that you wish.

Our Clinical Experience

The scientific assessment and development of ways of helping people have been of enormous importance both in our own work as therapists and researchers, and in selecting the techniques for this guide. But science does not have all the answers, and this book is the result of our extensive clinical experience. We believe that techniques and ideas that are useful come from a range of sources, as we have outlined in the next chapter on the *scientific background of the techniques presented here*. In our own work we make use of and synthesize this range in order to help each particular person as best we can.

In writing this book we have drawn extensively on our own experience. This experience has guided us in the choice of techniques, and we have tried to explain these using the methods that our clients have found helpful. We have thought for a long time that many of these techniques and ideas would be useful to everyone, because they can help in the process of keeping mentally fit; knowing about them will make it easier to take action quickly when you need to. Delay may perpetuate or worsen all sorts of difficulties. Another purpose of this book is, therefore, to make available to all the ideas and techniques which have been helpful to many, many others.

How to Use This Guide

This book is a practical guide to keeping fit—in your mind as opposed to your body. Its purpose is to help you to find more enjoyment in your life. For most of us, joy in life is at times diminished by too much worry, by periods of depression, or by other disturbing moods. The demands of modern life keep up a pressure which constantly threatens our psychological well-being. Keeping psychologically fit will help you to withstand these demands and will give you the flexibility and stamina to make the most of yourself.

This book is a guide for you to use in whatever ways you find helpful. We recommend that you read Parts One and Two first. Select from Parts Three, Four, Five, Six, and Seven as appropriate, reading them all if this is the way you like to read or browsing through them if you prefer.

- *Part One* explains the two principles on which our ideas are based.
- *Part Two* describes, in practical terms, the seven basic strategies, or skills, that will enable you to take positive control of your life.
- *Part Three* focuses on ways of developing fulfilling relationships.
- *Part Four* provides specific and practical guidance about ways of overcoming anxiety, depression, and loss which may otherwise interfere with pleasure and confidence.
- *Part Five* explains how to set in motion the process of recovery following distressing and traumatic experiences.
- *Part Six* gives guidelines on looking after aspects of the body that most closely relate to the mind.
- *Part Seven* is concerned with skills that will help you to develop your potential in an effective and creative way.

This guide is to be kept close at hand. To benefit most, you will want to refer to it again and again. Changes take time and persistence. At first, you will easily revert to old habits: to old ways of thinking, feeling, and behaving. As this happens, reread the relevant passages. Bear the following three points in mind:

1. Think of this book as a buffet table, and select those dishes which attract you. We present many ideas—those which we have found are helpful to the people we have worked with. Not all ideas are helpful for everyone. Pick and choose those which are relevant to you.

2. Learn the techniques which we describe so that you can apply them to your particular situation. Throughout the book we provide examples to show how the ideas presented can be used in real and specific situations. In some of these examples you will recognize a part of yourself; others will seem quite foreign to you. If the example does not seem to fit, do not dismiss the general method. For instance, in Chapter 8 we describe the technique of problem-solving using a specific example. The particular solutions this person used may not work for you; but it is the technique of problem-solving which is important and which you should think about using to solve your problems.

3. Do not dismiss ideas because they seem like common sense. Good psychology, once you know it, often seems like common sense, but it rarely seemed that way before you knew it. Common sense involves too many contradictions to always be right. Besides, in moments of uncertainty, when doubts set in, in the heat of the moment or in the depths of despair, most of us lose sight of common sense. It often deserts us in the hour of need. The ideas and techniques presented in this book have been chosen because they are helpful and effective when put to use. One value of this book is that it can nudge you into applying a technique you already know about but are not making proper use of. You may "know" the "Distant Elephants" rule (p. 40). It may be common sense, or you may have learned it before, perhaps in a management course. But you may not be using it. You may still be saying "yes" to things because they are so far in the future that you fail to work out just how large a commitment they will be. Think of this as a workbook that will help you to learn new techniques, and to apply techniques you already know but do not use.

The future is an exciting country. You need not be held back by the past. If this book can help you along the road, then it will have achieved its purpose.

2

The Scientific Background

The methods and techniques we describe in this book are derived from research in many different branches of psychology. They are derived both from basic research itself and from the application of basic research to helping people in practical ways. We also draw on scientific knowledge about physiology and physical medicine, to relate what is known about the mind to what is known about the body.

Experimental Research in Psychology

Fundamental research in psychology tells us an enormous amount about how the mind works. The painstaking, experimental work of psychologists, which started just over 100 years ago, has mapped out some of the basic processes involved in learning, remembering, and thinking. It has revealed the part we ourselves play in constructing our perception and understanding of the world around us. It has helped to explain how we develop, and to unravel the stages that we go through on the road from childhood to old age. It has thrown light on the relationships between our thoughts, feelings, actions, and sensations, and how these interact with the outside world: with the context within which we find ourselves. Its findings help us to understand more about the relationship between the mind and the body, about what motivates us and how we acquire new skills.

Psychologists have, through their scientific work, contributed to our knowledge about which aspects of ourselves we can change and which are fixed, and their work has revealed much about the processes of personal change. Applications of psychology, therefore, help us to control these processes, to use them to our advantage, and to recognize their limitations, in the same way as applications of physiology help us to keep our bodies in good shape without overstraining them. You do not have to be a physiologist to keep physically fit. Nor, nowadays, do you have to be a psychologist to make use of the science of psychology, even though the work of experimental psychologists is not over: many questions remain unanswered and new puzzles constantly emerge.

Applications of Psychological Science to Therapy

Over the last fifty years, therapists have developed new and effective ways of helping people with problems in living, most of which are relatively brief forms of psychotherapy. Following the decades after Freud, psychoanalysis was the main form of psychological treatment, but it typically required a long and intensive course of therapy, often extending over several years. In this book we focus predominantly on recent treatment methods, and we give most weight to those that have been scientifically evaluated and are based on scientific findings.

Psychodynamic therapies, including psychoanalysis, are based on extensive and sophisticated theories about human development, from infancy onward. The infant's development is understood in the context of relationships with others. Psychodynamic therapists have developed methods for increasing awareness of their own and of other people's feelings, in order to use the therapeutic relationship to help people to continue to develop. The theories underpinning these therapies were developed while experimental psychology was young, and they have not been amenable to scientific confirmation. Nor has it been easy to assess the effectiveness of the therapies derived from them, both because they take so long and because their goals are so complex. They have, however, provided therapists with a rich and fruitful source of ideas about emotional development and about relationships. Debates about the extent to which early patterns of relationships determine later functioning continue, but now have to be understood in the context of the proven effectiveness of other forms of psychotherapy.

BEHAVIORAL THERAPIES

The theoretical background to behavior therapy, which developed in striking contrast to psychoanalysis, comes from experimental psychologists' work on learning. It is based on what is called learning theory, which now recognizes that there are many ways in which learning takes place. The first type of learning found to have major implications for therapy was classical conditioning, first explored by Pavlov.

Discovering the rules of the different types of learning has led to the development of behavior therapies, such as exposure treatment for phobias. To take phobias as an example, learning theory suggests that a person's phobia can be overcome by breaking the association between the feeling of anxiety and situations that are basically harmless, such as seeing a spider or going to a supermarket. Research showed that an efficient way to do this is in step-by-step stages, practicing frequently and regularly. A person who is afraid of heights, for example, might start by walking up a stairway and looking down from progressively higher points. The next step might be to look down from a third floor window; then a fourth floor window; and so on. Depending on the severity of the phobia, it might take days or even weeks to progress from stage to stage. This step-by-step method is simple but effective.

Behavioral therapies originated in learning theory but have since developed beyond these beginnings and now employ a large number of methods for dealing with a wide variety of conditions. What they have in common is a focus on changing behavior in very specific ways. Behavioral methods can be used, for example, to help change eating, smoking, or drinking habits, to build self-confidence, and to improve time management and personal organization. Changing behavior can lead to changes in thoughts, feelings, and sensations, and also to changes in relationships. People who have recovered from a phobia are likely to *feel* more confident, to *think* better of themselves, to suffer less from the *sensations* of anxiety, and to *relate* more easily to others.

One of the most important contributions of behavior therapies is their focused attention on effectiveness and practicality. This is because they are based on specific, clear-cut, and observable changes. A therapy with goals can be tested to see if it works, and moreover, the therapy can be improved. Each of the improvements can then be tested to discover which precise methods are the most effective. In this way better and better therapies have been developed. This scientific evaluation of therapies has also revealed more about the processes involved in change, and has led to the recognition that changing behavior is only one way of initiating the process of change.

COGNITIVE THERAPY

Cognitive therapy developed partly as a reaction against the exclusive focus which behavior therapy places on behavior, and partly as a reaction to the unscientific aspects of psychoanalysis. It is based on the recognition that thoughts, feelings, and behavior are closely related. If you *think* something is going to go wrong, you will *feel* anxious and your behavior will be designed to protect yourself, for example by avoiding a situation that causes stress. If you *think* everything will go fine, you will *feel* more confident and you will *behave* in ways that express that confidence. By focusing on our patterns of thinking and on our beliefs, cognitive therapists have found many methods for helping us to change both our feelings and our behavior.

Cognitive therapy was first tried and tested as a treatment for depression. It has since proved to be effective in helping with many other problems, such as anxiety, panic, disturbed eating patterns, and difficulties in relationships. Cognitive therapy shares with behavior therapy the advantages of being a clearly articulated therapy, and this has meant that it has been, and is still being extensively and rigorously studied and improved.

The New Wave of Cognitive Therapies

Over the last few years there have been exciting developments in psychotherapy, with the integration of a variety of new ideas with cognitive therapy. Some of these ideas have been taken from the East—such as the methods of mindfulness meditation and a new focus on compassion both for oneself and for others. There has also been an increasing research interest in what has become known as "positive psychology." This developed as a reaction to the much greater attention given by rearchers to "negative" emotions and feelings, such as depression and anxiety, compared with "positive" emotions, such as happiness. Some of the most promising new developments in finding ways to help people to feel better and to flourish involve combining the strengths from a range of different sources. The situation is rather like "fusion cooking," in which a wide range of flavors and techniques, taken from all over the world, are combined in various ways. As with fusion cooking the results are sometimes stunning and sometimes disappointing. Research and increasing experience with this new wave of psychotherapeutic approaches is gradually helping to clarify what is effective and what is not.

THERAPIES FOCUSING ON RELATIONSHIPS

Relationships play a key part in our lives and contribute much to the ways in which we understand and feel about ourselves. They provide one of the main contexts for the things that we think, feel, and do. Many types of therapy focus on relationships, but unfortunately not many of them have been tested and evaluated. *Interpersonal therapy* has been evaluated and has proved to be effective, not only in improving relationships, but in overcoming depression and disturbed eating habits.

Applications of Psychological Science in Management

Many psychological findings are of particular value in the world of work, of action, and of management and have been put to practical daily use in a large number of settings. Most of these findings concern ways of using the mind effectively. Applying management techniques can help you to organize both your personal and business lives, make the best use of your time, communicate well, negotiate change, and make decisions. Research into logical thinking and into memory systems has been especially productive and applied most creatively in the field of management, but these skills are also of general use in managing ourselves and our lives outside work.

Research in Physiology and Physical Medicine

Mind and body interact. Perhaps, last night, you lay awake worrying. You think it is the worries which kept you awake; but it may have been the coffee you had after supper. In reducing alcohol intake you need to know about some facts of physiology in order to make use of the best strategies. There are also times when depression is helped by drugs. In this book we draw on the results of medical, as well as psychological, research, when relevant.

PART ONE

TWO PRINCIPLES UNDERLYING MENTAL FITNESS

Two principles guide the development of mental fitness. Success, however you wish to define success, can be achieved if you understand how to make use of these principles. The first involves *valuing yourself*. When this is difficult to do many aspects of life suffer. For example, it becomes hard to manage yourself and your problems, your relationships seem less satisfactory, you may feel anxious or depressed or sleep badly or eat too much, or you may find it hard to concentrate and make decisions. This book provides many strategies for learning to value yourself more.

The second principle involves *recognizing that you can change*. The process of change is, in fact, inevitable. Like time, it cannot be stopped. The ideas in this book are designed to help you to direct or control the way that you change, and to learn how to react differently to changes beyond your control. The various ways in which each of us reacts to change have advantages and disadvantages. Learning new ways broadens our repertoire and gives us more options. It can also help us when we feel stuck. These two principles together provide the basis for mental fitness.

3

Valuing Yourself

In that confident decade of the 1950s, Richard Hamilton titled one of his paintings: *Just what is it that makes today's homes so different, so appealing?* Sometimes we look around and everyone else seems to radiate the sense of success captured by Hamilton's title. We alone are haunted by the feeling that we are no good, by a sense of low self-worth. But we are wrong. Many of those who appear so confident from the outside are beset with doubts from within, just as most of us as we grow older still feel much younger than our looks reveal.

Why do so many of us believe we are of such little value—the belief that causes more misery than all others put together?

The Chef's Tale

Marc was a chef. He ran a successful restaurant but had one ambition: that he and his restaurant should be recommended in the *Good Food Guide.* He believed that he was not good enough for even a passing mention. Like so many people, he was riddled with self-doubt. Then, one day, the great honor came, and his excellence was recognized with a wonderful review. But he did not feel happy. He had wanted this honor all his working life and now when he attained it he felt wretched and miserable.

Why? Because, instead of valuing himself more as a result of this achievement, he valued the opinion of the *Good Food Guide* less. His reasoning went something like this: there can't be much to being in the *Good Food Guide* if they include the likes of me.

- **If you do not value yourself independently of your achievements, you will not value your achievements.**

We remain so vulnerable to losing the sense of our own worth because we tend to value ourselves by our achievements. The lesson of *The Chef's Tale* is a profound one. Finding within yourself a sense of value that does not depend on your achievements will make you more resistant to crippling self-doubts.

Unconditional Positive Regard

This inner sense of value can perhaps be best explained by using the analogy of parental love. The child may do things of which the parent strongly disapproves; the parent may not even like the child at times, but the love remains—whatever the child does. Carl Rogers called this sense of love *"unconditional positive regard."* The positive regard is unconditional in the sense that your personal, unique value does not depend on your origins or on your talents any more than it depends on what you do. It cannot be lost by doing something "bad" any more than it can be gained by doing something "good." You do not have to strive in any way to deserve it, and you cannot forfeit it by any of your actions. Losing sight of it is painful, while keeping it clearly in mind provides you with a sure foundation. It is helpful to try and hold onto this attitude of unconditional positive regard toward ourselves. It is not selfish, nor egoistic to do so. On the contrary, it provides the foundation for being generous and open with others. Feelings of guilt and a constant need for reassurance from others lead to egoism and selfishness—and to unhappiness.

This idea that each of us has an intrinsic value is one that forms a part of many religions. "Each of us is equal in the eyes of God" encompasses not only our intrinsic value but the idea, too, that at this fundamental level we all have the same value. The democratic principle—that each of us has one, and only one, vote—is the political embodiment of this idea; and we are all susceptible to the same feelings—of love, grief, fear, doubt, and so on.

Why Is It Important to Value Yourself?

Valuing yourself helps you to build your life on a secure foundation. This book is a guide to helping you become your own helper, adviser, friend, and therapist. You will gain most from it if you treat yourself with respect, as someone who has intrinsic value. Valuing yourself is different from liking yourself. We may respect, and even admire, someone whom we do not like. And we may accept that someone whom we do not like has intrinsic worth. Similarly, although it helps if you like yourself, it is not necessary to do so, and certainly you do not need to approve of all your actions. But you do need to value yourself, for unless you do, you will be taking away with one hand what you are giving yourself with the other. You will only undermine yourself, and dissipate your strength, if you allow yourself to believe that you are worthless or that your actions are pointless.

No Double Standards

If you tend to undervalue yourself, you are almost certainly applying double standards: underrating yourself just because you are you and not someone else. If you do value yourself less than you value other people, ask yourself "Why?" Is this fair? If you look at yourself from outside, as if you were someone else examining you as you are now, would you think differently? Are you downgrading your view of yourself just because it is you? Do you have one standard for others and a higher standard for yourself? If you do apply these double standards, you are constantly undermining yourself. It is like trying to build a house on top of a swamp. The house will not last, and its foundations will be constantly eroded.

Three Common Reasons for Undervaluing Yourself

1 I AM NOT A SAINT

Think of someone whom you admire because of how much that person has done to help other people. Do you use that person's goodness as a reason to berate yourself? Do you say: "I am not valuable because I have not helped people in the way that so-and-so has helped people. Now *there* is someone who really is valuable, unlike me."

We reply: "What this other person has done is to help people. That can only be valuable because the people she or he has helped are of value. Why do we admire such a person? Our admiration depends on our valuing the human beings whom this person has helped. It is only in the belief that each of us is of value that we can argue that anyone is of value.

2 IT WOULD BE ARROGANT

Arrogance is valuing yourself, your own opinions, and character *more* than other people. It is being unfair to others. If you undervalue yourself, you are making exactly the same error as the arrogant person, except in reverse. You are not being fair to yourself. Many an apparently arrogant person is in fact driven to behave in an arrogant fashion because of a deep-seated lack of self-confidence. Being fair to yourself, valuing yourself, is not arrogant, and it will help to protect you from behaving in an arrogant fashion.

3 I HAVE BEEN BAD

Sometimes we undervalue ourselves not because we are disappointed in our achievements, but because we are disappointed in ourselves, in our moral character. We have not come up to our personal standards of behavior, and we whip ourselves for this mercilessly. We set standards for our children and tell them off when they fail to meet some of these standards because we love them. But it is in the nature of standards that they cannot be lived up to all the time: if they could, they would perhaps be too undemanding. Failing to meet a standard is a reason for valuing yourself, for recognizing that it is worth trying to make changes and starting to make them; it is not a reason for ceasing to value yourself.

Where Do You Go from Here?

You already have the basis on which to value yourself; otherwise, you would not be reading this book. But you can also gain from building on that basis and from recognizing that you are of equal value with others. A sense of low self-worth will eat away at your life and at your enjoyment of life. This book will help you to put the principle of valuing yourself into effect. It will show you ways in which you can increase your effectiveness in achieving your personal goals, and ways in which to gain control over your moods. In Part 2 we explain many of the basic skills you will need, and Chapter 10 deals specifically with self-esteem. But before we tackle the skills, we will turn to the second principle on which to build: recognizing that you can change.

Chapter Summary

Valuing yourself will help you to build your life on a secure foundation: this book provides many practical ways to help you increase your sense of self-worth.

4

Recognizing That You Can Change

You have already embarked on an adventure. You are making a journey that has not yet ended, and peer as you will into the darkness you cannot discern what lies ahead. You did not choose to set out on this journey. You did not choose when to begin, or where, nor who some of your companions would be, nor the circumstances that surround your journey, nor the climate that alternately helps you to flourish or stunts your growth. It all happened without anyone consulting you—and indeed before you were able to make any sense or use of being consulted anyway.

The question is not whether to change or not; change is a part of all journeys. The question is whether the processes of change can be harnessed and mobilized to work for you rather than against you. Working with, rather than against, the inevitable process of change is easier if you know more about the way the mind works. This book will show you how you can use this knowledge to direct the ways you want to change. It draws on our knowledge of research, on our clinical experience, and on our understanding of our own culture and education. It is not that we can tell you how to change. That is something you will continue to decide for yourself. We do not know all the answers, but we can provide useful guidelines that, in your hands, can be used to recondition, strengthen, and update the rudder by which you steer. We believe that knowledge will give you the power to change in the ways that are right for you. As clinicians, engaged inevitably in the struggles and difficulties of others, we know this power is limited but is most effectively used when it is most clearly understood. Greater understanding, then, is what we are aiming for, so that greater confidence and control may replace feelings of helplessness in the face of the adventure on which we are all embarked.

The Climate and the Terrain

A guidebook to a new place is designed to provide information so that the reader can make choices. It starts with a summary of geology and geography, history, sociology and economics, and goes on to describe particular places to visit and how to visit them: how to travel, where to stay, whom you will meet, and what you might eat—if you know how to ask for it. It is designed to help you make your visit enjoyable, and it assumes your pleasure is determined both by external factors such as the scenery, the weather, people and their doings, as well as by internal factors such as your interests (in history, good food, or sport), your need for rest or excitement, your language skills, your sense of humor, and your stamina and adaptability when plans are frustrated. However, this guidebook, unlike others, will help you to link up internal and external factors, both of which influence how much you enjoy the journey. A guidebook can only be an approximate tool because both internal and external factors change as the journey, inevitably, continues. Your constant movement provides you with an ever-changing perspective, so it is wrong to assume that things are static, that we are stuck and cannot change. We are changing all the time as we encounter new challenges, new information, and new people. This book will help you make positive use of these changes.

INTERNAL FORCES FOR CHANGE

The mind as well as the body grows older daily, sweeping us along in the path of an inevitable process of change. There is some order in this change. As the dependence of childhood decreases, the turbulence of adolescence takes its place. Together with ever-increasing competence and independence, there comes the need to define an identity and to find one's way in the world. The middle years are often described as if they were static, as if once you had settled on a certain pattern of occupation and family and sexual relationships, you would stop changing. But knowing more about who you are and what you can do does not stop the process of change.

At times, you will feel on top of the world; at other times, out of your depth. You may alternate between being in the swim of things and being in a calm backwater. One day you may reach a peak, and the next plunge into the slough of despond. You may know that every cloud has a silver lining, and be able to look optimistically ahead, or you may lose sight of the light at the end of the tunnel. You may confidently stand your ground in stormy weather or nervously keep a wary eye out for thunder clouds looming on the horizon. The language we use to describe life's patterns and changes shows how naturally we think in terms of a journey through differing terrains, subject to varying climates.

EXTERNAL FORCES FOR CHANGE

The external world that provides the specific context for each of our lives is also constantly changing. We may play a part in influencing some of these changes, but many are beyond our control. We can all too easily come to think we are powerless: that, as there is little we can do about the external factors themselves, there is also little we can do about our reactions to them. This is a mistake. Changing our reactions to external events is one of the most effective ways we can change our experience of life.

Five Caricatures

We have written this book because we believe that change is possible. But, sometimes, all of us feel stuck in the situations we find ourselves in, not knowing how to bring about the changes we want. If that is how you feel, this book will help you find ways to move forward—it will help you to get unstuck.

You may, on the contrary, feel full of energy, full of the power to change and develop, but uncertain of the direction to take. Again, we hope that this guide will help by enabling you to find a path that leads you onward.

Different people respond differently to pressures for change. Here are five caricatures—you might recognize elements of yourself in one or more of these. They illustrate two points. First, most people learn to cope with change by developing a particular style of response. Second, each style has both advantages and disadvantages.

1 THE SAGE

The sage is the seeker after knowledge: the person who reads all about it.

Many people who use computers only use a small percentage of the options open to them. When learning to use a new machine they quickly master the basic skills, and then they go straight to work. They put the skills into practice, usually pleased and impressed with the speed at which they can do things like sending circulars to their clients, or invitations to their friends, and then they cease to learn about other features of their computer. The sage, on the other hand, knows that the more you know, the more options you have. Sages make full use of their computers, but the down side of this is that they may waste time learning about functions they do not need.

Sarah discovered the advantages of becoming a "sage." She had recently been assigned *Hamlet* at school, but when she started reading the play, she found the language hard to understand and she became bored. Her parents took her to a local performance of the play. This helped her to understand more about what was happening, and she started to enjoy it. She read it again when she had to write an essay, and then the class went through the play scene by scene, analyzing the language, the construction of the play, and the development of the characters. They had discussions about whether Hamlet was depressed and about his relationships with women: his mother and Ophelia. They found themselves talking about issues such as whether revenge is ever justified, about the meaning of forgiveness, and about what sorts of things might drive people mad. Sarah felt that a new world was for her beginning. A book that had been closed was gradually opening. The more she learned, the more she thought she understood—both about Shakespeare's play and about people and their feelings for each other. She began to find knowledge in unexpected places—knowledge that helped her to change.

2 THE TRAVELER

Travelers extend the journey and behave as if there is a purpose in the journey. They assume that because we are constantly on the move, we must be going somewhere, as if perfection, or nirvana, or the end of the rainbow could someday be reached. The quest goes on because no stopping place ever satisfies them for long. Travelers continue to search for the golden fleece, overcoming mountainous obstacles as they go, constantly hoping that they will find a resting place or that the grass will be greener on the other side of the fence.

Some sports enthusiasts show this degree of dedication, striving constantly to improve on their last performance, treating each new record or personal best as the next hurdle to jump. Provided they do not go overboard, and still enjoy the sport, they may indeed reach unexpected heights. Other people may think of their most intimate relationships in this way, as if the knight in shining armor or the fairy-tale princess is still waiting to be found, if only they keep on searching. They believe that the ideal person will be instantly recognizable and immediately responsive, and that when the knot has been tied the relationship will continue happily ever after. No wonder the quest continues.

Many of the changes that form part of our experience are cyclical. We get hungry, search for food, eat until we are satisfied, and then forget about food until we are hungry again. Or we look for a challenge, choose a mountain to climb, struggle to the top, and then start looking for the next challenge. We might become curious, focus on a particular puzzle or problem, wrestle with it until it is solved, and then our curiosity reemerges and we seek another puzzle. The process is never static, and the cycle may complete itself without any help from us. Our hunger, striving, or curiosity reemerges seemingly of its own accord and keeps us traveling onward.

David, to the outside, appeared a successful academic. He had progressed smoothly from doctoral student, to lecturer, to associate professor, and now to full professor. Ten years ago this would have been the peak of his ambition, for which he had strived hard, putting his career before personal relationships. But even now, as full professor, he could not enjoy his success: he thought only of being elected president by his professional association. His continual striving helped him achieve, but not enjoy his achievements.

3 THE DRIFTER

Drifters retire from centerstage, give up the struggle, and allow themselves to be carried wherever the current takes them. They bend to the inevitable and "go with the flow." They can be made to sound either weak or strong depending on how they are described, and on how their actions and decisions are viewed within their social contexts.

Tracy tried for four years to combine her work as a dental hygienist with caring for her elderly mother who suffered from Alzheimer's disease. Eventually something had to give, and she decided to quit her job. She devoted her energies to looking after her mother and hoped that in time she would take up her career again. Meanwhile, she would focus on keeping up contacts with friends. But many of Tracy's friends thought she had given up and submitted to pressure against her better judgment. Tracy herself, however, accepted that for a while the direction of her life would be determined by someone else's circumstances.

4 THE OSTRICH

The ostrich has two characteristics: it hides its head in the sand and it has a powerful kick. Refusing to accept the inevitability of change can lead to both of these reactions.

At some level, Christopher feared that his relationship with Lisa was over. He hardly dared to think about it, but the signs were there. It scared him when he noticed how little she had to say to him and how often she was busy at times when they might have been doing things together. He behaved as if nothing was wrong, carried on as normal, and continued to make plans for the summer vacation they had talked about earlier. Hiding his head in the sand might have helped Christopher to cope with the hiccup in their relationship, but perhaps he failed to read the writing on the wall.

Or take the example of Barbara, a laboratory technician. Barbara was accused by her boss of inefficiency, and she was furious. From her point of view she had been offered inadequate training. She had been left to her own devices to learn a set of complex procedures, and if she made mistakes, the fault lay more with her line manager than with her. She knew she did not have all the skills she needed, but thought that it was her boss's responsibility to help her acquire them. Barbara left the tasks she could not manage to others and was the only person in a busy office who regularly finished her work before the end of the day. From her point of view, this was efficiency. From her boss's point of view it was a failure to show the initiative needed to acquire new skills. She argued forcibly for what she wanted. She explained why she felt the accusations against her were false. Her boss was not convinced and warned her that unless she made the effort to learn from her more skilled colleagues, she would be fired. He gave her a month in which to change.

5 THE CONDUCTOR OF THE ORCHESTRA

Conductors work at harnessing the action of many different musicians, who if left to their own devices would produce cacophony. They know what they want to achieve, and provide the leadership that makes the difference. They take control and set out to make things happen. A conductor who loses control no longer has an impact. The conductor's success depends partly on being able to recognize which things are fixed and which are changeable. Good conductors may be able to work with ongoing processes of change and bend them to their will. Bad ones will use their energies ineffectively. Parents are conductors in the home, just as managers are conductors outside it.

Mike was a highly successful businessman. He went into the shoe trade immediately after leaving school, worked his way through all aspects of the industry, until, at age 56, he owned a chain of children's shoe stores. He kept a close eye on all aspects of the business, and no major decisions were made without consulting him first. In fact, his knowledge of the trade was encyclopedic. People at all levels relied on him to be able to answer questions, to solve problems, and to lead them in the right direction. Then he had a small stroke. He made an almost complete recovery but was dismayed to find himself having to search for the answers to people's questions. He stalled for time by keeping them talking until he remembered what he wanted to say. Shortly after returning to work, he forgot a couple of trivial things in quick succession: to return a phone call and to tell his secretary the time of an appointment. After catching a puzzled look on the face of a colleague and realizing that he must have told him the same thing twice, he asked his doctor to arrange a formal test of his memory. The results showed that the stroke had caused a slight, but nevertheless definite, impairment in his memory.

Mike's memory impairment interfered with his habit of being in complete control. He was a natural problem solver, however, and bought a book on memory improvement. With the help of his secretary, he devised some effective reminder systems. An unexpected consequence of his memory problem was that he also sought expert help in putting the information he held in his head onto the office computer, making it readily accessible to others. By recognizing the limitations placed on him by processes beyond his control, Mike discovered how to change himself.

Each of these caricatures shows a different style or attitude that people may adopt in the face of change. There is no one method that suits every person in every circumstance. We all tend to develop habitual ways of dealing with change. Use these caricatures to think about whether to enlarge your repertoire of styles for making changes.

Three Conditions for Fruitful Change

This guidebook will help you to direct the processes of change. Your journey is not yet complete; there is more to come, and none of us knows where it will take us next or what the weather will be like on the way. Circumstances constantly shift, demanding that we continue to adapt. On this journey we can use all that we know to give ourselves more options and better chances. No one way of dealing with change will fit all circumstances or all people, so the more you know about the various methods of helping yourself to change, and the better you understand yourself, the more you will be able to change in the ways you wish.

1 UNDERSTAND THE PRESENT

Choices about change can only be made in the present. That means that it is important above all to accept where you are now. The first condition, therefore, for fruitful change is that you see clearly where you are at the moment. Do not hide away from present reality. If there are aspects of the present you do not like, you can start to plan how to change: but if you pretend these aspects do not exist, you will never change them. Sometimes you will want to be energetic and active, and will need to know how to exert your will to direct or control the forces around you. At other times a quieter, more accepting form of change may provide what you need, and help you to steer away from turbulent waters into calmer ones. The potential for changing the future can lie only in the present.

2 STEP LIGHTLY FROM THE PAST

"If only things had been different." "I wish I hadn't said that." It is understandable to feel dismayed by the mistakes and concerns of yesterday, but it is a mistake to allow the past to become a prison. The past can no longer be changed, so the second condition for fruitful change is to step lightly from the past. The past is an information bank from which you can learn; it is not a web in which you are caught.

3 ACCEPT THE UNCERTAINTY OF THE FUTURE

We can only take one path and can never know what would have happened had we taken a different one. It is as if there were an endless branching of possibilities stretching out before us. The place we find ourselves in is determined by the past, but it tells us little about how things will turn out in the distant future. The path that appears to wind wearily uphill may provide unexpected rewards later on.

Thus, the third condition for fruitful change is to accept the uncertainty of the future. Many of the ideas in this book will help you to direct the changes you wish to make toward the goals you value. But we cannot foresee the future; much is outside our control and the unexpected is a continual possibility. In bringing about fruitful change, we need to leave room for uncertainty. An attitude of openness and confidence is needed for the future as well as the past.

It Is Better to Light One Candle Than Curse the Darkness

You can change, and we have written this book because we have seen how people can benefit from trying out new directions. We hope this book will help you make the choices you wish to make, and increase your ability to enjoy the journey on the way. It contains many ideas so that you can choose those which are most relevant for you. You may be thinking that you want to make so many changes, you do not know where to begin. Do not try to do too much all at once. Decide which change to make first. Lighting one candle is enough for a start.

Chapter Summary

The future is a journey, and change is a part of all journeys. This guidebook will help you to direct the processes of change.

There are three conditions for fruitful change:

1. *Understand the present.* Do not hide from reality but see the present clearly.
2. *Step lightly from the past.* The past cannot be changed. Do not allow it to weigh you down.
3. *Accept the uncertainty of the future.* Much of the future is not under our control. In order to learn how to face the future with confidence, we need to learn how to accept that uncertainly.

PART TWO

THE SEVEN BASIC SKILLS

To keep fit, mentally, you need seven basic skills. In this part, we show you how you can develop these skills. They will enable you to improve both your mood and your effectiveness.

As with all skills, you will improve with practice. Read and reread this section, using it as your workbook for mental fitness.

The seven skills are:

- Managing yourself and your time
- Facing the problem
- Treating yourself right
- Problem-solving: a strategy for change
- Keeping things in perspective: help from cognitive therapy
- Building self-confidence and self-esteem
- Learning how to relax

5

Managing Yourself and Your Time

Time Management Is Personal Management

Donald's full beard was as dark as his mood. He had been miserable since taking early retirement nine months before. He hung around the house with little to do, feeling bored and useless. His wife was at the limits of her patience. They both wanted the problem solved and hoped that there might be a medication that could cheer him up. He was taken aback when we started talking about the principles of time management. "Isn't time management what all those successful young business executives learn? That's for people who have too much to do. My problem is that I have too much time and not enough to do."

Hilary was just the kind of young businesswoman for whom time management courses are designed. From the outside she appeared happy and successful, but from the inside she felt anxious and out of control. That is why she had come to the clinic. Her work was an endless series of pressures, but she knew all about time management. She brought out her organizer which was full of appointments and lists of projects. It was easy to see why she felt stressed: she had so many urgent projects, and so many appointments, she was never still. It was fortunate that her clinic appointment had been rated as very important or she would never have had the chance to see where she was going wrong. She knew a great deal about some of the techniques of time management, but she did not understand the principles. At the end of the first meeting she said: "You are not talking about time management but about personal management." She was right. It is not time which needs to be managed; it is ourselves.

The Central Principle of Time Management

Enormous books and long courses are devoted to time management, but the central principle is simple and profound: *spend your time doing those things you value or those things that help you achieve your goals.* This is not an invitation to selfishness. The idea is not that you only do those things which are in your interests at the expense of others. Altruistic people want to spend time helping other people: this is what they value and this is one of their main goals.

Most of us would admit to spending a great deal of our time involved in activities which we neither value nor which help us to achieve our goals. Why is this? It is tempting to think that it is because of weakness of will, or laziness, or inefficiency. But although these can be contributing factors, they are rarely of major importance. The most important single reason is being unclear about our values and our goals. This was the case with Hilary. She was busy and she worked efficiently, but a great deal of the time she was doing things that did not contribute to her main goals. She did not choose which projects to take on and which to reject with reference to her values and goals, and this was because she did not have a clear idea what these values and goals were. The result was that she took on almost all the projects which were thrown her way; most of them worthy enough, but too many of them when considered together. She had no clear vision that could enable her to decide on her priorities. She ended up doing whichever tasks were the most urgent. The result: stress and dissatisfaction.

Clarify Your Values and Your Goals

To help clarify your values and long-term goals, carry out the following "thought experiment." Imagine your own funeral three years from today. What would you like people to say about you? What would you like a close friend, a member of your family, and a colleague or neighbor to say about you? The point of this exercise is not to think about your death, but about the kind of person you want to be and the kinds of things you wish to achieve. Three years from now is far enough away for you to do new things but near enough not to feel remote.

Do not try to guess what people would really say about you; the point of the exercise is to clarify what you would *like* them to say. Here is what Hilary wrote.

Results of Hilary's Thought Experiment

The family speaker. He said that I was warm, fun, and stimulating; that I spent time with the family and gave them the highest priority. He added that I was thoroughly dependable.

The friend. She confirmed that I was fun to be with and that I gave support when it was needed. She added that I was completely honest and sophisticated.

The colleague at work. She spoke of my integrity and productivity: I got valuable things done. She added that I brought out the best in my colleagues at work so that they flourished.

The purpose of this exercise is to help you to realize what is important to you. When you have done this exercise you are in a position to write a statement, for your own personal use, about your values and goals. Such a statement provides you with a touchstone against which you choose your priorities and decide how to spend your time. It need not be written on tablets of stone; it may change gradually as you grow older, or change suddenly at certain points in your life. But at any one time this statement reflects your values and goals. It may be something you wish to keep private, or something to share with those you are close to. It may be short or long. But we do recommend that you write it down and keep it in a convenient place so that you can read and reread it until you know it in your bones. Only then can you ensure that it illuminates your important decisions. Hilary was typically terse in her personal statement (see below) but it served her purpose well. It is clear how the funeral exercise helped her in producing her personal statement.

Donald had never thought about what he valued and what he wanted to achieve after his retirement. His life had revolved around his work, and when that stopped he just existed, bored and rudderless. He could not see the point of the funeral exercise but he agreed to do it anyway. He did not begin by thinking about what he would like his wife to say; he thought instead about what she was probably thinking at that point in time. "I wish

---

Hilary's Personal Statement

Central value of integrity and honesty
Caring for my family
Not, however, rigid and rule bound
Forgiving
Creative and imaginative
High value on hobby of painting
Stimulating and fun
Enabling others (for example, at work) to flourish
Main work objective over next three years: to expand my division of the company by 20%

---

he would go back to work so that he wasn't around me all the time getting in the way. He's so miserable it would be better if he were dead." He suddenly saw what he was like from her perspective, and he did not like what he saw. What would he like her to say in three years time?

"That's simple. I would like her to think that my retirement years were good ones for both of us. That the time which it gave us together was time we enjoyed and took advantage of. That I was helpful to her, but also that I was interesting to be with." Donald thought about what he would like his son to say, and his four-year-old granddaughter. By the end of the week he had not only written out a detailed statement of his values and goals, he had also planned how he wanted to spend his week.

Be Led by Your Goals and Values

Making a personal statement of your values and goals helps you to center your life around what you believe in. But knowing your values and goals is not by itself enough. You need also to *act* in accordance with them. The problem is that we often act as though we were being directed by someone else rather than by ourselves.

"But What If I Have No Control Over My Life?"

You might be thinking that this is all very well for someone like Donald, who is retired and can do pretty much what he likes. But what about those who do not have much control over their lives? Perhaps you are clear about what you value, and you know exactly how you would like to spend your time; but you have to earn your living, and in order to do this, you must spend a lot of your time doing things you do not really value.

It is a sad reflection on our society that there is much truth in this objection. We certainly all have to spend time doing things we neither enjoy nor find valuable. The central principle of time management tells us, however, that the only reason for spending time in this way is if it is necessary for achieving one of our long-term goals. If the only way of earning a living at the moment is by doing a job which we neither value nor enjoy, then it may be necessary to do this, at least for the time being. However, we need to look carefully at whether there are other ways of achieving our goals.

Anne worked as a secretary. Her father had always wanted her to be a secretary, but she hated the job. When asked why she did it, she said that she needed the money. We asked her what job she would prefer. She was quite clear about that: she would like to work in a travel agency. She had found out, however, that to do this she would have to work for a year at much lower pay, and even after a year, she was not likely to be earning as much as she was at that time. We discussed her values and goals. One of the things she really wanted to do was to travel. If she worked for the travel agent, she would be able to travel more cheaply, but she had not assessed the monetary value of this to her. It turned out that if she traveled a lot—and this is what she wanted to do—the cheap fares available to her went a long way to making up the difference in income between the two jobs. It did not make up all the difference. So what could the extra income in her present job help her to do that she would not do if she worked in the travel agency? For the first year, she would not be able to maintain a car. After that, the difference would have little effect on her day-to-day life.

Anne had thought that the ideas behind time management had little value for her because she had no control over how to spend her time. It turned out that by getting clear for herself what her values were she did have some choices. What it boiled down to was that she could continue in her present job, which she neither enjoyed nor valued, or she could do what she really wanted and sacrifice her car for a year. When put in these terms, she was certain that she would rather change jobs. It was through applying the central principle of time management that she had become clear about what it was she wanted.

A Piece of Pie

Donald discovered a technique that he found useful and that may be of help to you. He drew a pie chart of how he wanted to spend his time. In writing his statement of values and goals, he identified a number of different aspects of his life that he wanted to develop, and decided roughly how much time he wanted to spend on each. His pie chart looked like the one on page 37.

The Designer Week

Donald used his pie chart to design his week so that it had the elements that he wanted, in the proportion that he had chosen. He wanted to help his son and daughter-in-law. He looked at the pie chart and then he asked them: "If you could have four hours of my time, how would it be most helpful to you?" Their answer was simple: an evening of babysitting. So Donald wrote this evening into his weekly timetable.

He had wanted to learn French properly for years but with his work schedule he had never had the time. He went to his local library and found out about adult study programs. There was a local French class one afternoon a week, so he put this in his diary and also scheduled some time for homework. He talked with his wife. If he did the cleaning, she would do the cooking and washing. So she taught him how to clean the house, and this gave her more leisure time. They both enjoyed looking at antiques so they decided to plan outings to antique fairs and house sales, with a light lunch out. Donald put this on his weekly timetable.

His timetable did not provide a rigid list of musts, but was a helpful guide to make sure that, by and large, he spent his time following the pursuits he wanted. Having previously felt aimless and miserable with nothing to do, he started to think of his retirement as a purposeful rather than as an empty time of life, and began to feel more fulfilled.

The pie chart and the designer week are as useful for the busy person whose work seems to take up the whole of life as they are for those whose life seems filled with empty space. Often the busy person has lost touch with what is really important. So if you are very busy, take time to produce your statement of values and goals and then draw a pie diagram showing how much time you would like to spend on each of the main areas in your life: your family, your work, your friends, your hobbies and interests. How does the distribution of time shown in your ideal pie compare with how you are actually spending your time? One of the problems the busy person

Donald's time-management plan.

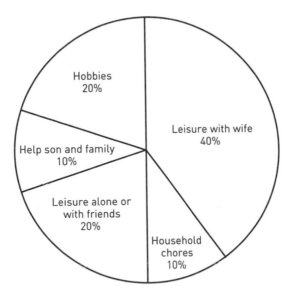

faccs is that work can take up an increasing and excessive amount of time at the expense of family and friends. Of course, economic factors often force people to work more than they would ideally like to. If your ideal pie and your actual pie show any marked discrepancies, think carefully about how you could bring them more into line. Do you really have to do as much as you are doing at work?

Classify Your Activities

Many books and courses on time management display a diagram much like the one on page 38. The idea is that each of the activities that occupy your week can be classified in two ways: in terms of how *important* they are and how *urgent* they are. Some authors devise elaborate rating systems, but for most purposes, it is enough to place each activity in one of the four quadrants.

The importance of an activity is determined by your values and goals. Urgent tasks, like returning phone calls or doing the household chores, pop up of their own accord until you find yourself snowed under by them. The nonurgent important activities, like developing new markets or keeping up with friends, never get done unless they become urgent. Because it

Weighing the importance of various tasks as a part of time management.

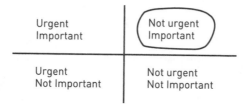

Urgent Important	Not urgent Important
Urgent Not Important	Not urgent Not Important

is so tiring living constantly with urgent tasks, we sneak into the "comfortable" quadrant of activities that are neither urgent nor important, like flicking through a magazine with no great enjoyment, whenever we can, just, as it were, to get some rest.

The central principle of time management is: *spend your time doing those things you value or that help you achieve your goals.* In other words, spend your time doing those activities that are important to you. The aim, therefore, is to spend no time on activities described as *not important*—whether urgent or not. Furthermore, it is desirable to spend as much time as possible on nonurgent activities, because it is more stressful to be working on urgent tasks, and then many of the most important activities never become urgent. If you spend most of your time doing the urgent things, these very important but nonurgent activities get continually put off. Such activities include spending time with family and friends, developing your interests and hobbies, and planning the long-term aspects of work. As you increase the time spent on nonurgent activities, gradually you will reduce the amount of time you need for the urgent tasks, because you will be carrying them out before they become urgent.

What about My Leisure?

You may be thinking that this sounds far too much like hard work—spending all your time doing important activities. What about time to stand and stare? What about time to be frivolous? What about time relaxing with friends? It is vital to understand what is meant by *important*. An important task might include lying on the beach in the sun, or having a drink with some friends, or putting your feet up to watch a football game on TV. In other words, relaxing and pleasurable activities are indeed important. In spending your time doing those things which are important to you, we are not advocating constant work and lifelong grind. Quite the contrary. Paradoxically, good time management often means spending less time on what is considered work. If the work is drudgery and not relevant to key goals, then it should be abandoned. This will leave you more time for doing those things you enjoy and value.

Important but Not Urgent in Two Steps

In order to shift to spending as much time as possible on important, nonurgent activities, you need to take two steps.

Step 1. Refuse to commit yourself to unimportant activities in the first place; and this means that you need to have clearly in mind what your values and goals are. Time management comes back, again and again, to this fundamental notion. Do not expect to ditch all the unimportant tasks that you have taken on overnight. You may need to carry them out simply because you have already committed yourself. But, from now on, do not agree to any unimportant activities.

Step 2. Use the time created by cutting out unimportant activities in order to engage in important, nonurgent activities. Do not fill this time with urgent tasks.

By applying this two-step process, over a period of a few months, you can ensure that most of your time is spent on important but not urgent activities.

Nine Tools and Rules of the Time-Management Trade

Once you are clear about your values and goals, you can use whichever tools you find helpful in order to get organized.

1 Use Your Starter Motor

An old Renault car runs as smoothly as cream once it gets going, but is a devil to get started, particularly in the wet weather. Most of us are like that car. A survey of students showed that the main difference between good students and average students was in the ability to get down to work quickly. The first tool of time management is to get to the task at hand. Do not spend time in that limbo of neither getting down to the work nor enjoying your leisure. For ideas about how to make it easier to get started, see Chapter 32.

2 Make Routine Your Servant

Routine can be your servant or your master. Mindless routine may become a prison and may curb your creativity. But routine, when used well, can release time and energy. Donald decided to learn French. He chose to devote half an hour each day, in addition to his weekly class, working on his French. He found that it was easy to skip a daily session, and if he skipped one, it was even easier to skip a second session. Two weeks went by, and he had only done his half hour of work on two days. We discussed ways to help him get down to work. He chose to make it a routine. After breakfast each day, he would work for half an hour. He established a routine. In fact, he had previously spent half an hour successfully delaying doing the work. Now he found that he had done his work before he had time to think about not doing it. He established the habit that, after breakfast, he would take his coffee into the sitting room and work for half an hour. It worked.

3 Every *Yes* Is a *No* to Something Else

Many of the best things in life arise by chance, and saying *yes* to an opportunity can lead to unexpected treasures. But the mistake most of us make is to say *yes* to too many things, so that we live according to the priorities of others rather than according to our own. We fail to recognize that doing one thing means that we are not doing something else. Every time you agree to do something, another thing you might have done will not get done. When someone asks you to do something, think to yourself: "If I say *yes* to this, from what other activity will I take away the time?" The problem is that almost all of us find it difficult to say *no* to other people's demands. The skills of *assertiveness* are necessary for the good management of time. These are described in Chapter 13.

4 Distant Elephants

From far away, even elephants look small; but when you come up close, they are as large as they always are. Peter received a letter asking him to give a lecture in Scotland. He knew it would take two days of preparation and a couple of days to travel to Scotland and back. It was not a lecture he particularly wanted to give, and if he had been asked to give it within two months, he would have had no hesitation in saying no. But he was being asked to give the lecture in a year's time. It was so far away he almost said yes without thinking, but then he remembered about distant elephants. In a year's time it would still be four days' work, and he would still have other priorities. This lecture was never going to be a top priority, and he would always have more important things to do with four days. *Do not commit yourself to unimportant activities no matter how far ahead they are.*

5 Salami

Large tasks can be so daunting that you either never start them, or having started them, you become dispirited and give up. The principle of *salami* is that large tasks should be broken up into a series of small tasks: like eating a whole salami over weeks, slice by slice. This principle is explained in detail on page 454.

6 The Curse of Perfectionism

Louise was a good scientist and was devastated when she failed to get the promotion she thought she deserved. The problem was that hardly anyone knew much about her work because she had published so little. Several of her colleagues had found it difficult to work with her because, when they came to write up their results for the professional journals, she was so slow. The reason for her slowness was her perfectionism. She thought so carefully about every word, and worried so much about every sentence, that her results remained lost to the world in half-finished, unpublished manuscripts.

There is a place for perfectionism. The great Dutch painter Vermeer worked with painstaking care and has left us a number of masterpieces. But for most activities, there comes a stage when there is not much to be gained from putting in a great deal more effort. It is usually possible to spot when this stage has been reached. This is the time to call a halt and focus on something else.

7 Once Past the Desk

Slightly unpleasant or tricky things, like letters we do not want to answer, seem to turn up again and again. What typically happens is that the letter arrives, we read it, and put it aside. Later we read it again, start to think about it, but put it aside again. We can even repeat the whole process and end up wasting yet more time. We could have dealt with it once and for all in the time we have spent putting off dealing with it. To prevent this waste of time, apply the rule of *once past the desk:* either deal with the task straight away, or decide when to deal with it and put it aside until that time. The successful application of this technique requires a certain discipline. The discipline is made up of four steps, all of which should be taken with deliberation, at least until they become a habit. The first step is a quick assessment of what you will need to do in order to deal with the matter: for example, to reply to the letter. This assessment should be brief. And in making this assessment, use your values as a yardstick: do not undertake tasks that are not important to you. The second step is to decide when to tackle what you need to do. One good reason for delaying completion of the task is that you need time to mull it over. Again, this decision should be made rapidly. The third step is to put the matter aside until the allotted time. The fourth step is to carry out the action at the allotted time. These four steps may often be carried out in quick succession—when you decide to deal with the matter right away. But do not keep revisiting the task without carrying it out. Deal with what is on your desk, whether literally or metaphorically, just the once.

8 Appointments Need to End as Well as Start

Be as aware of when appointments are due to end as you are of when they begin. For example, suppose that you are making a date to meet with a colleague to discuss an issue at work, or a date to have coffee with a friend. When arranging the time to meet, arrange also the time to finish. You will need to make some estimate of how long you need together, but the ability to make such estimates improves with practice. There are two reasons for scheduling the ends of appointments. The first is so that you know when you will be free for other activities and appointments. The second is that, if everyone knows when the meeting will end, you will all make better use of the time you have together.

9 Make Time to Plan

The final tool of time management is to schedule a regular time to plan your activities. Some people find it helpful to plan the day first thing in the morning. For others, it may be better to plan in terms of a week. The minutes spent in planning will be saved many times over. It is also useful to review your priorities from time to time. Holidays are a good time for this because you are away from the demands of everyday life.

Nine Tools and Rules

1. Use your starter motor
2. Make routine your servant
3. Every *yes* is a *no* to something else
4. Distant elephants
5. Salami
6. The curse of perfectionism
7. Once past the desk
8. Appointments need to end as well as start
9. Make time to plan

Chapter Summary

1. The central principle of time management is: *spend your time doing those things you value or that help you to achieve your goals.*
2. It is therefore important to know what your values and goals are.
3. You could clarify these by imagining what you would like a close relative, a close friend, and a work colleague to say about you.
4. Write down your personal statement of values and goals so that you can refer to it often.
5. Having clarified *your* values and goals, make sure that you are led by them. Do not be led by someone else's goals.
6. Classify the activities which fill your week in terms of their *importance* and *urgency*. Many leisure activities and time with family and friends will be classified as important.
7. Aim to spend as much time as possible doing those things that are important but not urgent. This is a two-step process:

Step 1: From now on, do not commit yourself to doing things which are not important.

Step 2: Use the extra time this gives you to do the *nonurgent* things. Gradually, fewer and fewer things will be urgent because you will have done them before they become urgent.

8. Make use of whichever of the *nine tools and rules of the time-management trade* are useful to you.

6

Facing the Problem

It is tempting to pretend that our fears and problems are not always with us. It is tempting to close our eyes to them, half hoping that they will, of their own accord, go away. But the problem with problems is that they rarely go away in silence. They usually need to be tackled and solved. If we pretend the problems do not exist, if we ignore their presence, then they will grow in the dark of our neglect. The longer the neglect, the larger, and more entrenched, those problems are likely to be. The earlier you recognize the problem, therefore, the better.

Much of this book is about the methods and ideas that have been developed for tackling the problems of everyday life. These methods can only help if the problems are brought out into the light.

If this sounds hard, it is important to take hold of the encouraging fact that most problems, when seen clearly, are a fraction of the size they seem when glanced sideways in a fearful or gloomy mood. Most problems shrink still further when confronted.

Crumbs Under the Skin

Paul had a demanding job as a junior member of the Parks Department, responsible for supplying both plants and equipment to the town gardeners.

Paul was also learning a new computer system for the control of these supplies. He had been doing this work for only two years and his responsibilities were growing. He had saved nearly enough to own a car, and he knew that his prospects were good—but he was not happy. He dragged himself out of bed to go to work, kept forgetting details of the new computer program, and was never satisfied with himself. It was becoming harder and harder to concentrate on the job, and he had to make ever-increasing efforts to keep going. His girlfriend noticed that he seemed depressed and asked him how he was feeling, but he simply said that everyone was overloaded by the changes in the office, and suggested that they go for a walk, hoping it would make him feel better.

Mandy had always been ambitious. She worked as a personnel manager, was married to a teacher, and had come back to work soon after having her first child, Lizzie, who was now two years old. She had excellent day-care arrangements for Lizzie, and liked to think that she could cope with whatever was thrown at her, both at home and at work. But she still felt troubled. She had started to worry about "silly" things, like whether Lizzie would make friends at school, and whether Lizzie was really as happy and contented as she seemed. Although she knew that Lizzie was fine, the worries continued, and she became increasingly bad tempered, both at home and at work. She resented it when people asked her what was the matter since it only made her feel worse. She was angry that they could not see how many demands were being made on her, and did not make allowances for her moods.

Storing Up Trouble

Both Paul and Mandy knew that they felt bad, but neither of them found it easy to face their difficulties. Like most of us, they found that avoidance was tempting. In the short term, avoidance felt like a solution because it made them feel better and because they could not face talking about the difficulties to someone else. But by not facing their problems, they were storing up trouble for the future for three reasons:

1. *Avoidance can make the problem worse.* The more Paul and Mandy avoided their difficulties, the more insurmountable the problems seemed and the more depressed and irritable they felt.
2. *Avoidance creates new problems.* Mandy's resentment and irritability were making her working relationships difficult, and Paul's self-confidence was being gradually eroded. He had convinced himself

that he would be no good at anything else, that he would be given a bad reference despite his obviously good work record, and that no one would understand how he could dislike a job that he obviously did well.

3. *Avoidance interferes with your life.* Neither Paul nor Mandy felt they could do what they wanted to do, nor enjoy the things that they were doing. The problems they did not face did not go away, but stayed to contribute to the storehouse of trouble.

Facing the Difficulties Instead

RECOGNIZE THERE IS A DIFFICULTY

For these reasons, it is best to face difficulties instead of avoiding them: to acknowledge the difficulty instead of denying it is there; to accept what is happening instead of trying to reject it; to recognize the facts for what they are without twisting or distorting them. These different ways of expressing the idea have slightly different shades of meaning but are tied together with a common thread: facing difficulties is helpful even though it may be alarming. To do this, you first need to recognize that the difficulties are there, or to recognize that you are avoiding them, and this is not always easy.

Paul's girlfriend did not give up when he suggested that they go for a walk. She helped him to talk more about his job, and eventually he explained to her how much he hated it. He had applied for the job because he was interested in gardens but now he had to spend the day confined indoors, pushing pieces of paper across a desk and fighting with a computer. There were many reasons why he avoided facing up to the difficulty: he feared a change would disappoint his parents or lead to a drop in salary, and he was not confident that he would find another job or, at any rate, one that he would like better. Besides, he was terrified of interviews, although he had hardly even admitted this to himself.

Mandy's situation was a little different. She was confused by her feelings and embarrassed when she let her irritability show in the office. She welcomed each weekend with relief, absorbed herself in family life, enjoying the pleasures of her days off, until Sunday evening, when she would "suddenly" realize that she had a briefcase full of work which she could not face opening. At first, she thought this was just a temporary phase, but one Sunday when her husband offered to put Lizzie to bed so that she could catch up with the work, she lost her temper. She was shocked and upset by the strength of her feelings. It took her a long time to calm down, and when she did, she said to herself, "I've got to do something about this." That evening when everyone else was in bed she started, for the first time, to think about what was going on.

CLARIFY WHAT THE AVOIDANCE IS REALLY ABOUT

Sometimes when we are avoiding difficulties, it is obvious what these are, but sometimes it is not. Paul avoided talking to his girlfriend about his predicament, and Mandy avoided thinking about the problem altogether. When Paul began to talk about how he felt, he realized that he was also avoiding many other things: upsetting his parents, admitting his unhappiness, making a change, taking a risk, and possibly going for an interview.

Mandy found it easier to begin facing her fears by herself. Once she had admitted to herself that the bad feelings were not just going to go away of their own accord, she started to wonder what was making her so tense and irritable. Gradually, her thoughts became clearer about what was happening. She had been surprised to find that her ambitions had dissipated since Lizzie was born. As a committed career woman she had returned to work as soon as possible, and now she was both confused and embarrassed to admit, even to herself, that she wanted to stop work to look after Lizzie. She had vaguely hoped that this was just a temporary phase, and when people asked what was bothering her, she felt criticized and angry with them. Deep down she was dreading what her friends would think of her change of heart, and she had not dared even to begin to contemplate how the family would manage if she no longer earned a good salary.

UNWRITTEN MESSAGES

There are unwritten messages we give ourselves whenever we avoid something. The messages are: "This is alarming and scary"; "I need to protect myself." Our attitude builds up an expectation that cannot easily be disconfirmed, because avoidance prevents us from finding out whether our fears are real. Imagine, for example, that you are feeling stressed at work to the degree that makes you think you will have to do something about it. You do not know what to do, and avoid talking to anyone about how you feel for fear of what they will think of you. Indeed, you try to work harder and harder so no one will notice that anything is wrong. Your avoidance prevents you from finding solutions to the problem since you never have time to stop and think, nor does it allow you to draw on the wisdom of others or to turn to them for support. Trying to protect yourself by working ever harder adds to the stress and prevents you finding out that there is no need to keep yourself safe in this way.

It is crucial therefore, in facing our difficulties, to pay attention to the bad feelings and use them as a prompt to look more closely at what is happening, to clarify exactly what those difficulties are. This might be done, as in the case of Paul, by talking to a trusted friend, or it might be done, as in the case of Mandy, by thinking carefully on one's own. But unless the difficulties are clarified, they cannot be effectively tackled.

ARE YOU AVOIDING DIFFICULTIES?

Sometimes it is hard to know whether or not you really are avoiding something. It is helpful, therefore, to be alert for signs of avoidance. These three guidelines may be helpful.

1. *Consult your feelings.* Your avoidance may show itself in subtle ways. If the reason you do not do something is because it makes you anxious or worried, then it is likely that you are avoiding it. If you persist in doing something you find difficult but feel no better for it, then you are probably avoiding some subtle aspects of the situation. Ask yourself this: "What would I have to do in order to feel more confident?"
2. *Observe your behavior.* If you find yourself stuck, or wavering, between two courses of action, then think about whether you are avoiding something, and if so, see if you can work out how to approach it instead. If you find yourself taking unnecessary precautions, or building protective walls around yourself, you may be avoiding finding out what would happen if you gave up these safety-seeking behaviors.
3. *Tune in to your thoughts.* Are you expecting the worst? Or predicting a disaster? Do you think something will go wrong, or that you will not be able to cope in some way? Such exaggerated, fearful thoughts can prevent you from even beginning to face the problem.

CATCH THE PROBLEMS EARLY

Avoidance not only keeps problems from being solved, it can also make them worse and increase the difficulty of facing them. The sooner that the problem is identified, the sooner you can start to tackle it and the more effective this is likely to be. Many of the problems that make you feel bad are not like clouds that appear out of the blue and blow away of their own accord; they are more like crumbs under the skin that irritate until they are removed.

ADOPT AN ATTITUDE OF APPROACH

Konrad Lorenz tells a story about a neighbor's dog which barked aggressively when safe behind its fence.[1] It seemed to be a terrifying and dangerous beast until one day part of the fence was removed for repair. As Lorenz and his own dog walked along the path beside the fence, the beast, as usual, barked furiously from the safety of the other side. But then they came to the place where the fence had been removed. The beast found itself bristling at Lorenz and his dog with no barrier between them. Its aggression immediately disappeared.

The avoidance of our problems is like the fence. From the safety of our neglect, the problems can bark at us with all their might. But if we take down the fence and meet them face to face, their ferocity will usually disappear. Ideas about how to overcome avoidance are described in more detail in Chapters 18 and 19.

Tackling the Difficulties

Facing difficulties and problems is the necessary prelude to tackling them. It is the first—and often the most difficult—step. Once the difficulty is clearly seen, a strategy for making you feel better is needed. The purpose of much of this book is to explain the variety of techniques available to you so that you can choose those which suit you best.

Related Chapters in This Book

Chapter 8   *Problem-Solving: A Strategy for Change*
Chapter 18   *Getting the Better of Anxiety and Worry, or Defeating the Alarmist*
Chapter 19   *Overcoming Fears and Phobias*

Chapter Summary

Facing difficulties is rarely as alarming in practice as it is in our imaginations, and avoiding them only perpetuates the difficulties.
Avoidance is unproductive for at least three reasons:

- It can make the problem worse.
- It creates new problems.
- It interferes with your life.

Facing difficulties involves recognizing that they are there. Only then can you work out what the difficulty is and think about what to do next. Catching problems early means that they have less chance of growing into imaginary monsters. Most problems shrink in size when they are looked at directly.

7

Treating Yourself Right

Most children are able to throw themselves into the smallest delights, abandoning themselves to the joy of the moment in a way that is, alas, all too easily hidden away and kept securely out of sight and out of mind as we grow to adulthood. We behave as if pleasures are so precious that they have to be kept for special occasions, as if they were in danger of being destroyed with use.

Two Reasons for Rewarding Yourself

Should we put away childish things as we grow older? Some things, perhaps, but not the readiness to enjoy simple pleasures or the ability to immerse ourselves in them. The ability to give yourself treats and rewards is one of the basic strategies for improving mental fitness, and this is true for at least two reasons. In the first place, they provide enjoyment and pleasure, which contribute to feeling good and confident. In the second place, treats and rewards create the very best environment for helping you to change in the directions you wish to change. A joyless time filled only with tasks done out of duty or guilt cramps your ability to develop, and feels more like a preparation for life than living life itself. It runs the risk of turning effort into drudgery—purpose into pointlessness.

For most of us, there are relatively simple things which can give us a great deal of pleasure—things which need not be expensive. A senior nurse in a psychiatric hospital went to her hairdresser once a week. She found that having her hair washed and styled was immensely relaxing and provided a much needed indulgence. She would forget all the stresses of work as she allowed her whole being to become immersed in the sensual pleasure of having her hair washed. She knew and liked her hairdresser, and having listened so often to the troubles of others, she thoroughly enjoyed being asked about herself. The time and money spent on her appearance gave her pleasure and confidence for the rest of the week.

Treats: An Effective Way of Adding Pleasure to Your Life

PERMISSION TO TREAT YOURSELF

The wonderful thing about treats is that they can give pleasure well beyond what would seem possible. The secret is to choose the right treats for *you*. Once we are adults, life can become so full of chores, both at home and at work, that it is easy to get bogged down in routine and forget pleasure. We can even come to feel that it would be frivolous to give ourselves treats when there is always so much to do. Or if the problems in life seem large, then the small things in life, which could give us pleasure, may seem unimportant, and so we fail to give ourselves any pleasure. It is when life's problems are getting on top of you that it becomes particularly important to reward yourself.

Adding treats to your life can be very difficult if you are not used to it, and you may have to start slowly. For example, you may need to start by ensuring that you give yourself a treat once a week, and work up to having a treat every day.

Giving yourself treats is a skill that needs to be developed. The first step is *to give yourself permission to have treats*. Treats bring pleasure, and pleasure is worth having purely because it makes you feel good. But treating yourself will also enable you to accomplish more, and enable you to change in ways that are right for you. *Giving yourself treats is the right way to treat yourself.*

THE WRONG KINDS OF TREATS

We have offered help to many people, from many walks of life, and it is amazing how few offer themselves the small rewards we call treats. Are

there wrong kinds of treats? Yes, those which either damage important relationships, or which fuel a problem. An example of the first kind might
be if the treat is going out with friends when this behavior is already causing marriage problems. An example of the second is when the treat is
drinking alcohol when there is already a problem with drinking too much
alcohol. In choosing treats for yourself, do not exacerbate any problems
you might have. Choose treats that give harmless pleasure.

OCCASIONAL BIG TREATS

Lucy and Jeff have two sons, aged seven and three. Jeff works full-time
and Lucy part-time, mainly from home. With two young children they
find themselves weighed down with endless chores. The one thing they always enjoy is vacations, but although they have the time for two short
trips a year, they only take one. Why, given that vacations can provide
them with so much pleasure? The reason they give is the cost.

Jeff's father is a widower living four hundred miles from Lucy and Jeff,
and they take him with them when they go on vacation. This arrangement
works well since it gives them all a chance to be together; Jeff's father can
spend time with his only grandchildren, and Lucy and Jeff can go out together knowing that their children are well looked after. But it does make
the vacation expensive because they pay for Jeff's father.

In fact, Jeff's father could afford to pay for himself, but he is saving the
money to pass it on to his grandchildren. Jeff and Lucy therefore pay for
him in order to leave their children's inheritance intact. Is this the best
arrangement? Jeff and Lucy had never asked themselves this question because, at the back of their minds, they felt it would be self-indulgent to
have two vacations. It was not until they realized what they were doing
that they could begin to think about what was best.

There is a great danger in our culture that we unconsciously block out
possibilities for fun because, at some level, we think that we ought not to
be enjoying ourselves. We are apt to think that other things are more important, or that planning for pleasure is too self-indulgent; but the reverse
is likely to be true. Having fun, giving ourselves treats, makes it more
likely that we will do those other worthwhile and important tasks because
we will have more energy, strength, and resilience.

Lucy and Jeff thought anew about the situation. They decided that vacations gave them the refreshment needed to tackle their demanding
lives. They worked out that they could afford two vacations if Jeff's father
paid for himself. All three of them discussed the situation and agreed that
it would be best all round if they had two vacations a year together, and

that Jeff's father would pay his share. This second vacation was a big treat and it was expensive, but it added an enormous amount of pleasure not only to Jeff and Lucy's lives, but for Jeff's father, and to the lives of the grandchildren, for whose sake, it once appeared, this second vacation was being denied.

USING TREATS TO SOFTEN UNPLEASANT TASKS

Few of us are lucky enough to avoid unpleasant tasks completely—either in our jobs or our personal lives. Unpleasant tasks, however, can be softened. For Jonathan, a general practitioner, the part of the job which he found most unpleasant was the nights "on-call." On such nights he might be woken at any time and have to deal effectively and compassionately with a medical emergency. When the phone rang, in the small hours of the morning, he would wake from deep sleep and immediately feel miserable having to drag his mind from the comfort of sleep to think about the medical problem, and more often than not to get up and drive to the patient's home. The problem he set himself was this: How could he soften that miserable feeling when the phone rang on his on-call nights? One of his great pleasures in life was listening to music, and he had just recently indulged himself and bought a new CD player. He hit on the idea of "giving" himself a CD token for every night visit. For every three tokens, he would allow himself to buy a CD of his choice. This system did not, of course, make night visits a total pleasure, but now, when the phone rings, a voice inside him says "another CD token—good." Getting up is still a strain, but he can think, as he drives to the patient's house, about which CD he will buy with the token he has earned.

Such a system, adapted to suit your own pleasures, can be used in many ways to soften the impact of unpleasant tasks. If there is something you have to do but are dreading, or if you find yourself dragging your feet, plan a treat for yourself for having accomplished the dreaded deed. Link the two: see the treat as being a result of having had the courage to face the unpleasant task.

USING TREATS TO OVERCOME BARRIERS

Planning a treat helps to knock down the barrier which gets in the way of getting the job done. It is much easier to get down to a difficult task if we promise ourselves a coffee break in a couple of hours. Treats should work as rewards and not as punishments. We are not saying that unless we spend a certain amount of time doing the dreaded task we cannot have the treat. The problem with making agreements with ourselves in that spirit is that they are so easily broken; we allow ourselves the treat even when we have not done what we agreed with ourselves to do. The treat is not, therefore, strictly speaking, a *reward;* instead the treat helps us to look over the barrier to the pleasure that lies beyond. Treats planned in this way are all the more enjoyable because they come after the dreaded, dull, or difficult task has been done, just as the beer tastes better after a trip to the gym.

Creating the Right Conditions for Change: The Carrot Not the Stick

It is by no means as hard to change as it often seems; what gets in the way is the "Dotheboys Hall attitude." This is the wrongheaded but deeply ingrained belief that the best way to bring about change is through punishment. Dotheboys Hall was the school, owned by Squeers, where the young Nicholas Nickleby took up his first teaching post. To quote from Dickens,

> "Bolder," said Squeers, tucking up his wristbands, and moistening the palm of his right hand to get a good grip of the cane, "you are an incorrigible young scoundrel, and as the last thrashing did you no good, we must see what another will do towards beating it out of you."[1]

Although we would no longer dream of behaving like Squeers to our children, we can still behave like Squeers to ourselves. Listen to your internal voice when you are trying to change or trying to learn something new. Do you hear yourself saying things like: "That's idiotic"; "Don't be so stupid"; "You should know this by now"; "Are you never going to improve?" It is curious how good we are at punishing ourselves—maybe because we know exactly how to hit where it hurts. Self-criticism and self-blame are two powerful and most discouraging forms of punishment which may be intended to goad us into action but which, more often than not, make it harder to change and to learn. The result of all these barbed and sarcastic comments is that you end up feeling disgusted with yourself, miserable, dejected, and disillusioned, having ignored the principle that *being kind to yourself makes it easier to change.*

One of our patients said: "I wouldn't treat a worm as badly as I treat myself." This insight was the beginning of an important change in attitude. But it was one thing for her to realize that she punished herself and another for her to do anything about it. Cultural attitudes, including religious ones, seem to make rewarding oneself seem bad, as if doing something for oneself or acknowledging one's good points is conceited, boastful, or dangerously self-indulgent. It seems that we are conditioned to put ourselves down. We cannot put the years of conditioning behind us all at once. But by *developing the habit of rewarding ourselves* we can gradually replace the automatic reflex of self-abasement with one of valuing ourselves.

Constructing a Personal Reward System

An effective system of rewarding yourself has three components: pick the treats that work for you; make your system work to your advantage; and avoid the punishment trap.

PICK THE TREATS THAT WORK FOR YOU

Think about the things that you enjoy, that give you pleasure, that make you laugh, or help you to relax. Think of small things like spending an extra few minutes over breakfast, and big things like taking a vacation. Think of things you could buy now or save up for and get later; things that you could do for yourself and things you could say to yourself; things involving others and things for yourself alone. Try and make a list of 20 things. The longer the list the better. The box on page 58 makes some suggestions for the categories you could adopt and offers some examples of possible treats.

MAKE YOUR TREAT SYSTEM WORK TO YOUR ADVANTAGE

1. *Get the timing right.* Treats work best when they come quickly after the specific goal. Immediately after forcing yourself to sort out the unpaid bills, give yourself a treat. If you treat yourself first, the bills will be even harder to face, and if you delay the treat when you have paid the bills, the connection between the two will be lost.
2. *Treat yourself often.* Everyone would benefit from a daily treat: small pleasures make life easier and more pleasurable. But make sure that you do not use treats which fail to satisfy. If rewards like shopping or having another cigarette, drink, or doughnut only perpetuate the search for pleasure, or make you feel better or less lonely only briefly, they may be the wrong kinds of treat for you.

Some Ideas for Treats and Rewards

Things to eat or drink:
Having a chocolate chip cookie, a can of beer, your favorite meal, a cup of tea

Activities:
Going clubbing, watching TV or a DVD, planning an outing, enjoying a hobby, doing a puzzle, playing cards with friends, gardening, going to a restaurant

Relaxations:
Listening to music, taking a long bath, calling a friend, reading a novel or magazine

Treats:
Buying a bunch of flowers or a bar of scented soap, going out to a movie, buying a new piece of clothing, getting up late

Time:
10 minutes on your own, a mid-morning break, a proper lunch hour, time to think, a weekend break, a vacation

Exercise:
Joining a gym, taking an exercise class, going for a swim, walking the dog

Self-talk:
"I'm doing fine," "I'm really pleased with . . . ," "well done," "you can make it," "you deserve a break"

Setting limits:
Number of chores, bedtime, a time to stop work, demands made by others

Other people:
Chatting with a friend (on the phone, or through the Internet); going out with a friend (for a drink, a meal or to a show or sports event)

---

3. *Saving up and cashing in.* You may want to save up for a big treat like a new piece of sports equipment, or an item of clothing, or a day's outing. If so, give yourself tokens toward what you want. Decide how many it is worth (for example, you could go out for a meal when you have earned 20 "tokens") and use a tick in your diary as the marker of when you have earned a token. As you collect more ticks, you can see how well you are doing.

4. *Give yourself variety.* You might get bored with the same treat just as with anything else, and then it loses its power to encourage. Like

a diet of pure chocolate, it could lose its appeal entirely. So update your treat system from time to time, remembering that different things feel like treats at different times. Going for a long walk may be your idea of fun in the summer, but in the winter you might prefer to watch TV. You may not value peace and quiet as much at 25 (when being on your own might feel more like a punishment than a reward) as you do at 35, when the thought of a few moments to yourself can feel like pure luxury. Or the challenge that you might enjoy at 50 (traveling on your own) may feel overwhelming at 19.

5. *Give yourself a break.* Not doing one of the chores when you are worn out can feel good even though you know you will have to do it later. Allow yourself such breaks, and remember that a change can be as good as a rest if you need one badly. It might feel better to swap chores with someone else from time to time.

6. *Turn routine pleasures into effective rewards.* Leaving all the things you hate doing to the last is like creating a quagmire to struggle through later—probably when your energy and enthusiasm are at a low ebb. For example, if you have a coffee break every morning, this will feel more enjoyable, and work better as a reward, if you do one hateful task before it rather than after.

AVOID THE PUNISHMENT TRAP

Do not make a virtue out of being a martyr. Do not fall into the trap of serving other people's needs so much at the expense of your own that you carry the sacrifice too far. Overburdening yourself "for the sake of others," treating yourself unfairly, makes others feel guilty and can become an undeclared way of punishing them. Saying "don't worry, I can manage" when you really mean quite the opposite punishes both you and others. In the long run everyone is worse off, and you may be building up resentment within yourself that will eventually burst out in anger, or push in on you as depression. Beating your head against a brick wall is another version of the same thing. It feels good when you stop beating yourself, but if this is your only reward for tackling the brick wall then persisting in punishing yourself is pointless.

Parting Thoughts

In our society, people have tended to choose self-punishment over self-satisfaction, with the result that they often fail to provide for themselves the kind of encouraging environment that makes for constructive change and development. Perhaps it is because of our Puritan inheritance that we can so easily think it wrong to indulge ourselves. Rewards and treats work better than self-criticism. They provide an important source of pleasure, and help in solving problems and overcoming difficulties. They also make it easier to learn new skills.

Chapter Summary

1. Give yourself permission to enjoy treats: they add pleasure to life and help you make the changes you want to make.
2. Replace habits of self-criticism with the habit of rewarding yourself.
3. An effective system of rewards has three components:
   - Pick those treats that work for you.
   - Make your system work for you.
   - Avoid the punishment trap.

8

Problem-Solving: A Strategy for Change

Susan

Susan was distraught when she came to the clinic, unable to cope any longer. Looking from the outside, she seemed a highly successful professional who combined work and home life with enviable skill; but this was not how she felt inside.

Susan worked half-time as a lawyer. She was married, had two young children, and her husband worked full-time as an engineer. When Susan was at work, her children were looked after by a babysitter. So what was the problem? The problem was that she felt that she was not doing anything properly. "I don't have time to read the law journals to keep myself up-to-date in my job; and the house is always a mess. I've had enough." Susan was feeling bad about her life and bad about herself. "The trouble is that I've never been a tidy person, but the house is getting me down. I feel quite hopeless about it."

Susan had gotten herself into a downward spiral and was focusing on her weaknesses. She felt bad about herself and so hopeless about the possibility of change that she was failing to tackle the problems.

MOST STRENGTHS ARE WEAKNESSES AND MOST WEAKNESSES ARE STRENGTHS

We tend to see things in black and white and from one perspective only. Fifty years ago, adventure films were often about cowboys and Indians: the cowboys were the good guys and the Indians were the troublemakers. Then came James Bond; the West was good and the USSR was bad. The same simplistic pattern has been used for adventure stories throughout the ages. That is fine for adventure stories, but it is a poor model for ourselves. *Whether a characteristic is good or bad depends on the situation, and on the way we view the situation.* Take Susan's "weakness" of untidiness. If she had been a very tidy person she may not have been able to go out to work at all because she would have needed to spend so long keeping the house clean. Tolerating some degree of untidiness enabled her to devote her energies to her profession. It is too simplistic to label her habits as good or bad, and doing so means seeing them from only one point of view. The categories of good and bad are too exclusive; life is messy.

Before teaching Susan the technique of problem-solving, we talked about how she hated the mess at home and wished she were a neater person. Perhaps tidiness seems like a trivial problem, but it is often the comparatively trivial things which get us down, and which lead to stress out of all proportion to the problem. She decided that she did not want to be the kind of person for whom tidiness was of great importance—she did not want to change her *personality,* but she did want to make some changes. The question was what changes to make, and how to make them. This is where the *technique of problem-solving* came in.

The Technique of Problem-Solving

Problem-solving is such a simple and effective technique that it is easy to dismiss it as just too simple. The fact is that most people hardly make any use of it, although it can be used to resolve many different kinds of problems. It is as though we tried to tighten and loosen screws using our fingernails when we could be using a screwdriver. Once you have mastered the technique, you will wonder how you managed without it. The key to success is to go through the various stages in a methodical manner, step by step.

STAGE 1: IDENTIFY THE PROBLEM

The most important stage of all is the first stage. The problem must be clearly identified, and it helps to give it a name. A vague feeling of unease, of anxiety, or of depression is hard to tackle. A particular problem is much easier. At first Susan could not name her problems. She just felt that it was all too much. "Life's getting on top of me, and I'm no good at anything," was what she said.

"You said that you didn't have enough time to keep up with the law journals. Is that the most frustrating thing in your work right now?"

Susan thought for a moment. "Yes."

"If you did have time to do this and were able to keep up-to-date, would you feel better about your work, or are there other things that frustrate you?"

"In my work, you mean?"

"Yes. In your work."

"It's mainly not keeping up-to-date. Other things can be frustrating but mostly I can cope with those. I think I could be good at my job but I won't be if I don't keep on reading and learning."

"Good. So you've identified the main problem at work. What shall we call it?"

"A name, you mean?"

"A name or a phrase to describe it."

"Let's call it simply: *Inability to keep up-to-date.*"

"*Inability* sounds as though the problem can't be solved. What about calling it *how to keep up-to-date?* Now what about the problems at home. What is getting to you most?"

"Undoubtedly the mess."

"What is this mess?"

"Lots of things. There are toys and half-sorted piles of clothes everywhere. The kitchen seems to be bursting at the seams and there's no place to put anything down without moving a heap of other things, so things keep getting lost. . . ."

"Do you have help with the cleaning and tidying up?"

"Yes. Someone comes in once a week to clean the house. But she can't do the tidying up because she wouldn't know where things go."

"Could you show her?"

Susan thought for a moment. Then she replied: "The problem is that we don't have enough space. Take the kitchen, for example. I buy things like kitchen towels and cereals in bulk and have to store these wherever I can find room, like on top of the kitchen cupboards, and this makes everything seem a mess. . . ." She stopped and fell silent.

"What name would you give to this problem?"

"The problem about the mess?"

"Yes."

"The main thing is that we don't have room for everything. If we could put things away then we wouldn't leave everything lying around in a mess."

"Okay. So what do you want to call that problem?"

"I suppose it is about *lack of storage space.*"

We have given the dialogue between Susan and the therapist in some detail to show you the thought process that led to identifying some of the problems. Do not be satisfied until you have done this. Talk the problems over with someone else if you can, and ask them to help you pinpoint exactly what the problem is. Then write out a list of the problems you want to tackle.

Tips for when it is difficult to specify your problems. This first stage sounds simple and sometimes it is, but often it is hard to clarify exactly what the problems are. The following tips might help.

Tip 1: Talk to someone you trust and who knows you well.

Tip 2: Take a break—a short one if that is all you can manage, or a relaxing vacation if you can afford one. Think about the problems from time to time while you are away from them. Difficulties can often be more clearly seen from a distance, and when you are not in the thick of them.

Tip 3: Trust your intuition. Think about what irritates you most—where the trouble spots are. This is particularly useful if you feel generally dissatisfied but cannot put your finger on where in your life the main problems are. Is it at work or at home? Is it the weekends or the weekdays that are the problem? If you are having great difficulty pinpointing the problem, *it may be because you are too frightened to admit it to yourself.* Do not be frightened. Acknowledging the problem puts you two-thirds of the way along the road to solving it. Running away from it means it will stalk you in the years to come. (See also Chapter 6.)

STAGE 2: THINK OF AS MANY SOLUTIONS AS POSSIBLE

Choose one of the problems that you have already specified clearly in Stage 1, and do a brainstorming exercise (see box on p. 65) to think of as many solutions as you can. Ask someone to help you if you can, and write down each of the possible solutions. The important point is: *Do not reject a solution at this stage however preposterous it sounds; just write it down and go on thinking about other possible solutions.*

This is how Susan tackled her second problem: the lack of storage space at home.

Brainstorming

Brainstorming is a useful method for generating possible solutions to a problem. It is best to brainstorm with someone else, buy you can also do it alone.

1. Write down a brief description of the problem you want to solve.
2. Use this description to get clear in your mind what the problem is.
3. Suggest a solution to the problem—any solution, whatever comes to mind.
4. Do not "censor" the solution—no matter how silly it sounds.
5. Make a quick note of the solution.
6. Suggest another solution, and repeat Steps6 4 and 5.

Do not "censor" any solutions even if they are similar to previous solutions. If there are two or more of you, allow your ideas to be stimulated by the suggestions of the other(s).

In brainstorming you allow your mind to take off in any direction—but always with the problem in sight.

"Well, I suppose I could buy fewer things, but the problem with that. . . ."

"Stop there. At this stage the idea is to generate as many solutions as possible without evaluating them. Write down: Solution 1: Buy fewer things. Now think about other solutions."

"Okay. We could increase the storage space in the house, but I'm not sure. . . ."

"Stop! Write down: Increase storage space in house. Go on."

"We could, I suppose, move to a larger house, but. Sorry. I'll write down: Move to a larger house."

"We could go on as we are and stop fussing about it."

"We could build a hut in the garden and just throw everything in there! Or we could build a cellar. We could leave the car on the street outside the house and use the garage for storage."

By the end of our brainstorming session, Susan's list looked like this:

PROBLEM: THE LACK OF STORAGE SPACE AT HOME

Possible solutions:

1. Buy fewer things.
2. Increase storage space in house.
3. Move to larger house.
4. Stack things all over.
5. Build storage hut in garden.

6. Build storage cellar.
7. Use garage for storage and put car on street.

STAGE 3: TAKING STEPs

Select a solution. *Try* it out. *Evaluate* what happens. *Persist* until you feel better.

Select a solution. Look through your list of solutions and decide which one looks the most promising. It may help to discuss this with someone you trust.

Susan quickly rejected solution 3. She enjoyed her garden and did not want to reduce its size by building a storage hut. The price of a storage cellar was prohibitive, and she was not keen on parking her car on the street since there had been a considerable number of car thefts in her neighborhood. Although she had lived in a messy house for several years, she was sure that she could no longer ignore the problem. This left her with two solutions to try. She thought that she could buy fewer things, and indeed get rid of a number of things she already had. Although this would help, she did not think that by itself it would be enough. She would still need more storage space. The solution she chose to focus on was solution 2: increasing the storage space in her house. There was one obvious part of the house which could be used for more storage: the loft. Susan decided that she would have the loft boarded over and a ladder put in the trap door for easy access. The cost was reasonable and the amount of extra accessible storage space would be considerable.

Try it out. Having selected your preferred solution, try it out. Work out exactly what it would involve, and take the necessary steps.

Evaluate what happens. The solution you have selected may be exactly the thing, or it may not be effective. If it works, you need to know this so that you can do it again if you need to, or persist if it looks as if it has put you on the right track. If it does not work, it is even more important that you know so that you can go back to your list of solutions and try something else. Many solutions are helpful but do not provide the complete answer. Again, you need to know so that you can work out whether to persist with the chosen solution or to look for further solutions to supplement it. Whatever the outcome, you need to evaluate it.

Two months after Susan had the loft space built, she evaluated the effect. She had decided to put all the things for which there didn't seem room in the loft. This had been easy and effective. She had managed to get rid of a lot of the piles which had previously cluttered up the house: her large suitcases, the children's sleeping bags, the Christmas decorations. The extra space available in the main parts of the house meant that she could start to make a place for other things. Her evaluation showed that there was still one part of the house which irritated her: the kitchen. This was still a mess. She needed to learn the last step of problem-solving.

Persist until you feel better. The evaluation may show that you are on the right track, but have not gone far enough. Problems are not often solved overnight. Some persistence is usually necessary. Susan's evaluation had made her feel good because she had made a great deal of progress. But the kitchen was still a problem and she needed to persist. She took another look at what the problem really was. Her kitchen was not large, but there was enough room for the things she used every day. She and her husband stood in the kitchen, glanced around, and discussed how much space was occupied by things they rarely used. Together they decided to put a large number of items up in the loft: gifts that had never been used, the barbecue grill, the cake decorating set, to make room for the things that they used every day.

The process of evaluating, and then persisting until the problem is solved, is ongoing. After another two months, Susan felt she was coping somewhat better and the therapist asked her to think again about the problem of the "mess" and the lack of storage space in the kitchen. This problem she had successfully solved, but how about the rest of the mess? Was the house now normally tidy? Did the mess still get her down? Her answer was that she had only partially solved the problem. She felt less overwhelmed and the kitchen was less cramped, but the house *was* still messy. There were toys lying around all over the place and most surfaces—for example, the tops of drawers and window sills—were cluttered with odds and ends. There definitely were still problems.

Susan was then encouraged to use the whole problem-solving method again, right from Stage 1, and she identified two new problems: the fact that many of the things lying around had no place where they belonged, and the fact that no one in the family had the habit of putting things away. These two problems were related: the fact that so many things had no "home" meant that no one saw any point in tidying up.

Susan started generating solutions to the new problems, and two months later, although the house was still not as tidy as she would ideally like it, it was significantly better than it had been. Meanwhile, she was also tackling her other problem—her inability to keep up-to-date. Her list of possible solutions looked like this.

PROBLEM: HOW TO KEEP UP-TO-DATE

Possible solutions:

1. Read journals every Saturday morning while her husband looks after the children.
2. Negotiate with babysitter to look after children for extra two hours and use the time for reading.
3. Arrange a babysitting "swap" with a friend—so that she looks after the friend's children one afternoon, and the friend looks after her children on another afternoon (giving her extra time for reading).
4. Negotiate three hours less work with her partnership and use the extra time to keep up-to-date.
5. Plan one evening a week to meet with one of her partners at work for an "update session" in which they each spend an hour and a half reading different journals and half an hour summarizing their reading to each other.

She first chose solution 3, but on evaluation, it had not proved very successful. In practice the extra time was filled with work related to her clients rather than keeping up-to-date. She went back to her problem list and selected solution 5. This proved far more successful. Sharing an "update session" with a colleague was more fun and she and her partner encouraged, or perhaps shamed, each other into doing the work.

The Uses of Problem-Solving

We have explained the method of problem-solving using a relatively straightforward case for the sake of clarity The key thing to learn is the technique, not Susan's particular problems, or her solutions, neither of which may be appropriate for you. The technique can be helpful when the problems are more complicated: when they involve your relationships with other people; or when they are more emotional in nature. If, for example, you are feeling irritated by someone with whom you live, the problem-solving method may help to clarify the problem and initiate some useful solutions.

Four Guidelines for Problem-Solving

Four Guidelines for Problem-Solving: Summary

1. Do not waste time on problems that cannot be solved: shift your focus.
2. Tackle one problem at a time.
3. Work on changing yourself, not on changing others.
4. Consider doing nothing, at least for the time being.

1. *Do not beat your head against a brick wall.* There is no point in trying to solve a problem for which there is no solution. One of our clients was finding it difficult to cope with looking after her mother who had Alzheimer's disease. We suggested using the technique of problem-solving. There was no point in trying to find ways of curing the disease; that was not possible. Instead, we helped her to focus on the aspects of caring that she was finding most difficult, such as the fact that she never had time off in the evenings for her own social life.

2. *Tackle one problem at a time, and tackle that in earnest.* If you try and tackle too much, you end up not solving any problem effectively. If your problems seem so numerous and so overwhelming that you need the rest of eternity to solve them all, do not lose heart. Remember the *80:20 rule: 80% of difficulties are due to 20% of problems.* If you tackle, one by one, the few most important problems, you will be overcoming a disproportionately large number of difficulties. *It is always worth tackling a problem no matter how many more problems there seem to be.*

3. *Work on changing yourself.* If the solutions you select force changes on other people, they are likely to fail. The person you *can* change is yourself: take responsibility for your part of the problem. It may be important to work on changing attitudes (see Chapter 9), or on learning how to be fair to yourself and others (Chapter 13), or at improving your negotiating skills (Chapter 15).

4. *You could consider doing nothing for the time being.* It is sometimes enough to accept a problem and decide that you can cope. For example, Susan could have decided to live with the mess in her house until her children were older, though this is not how she would ideally like it. The time and energy needed to solve a problem is sometimes not worth it.

When to Seek Help

The problem-solving technique is powerful yet simple. But there are times when you may need more help from others—for example, if you are so depressed that you cannot solve problems effectively. If this seems to be the case, read the chapters on *depression* (Chapters 22 to 24). Another signal that you may need more help is when your problems are causing serious troubles for you or those around you. *Addictive drugs,* and especially *alcohol,* can be like this (see Chapters 28 and 29). If addiction is an issue, you may need some professional help before you can solve your problems alone. Sometimes anxiety and phobias can be difficult to tackle without help. Read the chapters on *anxiety* (Chapters 18 to 21) if this applies to you. *Disturbed eating* (anorexia and bulimia) may also be best tackled with some professional help (Chapter 31).

Chapter Summary

Do not be put off by the simplicity of the technique of problem-solving. Be pleased that it is so simple and yet so effective. First, specify the problems clearly. Next, choose the problem you want to start on. Then brainstorm for solutions and start to take STEPs: *Select* a solution; *Try* it out; *Evaluate* how it went; and *Persist* until you feel better.

Problem-solving is a simple but powerful technique. Use the following box as a summary and reminder.

Three Stages of Problem-Solving

---

1. Identify the problem clearly.
2. Generate as many solutions as possible: do not reject a solution at this stage, however preposterous it sounds.
3. Take STEPs toward solving the problem:
   - *Select* a solution.
   - *Try* it out.
   - *Evaluate* what happens.
   - *Persist* until you feel better.

9

Keeping Things in Perspective: Help from Cognitive Therapy

> Men are disturbed not by things but by the views
> which they take of them.
> —Epictetus, A. D. 55–135

About 1900 years ago, Epictetus stated a profound truth. But only in the last 35 years has Epictetus's insight been developed into a type of therapy, called *cognitive therapy*—one of the most important recent advances in practical psychology. This therapy was originally developed by Albert Ellis and Aaron Beck.[1] This chapter explains how you can make use of the methods of cognitive therapy to change perspectives that have a negative effect on your feelings and actions. These methods will help you to tackle a whole range of problems and difficulties: those that affect your mood, such as feeling depressed, anxious, or angry; and those that affect your behavior, such as continually striving for success, eating too much or too little, or avoiding social situations. It is one of the most important tools available to psychotherapists and to you.

The Three Fundamentals of Cognitive Therapy

Cognitive therapy is built on three key principles. The first is understanding that the way you see things, the view which you take of them, is vital to your mood. Your perspective affects both how you feel and what you do. The second principle involves understanding how mood and thought are linked: change the one and you also change the other. The third principle consists of learning how to work on your thoughts and beliefs. The methods of cognitive therapy improve mood, but they do this not by working directly on your mood—they work directly on your *thoughts*. By changing your thinking, you can improve your mood. The first question to ask yourself is this: *Is there another way of seeing things?*

The Vital Importance of Viewpoint

If you visit a new place, or take a journey through a new country, you quickly accumulate impressions of what you see and develop your own point of view. You draw conclusions: "The people here are really friendly." And form opinions: "Life here is much less stressful than it is at home." Indeed, developing your own personal picture of the place and comparing it with the pictures others have developed contribute to the pleasures of travel. Each of us develops our own point of view, shaped by our particular, limited experience, and this experience is filtered and interpreted in our own particular way. We all use our own point of view, our own perspective, as a basis for our conclusions and our opinions.

Once on home ground again, however, it is easy to lose sight of this point. Our own ways of seeing things become habitual and compelling so that we easily forget that they are only one point of view. Imagine that you return from a holiday refreshed and throw yourself back into everyday life, maybe with one or two groans, but certainly with every intention of doing your best. Things go well for you. You get a lot more done and are given a pay raise and more responsibilities. You are pleased with your success, and the good mood that it brings pervades your life generally. You know you are a success.

Now imagine a different chain of events. You throw yourself back into the fray with energy and enthusiasm, but events beyond your control mean that things go wrong. Maybe someone gets ill, or jobs have to be cut and you are fired. There was nothing you could have done to prevent these things from happening, but all the same you blame yourself, feel helpless, and think of yourself as a failure. A mixture of feelings—sadness, anger, frustration, resentment, among other emotions pervade your life.

In one case you see yourself as a success, in the other as a failure. In both, the point of view seems to be the one and only truth. But this is not so. When you visit somewhere new, there is not just one possible point of view, there are many. Some perspectives may fit the facts better than others, or be more or less helpful to you, but each person's perspective has its own limitations and obscurities. The person who succeeds at work may do so at the expense of relationships. The person who lost a job may be a successful parent, friend, or musician. Neither of them is anything so one-dimensional as a "success" or a "failure," and both of them might see things differently looking from a different perspective. The point is this: *There is always more than one way of seeing things.* Not just sometimes, but always. You may feel at times as if you have no choice, but this is an illusion. So when the good mood evades you, learn to ask: How else could I think about this? How would someone else see it? What other points of view are there? Answering these questions is a mental exercise you should try from time to time. It flexes your emotional muscles, challenging you to expand your perspective, to think flexibly, and to search for a viewpoint that helps you feel better.

KEEPING AN OPEN MIND

If it is true that *there is always more than one way of seeing things*, then the difficulty is to find other points of view to choose from. One's own perspective is bound to feel most convincing, especially in the heat of the moment. The methods described in the rest of this chapter help you step back from your viewpoint and to see the facts clearly, to give yourself a choice of perspectives. As you shift your perspective, you will find that your mood also shifts. Looking for new, and wider, perspectives prevents you from getting trapped in a one-sided view and gives you more control over the way you feel. The spectacles through which you see the world are so familiar that you hardly notice that you are wearing them. By taking them off and trying out others, you can discover which things were out of focus and whether you have been looking through distorted or colored glass.

We are not recommending a kind of "cock-eyed optimism." We are not suggesting that whatever your circumstances you should look on the bright side. Our point is captured by Viktor Frankl, in his most moving book about life as a prisoner in a concentration camp when he describes "the last of human freedoms"—"the ability to choose one's attitude in any given set of circumstances."[2] Developing the habit, in the course of our more mundane lives, of searching for different and wider perspectives helps you to cope realistically and flexibly with difficulties as they arise. It gives you more options.

The methods of cognitive therapy are relatively new but the ideas behind them are old and familiar. Mr. Thornton, a successful industrialist described by Mrs. Gaskell in her 1855 novel *North and South*, decided not to talk to his mother about an interview she had with the woman he loved because "he felt pretty sure that . . . his mother's account of what passed at it would only annoy . . . him, though he would all the time be aware of the coloring which it received by passing through her mind."

The Links Between Feelings and Thoughts

Feelings influence how you think, and thoughts affect how you feel. These interrelations are quite dramatic. In one experiment different kinds of music were played to different people.[3] Some people listened to bright, happy music (an extract from *Coppélia*, by Delibes) to put them in a good mood. Other people listened to some very miserable music. In fact, it was an extract from the music for the film *Alexander Nevsky*, called *Russia under the Mongolian Yoke* by Prokofiev, and it was played at half speed to make it even more lugubrious. It sounded like Eeyore on a bad day. The people who listened to the bright music felt happy. The people who listened to the sad music felt miserable. That is not surprising. What was interesting was that those who felt miserable after listening to the sad music had different *thoughts* from those who had listened to the happy music. They remembered more bad things that had happened in their lives and thought that they were less likely to do a relatively simple task successfully.

Other research has confirmed these results and has shown *how* thoughts affect feelings. One of the most dramatic illustrations of this connection involved merely reading a list of words arranged in pairs.[4] This research was done in a therapist's consulting room during treatment for panic. When the subjects of the study were quite calm and at ease, people who experienced panic attacks read out loud a list of word pairs. If their list of words contained pairs such as "breathless-choking" or "palpitations-dying," they experienced sudden and intense waves of anxiety, and started to panic. This reaction demonstrated that episodes of intense anxiety can be precipitated entirely by thoughts.

These links between feelings and thoughts are being made all the time in our daily lives. For example, you feel miserable, and you think about the things that have gone wrong in your life, or you feel apprehensive and think you will make a mess of something. You think somebody you are fond of might be ill and you feel worried, or you think somebody is insulting you and you feel angry. Feelings and thoughts influence each other all the time—and there is a close match between them. If you think you have failed, you will feel disappointed, or sad, but you will not feel envious, since this emotion does not fit this stream of thought. If you did feel envious then you would have different thoughts, for instance about the good fortune of people who had been more successful than you.

Our very process of thinking—what we readily remember, what we think about, how we see things—is altered by our mood. The problem is that the bad mood in turn brings about more bad thoughts, so that the feelings get worse in a vicious cycle:

Here are examples of two common cycles, a "depressed" and an "anxious" one. In both of them you can see how the thoughts influence the feelings, and how the feelings trigger more thoughts.

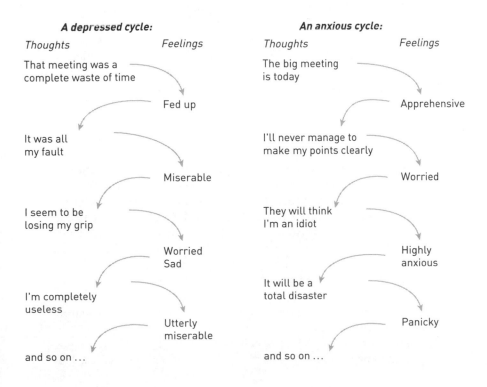

A depressed cycle:

Thoughts   *Feelings*

That meeting was a
complete waste of time

Fed up

It was all
my fault

Miserable

I seem to be
losing my grip

Worried
Sad

I'm completely
useless

Utterly
miserable

and so on ...

An anxious cycle:

Thoughts   *Feelings*

The big meeting
is today

Apprehensive

I'll never manage to
make my points clearly

Worried

They will think
I'm an idiot

Highly
anxious

It will be a
total disaster

Panicky

and so on ...

Working On Your Thoughts and Beliefs

If you were able to *think* differently, or to adopt another point of view, you would also *feel* differently. This is the key to cognitive therapy. Cognitive therapy tackles thoughts as a way of tackling mood. If instead of thinking you have failed, you recognize that everyone makes mistakes, the error you have just made will feel less like a sign of failure and more like a triviality. The skill lies in looking for ways of thinking differently, and the first step is to recognize your present viewpoint. First, you need to identify the specific thoughts that trouble you in the specific situations that make you feel bad.

STEP 1: HOW TO IDENTIFY PROBLEMATIC THOUGHTS—THE THOUGHT RECORD

Ashley came to us for help because she was often miserable and worried. She had accepted the offer of a new job and moved to a new place, leaving her boyfriend, Ben, behind, and she felt lonely and depressed. Over the last few weeks her feelings had been getting worse, until she felt utterly at their mercy. The vicious cycle had spiraled down until all she could think about was how bad she felt. At our first meeting we explained the relationship between thoughts and feelings, and asked her to keep a "Thought Record": a special kind of diary to help her pinpoint her thoughts and her feelings. She already knew the feelings well, and was giving far less attention to the thoughts that went with them. Each page of the diary was divided into three columns, as shown in the example of Ashley's diary (see p. 77).

We asked her to make an entry in the diary at least once a day. She had to focus on a specific situation, note down the feelings she experienced in that situation, and then ask herself, "What was going through my mind at the time?" Answers to this question revealed the thoughts that linked with her specific feelings. Although Ashley was suffering greatly, there were still times when she felt relatively good, but we could see that she easily lost sight of these. So we asked her to put in the diary not only the situations in which she felt miserable or worried, but also those when she felt relatively happy. She decided to add entries in the diary three times a day: taking ten minutes to do so at lunch time, when she came home from work, and before going to bed.

It is important to think of the specific situation you were in when you noticed feeling bad, and not just to dwell on the feelings themselves. This makes the task of identifying specific thoughts easier, because it tells you where in your memory to start searching for them. Doing this exercise is like becoming an expert mechanic who can listen to the sound of the engine, watch how the car performs, and then tune in to possible sources of trouble. Some of the entries from Ashley's diary are shown below.

Thought Record

Situation	Feelings	Thoughts
• Be specific.	• There may be more than one.	• Keep the different thoughts separate.
Traveling to work	Sad	1. I've made the wrong decision about accepting this job. 2. There's nothing I can do to change it.
Sitting at home after work	Depressed Lonely	1. I'm all on my own. 2. I don't have any friends.
After getting flustered talking to my boss	Miserable Anxious	1. I should be able to cope better than this. 2. I'm useless and feeble.
Ben telephoned when I was out	Worried Tense Upset Confused	1. I'm losing touch with him. 2. I'm not sure I want to stay with him.
Shopping	Cheerful	1. Ben is coming for the weekend. 2. No crowds in the supermarket. 3. Things might be okay after all.
Waking up	Wretched	1. No thoughts—but I know it's Monday morning.

It is often difficult to tune in to what is in one's mind. Sometimes the thoughts are not easily put into words. Or they can be so familiar that they "go without saying," like assuming others think you are stupid, or that they are too busy to be bothered with you. When cognitive therapists talk about "thoughts" they are using a kind of shorthand to refer to thoughts, beliefs, attitudes, ideas, images, and all the other contents of your mind—even including your dreams. So your thoughts may not have been put into words before, and they may not easily be expressed in proper sentences. Here are some key questions that can help you to identify your thoughts:

Key Questions for Step 1: Identifying Problematic Thoughts

What went through my mind at the time?
How am I seeing things now?
What is it about this that matters to me?
What does this event or situation mean to me?
Or what does it mean about me?

Look for thoughts that fit with the way you feel. Sometimes it is easy to make this fit: if you think you have done something wrong, or you remember doing something foolish, those things obviously fit with the way you feel—ashamed or embarrassed. Sometimes it is much harder: you feel discouraged even though nothing particular seems to have provoked that feeling today. Using the Thought Record can help you to solve this problem. Keep asking yourself the key questions, and try to stand back from the problem far enough to identify your personal perspective. Maybe feeling discouraged reflects a more pervasive attitude—lacking self-confidence or harboring dissatisfaction, for example. The links may seem obvious once you have identified them, but they are hard to recognize at first because it is so easy to become blinded by your own personal viewpoints. The more often you use the Thought Record, the easier this will become.

THIRTEEN KINDS OF CROOKED THINKING

Like looking through a prism, or a pair of distorting eyeglasses, some ways of thinking add a particular bias to your view of the world and are especially likely to be associated with feeling bad. Getting rid of the bias and getting your thoughts back into perspective will make you feel better, but first you need to recognize that the bias is there. These are the thirteen most common types of biased thinking which lead to feeling bad. *Which of these is contributing to your problems?* Most people have favorites, and readily fall into habitual patterns of thinking. Once you have identified, and named, the biases in your thinking, you are half way to defeating your bad mood.

1. *Catastrophizing.* Predicting the worst outcome. If something goes wrong, it will be a disaster. Every twinge is a sign of serious illness, every frown a sign of rejection. "If I make a mistake, I will lose my job." "I'll lose control completely." "My heart is beating so fast I could die."

2. *Overgeneralizing.* Assuming that because something happened once, this means it will always happen. "You always forget to do the things I ask." "I never seem to say the right thing." "We always do things your way." "I'm such a fool. I always blow it at the last minute."

3. *Exaggerating.* Giving negative events more importance than they really deserve, and positive events less importance. "I'll never get over it." "Any fool should be able to pass a driving test." "I can't bear it." "The way I look, nobody could take me seriously." "People never enjoy being with me because I'm too shy." "Landing this contract doesn't really mean anything at all."

4. *Discounting the positive.* Rejecting good things as if they did not count (or using a negative filter). "She only said that to make me feel better." "I could never have done that on my own." "It's just that I was lucky." "I happened to be in the right place at the right time." "What, this old thing? I bought it at a garage sale."

5. *Mind-reading.* Believing that you know what others are thinking. "She knows I've made a mess of this," "They all thought I was stupid." "He doesn't like me." "You only say that because you want to get at me." "They only asked me because they couldn't find anyone else."

6. *Predicting the future, or fortune-telling.* "Everything is bound to go wrong." "I won't be able to cope on my own." "I couldn't face it if something dreadful happened." "The interview went so badly I know they won't give me the job." "It's no use, I'll never get it right." "I'll never be able to do that sort of thing."

7. *Black and white thinking.* Switching from one extreme to another. "If I can't get this right, I might as well give up altogether." "If you can say that, then our relationship means nothing at all." "One mistake ruined the whole thing." "One false move, and the business will crumble."

8. *Taking things personally.* "They didn't ask me because they don't like me." "You're criticizing me" (when someone asks you to do something differently). "That waiter just ignores me." "If they don't get here it's because I gave them such bad directions."

9. *Taking the blame.* Taking responsibility when it is not yours. "It's all my fault." "Sorry." "They'd be happier if I'd been a better mother." "If only I'd done more for. . . ." "He failed the test because I was so nasty to him last night."

10. *Emotional reasoning.* Mistaking feelings for facts. "I'm so worried, I know something is going to go wrong." "I'm sure they've had an accident." "I love her so much she's bound to respond." "I don't care what you say, I just feel the way I do."

11. *Name calling.* "I'm an idiot." "You're completely heartless." "Anybody who could do that must be brain dead." "I'm stupid." "I'm bad."
12. *Scare mongering.* "Maybe she's really ill." "What if the car breaks down?" "Suppose they can't do anything about it?" "People do suddenly drop dead—you read about it in the papers." "Perhaps I'll fail." "I couldn't cope. . . ."
13. *Wishful thinking.* Supposing things would be better if they were different. "If only I were . . . younger . . . thinner . . . smarter . . . not the way I am."

Pressurizing words to watch out for. These words are often used when people want to motivate themselves to do better or try harder, but instead they tend to make them feel pressured and resentful so that motivation drains away and feelings of guilt set in.

- *Should:* "I *should* have done better." "You *should* have let me know."
- *Must:* "I *must* get this right." "I *must* not make a mistake."
- *Have to:* "I *have to* get there on time." "I *have to* keep this relationship going." "I have to hold things together."
- *Ought:* "I *ought* never to lose my temper." "I *ought* to lighten up."

Extremist words to watch out for. Extremist statements are (by definition) only very rarely true. Like meeting someone who is seven feet tall, it might happen, but it would be worth writing home about if it did.

- *Always:* "You *always* leave me to sort things out." "I *always* have to clean up after you."
- *Never:* "I can *never* do what I really want to do." "I'll *never* get what I want." "I'll *never* change." "You *never* listen to what I say."
- *Nobody:* "*Nobody* ever notices how much I do for them." "*Nobody* ever laughs at my jokes."

STEP 2: HOW TO LOOK FOR OTHER PERSPECTIVES—THE ALTERNATIVE DIARY

However compelling your thoughts and beliefs seem, there are other points of view as well: other angles from which one can look at the facts. After a couple of weeks of hard work with the Thought Record, Ashley was much better at identifying her thoughts. We then introduced her to the "Alternative Diary." Taking one thought at a time, she started the search for alternative points of view: the search for other ways of thinking that would make her feel better.

The Alternative Diary has only two columns: one for the thoughts and the other for alternative points of view. We asked Ashley to take one thought at a time, to write it down in the first column, and then to pose the following question: *"Is there another way of seeing things?"* She wrote down, in the second column, any alternatives she could think of, regardless of whether they seemed credible. An example of Ashley's Alternative Diary is given on page 82.

It is best to do this exercise on paper first. When you are good at it, you will be able to do it in your head. If you only do it in your head, and never write it down, you may forget how it went later. When the bad feelings sweep over you, it is only too easy to lose sight of the whole landscape and get lost in the mist.

The skill of looking for other perspectives lies in asking yourself some more key questions:

Key Questions for Step 2: Looking For Other Perspectives

Questions about thoughts: What other points of view are there? How would someone else think about this? How else could I think about it? How would I think about this if I were feeling better?

Questions about reality: What are the facts of the case? How can I find out which way of thinking fits the facts best? What is the evidence?

Questions about crooked thinking: Could I be making a mistake in the way I am thinking? Am I thinking straight? Am I using one of the thirteen kinds of crooked thinking? Am I pressurizing myself? Or using the language of the extremist?

Questions about coping: What is the worst that could happen? How bad is this going to get? What can I do when that happens? How can I get help?

Look for answers that fit the facts and that will make you feel better. If the answers do not fit with the facts they will not help because you will not believe them.

A note of caution: You are not looking for "the right" answers. You are looking for a way of seeing things that makes you feel better. There is no one right way, but there are many options (or perspectives). The problem is getting stuck with the option that makes you feel bad and forgetting that it is worth looking for others.

Alternative Diary

• *Reminder:* Look for alternatives that make you feel better.

Thoughts: Take one at a time.	Alternative points of view: There may be more than one.
1. I've made the wrong decision.	It seemed the right one at the time. It's too soon to tell. I probably think that because I feel so bad.
2. There's nothing I can do to change it.	Extremist words creeping in! Things I could do: Stick with the job and think how to make a go of it. Chuck it! Talk it over with Sandra (friend) and Alvin (brother). Get out and about more. Find somewhere to play squash.
3. I'm all on my own.	That's true. I *am* sitting here alone right now. But I'm not all alone in the world. There's Ben, even if I'm not sure about us. There are people at work even if I don't know them yet. Friends as well. I've made friends before, so I can probably make new ones too—it's ridiculous to think I always will be alone, and exaggerated to think it means no one cares.
4. I should be able to cope better than this.	The "should" really puts the pressure on. Maybe anyone would feel unsettled right now. Perhaps it's just a settling down stage. Anyway I *am* coping in some ways. The facts: Found somewhere to live; working things out with Ben; learning new things at work.
5. I'm useless and feeble.	If someone else said that about me, I'd think it was a complete exaggeration—and a real putdown. I know it's not true, and saying it only makes me feel worse.

How Does It Work in Practice?

Looking for the evidence. Mary was helped by cognitive therapy. She was a junior hospital administrator working in the accounts department and thought that she was being given too many of the rotten jobs at work.

She felt she was being used as a drudge. She had recently been asked to take on three major projects: to update the package of introductory material for people joining the department; to sort out the communal filing system; and to coordinate with other departments over joint projects. She felt she was providing the framework for other people to do the work rather than doing it herself. She tried to put a brave face on the situation, but nevertheless assumed that she was not considered very able. She dreamed about moving to somewhere where she would be better appreciated.

These were all Mary's assumptions, and she had not checked whether they were fact or fantasy. Her therapist asked her, "How could you find out whether these assumptions are right?" Together they discussed the possibilities, and Mary decided that she would talk first to one of her colleagues and then to her immediate boss. She found this difficult to do, but having thought about it carefully, decided that it was important enough to try. She was surprised to hear that no one realized either how she felt, or that she minded being landed with these tasks. From their perspective, they thought well of her skills and were exploiting her good nature. Everyone found these tasks boring and all of them were glad that they were in the hands of someone as efficient as Mary. Contrary to what she had thought, the evidence suggested that Mary's colleagues admired her abilities. After she talked about how she felt, her boss gave her more interesting work.

In Mary's case tackling the thoughts resulted in a plan of action which she carried out. As a result she felt much better. Sometimes the facts will be painful to hear, and not as reassuring as they were for Mary. This point will be taken up in the following section. Nevertheless, getting the facts straight is crucial, although it often takes courage to find them.

Looking for other points of view. After they had a fight, Nancy walked out of the house, leaving Jerry fuming inside. He thought; "Right. That's it. She's done with me for good. I might as well leave now." He was both angry and miserable. He did not want to lose the relationship.

What other views are there? Here are some of the possibilities from Nancy's point of view:

It's her way of cooling down. She does not realize how Jerry will interpret her behavior. She had to go out anyway, and did not explain because she was angry. She regrets the things she said and is blaming herself. She has difficulty controlling her temper and learned to walk away from it as a child. She is ashamed. She thinks he really means the unpleasant things he said about her during the fight. She wants to get back at him.

You can probably think of others—and the situation is very likely to be complex as well as explosive. The point is that, especially in the heat of the moment, one's own perspective has a blindingly obvious quality, while that of others becomes almost invisible.

Asking "What is the worst that could happen?" What if Mary and Jerry were both right, and their worst fears came true? So Mary finds out that no one thinks she is any good at the job, and Jerry discovers that he is going to lose Nancy.

If this happens Mary and Jerry will, almost certainly, be upset. But it is important that they do not turn their difficulties into catastrophes. If Mary thinks she will *never* be good at *any* job and Jerry predicts he will *never* find another relationship, then their thoughts will rub salt into the wounds, and the worse they feel the harder it will be to cope with the real difficulties they are in. If it seems to you likely that the worst really will happen, or if it has already happened, then the next step is to ask yourself how to cope: how to deal with this particular, difficult situation.

When problems seem insurmountable, or when they really are insoluble, it is tempting to give up—or to give in. Neither Mary nor Jerry may be able to find what they want in terms of "the right" job or a new relationship. Do they then *have* to go on feeling bad? Is this inevitable? What are their choices?

It would not be helpful to pretend that the difficulties did not matter. But Mary, and Jerry, may also have the resources to help keep the distress within limits. They each have personal assets and skills that could help: a sense of humor, an ability to accept what cannot be changed, persistence, flexibility, and so on. They have each coped with difficulties in the past and could think about what they did then—like looking to friends or relatives for help, advice, or support. They may need information, about openings for further training or where to meet people with similar interests. There may be more ways of looking for new jobs and different relationships than they have yet tried.

The point is that resources come in many shapes and sizes: personal qualities, skills and abilities, other people, general knowledge and information. Using them helps to keep the problems you encounter in perspective. If you do not use them when you feel bad, you will tend to feel helpless and be prone to self-blame, with thoughts in your head such as "I'm useless," "there's nothing I can do," "I should be able to cope better than this," which only make you feel worse, and make it harder to accept the reality for what it is: often not nearly as comfortable as one wishes it could be, but with smooth patches as well as rough ones along the way.

THE MEANING OF THE SITUATION

In Nancy's family, arguments were often violent: people got hurt physically as well as psychologically. She "knows" that it is better to get out while you can if you are involved in an emotional argument, and she ran away from Jerry in fear even though, in her right mind, she was confident that he would not resort to violence. She just thought, "I have to get out of here," and acted on this thought quickly, as she would have done as a child. This is an example of how one can be misled by one's thoughts. Nancy's thoughts made sense in terms of her past, but other ways of thinking would fit the facts far better in the present.

Many situations carry with them a load of meaning from the past, what is often called "emotional baggage." For example, when someone is angry with us, or critical, or when we are unable to get our own way, many of us behave and feel rather like we did as children. If we felt rejected by such things then, and wanted to run away and hide, then we may feel the same way now and want to do the same things. The old reaction is understandable but out of date. Present meanings may differ from old ones, and what felt like rejection in the past may be no worse than bad temper or a temporary reaction to a mistake in the present. This is another reason why it is so important to keep in touch with present facts and not assume that each new country you visit is just like the last one. Chapter 26 explains in more detail how to deal with the effects of distressing experiences in the past.

All sorts of activities carry with them meanings that trigger patterns of thinking that are associated with strong, and often disproportionate, feelings. When small children refuse to eat a meal that has been specially prepared, parents often feel surprisingly upset and angry, as if the well-being of the child depended on this particular meal, or as if the refusal to eat was a personal rejection. Losing a game of cards, or a competition for someone's business, can feel like a humiliating defeat rather than a temporary setback. Perhaps "winning" has become a way of gaining something important, like approval from others, or greater self-esteem. Or "losing" may have been associated with the kind of teasing from brothers and sisters that felt cruelly rejecting as a child. When relatively small events provoke much more strong feeling than you think they should, then it is likely that these events have some critical meaning for you. *This is when it is useful to go back to the beginning and ask yourself the key questions about meaning: "What does this mean to me? Or what does it mean about me?"* It is as if the meaning of these events has given them a disproportionate significance. Cognitive therapy helps you to feel better by getting your problems into perspective, and by testing your beliefs and assumptions against the facts.

Some Rules of Perspective

Having a problem can dominate your life. Whichever way you turn, the mountain or the cliff edge looms ahead, providing a dispiriting or alarming perspective. The following rules may be helpful when trying to find a more useful perspective.

1. *The 100-year rule (p. 221).* Will it matter in 100 years? Will anyone even remember what the problem was? Of course, this is something of an exaggeration, since few of us will be here in 100 years. It is meant as a reminder that those things that seem hugely important today may matter little when seen from a great distance. When you stand beside an elephant, it is extremely hard to see anything else. When you step back from it, the rest of the animal kingdom, the other visitors to the zoo and their surroundings, all come back into view.

2. *The measuring rod rule (p. 221).* Is the thing that is bothering you really the most important thing in your life at the moment? Imagine you have an important job to do today. You feel tense and worried about it, and the traffic jam on the way to work is enough to send you into a tirade of anger against all the bad drivers on the road. Of course, the traffic jam is important to you, but only as an impediment. Only as something that gets in the way of doing something that is of far greater importance in the long run.

3. *The middle of the night rule.* In the early hours of the morning, when you are lying awake, problems and worries assume insurmountable proportions. In the cool light of day, they can be more truly seen for what they are—molehills rather than mountains. The rule is: Think about them in the morning or during the day. It is always hard to keep things in perspective when lying awake worrying at night. Tell yourself "This is not the time." (See also Chapters 18 and 30.)

4. *The water-under-the-bridge rule, or the statute of limitations.* You feel bad about things that you did, or things you did not do. They continue to trouble you long past the time when they should. Let them flow by you instead, and look back on them as if they were someone else's mistakes or troubles. You may be carrying an

unnecessary load, weighing yourself down with troubles that are well past their sell-by date. There comes a time when you have punished yourself enough.

Chapter Summary and Reminder

• **There is always more than one way of seeing things.**

This means that although you may not be able to choose the facts you may be able to choose how you react to them, and help yourself feel better and act more effectively by looking at them differently. The methods explained here reveal how your feelings and thoughts are linked, and how these thoughts and feelings color your mood. If you practice using them, you will discover the kind of thinking that helps you to feel good. When practicing them, it is useful to ask yourself questions. The first one is this: "Is there another way of seeing things?"

• *Step 1:* Recognize your thoughts and the way your thoughts and moods link together.

Key questions for Step 1:

What went through my mind at the time?

How am I seeing things now?

What is it about this that matters to me?

What does this event or situation mean to me?

Or what does it mean about me?

• *Step 2:* Reexamine your thoughts. You will find that there are many perspectives from which you can look at a situation. Finding new perspectives gives you more options and helps you feel better.

Key questions for Step 2:

Questions about thoughts: What other points of view are there? How would someone else think about this? How else could I think about it? How would I think about this if I were feeling better?

Questions about reality: What are the facts of the case? How can I find out which way of thinking fits the facts best? What is the evidence?

Questions about crooked thinking: Could I be making a mistake in the way I am thinking? Am I thinking straight? Am I using one of the thirteen kinds of crooked thinking? Am I pressuring myself? Or using the language of the extremist?

Questions about coping: What is the worst that could happen? How bad is this going to get? What can I do when that happens? How can I get help?

10

Building Self-Confidence and Self-Esteem

Lacking Self-Confidence

Rachel believed she could never be confident. She was convinced that confident people had something that she just did not have, like blond hair or long legs. She was not sure how the differences between her and them allowed their confidence to remain strong in the face of adversity while hers remained fragile and elusive, even in good times. She suspected that confidence was unchangeable because it was written in the stars, or determined by chance. Confidence to her meant having a strong personality, which was either built in from the start or built up from encouragement at home and at school. Now that she was an adult of 32 it seemed to her that opportunities for becoming confident had gone for good. Lacking self-confidence was a cross she had to bear—whatever she did it was likely to remain with her and to let her down, in the same way as her short legs. She could wait for the lucky break (a complete change in fashion, or a world in which every shape was equally acceptable), but in her heart of hearts she believed she had no other option but to remain forever unconfident.

In the box on page 90, you can see how low self-confidence can affect the four aspects of life: your thinking, your feelings, your behavior, and your body. Being unconfident has surprisingly pervasive effects—it sneaks its way into hidden nooks and crannies and interferes with the things you want to do even when you least expect it. Look at the box and think about your own level of confidence. Adapt the list, if necessary, to fit your own experience.

Some of the Effects of Low Self-Confidence

Thinking
I can't.
That's too difficult.
I don't know how.
Maybe I won't be able to handle this.
It won't be good enough; someone else would do better.
I just can't decide what to do.

Feelings
Apprehension
Anticipatory anxiety
Worry, especially about forthcoming difficulties
Frustration and anger with yourself
Fear of the unknown, or of new situations
Resentment—it seems so easy for others
Discouragement and feeling demoralized

Behavior
More passive than active; keeping yourself in the background
Finding it hard to make suggestions, or put yourself forward
Prevaricating; being a slow starter
Avoiding taking on anything new or making changes in your life
Seeking help and advice even when you know the answer
Hesitating—and repeatedly needing encouragement
Taking a back seat
Asking for reassurance

Bodily signs of low confidence
Posture: tending to stoop, or retreating into yourself
Not looking people in the eye
Fumbling or fidgeting
Feelings of tension and nervousness
Sluggishness and lethargy

Becoming More Confident: Four Basic Insights

Rachel started to work on her confidence from the moment we first met her. Since confidence comes from *inside*, there was little point in giving her answers she might not believe, or could easily discount. She was ready with her favorite objection: "It's easy for you, but I'm just not like that." Instead, she took on the following assignment: to find out more about confidence from the point of view of others. This assignment made sense to Rachel because it could tell her more about the nature of this elusive concept, and carrying it out involved nothing more difficult than talking to people she already knew. She spoke to her brother; to someone who was starting her training as a nurse; to an aunt; to a colleague; and to various friends. She was surprised, once she developed ways of dropping the topic into the conversation, how many people had something to say about it, and how easy it was for her to sit and listen. Here are some of the things she asked: "What do you think confidence is?" "Where does confidence come from?" "Can you think of someone who is completely confident?" "How can you tell if someone is confident or not?" "How do you feel when you are talking to someone who is not at all confident?" "Does a confident person always feel confident?"

Rachel made both mental and written notes about her findings so that we could talk about them later. She found the following four points the most helpful—and they fit with what we know about confidence.

1 CONFIDENCE IS NOT JUST ONE THING

Confidence is not just one thing, it is many. Rachel was not confident when discussing a video she had watched with some friends, but she had no problem finding her way across the country to visit her aunt. She had stopped to ask the way when she needed to, and did not berate herself for getting lost along the way. Most of the people she spoke to said similar things. One of them thought she would never be able to make sense of her tax form, and had found learning to spell so difficult that she treated it as a lost cause, but she still led her daily exercise classes with energy and enthusiasm. The most confident person Rachel spoke to was her cousin, a buyer for a clothing store—but even he admitted that he lacked self-confidence from time to time, especially when training his junior staff, despite his acknowledged success. He knew he was good at his job, but he had learned it the hard way, by being thrown in at the deep end and having to get on with it. New recruits to his department now arrived with college-polished theories, talking a language that he told himself was "jargon," but that he feared, deep down, was too clever for him. He felt particularly at sea when the "common sense" he hardly needed to put into words was given textbook names that distanced him from the reality he knew. Rachel concluded that whether or not you feel confident depends on what you are doing. Labeling yourself as irredeemably unconfident is like failing to distinguish between all the different ways in which you can be confident or unconfident.

2 APPEARANCES CAN BE MISLEADING

Many people appear confident even when they are not. It is as if they know they might make a mistake, get things wrong, or put their foot in their mouth, but still behave as if everything will be all right in the end. When learning to give injections for the first time, Rachel's friend, the trainee nurse, said she thought about what she had been taught and about the more experienced people to whom she could turn to in a crisis. She hid her uncertainties for the sake of her patients. When she concentrated fully on what she was doing, she found there was little room left for doubts to creep in. Everyone Rachel spoke to could think of something that made them feel doubtful or shaky. Rachel learned that most people felt less confident than they looked.

3 CONFIDENCE COMES FROM DOING THINGS

Everyone Rachel spoke to agreed that confidence comes from doing things. Before you can ride a bicycle or drive a car, you have to learn how— confidence comes with practice, which makes it easier to recognize and accept that you really can do those things. Mistakes are inevitable when you are a novice. In fact, they are an important part of the learning process. Everyone makes mistakes, and they only get in the way if you let them undermine your confidence. Learn to shrug them off, or laugh about them with others who have found themselves in the same tangle (the video recorder that always misses the start of the program, the pasta that turns into a glutinous blob). If you try to avoid all mistakes, you run the risk of ceasing to learn.

4 PEOPLE TAKE YOU AT YOUR OWN ESTIMATION

When Rachel was using a friend's lawn mower, something went wrong. She was mortified. "I'm so sorry," she said. "I can't think what I could have done to it." She assumed the breakdown was her fault, and her friend went along with the assumption, hardly noticing that he had done so. Later it turned out that the clutch cable had snapped, and might have done so at any time. Her apologies, and her instant estimate of her own incompetence, led both of them astray: she convicted herself before she had committed a crime. He assumed a crime had been committed without even thinking about the cause of the breakdown. Rachel started to think again about her habit of apologizing—of assuming she was responsible for every mess she came across.

These four insights, coupled with the six guiding strategies which follow, provide the basis on which to start to build self-confidence.

Six Strategies for Building Confidence

1 PRACTICE

The first time you toss the pancakes they may fall apart—or onto the floor. But in the end, you will flip them over easily. Make building your confidence a habit—and that means practicing the other five strategies whenever you can. Do not think about building your confidence only when you are particularly vulnerable. Think about it when you are feeling buoyant, too. The more it becomes a habit, a practiced skill, the more secure your inner confidence will be when you really need it.

2 BEHAVE "AS IF"

When Cathy was sixteen years old, she flew with her family to Kuala Lumpur. A few minutes before landing they became engulfed in a severe tropical storm. There was insufficient fuel to fly to another airport. The pilot was forced to land after the runway had been flooded and closed to other aircraft. Sheet lightening surrounded the plane and fire trucks lined the airstrip. The lights went out. Someone screamed as the plane suddenly lost height. Cathy grabbed the arms of her seat. Her father, meanwhile, sat calmly reading his book. He turned the pages when he could see to do so; he kept his eyes on the print. The aura of confidence which exuded from him was almost palpable. It spread to those around him and helped others besides his family to cope with the fear of the moment. It also helped him. He, too, was anxious, but by behaving as if he felt confident, he helped himself, and others, to become confident.

Ask yourself, at an unconfident moment (preparing for an interview or a presentation to your boss), "How would I behave if I really felt confident?"

"How would so-and-so handle this?" where so-and-so is a confident person that you know. Adopting the behavior of confidence—the posture, the actions, and the thoughts—starts you on the upward spiral of increasing self-confidence.

3 TAKE THE ZIG-ZAG PATH

Confident behavior, especially when it is a newfound acquisition, can sometimes go to your head. This happened with Maggie, who had read about assertiveness and confidence building. She spent three weeks pushing herself to make new strides, making sure that others noticed her. In three weeks, however, she had become insensitive to how others felt. Concentrating exclusively on herself, she had no attention left over for them. Her colleagues withdrew from her—when they saw her coming, they thought: "Oh no, Maggie again!" And Maggie knew that this was how they felt. Not surprisingly, she was upset and confused about what to do next. She felt at risk of doing herself more harm than good.

It is important, therefore, to pay attention to what works, and watch out for the clues that come from others. Flexibility and confidence go hand in hand. Rigidity, even if it feels safer, gets in the way, as no two situations are exactly the same. Don't worry if you need to take a zig-zag path to your goal. People lacking in self-confidence often feel as if they have to steer a careful, well-planned travel route to avoid alarming pitfalls. But the pitfalls are largely imaginary, and the fear of taking a wrong step is inhibiting and becomes counterproductive.

4 MAKE THE MOST OF YOUR MISTAKES AND THEN IGNORE THEM

The mistake made by unconfident people is to think that mistakes matter. If you tried every day for the next year to make a mistake that nobody had ever made before, you would most probably fail. What matters is not doing something "wrong," nor doing something "badly," but whether you can recognize the mistake and use it to try to set yourself on a better path next time. Samuel Beckett said it for us: "No matter. Try again. Fail again. Fail better."

Errors are for learning. Only those who have ceased to develop never take a wrong step. Mistakes are a source of information. The newspapers were only too ready to tell us all about it when a U.S. president confused the Balkans with the Baltic. They made hay with the political implications of the error. But the furor blew over within a couple of days and hardly seemed to interrupt the president's flow of normally confident speeches, decisions, and actions. He learned from his mistake and then ignored it, getting on with the business at hand. Would any mistake you might make be more embarrassing?

5 LIMIT THE SELF-BLAME

Apply the "water-under-the-bridge" rule, and operate a statute of limitations (p. 86). Kicking yourself for past inadequacies, confusions, or failures gives fuel to your internal wavering voice—cut off its supply of oxygen and use an encouraging voice instead. Imagine you had a champion whose job it was to bring out the best in you. What encouraging things would this person be whispering in your ear? Amplify those messages, so you can hear them loud and clear.

6 BE KIND TO YOURSELF

Being kind to yourself is such an important strategy, and in our society such an underrated one that we have devoted a whole chapter to it (Chapter 7). It is a key strategy for building self-confidence. Problems with self-confidence are often rooted in a bad habit of punishing ourselves and of failing to seek out rewards and pleasures. If the habit of self-punishment is reversed, and you learn to treat yourself right, your confidence will be able to grow.

Six Strategies for Building Confidence

Use these six strategies often to build your self-confidence:
1. Practice.
2. Behave "as if."
3. Take the zig-zag path.
4. Make the most of your mistakes and then ignore them.
5. Limit the self-blame.
6. Be kind to yourself.

Self-Confidence and Self-Esteem

Rachel knew her self-confidence had taken a turn for the better when she booked a water-sports vacation with her friends. She was not a good swimmer, and only learned to put her head under water when she was 14, shamed into it at the time by school friends. But she was prepared to give it a try. She was even prepared to do only what she could manage and watch the rest. She no longer felt as if it mattered much how good or bad she turned out to be at the new venture. She had begun to believe in her ability to cope with success or failure as each came her way.

So she discovered that confidence spreads—from things you can do to the general feeling that you can learn to do things. This is why a good school provides such a variety of opportunities. The trip to explore an underground cave system provides important lessons in competence as well as in geology. Helping to introduce new students around school, or to make the stage scenery, or playing the trombone in the school orchestra gives children a chance to make mistakes with all the rest, and to learn how to correct them. Those who fall flat on their faces learn two important lessons: first, how to pick themselves up again; and second, that falling flat is not a *real* disaster. Protecting children from making their own mistakes does *not* help them to build their self-confidence: providing a safe environment within which they can make mistakes—and within which they can learn—is far more effective. It is sometimes harder for people who have sailed through early life with very little struggle and strife to cope with the difficulties and setbacks that eventually come their way, since they have had much less practice earlier on.

Self-confidence is concerned with how we feel about our abilities. But even the most confident people can feel that they are no good, or not good enough, or that they don't matter. Being good at something, believing that you can handle most of the problems that come your way, may still not make you feel worthwhile. So building up confidence is only part of the story. Self-esteem needs separate consideration. Self-esteem is about your values, and whether you live up to them; it is about your sense that other people value and accept you irrespective of your achievements; and it is about whether you value yourself.

Alice Walker, when she wrote *The Color Purple*,[1] started the book with a vivid and moving image of low self-esteem. Celie knew what others thought of her: "She ugly." "She ain't smart." Her feelings did not matter to anyone else. Her children were taken away. She was abused and forced into a relationship of subservience and disregard, not even recognized as sufficiently real to count as a marriage. She was reduced to saying "I don't know how to fight. All I know how to do is stay alive." "I don't fight, I stay where I'm told." The book tells the story of how Celie discovers (or rediscovers) herself and her ability to value herself. This is what self-esteem is about.

The value of self-esteem. Self-esteem is a difficult concept. If it is high we feel good about ourselves, and if it is low we feel bad about ourselves. This much is straightforward. The higher our self-esteem the more likely we are to achieve our potential, and the lower our self-esteem the more inhibited we will be. There is nothing so disabling as a sense of worthlessness. People who feel they are "worthless" or "do not count" also feel they have nothing to contribute. They hold themselves back and the prophecy becomes self- fulfilling.

Research has shown that children with low self-esteem don't try as hard and have lower expectations of success than others. A strong, positive self-esteem in adults is associated with being more assertive, with better physical health, with more satisfying relationships, and with an increased ability to tolerate and accept differences in others. People with lower self-esteem may denigrate others, including their companions, and thus get stuck in the "inferiority complex": "Anybody I like wouldn't like me; therefore, anyone who likes me isn't worth liking."

Sources of self-esteem. William James, writing in the 1890s, recognized that self-esteem depends on value judgments made about the self, and not simply on a list of qualities or achievements—being a good friend, mathematician, or swimmer. This was the truth which Marc, the chef, discovered (p. 15). William James realized that value judgments about oneself are closely associated with judgments made about us by others, and value judgments are associated with corresponding feelings. They make you feel good or bad.

What makes self-esteem such an elusive idea is that it is so central to our feelings. It is as though it provides the medium through which everything else is experienced, like seeing the world through a colored, or self-doubting, filter. It is perhaps not surprising therefore that the origins of our level of self-esteem go back to our childhood. Warm, intimates, and continuous attachments during childhood provide the kind of "emotional baggage" that helps to build self-esteem. This can be provided by *adequate* (not *perfect*) adults, parents as well as others. But it is not only our childhood which is important. Experiences in adult life, especially those involving warm relationships with others, are also important sources of self-esteem. Those who reach adulthood with low self-esteem are not, therefore, stuck in a dead end, but can take many steps toward feeling better about themselves—as did Celie in *The Color Purple.*

Five Strategies for Building Self-Esteem

You cannot change your childhood, but you can tackle those automatic thoughts—the legacy of your childhood—which work to undermine your self-esteem. Here are five strategies for counteracting these automatic thoughts. These make use of the skills of cognitive therapy described in Chapter 9.

1 ATTACK THE PREJUDICE

"Most women have no characters at all," according to Alexander Pope, putting into words a prejudice against which modern women have fought hard. Like all prejudices, it reflects the bias of the speaker far more than the qualities of the people spoken about. Once armed with this prejudice, the world seems to conform with it just as if the prejudice produced a biased way of seeing things. Women of character can be explained away as exceptions to the rule or by suggesting that they must have been provoked by exceptional circumstances. Or they might just be glossed over altogether—ignored to the point of invisibility. The information that fits with any other point of view has a hard time breaking through the barriers put up by a firmly held prejudice: instead, it is *discounted, deflected,* or *distorted.*

Low self-esteem is like a prejudice about oneself—seeing oneself as unworthy, or unacceptable. The self-perception is biased, or flawed, but the person with the prejudice has a hard time seeing it any other way. Learning to fight the bias involves acknowledging your qualities and talents rather than *discounting* them: "I like drawing. I was good at it even at school," "I've always been a good listener"; accepting compliments and signs of acceptability rather than *deflecting* them: "Thanks, I'm glad you liked my work/cooking/friends"; recognizing that you matter rather than *distorting* the evidence: "He really did seem interested in what I said."

Prejudices can be changed, but they are apt to reemerge at times of stress. Old habits die hard, but if you know them well and recognize their corrosive effects on the way you think and feel about yourself, you will have a better chance of fighting back when they start to reassert themselves.

2 STIFLE THE CRITIC

You were tired and shouted at the children—not just shouted, but yelled. They were storming about the house when you wanted peace and quiet.

Then the internal critic started getting at you: "Nobody should treat a child like that. You're a hopeless parent. They'll never learn to behave. No wonder their grandparents don't want to come here much . . . it's all my fault."

The critic within you is remarkably resourceful; so beat it at its own game. Think about what really happened, and clarify the facts. Accept what went wrong, but talk back to the critic to keep the "badness" in perspective. Explain that you were tired. Maybe you had good reason to be so! Ask how children learn to consider the needs of others. Can they do this without knowing what those needs are? Remind the critic of your good moments as a parent, of the times when you help your children in other ways to learn about consideration. Apologize if you need to, and put the critic, the exaggerator, back in the box with the lid shut.

3 BURY THE JUDGE

The judge is the person inside you who says: "I'm not wanted," "I'm in the way," "I don't matter," "compared to everyone else I'm a mere crumb—a grain of sand, a worm," "I'm not important." When you bury the judge, you learn how to replace the judgments with facts.

It may be true that you were always the last to be chosen when children were dividing each other up for a game or a contest of some sort. That fact has nothing to do with your chances of being chosen for the job you are going for now. In the new situation examine the facts carefully. You may, or you may not, have a good chance of getting the job. Try to weigh the chances for yourself. That way you can learn how to make realistic judgments and how to trust your own judgment.

The judge is also that part of you which says to a friend "You did really well getting that job," but when you get a job says to you "Getting that job was just lucky. You'll have to watch it, or they'll get rid of you as soon as they find out how useless you really are." The judge is flagrantly unfair by applying different standards to different people. Your judge needs to learn to apply the standard used for others to yourself as well.

The judge is unfair in other ways. It makes negative predictions, it biases your expectations, it makes snap judgments on the basis of superficial information. Your judge may lead you to expect to fail. It stops you from trying and brings you down. It makes you impervious to success, which is attributed to chance, and susceptible to failure, which is only to be expected. It is always finding "more successful" people with whom to compare you. Think of the child who rushes proudly home from school: "I came in second in class." "Who came first?" asks the parent, and the child retires crushed. The "judge of low self-esteem" is like that parent. Such judges could live happily in the same box as the critic, provided the lid was kept tightly shut on them both.

4 DO THE BEST YOU CAN

Ray used to say that he "had to do his best in every possible way." Then his therapist asked him what his aim was when he made that rule. He answered that it was to do his best. To do as well as he could. To get the best out of himself. Together they examined his rule to find out whether it did, in fact, help him to achieve his goal—which seems reasonable enough. The disadvantage was that it put him constantly under pressure. He set his goals so high that he almost always failed to reach them. It felt good when he did, but those moments were rare. The bottom line was that he knew he was no good. He just could not live up to his rule.

There is an important difference between having an ideal and making a rule to live by. The ideal may be perfect, unflawed, without blemish, a standard one would be proud to attain. Such an ideal provides you with a guide, but it should not be a daily standard. Making the ideal into a rule is digging oneself an elephant trap. If you constantly fall into the trap, you feel so bad about yourself that it becomes increasingly hard to keep going. The rule needs to be clear, and to direct you toward the ideal if that is what you want, but it also needs to be realistic, if it is not to undermine your self-esteem. That is why it makes more sense to *do the best you can*—rather than aim for perfection. Aiming for perfection in this life is a recipe for disaster. Aiming for better self-esteem helps you to do better, and also to feel better.

Some of the rules often adopted (half unawares) by people with low self-esteem are shown in the box on page 101. You can see how they might be counterproductive. Reject such rules, or revise them so that they work for you rather than against you.

5 DEVELOP FRIENDSHIPS THAT MAKE YOU FEEL GOOD

Other people play an important part in one's feelings about oneself. If low self-esteem is a problem for you, think about your current relationships. Who helps you to feel good about yourself? Who undermines your self-confidence? Make a list and estimate how much time you spend with people in each group. How could you increase the time you spend with those who make you feel good; and decrease the time with those who make you feel bad? Making changes in your relationships may be one of the most effective ways of increasing your self-esteem—but making changes in relationships is rarely straightforward. In Part Three we describe a number of skills to help you to develop fruitful relationships.

Some Rules that Perpetuate Low Self-Esteem

- I have to do things right.
- People should always help each other.
- Do what others suggest: they know best.
- I should be better, or more skilled, or wiser . . . and so on.
- A woman should be helpful.
- Men should never cry.
- If I don't do excellently well, I should try even harder.
- Mistakes should not be forgotten or forgiven.
- One should never burden others with one's problems.
- You have to accept the way you are; there's nothing you can do about it.

A Logical Fallacy, or a Legacy from the Past

Self-esteem is not a constant. It is not something that is impervious to knocks and never varies. Even people with the toughest systems feel better about themselves some days than others. But there is one particular fallacy that is especially hard to uproot. For most people, when they were young they were sometimes punished in one way or another, at home or at school, and they learned the lesson well. If you do something wrong, you deserve to be punished. If you do something wrong, it means you have been bad, or that you are bad.

For some people, especially for those with memories of painful experiences in the past, for people who suffer from depression, and for those whose concerns about their weight and shape have led to disordered patterns of eating, it can be hard to break the link between being treated badly and believing that you are bad (see Chapter 26 for more ideas about how to break these links). If life is bad to you, you may be tempted to think that you are bad—that you have deserved "punishment." This is not so. Life is not a courtroom. Our experiences are not the just desserts for our characters. If you have been badly treated by others, or have suffered from bad luck, do not compound your problems by taking the blame—by seeing your suffering as a proof of your unworthiness. Learn to value yourself, and this will give you the strength to face your suffering.

Related Chapters in This Book

Our sense of self-esteem and self-confidence has a great impact on our enjoyment and success. This is why valuing yourself is one of the two fundamental principles explained in Part One (Chapter 3). There are few chapters in this book which will not help you to increase your self-esteem and confidence. Six chapters are, perhaps, of particular relevance:

Chapter 3	*Valuing Yourself*
Chapter 7	*Treating Yourself Right*
Chapter 13	*Be Fair to Yourself and to Others*
Chapter 23	*Digging Yourself Out of Depression*
Chapter 26	*Dealing with the Past*
Chapter 31	*Good Eating Habits*

Chapter Summary

You can build up your self-confidence, even if you have lacked confidence since childhood.

The *four* basic insights are:

1. Confidence is not just one thing. Each of us lacks confidence in some areas of our life, and has confidence in other areas.
2. Apparently confident people may not be as confident as you think.
3. We gain confidence from doing things.
4. If you tell people you're no good, they might believe it!

These *six* guiding strategies will help you to build up your self-confidence:

1. Practice.
2. Behave as if you are more confident than you feel.
3. Be flexible in your behavior.
4. Learn from your mistakes. The only way of avoiding mistakes is to become stagnant.
5. Silence the voice of self-blame, and speak encouragingly to yourself.
6. Be kind to yourself.

Self-confidence is concerned with how we feel about our abilities. Self-esteem is subtly different: it reflects the degree to which you value yourself.

These five strategies will help you to build your self-esteem:

1. Attack those prejudices which lead you to undervalue yourself.
2. Stifle the inner critic.
3. Bury the judge within you that applies double standards: an unfairly strict standard to you, and a generous standard to others.
4. Do the best you can, but don't berate yourself for not being perfect.
5. Spend time with people who make you feel good.

11

Learning How to Relax

The last thing Jess wanted to be told when she was feeling wound up was to calm down. The very demand was counterproductive, and ran the risk of winding her up further. At the time it seemed to her both impossible to do and the wrong thing to do. She admitted that she usually got tense and on edge when she felt under pressure, and worried that she was not going to be able to get things done, or that she would forget to do something important. What she really wanted to do was to keep going as fast as she could. In the heat of the moment she swept aside any helpful suggestions from others, dismissing them as insensitive intrusions into her personal affairs, or reacting as if they were fundamental criticisms of her as a person. But in the end she usually had to admit that the suggestion was right. She needed to calm down, and to do so sooner. If she went on too long, she became overtired, even more tense and strained, found it hard to sleep, and wondered if, having managed long ago to turn herself on so as to function on all cylinders at once, she had now lost the "off button." She found it extremely hard to switch off—but learning how to relax was a great help.

Learning how to relax is not one thing, it is many. It is an *attitude:* taking things calmly and in your stride, or keeping cool; or accepting what you cannot change. It is a *physical skill:* learning how to recognize and release tension, both physical and mental. It is a *habit:* developing routines that work for you rather than against you. It is a *restorative:* a way of giving yourself rest and recreation, and refilling the systems that are otherwise constantly being depleted. We will touch on all these aspects of relaxation in this chapter. If you would like to learn how to take things more easily in your stride, read this chapter carefully, but look also through the rest of the book for chapters relevant to those things that make it especially hard for you to relax.

Relaxation is one of the most general ways of making you feel better. When you have learned to do it, you will find that it makes a noticeable and extremely worthwhile contribution to your mood and to your energy, not just when you are feeling tense or agitated, but at other times as well. Developing relaxed attitudes and habits also has a preventive, or protective, effect, so relaxation provides one of the main building blocks of psychological fitness.

Why Bother with Learning How to Relax?

TENSION IS PAINFUL AND UNPLEASANT

You should learn to relax because tension, the opposite of relaxation, has so many painful effects. It produces aches and pains, perhaps most commonly in the neck and back. The shoulder muscles for many people provide a kind of internal thermometer of their tension level. Learn, during relaxation exercises, to relax your shoulders and you will be surprised to find, if you tell yourself regularly to "drop your shoulders," just how often there is something to drop. Having aches and pains adds to your troubles and give you something extra to worry about.

Being tense also makes people irritable and tired. Everything that you do while feeling tense takes more energy than it would if you were feeling relaxed, and of course this is energy wasted. Tension tends to speed people up, like a clockwork toy: the tighter the spring is wound, the faster the machine will run. Learning to relax slows you down again, and helps you to cope more comfortably with the demands of daily living. So learning to relax soothes both the mind and the body.

RELAXATION IS A SKILL

You should also learn to relax because, for many people, this is not something that comes naturally. It is no use just telling yourself, or someone else, to "calm down" and to "relax" because relaxation is a skill that has to be learned before it can be applied. It's unlikely you will be able to do it effectively unless you first spend some time learning the skill, and then practice applying it in easy situations first. These principles are the same for learning all physical skills, such as riding a bicycle.

How to Relax

Did you ever lie awake at night feeling tired, tense, and worried, making every possible effort to switch off and relax only to find that the harder you tried the more elusive such a peaceful state of mind seemed to be? There is certainly something paradoxical about learning to relax: it is like making an effort not to make an effort; working hard at not working; or taking control in order to let go. Maybe this is why, for many people, the state is so elusive: the harder one tries to do it, the more frustrated one becomes when it seems not to work.

The first thing to remember is that you can rely on both your mind and your body to do the job for you. If you can deal with those physical and mental tensions that interfere with your ability to relax, then the process will take care of itself. Your job is to deal with those things that, for you, get in the way of letting go. The four steps to go through are described next, followed by an example showing how these steps fit together.

STEP 1: PREPARATION

Preparing to Relax

- Choose the method which attracts you, and stick with it.
- Schedule a time each day when you can practice, undisturbed, for half an hour.
- Find a comfortable place for your daily practice.

There are many methods of relaxation and very little research on which ones work best. Research does show that learning to relax helps people become calmer, less tense and less anxious, so it may not matter which method you choose. What does matter is that you *choose one method and stick with it until you have learned it properly.* If you want to try out other methods, then do so later. Some of the main options include deep muscle relaxation, yoga, various types of meditation, and the Alexander technique. You may be able to find classes, videos or CDs that teach these methods. Here we describe how to learn deep muscle relaxation.

Learning to relax takes time—at least half an hour a day for the first few weeks. But if you feel tense, learning how to relax should become a priority. *Decide first which time of day suits you best.* You need to find a time when you can make yourself warm and comfortable, and when you will not be disturbed, either by other people or by the telephone. If it is difficult for you to see how you can fit a relaxation practice time into your day, then ask yourself what you could give up in order to make time, or how others could help you protect the space and time that you need. Making relaxation into a routine, and practicing it at the same time, every day, can relieve you of the task of deciding each day when you will do it, and make it easier to remember to practice. It is usually best not to do it last thing at night, when it may put you to sleep. This is because you need to use the practice to learn how to recognize your personal signs of tension, to learn how to let them go, and therefore you need to remain aware of what you are doing. Also, should you fall asleep doing the exercise you will have to disturb yourself afterward in order to go to bed. Once you know how to relax, then you can, if you wish, use the method to help you settle down and to sleep better.

Learn to relax at your own pace. Just as with anything else, some people can learn a method more quickly than others. But when learning to relax, trying to hurry is counterproductive. The more you rush, the harder it will be.

Deep muscle relaxation uses the pendulum method—if you want the pendulum to swing in the opposite direction, you first have to pull it back. So practice involves tightening up muscle groups and then letting them go. The aim is to work systematically through the body, and it is usual to start with the hands, work up to the shoulders, then back to the feet and up to the shoulders again, leaving the face and neck to last. We have no reason to suppose that it matters if you go through the body in another order, but it may be difficult to start with the areas in which physical and emotional tension seem to concentrate, such as the shoulders, neck, and face, and it may also be helpful at the end to repeat the exercise for any parts of the body that are especially difficult for you to let go.

Settle down in your warm and comfortable place. Undo any clothing that feels tight, especially around your waist or neck. We recommend that you lie down on your back and close your eyes. If you find this hard, then do whatever feels most comfortable, such as sitting in an armchair and starting with your eyes open. Give yourself a moment or two to settle, and then tune in to your breathing. When you are breathing in a relaxed way, your stomach will move gently up and down as you breathe in and out. If all the movement comes from your chest, then your breathing is less relaxed. To relax your breathing, tell yourself to "let go" as you breathe out, as this emphasizes the natural body rhythm. Telling yourself to "let go" as you breathe in is going against the grain, and therefore harder to do. You can find out how you are doing by putting one hand on your chest and the other on your stomach and feeling them move. Aim for the relaxed, diaphragmatic type of breathing during which the hand on your stomach moves most, but accept calmly whatever is happening at the time. As you become more relaxed, your breathing will take care of itself.

When you are settled, start to work through the muscles one by one. You can work out ahead of time which order to go in, or you can make yourself a tape recording of the instructions which follow.

STEP 2: PRACTICE

The basic exercise. Turn your attention to your hands. When you are ready, tighten up all the muscles in both your hands. Clench your fists, and hold the tension while you count slowly up to three (pulling the pendulum back), then let the tension go. Feel the tension drain out of your fingers, and let them come naturally to rest. Each time you breathe out allow your hands to become heavier. Let the blood circulate freely right to your fingertips, as you feel more and more deeply relaxed. Give yourself as much time as you like to focus on your hands before you repeat the exercise with the next muscle group.

The muscle groups. This is the order we suggest, together with some ideas to help you tighten the right muscles. Work up to your shoulders from your hands, and then all the way from bottom to top. It does not matter if you make a mistake, or miss out on a muscle. It is more important to learn how to recognize tension and how to let that go, in order to achieve a state of deep muscular relaxation.

Finally, tune into your breathing once more. Every time you breathe out imagine you can reach an even deeper state of relaxation. Enjoy feeling more relaxed for a moment or two before you move about again, and then rouse yourself slowly. If you leap up quickly after the exercise you may feel slightly dizzy, and you will also undo some of the beneficial effects. The whole exercise should take about 20 to 30 minutes.

Later in the chapter we will explain how you can shorten the time needed.

Deep Muscular Relaxation

Here is an order that we find easy to remember which will help you not to forget any muscle group. Remember, after tensing each muscle group, let go slowly, feeling the tension drain away and the blood flowing freely. Don't forget to breathe.

- *Hands*: Clench the fists. Now, let go.
- *Arms*: Tighten biceps and lower arms together, without the hands.
- *Shoulders*: Raise your shoulders as if they could touch your ears.
- *Feet*: Screw up your toes.
- *Front of legs*: Point your foot away from you so that it is almost parallel with your leg.
- *Back of legs*: Flex your feet upwards, stretching your heels down.
- *Thighs*: Tighten them while pressing your knees down into the floor.
- *Bottom*: Clench your buttocks together.
- *Stomach*: Hold your stomach muscles in tight.
- *Lower back*: Press the small of your back into the floor.
- *Chest*: Breathe in, hold your breath, and tighten all your chest muscles.
- *Shoulders*: Breathe in, hold your breath, and raise your shoulders as if they could touch your ears.
- *Neck*: 1. Stretch your head up, as if your chin could touch the ceiling.
  2. Bend your head forward until your chin reaches your chest.
- *Mouth and jaw*: Press your lips together and clench your teeth.
- *Eyes*: Close them up tight.
- *Forehead and scalp*: Raise your eyebrows as if they could disappear.
- *Face*: Screw all the muscles up together.

Relaxing mentally as well as physically. Some people find they can relax more easily physically than mentally. They keep thinking about worrying or upsetting things, even after all their muscles are deeply relaxed. This is when making use of relaxing imagery may be helpful (see also Chapter 30, pp. 429–432). Make a list of places or situations that you find calming or relaxing, and as you relax after doing your exercises, imagine that you really are in one of them. Do not worry if the images keep changing—imagery is rarely static. Just guide the images into calm waters, and away from sources of trouble. For example, you may be imagining a calm spot on the banks of a river where you once fell asleep in the sun. But your concentration might waver so that you find yourself thinking about tomorrow's problems. Gently bring your attention back to the river bank.

Making your own relaxation tape. Write yourself a basic script, or prompt sheet, based on the ideas above, before you record it. Start by reminding yourself how to settle down. Then talk yourself through the whole thing, including all the instructions about how to tune in to your breathing. Tell yourself which muscles to tense up, remind yourself how, then tell yourself to let go. As you are letting go, talk to yourself about what you are trying to achieve. Give yourself reminders like this: "Let all the tension drain away. Allow the muscles to feel warm and heavy, as your relaxation becomes deeper and deeper. Each time you breathe out, let go a little further. Imagine that your limbs have become too heavy to move, and that you are completely, and comfortably supported" . . . and so on. You should talk to yourself slowly, in a quiet and calming voice, and of course you can add your own variations, like repeating exercises you find difficult, or some music you find relaxing to listen to before you begin or after you have finished.

Occasional problems with physical relaxation. People who suffer from pains in their joints, such as those caused by arthritis, may not be able to use the pendulum method as it may hurt to tense up before letting go. If this is a problem for you, you can learn to relax just by focusing on each muscle group in turn, or by using one of the forms of relaxation more closely related to meditation.

Some other people find the sensations they experience when starting to relax rather alarming, as if they were about to lose control, rather than sink into a state of restfulness and calmness. Usually it does not take long to realize that nothing alarming happens when you relax, especially if you proceed at your own pace, and follow these exercises with those described in Step 4 below.

STEP 3: APPLICATION

Once you are able to achieve deep muscle relaxation using the whole exercise, you need to learn how to use this new skill in ways that make you feel better. It is not possible to remain in a deeply relaxed state as you go about your daily life, so you may gain little benefit from Steps 1 and 2 alone. How can you drive a car, talk to people, or put the children to bed if you are deeply relaxed? The next stage involves learning how to recognize small degrees of tension early and how to let them go before they build up. This is achieved by shortening the exercise, so you can relax quickly, and by practicing in increasingly difficult situations.

Shortening the relaxation exercise. Shorten the exercise gradually over the next three to six weeks. For example, you could try collapsing some of the muscle groups until you only work on your arms, legs, abdomen, chest, and face. Or you could settle down and see how relaxed you can get just by tuning in to your breathing, then work on any muscle groups that still feel tense. You could work through the first half of the exercises and then see if you can do the rest just by becoming aware of all the different parts of the body one by one. You could leave out the tension, and work only on the relaxation. Eventually, you want to be able to relax quickly and when needed—the thing that seemed impossible to start with. Use your imagination to find any way of shortening the exercise that works for you. You can see why first you need to use the whole body exercise to learn to recognize the signs of tension and let them go, however small they are.

Continue to practice daily, but as the practice times become shorter, look for opportunities to practice more frequently.

Practice in increasingly difficult situations. Once you are reasonably good at basic relaxation, try doing the exercises in different positions, such as sitting instead of lying down. Try to relax sitting in an armchair, and then try it sitting at a table, or walking around the garden. Try it when you are reading, watching TV, or washing up. Think about only using the muscles that are necessary for the job at hand. If there is tension elsewhere, for instance, in your stomach when driving the car, or in your shoulders when listening to music, then try to let it go. Tense the muscle up more to begin with, to make use of the pendulum effect, then allow the tension to drain away.

Once you can relax while engaged in normal daily activities, try to relax in the situations that make you tense—in those situations that trouble you. You will not be able to apply the relaxation successfully in the most difficult situations without a great deal of practice, so do not expect this to work the first time you try. Work up to the hardest situations by relaxing in the easier ones first, and remember it is always easier to relax if you catch the tension early. Check your tension levels regularly to begin with, and tell yourself to relax every time you check. You will be surprised to find how often there is unnecessary tension to let go.

A Quick Relaxation Routine—The Quick Fix

---

1. Tune in to your breathing. Take one deep breath in, hold it, then tell yourself to let go as you breathe out. Breathe naturally for a while, repeating the instruction to let go with every outward breath. Choose an instruction that fits for you: "Keep calm," "Hang in there," "Take it slow," "Let it go," etc.
2. Tense up and then relax a single muscle group such as your hand, foot, or stomach. When you let go, try to let all the unnecessary tension slip away.
3. Drop your shoulders.

If you start with the full relaxation exercise, shorten it to a quick routine, and then apply your relaxation skills in increasingly testing situations; you will soon begin to feel the benefit. Occasionally, go back to the whole exercise just as a reminder.

STEP 4: THE EXTENSION COURSE: SIX WAYS OF DEVELOPING A RELAXED ATTITUDE

Relaxation is an attitude, a habit, and a restorative as well as a skill. Make it part of your life in every way.

1. *Adopt a relaxed posture.* Do you catch yourself sitting on the edge of your chair? Fidgeting and fiddling with things? Tension can waste so much energy, so allow your body to rest when you get the chance.
2. *Stop rushing about.* It only winds you up. Most people find that they get just as much done when they go slowly as when they rush, and they can also keep going longer. Doing things calmly is much less tiring.
3. *Make a habit of doing the things you find relaxing.* Whether they are peaceful and calm things (like reading or doing nothing much of anything) or strenuous things (like exercising or going to parties), do the things that relax you.
4. *Seek out pleasures and treats.* The more you are enjoying yourself, the more relaxed you will feel.
5. *Spread the risks.* If you put all your eggs in one basket, you will feel extremely tense and on edge if that basket is threatened.
6. *Give yourself breaks.* Take short breaks, like half an hour talking to a friend, as well as long ones, like regular vacations.

Many of these ideas are expanded in the example below as well as in the other chapters listed at the end of this one.

How Relaxation Can Work in Practice

Graham was the salesman for a small light-engineering company. His salary was paid on a commission basis, which meant that the more he sold the more he earned. He was always at the mercy of economic trends: if business was good he did well, and when it became scarcer his salary dropped. He came to the clinic after he had recently married and had taken on his first mortgage. As a downturn in business had developed, he had felt increasingly tense and pressured. By the time we met he sounded frantic. He had been working extremely long hours, traveling to see potential customers, leaving little time for paperwork in the office, and an old injury to his neck was causing him considerable pain after he had twisted it lifting his briefcase out of the car. There seemed to be many sides to Graham's problems. However, his tension was visible, and he was no longer able to relax on the rare days when he was not working. He wanted to learn how to relax, so this is how we started. These are the stages he went through.

1. *Preparation.* He started by wrestling with his timetable, and talking to his wife, trying to find a regular time to practice. On working days he chose to do it as soon as he came home from work, regardless of whether he had eaten, and on other days, immediately after breakfast. He wanted to use the relaxation exercise to help him mark the difference between "time on" and "time off." Then he asked his wife to help him make his own relaxation tape. He knew he might forget to practice, or try and argue himself out of it when he felt rushed, so he stuck a small card on his shaving mirror with the days of the week written down the side, and ticked off the days when he practiced (five out of seven in the first week; every day in the second).

At first, he gained little benefit, since the more he relaxed the rest of his body, the more he noticed the pain and tension in his neck. He found himself struggling against the pain, frustrated at not being able to let the tension go. He had forgotten how important it is to accept feelings for what they are, and work at removing the blocks that get in the way of allowing the body to take care of itself. We suggested that he take special care to make his head and neck comfortable before practicing, using extra support, and also that he should do an experiment to find out which method of relaxation was most helpful: doubling the neck exercises to give himself more practice, or working on his neck without the pendulum—relaxing his neck by becoming aware of the tension already present and allowing that tension to drain away without first tensing up.

By the end of the next week, Graham had started to make noticeable progress. Doubling the neck exercises had given him the most help, and he was surprised to find out how much his general level of tension had been adding to the discomfort caused by his original injury. He also discovered that he needed to allow about double the average amount of time to let the tension in his neck drain away when he was letting go. Knowing that the next step involved shortening the exercises and using them in more testing situations, he repeated the tension and release exercise for his neck at other times during the day when he noticed the tension building up.

2. *Practice.* Shortening the exercises posed little problem for Graham since he was so busy; he was glad to cut down on extra commitments, including this one. There was a danger that he would try to run before he could walk, and easily fall back into old habits. He needed to make the relaxation part of his daily life as quickly as possible. By the time he had learned to let the tension go while sitting at his desk, he agreed that it was worth devoting half an hour a day to relaxing, but he decided to break the time up over the course of the day. He worked out his own "quick fix" routine, then he put this into effect every time he sat down. Sitting down became a cue to practice, whether he sat down to eat, to work, or to drive the car. Even sitting in a bar or in front of the television, he ran through his quick routine (which was totally invisible to those around him) the moment he got the weight off his feet. Altogether, he probably practiced far more than half an hour a day at this stage.

3. *Application.* For the first four weeks Graham had been working predominantly on the preparation and practice steps. He then moved on to applying his developing skills in more difficult situations related to work. We reminded him how important it was to catch the tension as early as possible, and together we devised a monitoring system. Graham needed to remind himself to check his tension levels very frequently during the day, but he was so pressured that he kept forgetting. He bought a sheet of colored sticky dots to use as reminders. He stuck them wherever he would see them: on his watch face, his diary, the telephone, the rear view mirror, his bedside lamp, the kitchen window, and so on—about 30 of them altogether. These were his messages to himself: "Whenever I see a dot, check my tension level, and let the tension go." He found the dot on the telephone at work was the most useful, and realized that he was often so tense by the time he reached the office that he avoided using the telephone for fear of discovering more problems and adding further to his

difficulties. By feeling relaxed when he used the telephone he was able to bring more of his work under control.

4. *The Extension Course.* By now, Graham had developed the habit of checking his tension level frequently and relaxing quickly when he needed to. If he put off doing his relaxation exercises for too long, he found it harder to let go, so we encouraged him to keep practicing. At this point he started extending the relaxation in other ways. By the middle of the working day, he was usually pushing himself along at full speed. We persuaded him to take a proper lunch break away from work—to find a way of leaving the problems behind even for a short time. So he decided to try, literally, walking away from them. Wherever he was, rain or shine, he went for a brief walk. If a meeting got in the way, he took the walk earlier or later. He gave himself a breathing space away from the pressure. And he did similar things at home and on Sundays. He started to do some work on the house. This does not sound relaxing, but he enjoyed the physical and relatively undemanding activity. It stopped him from thinking about other things, and felt more constructive to his wife as well as to him. Together they decided that it would be a good idea to fit in more exercise, and so they planned some long country walks. The exercise felt good, but they soon discovered that this was not their kind of thing. They enjoyed more social activities, like bicycling with friends or dancing at a club in town. The more they engaged in relaxing activities, even tiring and strenuous ones, the more Graham shed the load of tension, and—to his surprise— the better he found himself coping at work. Even the pain in his neck disappeared. He had spread his interests wider again, and doing so helped him to develop a more relaxed attitude to the pressures at work.

RELAXING OUT OF PAIN

It is well known that prolonged physical tension is painful, even if the tension is as mild as that caused by sitting all day at a word processor. It is also well known that tension exacerbates pain. If you are in physical pain, then the more tense you are the worse this pain feels. This information has been of great value to women during childbirth, many of whom benefit from relaxation classes during their pregnancies.

It is less well known that relaxation, and other skills such as mindfulness-based meditation, can also be helpful to people with other sorts of pain, such as the pain of arthritis or persistent headaches. The exercises described here, including the ways they can be applied and extended, can be used in these circumstances too.

Other Chapters to Turn to If You Feel Tense

Chapter 7   *Treating Yourself Right*
Chapter 9   *Keeping Things in Perspective: Help from Cognitive Therapy*
Chapter 16   *Anger in Relationships*
Chapter 18   *Getting the Better of Anxiety and Worry, or Defeating the Alarmist*
Chapter 20   *Stress: How to Live with the Right Amount of It*
Chapter 30   *Overcoming Sleep Problems*

Chapter Summary

1. The techniques of relaxation do not come naturally: they have to be learned.
2. Practicing relaxation will give you more energy; decrease anxiety and irritability; and reduce pains due to tense muscles, such as neckache, backache, and headache.
3. Learning to relax is: an *attitude*; a *physical skill*; a *habit*; and a *restorative*.
4. Learning to relax involves *four* steps:
   * *Preparation.* A regular time and place for daily practice is needed until you become competent.
   * *Practice.* The basic method involves first tensing each muscle group and then letting go.
   * *Application.* Once you are skilled in the basic method, you can shorten the daily relaxation period and carry out mini-relaxations throughout the day
   * *Extension.* Make relaxation a part of your way of life by extending it to include relaxing and recreational activities.

HOW TO IMPROVE YOUR RELATIONSHIPS

Satisfying relationships are a major source of happiness, but they can be difficult to achieve. When relationships go wrong, our whole life can feel as if it is in shreds, and one response to problematic past relationships is to avoid becoming close to anyone again.

We relate to others in almost all aspects of our lives. Close personal relationships can be a source of strength and of continuous renewal. But it is not only these close relationships which are important. Both in our work, and in our everyday pursuits, we are constantly relating to other people. How we do this will determine our effectiveness as well as our pleasure.

Part Three will help you develop skills that lead to good relationships. We have found that the following three keys are central in developing satisfying relationships:

1. Develop the skill of *assertiveness* so that you can be *fair* to *yourself and to others*.
2. Learn to recognize and understand the *voices from your past* so that you can use them constructively.
3. Understand that *relationships are systems* so that you can make changes in the way that you and others interrelate using *negotiation skills*.

We devote a chapter to each of these keys, and then turn our attention to two important sources of difficulties in relationships: anger and worries about sexuality.

12

The Importance of Relationships

We are, to a great extent, social animals. Our happiness, our self-esteem, our moods, our capacity to flourish, all are influenced enormously by our relationships. Relationships are so central to our functioning that one form of psychological therapy—interpersonal psychotherapy—focuses entirely on ways of relating to others. It is tempting to think that in order to improve our relationships we need to change other people. It usually seems only too clear that the problem lies with the other person. But this is exactly where many people go wrong. In order to improve relationships we can only work on ourselves, and then others will change the ways in which they relate to us. So this part of the book, although about relationships, is just as much about ways of changing yourself as is the rest of the book. It is about changing yourself in the ways you relate to others.

We start this section with a story chosen to illustrate the following points:

1. Your relationships will work best if you are able to be yourself within them. Relationships in which you can be yourself are likely to feel more comfortable and to make you happier. This is not to say that you should throw tantrums when you feel like it, and be as rude to people as you wish. Nor is it to suggest that all relationships should be comfortable. Some very good ones can be provocative and

challenging. It is rather that relationships tend to become unstable and to be less satisfying when you are not yourself. It follows that it is helpful to be curious about your relationships and to try to understand them.

2. Bringing about change in a relationship can be seen as a four-step process:

Step 1: Look for the patterns.
Step 2: Focus on specific areas of difficulty.
Step 3: Learn to pilot your own ship.
Step 4: Notice how others change in response.

The story which follows shows how to use these steps to bring about changes in your relationships. The steps are the threads that run through the other chapters in this part of the book.

The Story of Debbie

DEBBIE'S DIFFICULTIES

Debbie had been given a black eye. She was 22 years old and worked as a receptionist and typist with a small firm of lawyers. She lived with her parents and younger sister, who thought of her as a rather quiet, uncommunicative person. Much of the time she was miserable. She felt that she was disgustingly overweight, and she hid herself in swathes of baggy, dark-colored clothes, always in the process of starting new diets only to give them up a few days later. She resolved to go to the gym after work and berated herself whenever she failed. She felt stuck, hopeless about being able to change, and convinced that nothing would get better unless she could change the way she looked. Her self-esteem and self-confidence seemed to have reached rock bottom, and over the past few months she had started to drink far more than was sensible. She drank nearly two bottles of wine when out with her boyfriend Nigel and then had an argument with him. They had arranged to meet on Saturday night, but instead he had gone out with some male friends to a football game and on to a party where they had all got drunk. When she did see him the next evening, she hit him on the head with a glass ashtray. He punched her in the eye. The shock of the fight with Nigel forced Debbie to stop and think. Her doctor referred her to a therapist who used interpersonal therapy, and together they worked through the following steps.

STEP 1: LOOKING FOR PATTERNS

Debbie recognized that her attempts to diet and to exercise were getting her nowhere so she concentrated instead on trying to understand what was happening. She blamed herself and felt guilty every time she failed to live up to her good intentions, but realized deep down that this was not the whole story. She needed to take a wider, and a longer, look, and she asked herself questions like these: *"When do I feel at my worst? What is happening then?"* and *"When do I feel at my best?"* She asked, *"Do the same kinds of things keep happening to me? Do I seem to keep going round and round in a circle?"* The first pattern she noticed was this: she felt especially bad when left out, ignored by her friends, and when anyone at home or at work said something critical about her, but she felt worst of all about herself after an argument or fight. These were the things that seemed to be happening when the diets went out of the window.

She felt better about herself, regardless of her weight, when other people were kinder to her and more friendly. The main pattern seemed to be that her relationships were calling the tune, and she suspected that all the important knobs and buttons controlling the mechanism of her relationships were in the hands of other people. However, she was now curious about how this worked. Instead of concentrating on her size and how much she ate or exercised, she started to think about the patterns of her relationships.

STEP 2: FOCUSING ON SPECIFIC AREAS OF DIFFICULTY

Interpersonal therapy recognizes three different types of relationship problems. It is useful to know about them because it helps to separate one problem from another so that you can think about them one at a time. Start by focusing on specific areas of difficulty and then label each as a problem of a particular type. The three types are:

1. Disputes—for example, frequent arguments between husband and wife, or parent and teenager
2. Role changes—for example, growing up and leaving home, or retirement
3. Loneliness—or a lack of close friends

Debbie focused on three particular areas of difficulty.

1. *A problem of loneliness.* Debbie noticed that her friendships, with both men and women, tended not to last (another pattern). She would spend a lot of time with new acquaintances for a short period and then fall out with them, often after a series of arguments and fights, and she did not have any long-standing close relationships. It was as if she was standing still in the midst of a constantly moving crowd of people who all knew where they were going and only stopped briefly within reach of her before moving on again. She had not noticed this loneliness before because she often went out, but not with people she was close to. The problem was so long-standing that she anticipated falling out with people almost as soon as she got to know them. She had become passive, and tended to agree with whatever other people wanted so she would not precipitate a falling out.

2. *A dispute problem.* Debbie's relationships were undeniably stormy; the black eye was only a visible reminder of this—and it was easy to see how her tendency to have arguments led to her loneliness.

3. *A problem of changing roles.* Debbie's third area of difficulty concerned differences in her relationships with men and with women. She felt unable to get the balance right, as if this part of the mechanism was completely out of her control. If she met a new boyfriend, she went out with him every night and completely stopped seeing her girlfriends (another pattern). But when the relationship broke up, she found her girlfriends had not hung around waiting, but had gone their own way without her, leaving her feeling inadequate and lonely.

Focusing on specific areas of difficulty showed Debbie that there were even more patterns at work than she had at first realized. For example, she recognized that, even though she was always having fights, she also felt helpless to do anything about them, and was constantly trying to please other people. The fights only served to make her feel worse about herself—more evidence that she had failed, but this time in her relationships instead of with her diets and exercise plans.

She tried to please people by agreeing to do whatever they wanted, as if what she wanted did not count, or as if she did not really matter. This meant that if someone asked her out she agreed to go, and did whatever they suggested, behaving in exactly the same way, regardless of whether or not she liked them. She passively followed anyone who asked because she felt so unattractive and shapeless, and thought so little of herself that it never occurred to her that she might have a choice. She assumed that people would eventually reject her. Trying to please people was a way of staving off the inevitable loneliness and isolation. Fights erupted when she felt trapped, or when others became fed up with her passivity and pro-voked a confrontation. She even wondered whether she engineered some of the fights with men to escape from a situation that alarmed her, or to make sure she rejected them before they had a chance to reject her. Deb-bie discovered a truth about herself which is almost universal: suppress-ing our own desires for too long will lead to an explosion.

STEP 3: LEARNING TO PILOT YOUR OWN SHIP

The idea that Debbie could have some control over what happened in her relationships was not easy for her to accept. She felt as if other people had all the choices. She felt that socially she would have to be content with whatever came her way, and be thankful for small pleasures. But as Debbie thought more about her specific difficulties, she came to realize that her passivity, her tendency to go along with what others wanted without thinking of herself, might be affecting what happened in her rela-tionships. Part of the responsibility for what was happening might lie with her.

For the first time, Debbie asked herself what she wanted from relation-ships. Instead of focusing on her outward appearance, she started to think about the inner person—about the Debbie she thought she would like to be. Instead of blowing with the wind, she began, in small ways, to take control. For example, she arranged to go out with a group of girl-friends and joined them in a regular, weekly outing. Instead of worrying about displeasing someone when she went out on a date, she thought about what she wanted to do, and began to speak up for herself. When she found herself in a relationship that she did not like, she had the courage to end it. She learned how to keep a better balance between her friendships with men and with women.

STEP 4: NOTICING HOW OTHERS CHANGE IN RESPONSE

One of Debbie's big fears was that if she disagreed with someone it would end in an argument. What she noticed, however, was that the more she took control and allowed herself to be herself, the more others respected her and the fewer fights she had. She started to meet girlfriends for lunch, and to her surprise found that they spontaneously kept in touch, and showed that they wanted to see her. At home it was a little harder to pilot her own ship because her mother was worried that Debbie was setting a bad example for her younger sister. After the episode with the black eye, she demanded that Debbie tell her where she was going in the evenings and tried to make her stay in for fear that she would get drunk again, or get hurt. Debbie was in a conflict: she wanted to please her mother, but she also wanted to live her own life. She had another *role change* problem on her hands. But this time she understood herself and her relationships better. She continued to go out as much as she liked, but she talked to her mother more about whom she was with and what she did. She continued to develop her independence, but this time opened herself up instead of hiding herself away. As her mother learned she could trust her, she too started to relax the effort to restrain her.

THE CHANGES DEBBIE MADE

Although Debbie had focused on the four steps to change her relationships, the benefits she felt were far wider than this. The better she became at playing her full part in relationships, the better she felt about herself. The better she felt about herself, the less she wanted to hide away behind layers of shapeless clothes. Others seemed pleased to see her, and she made new friends, so she stopped worrying so much about her weight. The changes Debbie made in her relationships set off a chain reaction, helping her to make many other changes. Once she accepted herself, others also found it easier to accept her.

Solitude

In emphasizing the value of good relationships, we do not wish to underrate the importance of solitude—the ability to enjoy, and to find creative strength, in our own company. To be at ease with yourself, alone, can be a source of refreshment and energy. It is a necessary component of many creative activities that require us to draw from our own inner depths. Solitude is not the opposite of good relationships. Indeed, if we are continually seeking company because we are uncomfortable with ourselves, this is likely to tarnish our relationships. If we are at ease with ourselves, we will be at ease with others.

Three Guidelines for Improving Your Relationships

We tend to be at our most unrealistic when looking at what went wrong in our relationships. This is probably because they are so important to us and we have so much invested in them. If you want to change, or to develop new ways in which to relate to others, then you will have to start with a good dose of reality. Three guidelines will help you focus on what is realistic.

1 WORK ON CHANGING YOURSELF, NOT ON CHANGING OTHERS

The temptation, particularly if a relationship is stormy, is to insist to yourself, and to others, that it is not you that needs to change but the other person. Now it may well be true that the other person should change, but since you can't change other people, it is not worth trying. Or perhaps it would be more accurate to say that the only way you can change another person is to change yourself—to change the way in which you relate to them. Working to change yourself is always difficult. Working to change your relationships is doubly difficult because it is so tempting to think that other people are at fault, and that they rather than you should make the effort. Do not be distracted by trying to change others: change yourself, and change the way you relate to others. The changes you make will precipitate changes in others. Leave these changes up to them, and the relationship will feel better to both of you.

2 CHANGES TAKE TIME

When you change the way in which you relate to others, they may resist that change and do things to make you change back. So making changes in relationships can take longer than making changes in yourself alone, and it certainly requires persistence.

3 WORK WITH PEOPLE AS THEY ARE

When you find yourself saying "If only he would tell me what he's thinking," or "If only she didn't criticize so much," stop yourself and remind yourself to be realistic. If you want to bring about some changes in those relationships, you should put away these "if only's" and accept people as they are. Once you start to make changes in yourself, the other person is likely to begin to change. Then you will be able to find out if you can accommodate each other and get on. If after you have tried to change you still find the relationship is no better, and you still keep wishing the other person were different, then it might be better to end the relationship.

The Three Keys to Good Relationships

Scores of books and articles have looked at ways of improving relationships. If you were to comb through all these works, you would find three recurrent themes, or keys.

The first key is: *be fair to yourself and to others.* The core skill in ensuring that you are fair within your relationships is the skill of *assertiveness.* The second key is: *understand the voices from the past.* A central insight from psychoanalysis is that our past is always with us. When we recognize the presence of these voices from our past, and learn how to think about them, we can choose to ignore them or choose to listen to other voices instead. When we fail to recognize them, they can cause havoc within our relationships. The third key is: *understand that relationships are systems.* We have already seen that when we make changes in the ways we relate to others, those others will tend to respond to, and resist, the changes. In a system, one change leads to another and the skills of *communication* and *negotiation* help to ensure that the changes we want match the changes others want—so that the relationship system can adjust and adapt. The following three chapters explore each of these three keys in turn.

Chapter Summary

Our happiness, self-esteem, and capacity to flourish are influenced enormously by our relationships.

In order to improve your relationships:

1. Work on changing yourself, not on changing others.
2. Expect changes to take time.
3. Accept other people as they are.

The three keys to good relationships are:

1. Be fair to yourself and to others.
2. Understand the voices from the past.
3. Understand that relationships are systems.

The following three chapters deal with each of these keys in turn.

13

The First Key to Good Relationships: Be Fair to Yourself and to Others

Being Fair Requires Being Assertive

Rita was 48 when she first became a grandmother. She was desperate to see the new baby and had been planning for months to take the necessary time away from her busy schedule. She was the principal of the local school, and involved in helping to raise funds for a kidney machine. Her husband, Daniel, buried himself in his work.

Rita telephoned her daughter-in-law, Karen, hoping to be asked to visit. Karen chatted happily about the baby's antics, sleepless nights, and feeding schedules. Rita started to worry that the invitation she wanted was never going to come. She listened, waiting to be asked. Then she said, "You must be frantic," and "I know there's no time to think of anything else with a new baby around." She talked about her husband's busy life, saying "He sometimes says he can't do without me." The message she wanted to get across was how useful she could be. The message Karen heard was that Rita had no time to spare. So Karen said questioningly, "I suppose you couldn't leave Daniel on his own?" Rita answered, "I sometimes think he hardly notices I'm here." Both Rita and Karen wanted the same thing—and they did not get it because they both beat around the bush. Neither was able to state what she wanted in clear language. Neither was fair to herself.

Rita's husband, Daniel, was very different. He was a hospital consultant. He told others exactly what he wanted without bothering to find out anything about their perspective. He had working for him a junior doctor, Richard, of whom he thought very highly. Daniel was quite often away at conferences and he would tell Richard to look after those of his patients he was most concerned about. Daniel would burst into Richard's office, without knocking, holding a pile of patients' records. Saying "These ones are yours for the clinic next Thursday" and dumping the files on Richard's desk, he would turn on his heels and walk out. Richard felt he was being treated like a servant, not like the competent doctor he was. Things came to a head when Richard booked his skiing vacation for February. He had negotiated the timing with his colleagues—the other junior doctors—so that his vacation did not clash with theirs, following the normal procedure. When Daniel heard of Richard's vacation dates, he was furious. They coincided with his own vacation and he had come to rely on Richard to cover his difficult patients. He marched into Richard's office and told him point blank that he could not take his vacation in February. He brooked no discussion. Richard felt he had little choice, and he changed his vacation dates. Six months later he had found a different job, and Daniel lost the junior doctor he most respected.

Most of us will recognize aspects of ourselves in either Rita or Daniel—even in both. Their stories illustrate how different kinds of unfairness prevented them from building up the kinds of relationships that are rewarding for all concerned. It is easy to be unfair either to oneself or to others, and surprisingly difficult to find the middle ground on which we can stand up for ourselves without putting others down. We tend to be better at this in some situations than in others: we may be decisive, openminded, and assertive at work but passive at home. Being fair depends on being able to be assertive.

What Is Assertiveness?

Assertiveness is a skill based on the idea that your needs, wants, and feelings are neither more nor less important than those of other people: they are equally important. You should, therefore, make claims for yourself appropriately, honestly, and clearly. Learning how to do this helps ensure that you do not come away from situations feeling bad about yourself, or leaving others feeling bad.

The alternatives to assertiveness are either passivity or aggression. If you adopt the passive approach, you will either fail to get what is your due or become manipulative: "I'm useless at anything mechanical, I'll only make a mess of it," "I'm sure you'd do this better than me," "I just can't go on—I've got such a headache." Out of frustration, passive people may cajole, sulk, or cry to get their way. The aggressive approach becomes overbearing: "Get this done right away," "Like it or not, my parents are coming to supper," "That's your concern. It's got nothing to do with me." Aggressive people may fail to listen to what others say, or dismiss the views of others as irrelevant. Neither passivity nor aggression are ultimately satisfactory, both because of the bad feelings they engender and because they are unfair: and in the long term, they usually fail to get you what you want. Michelle, who went along with the crowd to an Indian restaurant, though she hates curry, ended up feeling resentful and inadequate. Brian, who demanded angrily that a project should be scrapped and started again from scratch, ended up feeling stressed and alienated. It is not that Michelle needs to learn about assertiveness and Brian needs something else, but rather that assertiveness provides a more effective solution to both kinds of problems. Assertiveness is about being fair both to yourself and to others.

ASSERTIVENESS INVOLVES CLAIMING YOUR RIGHTS

You are entitled to your own feelings and opinions. Other people may want you to feel and think differently, but this is their problem, not yours. If you value yourself and trust your own feelings you will express yourself to others effectively. The strange thing is that other people will then value and trust you more than if you bend over backward to try to please them. Passive people, and a surprising number of aggressive people, want to be liked by everyone. This is rarely possible and it is usually counterproductive to try to be liked by all the people you meet. *Instead of focusing on being liked, focus on being fair.*

Study the "Assertive Rights" given in the box on page 129. They express the freedom you have to be yourself. Do you agree with them?

Assertive Rights

I have the right:
- To say "I don't know."
- To say "no."
- To have an opinion, and to express it.
- To have feelings, and to express them.
- To make my own decisions, and deal with the consequences.
- To change my mind.
- To choose how to spend my time.
- To make mistakes.

ASSERTIVENESS AS A BALANCING ACT

Assertiveness skills can be seen as providing three important kinds of balance:

1. The balance between aggression and passivity.
2. The balance between yourself and others.
3. The balance between reflecting and reacting.

The balance between aggression and passivity. Aggression and passivity reflect two extremes, neither of which makes for good relationships. Assertiveness provides a better way because it helps people to make their own point of view known while recognizing and accepting the views of others. It is essential to understand the differences between passivity, aggression, and assertiveness. The following three stereotypes crystallize the main differences.

Roger was a passive person. He tried to please others and avoid conflict; he found it difficult to make decisions, and constantly criticized and blamed himself. He never accepted compliments and tended to foster guilt and frustration in others, who saw him as a bit of a pushover. He was liked but not much respected because people knew he could be pushed around, and he seemed not to respect himself. He did what those around him wanted and put his own interests last. When talking to others he cast his eyes down, and there was a note of pleading in his voice. His conversation was filled with such phrases as: "Would you mind if . . . ," and "Maybe you could . . . ," and "Sorry, sorry."

Bruce was an aggressive and extremely competitive person. He readily confronted others, talking loudly and forcibly, and tended to belittle others by picking on their thoughts, actions, or personal qualities. He often offended people and they tended to avoid him. Few people liked him because he was too aggressive, always out to win and minimizing the contributions made by others as if he deserved to take all the credit. His conversation was peppered with such phrases as: "You'd better . . . ," "That's stupid . . . ," "Typical!" and "or else. . . ."

Caroline was assertive. She said clearly what she wanted, and made the claims she wished to make while listening to others and recognizing their claims too. She could express her feelings strongly when she wanted to, and she could also cope calmly with disagreements. Caroline was easy to get along with whether you liked her or not. People felt they could trust her, and communicate with her well even when feeling confused or angry. It was easy to laugh with Caroline. In her conversation she used phrases like: "I think ... ," "I believe ... ," "What do you think?" and "How could we work that out?" *The assertive person uses the word "I." The others focus on "you."* The focus on "you" is damaging because it rarely changes anything—we do not have much control over others—and because it usually builds up resentment. The focus on "you" lays the blame at the other person's door, and one way or another, the other person is likely to strike back. By focusing on "I," you are taking responsibility for yourself, and leaving others to take responsibility for themselves.

No one behaves in exactly the same way all the time. Aggression comes more naturally when one is angry or after being frightened—for example, by someone stepping carelessly into the road in front of your car. Feeling low and unconfident makes people withdrawn and passive. No one can behave assertively all the time, but we can increase the frequency of doing so. Assertiveness is a skill, or set of skills. But underlying these skills is an attitude about yourself.

Low self-esteem, thinking badly about yourself, makes it extremely difficult to be fair. How can you be fair if you believe that you "don't count" or "don't matter," or if you fear that your weaknesses will become glaringly obvious unless you keep on trying to win? Or if you believe that failure is always just round the corner? The ability to stand up for yourself appropriately—and to make sure that your relationships, however unequal in social or other ways, reflect your assertive rights, depends on having a healthy, well-functioning basis for your self-esteem. Chapter 10 concentrates on ways of building self-confidence and self-esteem. This chapter is about fairness and assertiveness. The two fit well together.

The balance between yourself and others. When it comes to your right to have feelings and opinions, you are just as important as other people. This is one of the central lessons of this book (Chapter 3). The interesting point is that there are two sides to this lesson. One side is that you are not less important than other people; the other side is that other people are not less important than you. Passive people usually value themselves less than others, and this often shows in what they say: "I'm sure you're right"; "I'll leave that up to you"; and so on. With aggressive people it is often not so simple. Some are aggressive because they undervalue others. They ride roughshod over the opinions of others and treat them as if they did not matter. They say things like: "That's completely irrelevant"; "Stop complaining and get on with it"; or "You can take it or leave it." But aggressive behavior can also come from feeling inferior oneself, especially for people who have learned to "hit before they get hit." Those who have been bullied, or repeatedly treated badly, may feel vulnerable and readily lash out, verbally or physically, in order to protect themselves (see chapter 26). Assertiveness is about recognizing the symmetry between yourself and others, and valuing all people—even when you disagree with them and have completely different feelings. It is not about *liking* everyone (we all have likes and dislikes), but about how to negotiate with them fairly. Assertiveness makes it unnecessary to resort to subterfuge or to adopt unnecessary armor in order to protect yourself. It helps both you and others to recognize and respect your mutual rights.

The balance between reflecting and reacting. Assertiveness may sound like a thoughtful, laborious, and rather unnatural kind of activity. It is not so much about reflecting *instead of* reacting, but about finding the balance between the two. If someone makes you angry—for example by borrowing something precious to you and damaging it—you might explode with a tirade of expletives, and end up saying many things that have little bearing on the present incident: "You are *such* a careless idiot. I don't want anything more to do with you—ever." The opposite extreme might involve thinking about how upset they must feel, avoiding making a scene, and hiding your feelings of anger under a veneer of friendly smiles. You might even accept part of the blame: "I should never have lent it to you." The balanced, assertive response would involve expressing your anger clearly and appropriately, focusing your anger on the behavior rather than the person: "That was a really careless thing to do" rather than "You're completely irresponsible." Then you can follow up by finding out how the other person feels (embarrassed? remorseful? unconcerned?) in order to decide how to resolve the difficulty, taking into account how you wish the relationship to continue after this hiccup. In Chapter 16 we focus on the problems caused by anger in relationships and explain in more detail how assertiveness can help.

ASSERTIVENESS BUILDS STRENGTH

The skills of assertiveness help you to build the stamina and strength to stand up for yourself, and so they also strengthen your relationships by placing them on an equal and robust footing. Linda was a high school teacher, with her own teenage children at home, who found that as soon as she left work and set foot in her home, her family would begin to make demands on her. Because she was tired, she often snapped back and was irritable, and then the tensions would quickly escalate. She decided to make use of assertiveness skills. She explained that she was tired when she came home and needed a few minutes of peace and quiet. She said she would make herself a cup of tea and take it into the living room, where she would drink it slowly by herself before joining the fray once more. At first her family continued to make the usual demands and interruptions, assuming that she would soon return to her old familiar, and irritable, self. But she persisted, chasing them out of the living room if necessary, until the new ways became second nature, both for her and for her family.

Risking even small changes takes courage—for an aggressive person as much as for a passive one. "Giving way to feelings," and "allowing your heart to rule your head" are only too readily labeled as signs of weakness. But taking the risk helps people to build confidence and self-esteem, and to take pleasure in feeling stronger. Being fair to yourself in this way also demonstrates your worth—to yourself and to others. It shows that you are worth considering and caring for in the same way as others. If you make your own needs clear, you are less likely to be irritable and more likely to have the strength to respond to the demands others make on you. If you fail to make your needs clear, but instead bottle them up or sit on them, or hide them under a self-deprecating smile, they will not go away but will gnaw at you inside, and make you feel resentful toward others. This resentment may eventually burst out as aggression. Indeed, many unassertive people fail to speak up for themselves precisely because they fear that, if they were to do so, the floodgates of their anger would open. Expressing yourself assertively defuses and bypasses the resentment and the anger, which quickly dissipate in the light of fair play (see Chapter 16).

ASSERTIVENESS LEADS TO FLEXIBILITY

The rigidity of both passive and aggressive responses means that they encourage only one type of behavior in other people and only one kind of solution to problems. Both tyrants and doormats are dominated by control: they either need to be in control or to be controlled. Assertiveness produces flexibility. It helps people to understand each other and to think about how they can both get what they want. It helps people adapt to each other and prevents them from getting stuck in fixed positions. Initial conflict followed by assertiveness leads to creative resolution. Aggressiveness and passivity both invite the opposite response, and close down other options. Assertiveness opens more possible paths and leads to a more satisfactory kind of adaptation. Assertiveness provides the secure foundation for effective negotiation (see Chapter 15).

Steps Toward Fairness

Treating yourself and others fairly involves combining the *attitude* of fairness with the *skills* of assertiveness. The attitudes provide the framework for the skills which, as with all skills, need to be practiced. The analogy with sports is a useful one here. In order to perform well in sports, you need both to train on a regular basis and to prepare for a specific important event. So it is with assertiveness. Three steps for building the framework are described in the next section, followed by six specific skills. We also suggest some exercises that you can do at any time and can repeat in order to become highly skilled. Pick and choose those exercises that appeal to you, and combine them in the ways you find useful.

Nine Ways to Become Fair to Yourself

Building the framework:
1. Build up your confidence and self-esteem.
2. Clarify what you want.
3. Lay claim to your rights.

Learning six specific skills:
1. Listen to others.
2. Use the "unselfish I."
3. Stick to the important points.
4. Manage criticisms and complaints.
5. Use your body to back you up.
6. Say "no" with assurance.

Three Steps for Building the Framework

STEP 1: BUILD UP YOUR CONFIDENCE AND SELF-ESTEEM

If your self-esteem is low it tends to undermine you at every turn, as if your inner voice produced a stream of unfair comments, determined to cut you down to size: "I'm weak—stupid—a failure—making a fool of myself—upsetting the applecart," "People will—think I'm no good—dislike me—ignore me," and so on. A whole chapter is devoted to this important subject (Chapter 10), and three exercises are provided here.

Exercise 1. Make a list of your good points. Include things about your appearance, a skill that you have developed, something about your personality, and at least one achievement that you are proud of. Remember only you can know just how hard these were for you to achieve, so give credit where it is due, as well as where you think others might give it.

Exercise 2. Keep a diary for a week in which you write down only positive things—your achievements; struggles overcome; people who were friendly, helpful, or kind to you; things you enjoyed. Look back over the diary. Add to it when you feel good; read it when you feel bad.

Exercise 3. Practice saying clearly what you truthfully think by paying someone a compliment every day. Make sure your compliments are honest and appropriate: you are not learning how to use flattery, or false praise, but to give fairly and to receive what is your due. Notice the different ways in which compliments are received. When it comes to your turn to receive one, do not dismiss it, or laugh, or say "Oh, I was just lucky." Accept it as a genuine expression of someone else's feelings—as being perfectly fair and not a reason for feeling embarrassed or uncomfortable.

STEP 2: CLARIFY WHAT YOU WANT

Assertiveness is about stating clearly what you want, without either retreating into your shell or bullying others. Passive people may know what they want but are unable to ask for it. Aggressive people often bluster about aggressively because they do not really know what they want, like those customers who complain loudly about the poor service they think they are getting. They get angry with an inappropriate person, and are then so rude that everyone is upset and nobody feels satisfied. The problem arises from failing to think beyond the anger to what they really want: to cancel the transaction? a price reduction? a replacement? an apology? Assertiveness involves tuning in to what you want (this comes more quickly with practice), and then making requests without bringing unnecessary emotional baggage. This is much more effective than unfocused anger. *Keep asking yourself: What is it I really want?*

STEP 3: LAY CLAIM TO YOUR RIGHTS

Assertiveness requires that you truly believe that you have the same rights as others to have your interests and views respected.

Exercise 1. Reread the table of Assertive Rights (p. 129) and think about whether you believe in them or not. Remove any that you think should not be there, and add any that you think should be there. Relevant areas to think about might concern your independence; your needs; asking for help; time to rest, relax, or be by yourself; your right to enjoy yourself; or your right to change. Think about these questions: What rights do you have in an argument? Or if you want to end a relationship? Or start a new one? Your rights and those of others should be the same.

Exercise 2. Talk to others about whether they have the same rights as you; ask them what rights they think are important. If you think others have rights which you do not have, then you are probably not being fair to yourself. If you would find it difficult to allow others the rights you claim for yourself, then you may not be being fair to them.

Six Specific Skills

Attitudes and skills go hand in hand. Sometimes working on skills helps to develop attitudes, but sometimes it works the other way around and building attitudes makes it easier to develop skills. Liking the French encourages you to learn their language, just as learning the language helps you to get to know, and to like, French people. Assertiveness is, in fact, much like a language, or a tool, that facilitates communication and understanding. Like a language, it has many different facets and uses, and involves many different skills. Here are six skills that can build assertiveness.

1 LISTEN TO OTHERS

Think again about the behavior of aggressive people who make blustering demands without having any idea what others think. Instead of succeeding in the attempt to dominate others, these people often put themselves in a weaker, more vulnerable position and fail to listen. Listening carefully to what someone else is saying means giving them your undivided attention. A good listener will understand the words said, but will also be able to pick up on how the person is feeling. You may need to verify whether your guess is right: "You seem really worried about that," or "That sounds extremely irritating to me."

Guides to Good Listening

- Show that you are listening by looking at the person who is speaking, or nodding, or saying "Uh-huh."
- Reflect, or repeat, a few words: "You were tired," "You didn't?"

Guides to Good Listening—cont'd

- Summarize what you have understood: "They asked you to join them."
- When you agree, say so. Especially when discussions get heated, it is very easy to concentrate on what you want to say in your turn and to assume other people know you agree with what they said. Then they feel that they have failed to get the point across, and repeat themselves or become irritated.
- Listen for what people mean by what they say, or to what is not voiced, and verify whether you are right. "You're late" could be an accusation or a sigh of relief; a monosyllabic answer could be a sign of being distracted, depressed, uninterested, bored, or in full agreement.
- Listen to the end. There may be a twist in the tail of the message.
- Take off your blinders: the assumptions that tempt you to jump to the wrong conclusions, like supposing when someone says "please help" that they want you to solve the problems for them rather than provide support and encouragement. Or supposing, when someone says they have had a dreadful day that they want to unload the agony on you, or that they are feeling overwhelmed or depressed. Maybe they just want to be heard and understood. Maybe saying it helps them to leave it behind.

---

2 USE THE "UNSELFISH I"

Saying "I want to go home at five tonight" is being fair to yourself if that is what you want; it is not being selfish. It is only fair to express yourself clearly, especially when you want something. There is no need to beat around the bush, nor to be vague, coy, or embarrassed. If others have the right to speak up for themselves, to express themselves, and to expect their viewpoint to be respected, then so do you.

Imagine you want to talk to someone about something that is troubling you. You may be able to get the help you want quite easily, but it is often far more difficult than it appears unless you explain what you need: "I need help in making this decision," "I need to let off steam," "I need a hug," "I need—space to breathe—to talk about the weekend—advice—to complain."

Accept your feelings for what they are and not as if taking account of them makes you selfish. If you feel stressed, then that is what you feel. There is little point in telling yourself you *should not* be stressed. Acknowledge the feeling, so that you can express it or manage it appropriately. The same goes for others. They have the feelings they have, and the right to have those feelings, to acknowledge and accept them—but they do not have the right to bombard you with them against your will. A feeling needs to be acknowledged. But do not confuse the feeling with the belief that may accompany it. If you feel stupid, that feeling is *real*, but it does not follow that you *are* stupid. You will find more about the relationship between thoughts and feelings in Chapter 9.

3 STICK TO THE IMPORTANT POINTS

Anthony Flew, the philosopher, used to talk about "the ten leaky buckets argument." This is putting forward many weak arguments in the hope that together they will add up to one good one—which of course they never will. What you want is one watertight bucket, not ten leaky ones. In reality, many leaky arguments actually weaken a good case. Leaky arguments turn your whole case into excuses rather than arguments.

Imagine that someone invites you to a party this coming weekend. Suppose you are off on vacation for two weeks starting tomorrow. You simply say that you cannot accept their invitation because you will be away. This is one, utterly convincing, reason for not being able to go to the party.

Now imagine that you are invited to a party but do not want to go because you have too much else on that weekend. You are actually free to go, but would rather not. You start to make excuses: you are not quite sure what you will be doing; you have to go out earlier in the day and are not certain whether you will be back in time; you have to get up early the next day and don't want a late night; you feel you might be developing a cold and would not like to give it to anyone. None of these excuses is entirely convincing and all could be challenged. If you are not sure what you will be doing, why not make yourself sure by accepting the invitation? You could turn up late, or leave early.

The most convincing reply is the straightforward and simple one: "Thanks, but I've got too much else going on." There is no comeback for that. You have stated your decision and have given a single clear reason. If your answer is not accepted, then repeat the message, either using just the same words or slightly different ones to say the same thing. "No, I'm afraid I can't," "I'm sorry, but I am too busy," "I would like to, but I can't." This is an extremely useful strategy that can be adapted for many different situations.

Learning to stick to your guns, to stay on track, and to use watertight arguments takes practice. The exercise in the following box describes three steps to take and provides examples of situations in which you could practice taking them. Think carefully about each of them. You could write your ideas down, or talk them through with a friend, or ask someone to help you with a dress rehearsal. This might be useful for particularly difficult events, such as telling someone their work is not good enough, or insisting that your request for a pay review be dealt with.

Exercise for Sticking to Important Points

Step 1: Decide what you want.
Step 2: Express this clearly.
Step 3: Think of as many other ways of expressing your decision as you can.

Practice situations:
1. Refuse to look after someone else's cat while they are away.
2. Ask for your money back.
3. Change some theater tickets.
4. Turn down an invitation or date.
5. Get your children (or someone else) to pick up their clothes.

---

4 MANAGE CRITICISMS AND COMPLAINTS

Criticisms and complaints make feelings run high whether they burst out aggressively—"That's typical of people like you," "You're useless," "You've never been any good at . . ."—or run more passively through underground channels of resentment, anger, and blame. Exploding with fireworks or seething with unexpressed emotion are two destructive extremes that being fair to yourself and to others helps you to steer between.

First, it is essential to make a distinction between criticism and character assassination. Everyone does things wrong at times, makes mistakes, gives offense, behaves thoughtlessly or rudely, but these are all particular types of behavior, provoked by particular situations. It makes no more sense to draw general conclusions from them (and to label the person who does them as "bad") than it does to draw equally general conclusions when someone does something helpful or considerate. Counteracting false accusations is easier if you can admit to weaknesses *accurately,* without exaggerating their importance and without dismissing them as irrelevant. Three different strategies that help in responding to criticism are explained here.

Refuse to be labeled. Your critic says "You're always so illogical. You can't keep an idea straight in your head for more than ten seconds," and you reply "Sometimes I say illogical things. Mostly I make perfectly good sense."

Agree with the critic and apologize appropriately. The critic says "You're late again," and you reply "Yes, I'm sorry—I've been running late all day."

Ask for clarification. The critic says "You're muddled and disorganized," and you reply "What makes you say that?" or "Is something in your way?" or "What would you like me to sort out?"

When the shoe is on the other foot and you want to make a complaint, a three-step process is helpful.

Step 1: Name the problem. "Your music kept me awake last night"; "I have not had a pay increase this year"; "This order is incomplete"; "You have sent me the wrong tickets."
General rules: Be brief, specific, and clear, and do not make guesses about the other person's attitudes or motives. Stick to the facts.

Step 2: State your feelings or opinions. "It was really irritating"; "I am very disappointed"; "I think there must be a mistake somewhere."
General rules: Only state your own feelings and opinions, and take care not to exaggerate them. Keep it low key, without blaming or shaming others. Remember to focus on "I" not "you."

Step 3: Specify what you want. "Please could you turn it down after midnight?"; "Can you tell me why that is?"; "I need replacements by Wednesday."
General rules: Ask for clearly specified changes, one at a time, that others can reasonably be expected to manage.

On both the giving end and the receiving end of complaints and criticisms, it helps to remain calm. When feelings run high, they obscure our vision of other people, and distort our ideas of fairness. Shooting from the hip, saying things that you will later regret, tends to escalate conflicts. If your requests have been ignored, or someone is gratuitously unpleasant or critical, and you feel frustrated or undermined or angry about someone else's behavior, you may need to calm down before you can reflect as well as react. Ideas about dealing with conflicts and disputes can be found in Chapters 15 and 16.

5 USE YOUR BODY TO BACK YOU UP

There is a physical aspect to assertive behavior. How assertive you feel shows in your posture, eye contact, tone of voice, gestures and movements, facial expression, and the distance you place between yourself and others. The following exercises help to increase awareness of these factors. There is no one right way of being assertive. The exercises are meant to help you think about the signals you observe in others and those you send out. In general, more assertive behavior involves holding yourself straight, looking at people openly, and neither giving them a wide berth nor crowding them.

Exercise 1. Think of someone you know who behaves assertively (not aggressively!). Get up and walk across the room in the way that they would walk. When you have the chance, observe what assertive behavior looks like. What do you notice?

Exercise 2. Repeat these exercises, thinking instead of aggressive and of passive behavior. Exaggerate the differences between them. For instance, when feeling passive, people tend to avoid eye contact; when feeling aggressive, they tend to stare. Try out each type of behavior in a conversation with those you know well, and observe the reaction. Ask them whether they notice the differences. Then see if you can find an "assertive compromise"—the right balance for you. Can you recognize your own body language? Is there anything you would like to change in the way you use your body? If there is, specify clearly what, and practice the new behavior as often as possible.

6 SAY "NO" WITH ASSURANCE

When others ask us to do things, we usually feel under pressure to say *"yes"*—a pressure which we often yield to against our better judgment. Why is this? There are probably three main reasons. The first is not being clear about our priorities. The second is fearing the other person will be displeased or think badly of us if we say "no." And the third, if the other person is a friend, is to make them happy.

Clarifying priorities. Every time you say "yes" to one thing, you will have to say "no" to something else. This is true even if you are not leading a busy life. So be sure that you say "yes" to those things that you want to say "yes" to. Do not say "yes" for the wrong reasons: just to please the person who asked you; or to get them off your back; or because it appeals to your sense of self-importance. When you say "yes," you should be agreeing to something which, given all your priorities, you truly want to agree to. What you agree to should be more important to you than what you have to give up (see Chapter 5). You might refuse to take on something extra because you are not prepared to drop other commitments that are more important to you—or that you would prefer to do. You might say no to helping a neighbor on Sunday because you want to relax with the Sunday papers.

Be fair to yourself, balance your own needs and wishes with those of others. Saying "no" is not being callous and uncaring, but treating your needs and wishes as equally important as those of others.

Saying "no" nicely. If someone asks you to do something that you do not wish to do, then all you need to do is to say "no." You are under no obligation to explain yourself. You have as much right to say "no" and leave it at that as the next person. However, many people find it easier to say "no" if they know how to do so without provoking pressure, persuasion, confrontation, or dismay. Some people make it hard for us by refusing to take "no" for an answer. Strategies for saying "no" nicely can, therefore, contribute to your sense of fair play.

Here are a few ways of making a refusal easier on you and easier for someone else to accept.

- Make it clear that you appreciate being asked: "Thank you for asking me"; "That's nice of you"; "I'm really pleased to be asked."
- Acknowledge the other person's priorities and wishes: "I know that it is important"; "I understand the difficulty, but. . . ."
- Give a clear reason for your refusal: "I am already committed to doing . . ."; "It would take more time than I've got"; "I don't know how."
- Help the other person to resolve their difficulty. One way of doing this is to make a suggestion—for example, suggesting someone else they can ask instead. The aim is to find the balance between saying (or thinking) "This is not my problem" and taking on other people's problems as if they were your own.

The sleep on it rule. Make it a rule not to commit yourself to anything important until the next day at the earliest. This gives time to think through whether, taking all your priorities into account, you really do want to say "yes" or "no." This one rule saves many later regrets. A night's sleep is a powerful way of getting things into perspective.

Chapter Summary

Assertiveness is the core skill to being fair to yourself, and to others.

Assertiveness is different from aggressiveness.

Assertiveness provides a balance between:

1. Aggression and passivity
2. Yourself and others
3. Reflecting and reacting

Here are three steps for building the framework of assertiveness:

1. Build up your confidence and self-esteem.
2. Clarify what it is that you want.
3. Lay claim to your rights.

And here are six specific assertiveness skills:

1. Listen to others.
2. Use the "unselfish I"—express your wishes clearly and simply.
3. Stick to the important points.
4. When criticizing others, criticize their actions, not their character.
5. Use body language to reinforce your message.
6. Say "no" with assurance. Never commit yourself to something important or time-consuming without first "sleeping on it."

14

The Second Key to Good Relationships: Recognizing Voices from the Past

The past is always with us. It provides the base from which we start and the framework through which we see the world. It can be a source of creativity, but also a source of confusion and pain, particularly when we do not understand how it is affecting us and how to free ourselves from its limitations. In our current relationships, or in our lack of relationships, there will be voices from our past. These voices can be the source of problems, and the problems may only be effectively tackled when we learn to recognize—to hear—the voices from the past. In this chapter we focus on ways of identifying, and taking control of, these voices and in Chapter 26 (*Dealing with the Past*) we explain how to move forward when the effects of past distressing experiences are holding you back. These two chapters complement each other.

Our past is laid down in layers. We are like the earth, whose layers can be revealed by looking at a cliff face. Looking back through time at the layers of rock, we can see the layer that was once the floor of a lake, where small creatures drifted to the bottom; the layer where the forest grew, now crushed by the weight of rock to a thin black line; and in places, because of the crush of the land, older layers are pushed through to the surface.

We too have layers, and as with the earth, past layers can rise gently to the surface or they can burst through unexpectedly, visiting us with disturbing images and feelings. The things that happen, or do not happen, in our relationships readily activate and reveal this movement between the present and the past.

Our past layers are of course complex, but simplified models can help us understand more about them, and also help us in our relationships. One method, transactional analysis, provides a model of ourselves, designed to be of practical value in understanding the voices from the past.

Help from Transactional Analysis

Our complex, layered personality can be thought of as having three *voices: parent, adult,* and *child* voices, as if you were made up of three parts: a parent, an adult, and a child. The parent is not you as a parent of your children, but consists of the voices of your own parents or parent-like figures from the past. When you relate to others, all three parts might come into the picture. All three are important and none should be blocked out. But, in some situations, these "voices from the past" can cause trouble.

For our present purposes, we want to help you to focus on listening to, and understanding, these voices from your past. Listen to yourself. When can you hear the child's voice? When you're throwing a tantrum, for example? ("I'm not going to do what you say!") When are you listening to the voice of your parent? ("Pull yourself together and stop whining!") When relationships are problematic, it helps to replace the voices and behavior of the child and parent with those of the adult. This is not to say that there is no room for the child and the parent; the child within us is often the source of fun and of creativity and often good at warning us when we are in danger. The parent may provide us with useful discipline, or with goals and ideals to work toward. But the parent and the child will be more useful to us, and less troublesome in our relationships, if they are under the control of the adult. If the child or the parent takes over, problems arise, causing major difficulties in relationships.

The Adult's Voice

The adult voices the mature part of your personality—the part that has developed as a result of your own explorations of the world. It is the part of you that can think and reason about your experience and can learn to make predictions about how things will be in the future. It can make decisions based on reality. When the adult is in control, it can put the voices of the parent and the child to constructive use. There is no need to stifle the voices of the child and parent; but you can prevent them from making themselves heard in destructive and unwanted ways by becoming more aware of what they are saying. The voice of the adult can help you to stand aside from them, or to use them constructively rather than be swept along by them.

The Child's Voice

The child voices those feelings and responses that were mainly laid down during the first years of our lives. The child's voice can express the whole range of feelings, as children can experience intense and complex feelings long before they can talk about them. It can also express many childish, positive aspects of our personality, such as our curiosity, the ability to throw ourselves wholeheartedly into things, and the capacity for sheer fun. People who no longer experience much of this kind of fun may have repressed the child within themselves. But childish voices can also be the source of problems, particularly problems in our relationships.

When you listen to children, you will hear certain patterns of speech which are common: "Leave me alone"; "You never let me do what I want"; "I'm not going to do what you say." We may think that these complaints are gone now that we are adult. However, this is unlikely to be true. The voices, and the behavior, of this child can still be heard, but in less obvious ways.

COMMON VOICES OF THE CHILD

Mine's better than yours. Children often compare their belongings with those of other children, insisting that they come off best—"I've got the biggest one"—and exaggerating its advantages—"it takes ten minutes to walk around my Dad's car." This voice can be heard when, as adults, we compare ourselves with others and emphasize how much better we are doing or insist on our superior equipment. Such comparisons often conceal underlying fears, and serve, as they do with children, as a rather ineffective type of reassurance: "At least my desk isn't such a mess as hers." The fears seem to reflect the assumption that if I am not the top dog then you will be, leaving me in danger of being trampled on, or of not being able to control what happens. The fear also breeds insensitivity to others: "I can rely totally on Dan in a difficult situation. It must be dreadful for you not having someone like him to turn to."

This voice, when dominant, leaves us with an underlying bad feeling, which is why it is not so very different from jealousy.

I want yours. Children are often jealous of the better possessions of other children and become rapidly dissatisfied. One of the tasks of parenthood is to help children to learn to be satisfied with what they have rather than demanding the possessions of others. It is a difficult task, and few of us grow to be adults without this childish voice still making itself heard.

You hear of a friend's success, and instead of feeling happy for them it "gets to you." Is this your inner child playing: "I want yours"? Perhaps you have observed in yourself, or seen in the behavior of others, the desire to have *everything* that others have, ranging from a newfangled potato peeler or bottle opener to a new car; from gadgets to status symbols of all kinds. Just as when we take our children to toy stores, almost everything seems eminently desirable.

Here is yet another variant.

It's not fair. This is seen in particularly powerful form between siblings. "You gave her a new drawing book, but you didn't give me anything." We can think, as we grow older, that this kind of rivalry with our brothers and sisters disappears, but it can come out in subtle and unrecognized ways. "It's my turn to throw the party, chair the meeting, get on the housing committee." "It's your turn to fold the laundry, pay for the drinks, come out with my friends."

The feeling of unfairness can be even more powerful when it is about *time* rather than *belongings*.

What about me? This can seem a particularly unfair accusation to parents with two or more children! You spend an hour reading to one child while ignoring the others; then you spend a few minutes drawing with another and the first says, "What about me?" All children need attention, but not all to the same degree, and all children can at times have an almost insatiable desire for the attention of their parents. This desire can break through the surface when we are adults, especially in relationships with key people such as partners. In most close adult relationships, there are times when the voices of the child within us demand attention, and appeal to the adult or parent part of our partner for time or consideration. This is not a bad thing as long as it does not dominate the relationship, but it can be a source of jealousy and friction when it is not recognized for what it is, and especially if there is a very unequal balance between the partners in the parts they play.

Voices of complaint: Temper tantrums and deep sulks. Few children do not respond to frustration, from time to time, either by throwing a temper tantrum or by going into a deep sulk—inviting parents to cajole them out of it but simultaneously determined not to be appeased.

The temper tantrum can be seen in adults in the form of almost uncontrollable rage, or the kind of angry shouting that seems to combine anger with pleading. The deep sulk may persist with some couples for days and be precipitated by apparent trivialities, such as finishing up the last of the bread or forgetting to give someone a message. The unrecognized meaning of these events is often the important factor: "You didn't consider me"; "I'm not important to you." The atmosphere created by this deep-seated response can be almost palpable: "You could have cut the tension with a knife."

The Parent's Voice

The voice of the parent reflects the voices we internalized as children, on the basis of the messages we received from our own parents, from the other adults who surrounded us as children, and even from television and radio. These are the voices of authority that we derive from internalizing some of the views we heard expressed. Most of what these adults said, if we were lucky, was sensible and helpful. But there will also be unhelpful, outmoded, or painful messages coming to us through the voice of the parent within us. Amy and Thomas Harris, who have made the ideas of transactional analysis generally available, wrote:

> One of the most powerful ways in which the Parent enters our lives in the present is the internal dialogue in which we hear the same applause, warnings, accusations, and punishments we heard when we were toddlers. The person in us who is at the other end of the dialogue is the Child, the preschooler in our heads. We can feel as bad today as we did then, when negative recordings in either Parent or Child are activated, and we hear the internal, unceasing voices of regret or accusation.[1]

Some Common Voices of Childhood

A childish version	An adult version
I'll tell my teacher about. . . .	I shall have to speak to the authorities.
If you don't, I'll. . . .	Unless . . . I may have to. . . .
I'll scream and scream and scream until I'm sick.	I'll continue making a fuss even if it kills me.
Everyone else has	Our competitors are using. . . .
Crybaby!	Softie! Moaner! Wimp!
I'm bigger than you are.	Of course, speaking as someone who knows, . . .
I'm king of the castle. . . .	I'm in charge here. . . .

Some Useful Questions to Ask Yourself

- What am I feeling in these difficult situations? (For example, just before a fight.)
- When have I felt like this before?
- When was the very first time I felt like this?
- What was happening at the time?
- What is it I want in this situation?
- Who else in my childhood behaved like this (am I copying my sister . . .)?

COMMON VOICES OF THE PARENT

You can do better than that. Even though this is meant as encouragement, the message the child often receives is "That's not good enough." When no performance or achievement seems to satisfy, the parental voice may be acting as a goad and a reminder. If you are very distressed when something small goes wrong, or when someone points out that you have made a mistake, you may be listening to this voice from your past (see also Chapter 26).

Stop making a fuss. Parents usually want to help their children develop self-control and the resilience to withstand knocks and setbacks in life. They may also have little time or energy to give to their children when things go wrong and they are distressed. Or they may be too troubled and preoccupied to attend to their children. They may even not care much about them. For some or all of these reasons, they may discourage children from showing their distress.

The voice of your parent telling you not to make a fuss may reveal itself in various ways—for example, if you feel guilty or embarrassed whenever you make a claim for yourself, or if you are tempted to apologize and hide your feelings when someone forgets to keep an appointment.

Don't be angry. This message is often backed up by actions or threats, such as banishing children from the room when they are angry, or refusing to speak to them until they have calmed down. Children brought up hearing this voice may later be frightened or alarmed by strong feelings of anger, and come to believe it is wrong to feel anger and to express it. They may find it hard to develop adult ways of expressing anger that allow them to acknowledge the feelings without damaging relationships that are important to them.

We can recognize our parent's voices within us particularly when we come out with inflexible rules and clichéd statements, and when we put others or ourselves down in a peremptory fashion. If you are vulnerable to being hurt by a particular person, or inexplicably go to great lengths to please someone else, it may be because that person speaks to the child within you with the authority of your parent. Becoming aware of what the messages from these voices are telling you helps you to mobilize your adult voice, and either adapt or reject them as, on consideration, you wish.

How Voices from the Past Can Interfere with Current Relationships

ARGUMENTS WITH A PARENT

Arthur was 36 years old, married, with two sons. His parents lived far away, in the same town as their other son, Arthur's older brother. Arthur was only able to visit his parents about twice a year, and although Arthur was very fond of his parents and would normally get along well with them, at some stage during these visits he would have an argument with his mother. The topic of the argument would vary, but the quality was the same each time. It was as though he and his mother could not help having this argument, and it left them both unhappy. Arthur saw so little of his parents that he greatly regretted having these arguments since they spoiled what little time he had with them.

Arthur used the ideas of transactional analysis and this gave him the understanding he needed.

He realized that the main voice to be heard during his arguments with his mother came from the child within him. What underlay all these arguments, whatever their ostensible subject matter, was that powerful child voice of *sibling rivalry*: he was jealous that his brother was getting more attention from his parents than he was. His brother saw his parents daily and had help with babysitting, taking the children to school, gardening, and much else besides. Arthur felt left out, just like the child crying out "What about me?" "Why are you spending all this time with my brother and ignoring *me?* "He was quite upset to realize that he still felt like a five-year-old. The fact that he did not need help from his parents now was irrelevant. The fact that these arguments were spoiling some of the precious time he spent with his parents was irrelevant. The child within him was simply jealous of his brother ("He's getting more than I am"), and it pushed him into the arguments with his mother.

Some Parental Voices That Can Be Unhelpful to Adults (These Can Be Spoken by Friends, Teachers, and Others, Too)

- Stop moaning and groaning and get on with it.
- Hurry up, or you'll get left behind.
- Be careful. Make sure you get back safely.
- Don't interrupt.
- You can't just have whatever you want.
- Don't be selfish.
- Don't answer back.
- You're on your own now.
- Wait for your turn.
- Never an idle moment.
- If you've started it, finish it.
- You're clumsy, silly, a crybaby, irresponsible, bad.
- You're in the way.

There Are Just as Many Helpful Parental Voices as Unhelpful Ones

- You'll be okay.
- I'm sure you can manage.
- You can do it if you want to.
- Keep trying—I'll help if you get stuck.
- Nobody can do more than their best.
- You're wonderful, important, lovable, funny, etc.

Can You Recognize the Voices That Speak to You?

1. Think of the adult people in your life when you were a child: parents, relatives, friends, teachers.
2. What are the main messages you picked up from them? If they could say one thing to you, what would it be?

Once he understood what was happening, he was able to cease arguing. The adult part of him could take over, recognizing, as it did, the jealous child within. The adult part could understand that the child's jealousy was misplaced, and he could then relate to his mother as adult to adult rather than child to parent.

A TEMPER TANTRUM

Sandra was normally a well-tempered and patient person. But just occasionally she would lose her temper. It was usually when she was particularly tired. To her it felt as though she suddenly "snapped," and when she lost her temper, she would shout, almost scream, at her partner. It seemed quite out of character, and it troubled her because she did not like it and felt out of control. It was as though someone else took possession of her during these temper tantrums.

A friend gave her a clue about what was going on when he told her that she sounded just like her elder sister during these temper tantrums. Sandra asked herself how she felt at the times when she lost her temper. Did how she feel seem like any times in her childhood? She considered this. When she lost her temper she felt utterly helpless inside, just as she used to feel when her sister lost her temper with her. As a child this made Sandra feel both frightened and powerless—helpless. The feeling of helplessness was very similar to how she now felt, occasionally, when her partner insisted on having his own way regardless of what she wanted. She felt so helpless that she wanted to scream, just as her sister had screamed at her.

Recognizing this voice, which had seemed so alien to her, as the voice of her sister, and understanding the similarity in feeling between how she had sometimes felt with her sister and how she now sometimes felt with her partner, reassured her and helped her to manage her uncontrollable tempers. Understanding their origin had a profound effect because it enabled her to make use of her adult voice to free herself from the old pattern. These are some of the things she said to herself: "I know where this comes from"; "There's no need to stay the same way now"; "When I feel helpless or powerless I can think of how to pilot my own ship" (p. 123). Her temper tantrums became less dramatic, and less frequent.

A MARITAL DIFFICULTY

Andrea had a good relationship with her husband, Rick, but whenever they visited Rick's parents, irritation with him seemed to come out of nowhere until hardly a civil word passed between them. He retreated into himself while she worried about what her mother-in-law was thinking. She could not put her finger on what the problem was. They did not have open arguments, and she could not honestly say that he did anything to upset her. On the contrary, he seemed to treat her just as he usually did. The problem seemed to be her fault, but what was it? Why did she feel so uncomfortable and irritable whenever she visited her in-laws?

Then she noticed something interesting. When Rick visited his parents, his behavior seemed to change. He reverted to childhood patterns and his behavior became dominated by the child within him. His adult part became submerged. That is what Andrea found so difficult. When at her parents-in-law her husband sat in the living room and waited to be looked after. He allowed his mother to serve him hand and foot. She pampered him and he just let her do it. Indeed, she even repeated some of the parental messages that he must have heard in his childhood: "You're in the way dear. Keep out of my kitchen. You wait there and I'll bring you a cup of tea." It was this childish behavior in him that Andrea found so irritating, and until she talked to him about it, Rick had been completely unaware of what was happening. He had just fallen back into old habits automatically. Their problem was easily resolved once they noticed the pattern.

RECOGNIZING THE PATTERNS IN RELATIONSHIPS

Do the voices and messages from your past reveal patterns? And are these patterns helping or hindering your relationships? At the simplest level, if you grow up believing you are likable, your friendships are likely to reflect a more satisfactory pattern than if you grow up believing you are not likable (see Chapters 10 and 26). Learning how to free yourself from destructive voices from the past involves learning how to recognize these patterns. If your brothers and sisters always ridiculed your opinions, you may develop a pattern of keeping them to yourself, and not even notice this pattern until you find yourself in a conflict of opinions that really matters to you. But most situations are more complex than this.

When Steven and Denise started a relationship, they had a great deal to say to each other, and also went out a lot with their friends. Then Steven moved into Denise's apartment, and their relationship became strained. Denise thought Steven no longer cared for her. He stayed home most evenings, they cooked together, and they shared the bills, but he hardly ever started a conversation. He seemed to her to have run out of things to say about himself and to have lost interest in asking about her.

But Denise was wrong. In his way, Steven *was* showing that he cared about her. Doing things together and sharing responsibilities were, for Steven, signs of caring. Signs of caring, for Denise, were different. She wanted to know how Steven felt and to be able to talk to him about her own feelings. For her, communication—talking—was a sign of caring. These differences reflected the different messages they had received as children. Parents can show that they care in many different ways: for example, by talking, paying attention, hugging, doing things together, paying for camping trips and music lessons, allowing a child its freedom, and just by being there. Children also pick up patterns of relationships from their friends, and the differences between Steven and Denise are common reflections of the different ways men and women behave in western societies generally. It is a common pattern for women to talk more about their feelings than men do. The point is that unless Denise and Steven learn to notice and understand their own patterns, their relationship will continue to produce emotional strain. Denise will continue to think that Steven does not care when really he does.

Recognizing the patterns provides the understanding that can start to take away some of the strain. Once Denise understood how Steven showed that he cared, she felt less rejected by his silences and would ask him directly for what she needed.

Changing the Patterns

Changing the patterns of thinking and behaving which originate from the child or parent within you may be quite easy and straightforward. You may be able to free yourself from their problematic aspects simply by recognizing that they are there, and realizing that they are an unnecessary piece of baggage that can be dumped. Their power may dissipate in the light of your new understanding. However, old habits sometimes die hard.

Patterns can be broken, but this sometimes requires strategic planning and constructive work. A wide variety of skills that can help you to do this work are described in this book. It is unlikely that you will need all of them, so pick and choose, and use the index to give you some good ideas. The main steps are as follows:

Step 1. Understanding is the first step. Use the ideas provided in the boxes in this chapter to help with this. If you can understand how the problems

---

Some Common Patterns

Someone is angry with you. → You feel rejected.

You are criticized. → You think you are no good, or unacceptable.

Someone ignores you. → You feel no one cares about you.

You receive a complaint. → You feel incompetent or blame yourself.

Someone asks you to change. → You feel insecure or frightened.

Someone tells you they feel bad. → You feel responsible for making them better.

Someone notices your mistake. → You feel like a failure or give up trying.

Note: These are only a few of the many patterns that can interfere with relationships. To some degree, they are present in all of us. It is only when they become dominant—when present in extreme forms—that they cause major difficulties.

---

and difficulties make sense, in terms of the framework of your past, in terms of the messages it gave you and the voices that continue to speak to you, then the adult part of your personality can start to adjust and to deal with the problem.

Step 2. If you want something to change in your relationships, then think about what *you* can change, not about what you would like someone else to change. Being able to change, to become more flexible, for example in the way you show affection, places your relationships on a broader, and firmer, footing.

Step 3. Accept that other people will have heard other messages in their past. There is no more point in blaming them for what they were told than there is for blaming yourself for what you were told.

Step 4. Learn about your "trigger points." Imagine that some small event triggers off some unexpectedly strong feelings: someone asks you to do something again and you feel deeply criticized; your friends go out for a drink without you and you feel completely rejected; someone fails to do what you ask and you feel wildly angry. These triggers are useful cues. They may make others accuse you of overreacting, but they may help you figure out what is going on. The idea is that the strong feelings you have in these situations arise because of what the situations *mean* to you. When working on meaning the messages of cognitive therapy are useful (see Chapter 9) and may be combined with the ideas in this chapter. Some questions you might ask yourself include the following:

Questions for Unraveling Meaning

What does this mean about me?

What does this mean about how others see me?

What can this tell me about myself?

What does this mean to me?

How might this link with the past?

Who has said that sort of thing to me before?

What is important to me about this?

Note: You will find more useful questions in Chapter 9.

Not all the situations to which people overreact are ones that make them feel bad. Some people feel quite ridiculously pleased with certain kinds of compliments—and often that is because of what the compliment means to them. "You did really well to manage that so quickly"—you glow with pleasure knowing that you are efficient and competent. "I am so grateful for your help"—the feeling of being needed stays with you all day. "You look wonderful"—and you spend the rest of the day behaving as if everyone loved you. Someone you respect says, "Well done," and you bask in the pleasure of knowing you are an okay person. There is nothing wrong with any of these reactions. But you can use them as clues as well. They can tell you which are the important issues, which are the themes and patterns likely to weigh most with you. These are also the ones that will make you feel the worst when something threatens them.

Related Chapters in This Book

You will need to reflect on and think about what concerns you, so you can identify the patterns. Other ways of doing this are described in *Chapter 12, The Importance of Relationships* and *Chapter 26, Dealing with the past.*

It helps to be fair both to yourself and to others. Skills for helping with this are described in the previous chapter.

When caught up in the web of the past it is easy for you to lose perspective. *Chapter 9, Keeping Things in Perspective: Help from Cognitive Therapy,* explains how to look at things in new ways.

Communication skills of all kinds (listening skills, pp. 136–137; the skills of assertiveness, pp. 134–143; negotiating skills, pp. 161–166) will be some of your main tools.

Ways of using these tools when anger is a problem in your relationships are discussed in Chapter 16. These ideas are also useful when difficulties arise in initimate sexual relationships (Chapter 17)

Problem-solving skills, which are discussed in Chapter 8, may be helpful if you feel stuck.

Chapter Summary

The past is always with us.

It can be helpful to think of ourselves as consisting of three parts:

- Parent
- Adult
- Child

The "voice" of the "parent" within us reflects the messages we internalized as children from our parents, and other figures of authority.

The "child" voices those feelings and responses that we had as young children.

The "adult" voices the mature part of our personality.

The "voices from the past"—those of the "parent" and the "child"—can be a source of strength and creativity. But if they are not recognized for what they are, they can also be a source of problems in our current relationships.

By recognizing these voices from the past, we can prevent, or limit, the damage they can do and make use of their constructive possibilities.

- **The main message is this: although there is nothing you can do to change the past, you can change the way you look at it, and you can take control of the way it affects you in your relationships with others in the present.**

15

The Third Key to Good Relationships: Relationships as Systems

Marjorie had married at the age of 18, and by the age of 34, she had three children between the ages of 11 and 14. She had not worked since her first child was born because she was busy and because her husband neither expected nor wanted her to work. He was an electrician employed by a small firm of builders. Marjorie kept the household running well and was the center around which her family revolved. She provided clean clothes, meals, a safe base to which everyone else returned each day, friendship, and most of the organizational energy needed for the family's functioning.

Marjorie loved her husband and her children and they loved her, but now that the children were getting older, she felt in need of a change. Indeed, she felt she had put off making changes for far too long, mainly because her husband said *no*. He was earning good money and told her she was needed at home. He thought she should put the family first, at least until the children had left school. The children joined in the chorus, saying "What about us?" and "Who will be here when I get home?" She found she could not raise the question, nor even talk to them about what she might do instead of housework, since the topic was slapped down as soon as it was brought up. She felt helpless, frustrated, and depressed; stuck and feeling as if everyone was conspiring against her.

Marjorie was caught in a system: the system of relationships within her family. And it was a system that, clearly, did not want a change.

What Is Meant by Seeing Relationships as Systems?

The idea is that what we are, how we relate, how we behave is partly determined by the role we fulfill in a system. Taking us out of the system changes our shape, so that putting us back in the system means that we no longer fit the old slot. The slot in the system which used to be our old shape changes, too, so it no longer provides the comfortable fit that it used to. When one part of a system changes, the other parts cannot help but change with it.

There are three practical consequences of understanding relationships as systems.

1 THE PRINCIPLE OF JOINT RESPONSIBILITY

Problems within a system of relationships are not the sole responsibility of one person: responsibility for relationships is shared. This is recognized in the language of our proverbs—It takes two to tango; It takes two to fight—and it is also recognized in modern methods of family therapy. The following brief sketches provide a glimpse of this principle at work.

At the age of 16 Ned was noisy, messy, and gregarious. He played loud music late at night; stayed out with his friends until the early hours of the morning without permission; slept most of the day on weekends; and his parents feared he would never get to school at all if they did not forcibly shake him awake. The rest of the family were fed up with being bombarded by uncivilized music and falling over the junk he left lying around. Exactly who has responsibility for what depends on the particular people involved and their actual situation. What is clear is that they share the responsibility for their interactions. Each of them plays a part in creating, and in changing, this situation: solving the problem depends on whether they can adjust to each others' ways. We will show how to manage such change later on.

Ruth was devastated when Jake lost his job. There seemed little possibility of his finding another. His early optimism soon evaporated and he wandered around at home with nothing to do, feeling depressed, unwanted, and miserable. The usual patterns of their relationship seemed to have been swept away at a blow. Ruth became the main wage earner and Jake ran the house, but they fought and argued as each one thought the other was doing a bad job that the other thought he or she could do better.

Wayne, age 12, was brought to the clinic by his parents because his behavior was out of control. He scribbled over wallpaper at home, damaged the furniture, and had started to wet his bed seven years after he first learned to be dry. He was brought to the clinic because he had a problem that his parents wanted solved. With careful work, other problems emerged: difficulties caused by his father's night shifts; disagreements between his parents over the money his father spent on old cars; other children in the family demanding the lion's share of attention, and other problems too. Wayne's problems resolved as other members of the family worked on these problems, and the tension in the house decreased.

Alex lived in a house shared with three others. When one person left, she asked a friend to join them, but this friend failed to pay her share of the bills. She had a reasonably good job, but she spent her money on new clothes and vacations with apparently no thought to her responsibilities. Everyone else was angry, and blamed Alex for the problem. Although Alex was embarrassed, she did not think it was her fault.

Relationships of all kinds can be seen as systems, because one person's behavior impinges on that of others. All relationships within a system may be affected by changes that have started outside the system (e.g., losing a job), or by the behavior of one person (e.g., Alex's friend who failed to pay up). And one person's behavior (e.g., that of Wayne) may be the result of many interacting features of the system.

The first practical point is, therefore, that *it is essential to avoid "scapegoating"*—seeing either yourself or others as the sole cause of problems in relationships. The implications, when you have a problem, are:

1. You are probably under pressure from some quarter to change—to be different.
   • Where could this be coming from?
2. To solve the problem you will have to play your part in adapting to new solutions.
   • How can you adapt?
3. If you can change, the system around you will inevitably change, too.
   • What changes would you like to bring about?
   • Which changes can you initiate?
   • How will others react?

2 THE PRINCIPLE OF HOMEOSTASIS

Our bodies have a remarkably efficient way of keeping the inside temperature constant—within quite small limits. Whether we lie in the sun or roll in the snow, whether we go to an exercise class or sit watching a video, our internal body temperature stays pretty much the same. The system makes constant adjustments, sweating or shivering as necessary, to keep the temperature right.

A system of relationships works in a similar way. When one person within the system changes, the others will react by resisting the change in order to keep the system functioning as before. They say things like "That's not like you to do . . ." and "It's nice to see you back to your old self." Of course the system, just like the central heating, also has limits—it is possible to freeze someone out, or for someone or something to be too hot to handle within a particular system. But, generally, unilateral changes provide the impetus for corresponding changes of the opposite kind—so that the system returns to its previous state.

This principle has two important implications. It forewarns you that unilateral changes in your relationships will be resisted by others, and it emphasizes the value of making mutual and compatible changes, so that the changes you make are complemented by changes others make. In this way your changes "fit" with those of the others, so that the system continues to function, but in a new way. This is why learning how to negotiate will help the system both to keep functioning and to change.

3 THE PRINCIPLES OF NEGOTIATION

The term *negotiation* is usually applied to business and management. But we are carrying out negotiations all the time in our personal lives. We may use the word *discussion,* or *argument,* but often what we are talking about is negotiation, carried out more or less skillfully. Good negotiation is often thought of as if it were about getting the better of someone else, and as if it were about making (more or less unwelcome) compromises. The image that comes to mind is of dividing a cake—if one person gets more, the other gets correspondingly less.

Good negotiation, however, is not about dividing the cake, but about baking a new one. The principles of negotiation are based on the idea of abundance, on the idea that in relationships the size of the cake is not fixed at the start. Dividing up the spoils, so to speak, or competing for relative gain, ends up being counterproductive because it focuses attention on the costs and not the benefits, on what everyone may lose, or have to give up, instead of on what, by putting their heads creatively together, everyone stands to gain.

The implication is that negotiation is not about getting the better of someone else, or of thinking about what all parties to the negotiation are in danger of losing. Using the language of competition, the aim is for both of you to come out of the negotiation having won. This is not as silly as it might sound. Indeed, it is the attitude taught in management studies at Harvard Business School and at many other progressive schools of management. This attitude provides a firm basis for long-term relationships, especially when skillfully put into practice.

Negotiation Skills

Being able to negotiate skillfully is one of the most valuable assets you have when developing relationships. It is relevant to all kinds of relationships, in all kinds of settings. We are carrying out negotiations all the time—whenever two of us disagree about which movie to go to, or which TV program to watch, or who left the mess in the kitchen. Children are born negotiators: "Only one more sweet, then you must put the package away." "No, two more" comes the immediate response.

Relationships are rarely static, so that those involved in them always need to know how to negotiate change. Negotiating skills help relationships to change smoothly and they help to steer them around the hairpin bends. They provide us with an approach to difficulties in relationships that is fair to all because they focus on helping everyone to get what he or she wants.

THE COOPERATION GAME

Here is a game that is played with two sides. The main aim is to end up with positive points; a secondary aim is to end up with more points than the other side. Both sides make their moves at the same time by playing either a round or a square token. For each turn, each side places one token in its bag. After each round, the two bags are opened and points awarded as follows:

- If both tokens are round, both sides score –2.
- If both tokens are square, both sides score +2.
- If the two tokens are different, the values of the tokens are reversed and doubled. This means that the side that played a round token scores +4 and the side that played a square token scores –4. Both sides know this scoring system from the beginning.
- After the first few rounds, the two sides *negotiate* their next moves.

The interesting aspect of this game is that both sides can win if they both play square, but this requires cooperation. Focusing on beating the other side results in both sides losing, since they both go for the highest possible score (a single round token scoring +4), and both play round all the time, which means they both score –2. The point is that *lack of trust* and the *desire to do better* lead to mutual destruction. Play it and find out. Only groups that are prepared to trust others, and are prepared from the outset not to do as well as the other side (to risk playing a square token when the others play a round one), can end up with positive points.

This game illustrates in stark form one of the ways in which we destroy valuable relationships. If we go into relationships to compete—to get more out of the relationship than we put in, or to win so that the other person loses—then we will develop a set of relationships in which everybody loses. Successful relationships are built on the idea that everyone in them will gain, and they require the skills of cooperation.

Some Pointers on How to Cooperate

- *Try looking at the situation from the other person's point of view.* Use your imagination to step into the other person's shoes.
- *Build up trust.* Risk saying how you feel and talking about what you want. Show you believe what other people say. Leave them the space they need to be their own person.
- *Keep in contact.* Do not allow yourself to slip into the habit of not being able to talk. Do not avoid thorny issues.
- *Recognize that people vary in their needs.* People need different amounts of closeness, silence, sharing, and independence. They enjoy different forms of physical and sexual contact. They may, or may not, need to let off steam.
- *Provide what you know you want.* Acknowledge another point of view; take what someone else says seriously; respond with warmth and encouragement.
- *Cut out the blame.* "You make me so angry/nervous/upset. . . ." Ask instead, "What is it in me that makes me so angry?"

FOUR RELATIONSHIP PATTERNS

1. *There is plenty for all.* Everyone in a relationship has something to gain, and this attitude of abundance is, in the long run, the most satisfactory way of relating. It is based on the realization that working together with other people can make things happen that could not otherwise happen. Thinking about ways in which everyone gains engages two heads rather than one, and generates more options and more solutions

to problems. It ends up being more *creative* than the other patterns, and this provides more potential for satisfaction.

2. *I win: you lose.* This is not only intrinsically unfair, it is also not to your long-term advantage. Either the people who lose when you win will draw away from you, or the ones who remain close are the ones who complement you by showing you the next pattern.

3. *You win: I lose.* This attitude builds up resentment and anger, and is therefore satisfactory to neither party: "If you act like a doormat, don't be surprised if people walk on you."

4. *Lose: lose.* This is a totally destructive pattern, and not likely to result in lasting relationships.

THERE IS ALWAYS THE POSSIBILITY OF NO DEAL

The bottom line in all negotiations is that you are free to make no deal and walk away. The bottom line in all relationships must be that if you cannot both make the changes needed for the relationship to give you both what you want, then the relationship is off. It takes courage to end relationships, but it must always be a possibility. The alternative is that you make unwise deals, or deals that maintain relationships which are destructive (see also Chapter 17, pp. 202–209).

PREPARATION FOR SKILLFUL NEGOTIATION: MAPPING THE TERRITORY

Step 1: Find out what everyone wants. Relationships are systems, which means that if you think only about what you want, you see only half the picture. You need to think both about your own perspective and that of others. If you are too inflexible about what you want, it may be harder to negotiate. For example, if you want help cleaning up and others are not bothered about being messy, your negotiations may quickly get bogged down. What is it about the mess that bothers you? Would you feel satisfied if it was kept to certain places? Or removed only on special occasions? Or do you want most of all to feel that your burden of chores is shared? The three main ways to answer these questions are to *think*, to *ask*, and to *listen*. You need to do all three of these things, not just one of them.

Step 2: Look for common ground. Common ground is useful in establishing what you are *not* negotiating about—we both want to go out, but we cannot agree where to go; we both want to live here, but disagree about who makes the rules. When negotiation is in danger of failing return to the common ground. If you both want to go out tonight it would be silly to stay in because you couldn't agree on where to go.

Step 3: Broaden the basis of the negotiation. A negotiation often founders because it all hinges on one thing, such as who is responsible for servicing the car, or whether one person's necessity is another person's extravagance. But often there are many negotiable aspects of a situation. In the commercial world, for example, a negotiation may center entirely on fixing the price, but there are many other aspects to the deal, such as delivery time, payment time, after-sales service, further orders, and promotion of products. This is often true of relationships, too. A narrow negotiation about heating bills might focus on closing the door when you leave the room. A broader one, leaving more room for considering what everyone wants, might also focus on resetting the time clock or thermostat; sharing the bills a different way; fixing the drafts in the house; or buying a warm sweater.

Step 4: Look for opportunities to trade. Identify the important issues for both of you. It is rare for two people to place exactly the same importance on particular issues, which means that you might be able to gain what is most important to you by giving way on what is most important to someone else. "I'll turn the music down after 11 P.M. if you agree not to fuss about the mess in my room." The broader the basis for the negotiation the more opportunities for trade.

FIVE STRATEGIES FOR PUTTING THE SKILLS INTO PRACTICE

1. *Clarify.* Be sure to clarify what the other person means and what you mean. "Are you cross with me, or has something else upset you?" Make your points clearly: "I'm angry that you didn't telephone me." Not "I'm fed up with you. You never bother to let me know where you are."

2. *Build on what the other person says.* Instead of reacting to what you do not like about it and instantly saying "no," look for what you can accept and start with a "yes," or an "OK, how could we manage that?" This takes you out of conflict and straight into negotiation.

3. *Cut out the blame.* Think of there being different points of view rather than one wrong one and one right one. Instead of thinking in terms of "fault," think in terms of shared responsibility. This might sound overly optimistic: sometimes one person is wrong. But a flurry of accusations, derogatory name-calling, or insults only raises the temperature, and

makes this harder to admit. Cut out the blame, and look for possibilities for mutual change. Remember that there is always the possibility of *no deal*, but *no deal* is taking your share of the responsibility, not heaping all the blame on the other person.

Some Rules for Fair Fighting

1. *Stick to the concern of the moment.* Don't throw out the kitchen sink and any old "unfinished business."
2. *Don't overgeneralize.* "You *always* complain . . . or *never* listen to what I say."
3. *No name-calling.* "You're stupid . . . completely heartless . . . domineering . . . childish. . . ."
4. *Use the cooler.* Take a break from a fight. Count to ten before you answer back. Go somewhere you can calm down. Explain what you are doing—do not just storm out.
5. *Ask: What's my part in this?* Start your sentences with "I": "I'm furious," not "You make me wild."
6. *Avoid going for the jugular.* Hitting where it hurts mostly just adds to the pain, hurt, and anger. It makes it harder to forgive and forget.
7. *Do not use threats, verbal or physical.* They lead to escalation not resolution.

---

4. *Watch out for escalation.* Anger easily spirals upward, especially when people are hurt by the angry things others have just said to them. Anger generates the sort of vicious cycle that stops all reasoned discussion and prohibits agreement (see Chapter 16). It usually leads to the "lose: lose" pattern.

It can sometimes be useful to tell the other person that what they say makes you feel angry, and it is also helpful to look behind the anger. Often people behave angrily when they are hurt (feel wounded by the angry things said to them) or frightened (by the implications for the relationship, or by threats of being hurt). It may be the hurt and the fear that need addressing rather than the anger.

5. *Bottle up the insults.* Offensive comments impede negotiation until feelings subside. Examples of such comments are: "I can't talk to anyone as illogical as you," "You're so arrogant/pigheaded/clumsy," "You're as bad as your mother/father/sister," or putdowns such as "Everyone knows that . . . ," "I think you will find . . . ," "Any sensible person would realize . . . ," "I'll be generous, and leave that out of consideration/give you the benefit of the doubt." It is best to avoid making these offensive or irritating comments, and to try to ignore them when they are thrown at you.

When Others Ask for Your Opinion

Most people at times talk to others about their relationships, and they are especially likely to do so when the relationships are stormy or difficult. In the following box we offer some guidelines for the times when others want to talk about their relationships.

Talking to Others about Their Relationships

- Listen.
- Ask questions.
- Clarify what is going on.
- Do not judge, but show that you understand.
- Remember you can only change yourself: they can only change themselves.
- Ask how the person you are talking to feels.
- Ask how the other people involved feel.
- Think of yourself as offering support, not taking sides.
- Help them to decide what they want.
- Help them to mobilize their resources for coping.
- Help them to start the process of problem-solving.
- Avoid giving advice.

Avoid taking sides because this can end up with one person feeling more isolated, rejected, and hurt, which will only perpetuate high levels of distress. Instead, your role is to help the other person to clarify and solve his or her problems. Trying to impose your solution on someone else's personal problem rarely works, and can end in disaster. If you strongly support one person rather than another, it may help to say so, but it rarely helps to add your barbs of criticism to theirs. There always are two sides to a story, and responsibility is always shared to some degree (see also p. 177).

Sometimes the problems of another person are too much for us. Remember that if you do not want to get involved, you have a perfect right to say "no." If you find this difficult, see pages 141–142.

Two Common False Beliefs about Relationships

There are two common false beliefs that can prevent people from adopting a constructive approach to developing relationships.

• **"A relationship that needs working at is not worth having."**
"I shouldn't have to work at it" is a reservation that gets in the way of solving relationship problems. The reservation takes many forms: the belief that working at a relationship removes the spontaneity from it, and makes it false, artificial, or contrived; or that if you have to work at it, it cannot have been much of a relationship to begin with; or that working at it is treating it like a kind of pathology, suggesting that the people in the relationship are suitable cases for treatment; or that a single sign of discontent is enough to show that the relationship is doomed anyway.

All these versions of the truth are false. Quite the contrary, relationships need work; satisfying relationships are unlikely to develop unless all concerned are prepared to be committed and to make an effort. The problem is perhaps in the terminology: in the use of the word "work." If relationships are systems, and systems of joint responsibility, then instead of work we can just think of adaptation. It is important to realize that such adaptation takes effort, but the effort is likely to be amply rewarded.

• **"You should know how I feel."**
This reservation comes from supposing that feelings between people who are close to each other are readily observable, and that being close means that one should understand, as if by telepathy, how each other feels. Indeed, relationships often take off precisely because two people do easily understand each other, and later on a sense of disappointment and sadness arises because the understanding seems to get lost. Nevertheless, we cannot see into each others' minds, and however close you are to others, they will never be able to know exactly how you feel unless you let them know. It is easy to make mistakes, and also to take things personally: to confuse depression with irritability, preoccupation with indifference, frustration with the outside world with hostility, and so on. An important feature of close relationships is not telepathy, but the ability to say to each other, honestly, how you feel.

Chapter Summary

Relationships are systems. This has three implications:

1. The principle of joint responsibility
   • Within a system, the responsibility for the relationships is shared by everyone.

2. The principle of homeostasis
   - If you try to change the way you relate to others, your changes will be resisted.
3. The principles of negotiation
   - You can make changes within a system of relationships through negotiation.

Good negotiation is not about dividing the cake; it is about baking a new one. Preparing for skillful negotiation involves *four* steps:

Step 1: Find out what everyone wants.
Step 2: Look for common ground.
Step 3: Broaden the basis of the negotiation.
Step 4: Look for opportunities to trade.

The five strategies for skillful negotiation are:

1. Clarify.
2. Build on what the other person says.
3. Cut out the blame.
4. Watch out for escalation.
5. Bottle up the insults.

16

Anger in Relationships

Anger makes problems for relationships when there is too much of it, when it happens too often, and when people are unable to control the way they express it, and become, for example, argumentative, aggressive, or violent. It also causes problems when people cannot, or dare not, express their anger and try to keep it hidden. Too much anger hurts everyone: both those who experience it and those on the receiving end. Anger may be expressed by sulking, or by talking about it, as well as by shouting or yelling. It may also result in physical violence.

It is normal, however, to feel angry at times, and it can also have useful effects. Anger can mobilize you to take action, for example to set limits to the demands others make of you, to think about why something matters to you or to defend yourself if attacked. It can be constructively expressed, and prompt you to explain what it is that is distressing or alarming you, and to ask for what you need. Anger may be behind such actions as setting up a local neighborhood watch group, or a safe refuge for victims of domestic or political violence. It can also prompt people to face their differences and difficulties and seek resolutions. So anger does not always cause problems, even though for many of us, especially in the relationships that matter, it can be difficult to keep the more constructive aspects of anger in sight.

Intimate relationships are a potent source of anger because such relationships are important. They contribute to the way we feel about ourselves. It matters if the people who are close criticize the way you do things, or ignore you, or dismiss your ideas as worthless. Proximity brings with it strong feelings and (often unspoken) expectations. People who live or work together are bound to experience irritations, disappointments, and disagreements. They will at times misunderstand each other, or misperceive the facts. Those who readily become explosively or uncontrollably angry when this happens may be seen as unpleasant, difficult, or dangerous, and the people around them may become watchful and mistrustful or retaliate, becoming aggressive and hostile themselves. In the end, the main options in responding to a person who expresses intense anger are to fight back, to build up defenses, or to withdraw. Hence the damaging effect of anger on relationships.

So too much anger is bad for you: it eats away at self-respect, damages relationships, and can contribute to ill health such as stomach ulcers and cardiac problems. In this chapter we will start by explaining four key facts about anger. We will then provide practical suggestions, both for those who think that their own anger is a problem and for those who are on the receiving end of someone else's anger.

Four Key Facts about Anger

1 ANGER MAKES YOU BLIND

Anger blinds you to other ways of seeing things. It produces rigidity in mind and body—as if it gets a grip on you. It is then difficult to see things any other way: for example, someone forgot to give you an important message, and as far as you are concerned this means that they are utterly careless and irresponsible.

Anger blinds you to your share of the responsibility. When angry we shift the blame onto others. "It's your fault. You didn't do what I asked . . . you made me look ridiculous in front of my friends . . . you left me in the lurch." The message to others is: "you made me angry," and sometimes also "you knew that would upset me, so you must have done it on purpose." Thinking, or assuming, "I didn't do anything wrong. It's your fault, not mine" goes with demanding that others take responsibility for putting things right.

Anger blinds you to other (more peaceful) options for dealing with it. Anger makes you think: I know I am right, and the anger is justified. I *should* let others know how I feel: give them a piece of my mind; make it clear that I never want that to happen again. The more forceful you are the more likely (it can seem) that you will succeed in making others do what you want. But this way of thinking blinds you to more effective, and more peaceful, ways of dealing with the problems that made you angry.

2 ANGER ESCALATES

Left unchecked, anger progresses through stages: from the first perception of having been wronged, to becoming angry, to feeling impelled to attack, to an attack, and at its worst, to violence. Once anger is expressed, only too often the genie is out of the bottle. Attacks are met with counterattacks which add fuel to the flames: if you hurt me then I want to punish you, and hurt you back. Seeing you suffer brings me a measure of relief. But you also want to find relief, so you want to make me suffer more. Combativeness escalates rapidly as each of the warring parties tries to strike the winning blow and avoid a humiliating defeat. The longer this goes on, the harder it is to stop and the stronger the desire to inflict pain before letting the matter rest. This common process, which may seem childish when its bare bones are revealed, partly explains why angry people in close relationships can do increasingly damaging things to each other, and sometimes be consumed with guilt and self-recrimination afterward.

3 ANGER IS PAINFUL (ANGER HURTS)

Anger is a reaction to pain that causes more pain; layers of pain. People become angry as a reaction to the pain of insults or put downs, to being treated unfairly, disrespectfully, or with condescension. All of these can hurt, whether or not they were intended to cause pain.

Underneath this first layer of pain lies more pain, often in the form of fear. Someone who insults you might not care about you or value you. If you see the point of their accusations then you will feel hurt, and your self-esteem will be threatened.

Behaving angrily toward others causes them pain. It may be meant to hurt, or you may be completely unaware of their reactions; so caught up in letting off steam that you can only think of yourself. Your anger may also be intended to make others change their ways or behave as you think they should.

Your own anger may increase your own pain. We do not use the term "hot and bothered" for nothing. Feeling intensely angry is not pleasant, which is why it goads us into action, and mobilizes our forces to combat the cause of our anger. Moments of satisfaction may occur when we think we are winning, or diverting further attack, or if it feels better to be doing something than nothing. But the longer term consequence of our anger is often more pain both for ourselves and others.

4 DANGEROUS DOUBLE MESSAGES: IT'S NOT JUST THE WORDS THAT COUNT

What we are thinking is conveyed to others by our words and also in subtle, nonverbal ways (the ways we look, sound, and move), and the two kinds of messages often convey different meanings. Here is a common type of exchange between two people who are close to each other. Alexa asks Shaun the verbally innocuous question: "Have you paid the phone bill?" Shaun responds to what he knows is a reprimand, and says: "What have *you* been doing all day?" The reprimand and resentment escalate into overt anger and Shaun and Alexa start shouting at each other. Alexa yells at Shaun: "You're useless, and take no responsibility." He shouts back "You have no idea how hard I work, and seem to care less." Alexa retorts: "I only asked if you'd paid the phone bill." When we give double messages, so that the verbal and the nonverbal messages differ, people usually respond to the *nonverbal* part of the message—to the resentment or irritation behind the words. The feelings behind the messages leak out, and people jump to conclusions. Anger tends to dominate the scene, and feelings are easy to misconstrue, even in those we are closest to. Sadness, misery, and confusion can all look like anger, and unhappiness of another kind can easily be translated into anger.

The Main Effects of Anger

Anger affects your body, your feelings, your behavior, and your thinking in many negative ways. It also affects your relationships. In order to deal with it, start by focusing on yourself, rather than on the person who made you angry, and work out the ways that anger affects you. With a real example in mind, look for at least one symptom in each of the categories in the box on page 173, adding to the list as necessary. As you read the rest of this chapter, keep in mind those effects that you find especially upsetting or difficult to handle, so that you can start looking for solutions as you read.

Five Effects of Anger

Effects on your body:
Tension, shaking, heart racing, going red in the face, restlessness

Effects on your feelings (these can erupt suddenly or build up slowly):
Resentment, confusion, frustration, fear, pain, feeling detached or uncaring

Effects on your behavior:
Glaring, shouting, demanding that others change, fighting, hitting, sulking, calling people names

Effects on your thinking:
It's your fault; you *shouldn't* have done that; people *should* do what they say they will; I've a perfect right to show how I feel
Ruminating about wrongs received and about what you would like to do as a result

Effects on your relationships:
People keep their distance, reject you or complain about you; they retaliate and cause you pain; wariness creeps in between you, and trust diminishes

---

Six Myths about Managing Anger

There are some common myths about how to deal with anger, and these often lead people astray. In each of them, however, there is a grain of truth.

1 THE VENTILATION MYTH

According to this myth, ventilation—for example by punching a pillow, shouting or kicking something—makes you feel less angry. It gets anger out of the system, lets off steam, and clears the air. The image behind this myth is false: anger is not like pressure, building up inside until (if not ventilated) it explodes out of you. Ventilation does not provide a safety valve; it increases angry feelings. Ventilating anger often makes people less inhibited about what they say, when they say it, and what they do when they feel angry. It can work like a training session in aggression, removing restraints that might otherwise have been there. In the home, the more that anger is expressed verbally, the more likely it is that it will lead to physical violence. Ventilation makes things worse, and infects the atmosphere. Rather than clearing the air, it can trigger a host of negative feelings such as hostility, unhappiness, depression, anxiety, irritability, and resentment—in other words a great deal of misery, turmoil, and confusion.

The grain of truth in the myth that ventilating your anger is useful is that it may help you to acknowledge and accept your angry feelings. But it is better to do this without the ventilation.

2 THE SHARING MYTH

The sharing myth is that it helps if people with the same problem—colleagues with a bullying boss, for example, or women who feel exploited by men—share their anger. Sharing anger, however, works like group ventilation. It reduces inhibitions, helps people to imagine what it would be like to express the anger, and acts more like a rehearsal than a safety valve. Shared expressions of anger make the anger seem increasingly justified, and result in people apportioning blame with greater certainty. Feelings escalate, the mind shuts down to other points of view, and seeking solutions falls off the agenda.

The grains of truth in the sharing myth are that it feels good to know that you are not alone, and it can help to join forces in solving problems and taking action.

3 THE INSTINCTIVE IMPULSE MYTH: "I CAN'T HELP IT"

According to this myth, anger is like an animal instinct, and as automatic and uncontrollable as a reflex. This myth is plausible because anger can erupt so suddenly. However, much about anger is not instinctive. Different things make each of us angry because we perceive, interpret, and understand them differently. What provokes anger and maintains it, how we express it and respond to it, are all influenced by our individual experiences and cultures: by our thoughts, assumptions, and beliefs. Whether we shout and scream, or glare, or cry, or withdraw, are things we can reflect upon and adjust in a cool moment. They are not reflexes.

The grain of truth is that you might feel powerless to prevent yourself getting angry, but this truth should not blind you to the fact that you can control what you do when you are angry. Controlling what you do—and say—may even help you to react less "instinctively" next time.

4 THE MYTH ABOUT GENDER DIFFERENCES

Men are supposedly more angry than women, and more likely to be violent and uncontrolled. Women are supposedly more likely to sulk, grumble, and manipulate. But in Western cultures now there are few gender differences between men and women both in the degree of anger experienced and in ways of expressing it. Both men and women express anger openly and violently, and both can suppress it while continuing to bear grudges or running an internal critical commentary through their minds.

The grain of truth is that men are (or were) a bit less inhibited about expressing anger publicly, and women are more cautious about letting their anger show, probably because when anger flares up women are more likely to be injured and to need physical protection. And of course cultural differences persist.

5 THE MYTH THAT YOU CAN DECIDE NOT TO GET ANGRY AGAIN

This myth is a recipe for failure. Could you decide never to laugh at another joke? Feeling anger is normal and it is bound to happen again, to all of us. There is nothing to be gained from trying never to be angry again.

But the grain of truth—perhaps it is more than a grain—is that you can decide how to control and express your anger, and it might be important to do so.

6 THE REVENGE MYTH

Paying people back, getting even with them, and seeking revenge are dangerous games to play. They fuel the cycle of escalation, and they inflame situations rather than resolve them. Thinking about revenge poisons the atmosphere. It gets hard to think about anything else, and rumination leads to increasingly elaborate and vivid images of possible actions. So the myth that it is helpful to engage in a payback cycle or embark on a trajectory of revenge is both false and dangerous.

The grain of truth is that getting even, or winning, can bring temporary relief, but only at a terrible price. Revenge escalates and turns back to hurt the avenger.

Dealing Better with Your Own Anger

Learning to manage anger involves recognizing it, accepting it, and practicing expressing it without doing damage. It is not a question of starting another fight, this time with yourself; of battling with yourself not to feel angry, or of deciding not to let your anger show. It is more a question of learning how to notice and pay attention to it so that it does not grow or escalate dangerously out of control.

There is value in anger and it may be right to feel angry. Your anger may point to a problem that needs to be faced and dealt with (see Chapter 8 on problem-solving). The purpose of this chapter is to enable you to manage your anger when it is not helpful and when it makes difficulties for you or for others. We will describe several methods so that you can choose those that suit you best. However, from the start it is helpful to keep one key aim in mind: *Express your anger in the right way, at the right time, and to the right person.* This means, for example, without violence, not when you are exhausted or have been drinking, and to the person who made you angry rather than to others. This does not mean that there is only one right way but that there definitely are some wrong ones.

ACCEPTING RESPONSIBILITY

The first step is for you to accept some responsibility for your anger. Otherwise you will remain at the mercy both of others and of your feelings.

Usually people think: "But it's their fault, not mine," and sometimes others are unreasonable, insulting, or completely outrageous. They may clearly be in the wrong, and being angry with them may also help to change their behavior. But without taking responsibility for your own anger you will not be able to control it. Being angry focuses attention on what others have done wrong and blinds you to your part in exacerbating the problems.

First, it is helpful to separate responsibility from blame. Blame goes with accusation, resentment, or escalation, and often gets in the way of solving the key problems. Whether or not the other person is mainly to blame, you can take responsibility for:

1. *Recognizing that you are angry.* The earlier that you can do this the better. Aim to recognize your anger before it intensifies and does damage.
2. *Deciding what to do when you are angry.* In the heat of the moment this is hard so you will need to plan ahead. We will say more about this below (p. 179).
3. *Calming yourself down.* Waiting for other people to put things right leaves you in their hands. Focusing on them can keep your anger simmering. The value in accepting responsibility is that it puts you in charge of what happens next. If it was not your fault in the first place, then accepting responsibility provides you with choices of effective

ways to move forward. If it was (partly) your fault, then accepting responsibility makes it easier to find out where you might have been mistaken, for example by misunderstanding the other person, or misperceiving what happened. Did you jump to conclusions? Or take something personally when it was not intended that way?

In short, if you wish to decrease your anger, deal with yourself before you deal with others. Indeed it is by changing yourself that you can have the most powerful effect on other people. Eight ways of dealing with anger are listed in the box below.

Dealing with Anger

1. *Address the inner cause.* Instead of focusing on the wrongdoers and their actions, think about what it was that hurt you, in mind or body.
2. *Recognize your own flashpoints.* These might be feeling disrespected, unfairly judged, disregarded, exploited, uncared for.
3. *Identify the specific damage done by anger.* For example the pain and suffering for you and for others; the damage to your relationships.
4. *Develop your conflict-management skills.* Learn how to be assertive rather than passive or aggressive. Make use of negotiation skills (pp. 161–166), and obey the rules of fair fighting (p. 166).
5. *Search for the other person's perspective* (even if you don't agree with it). Listen to the other person in the spirit of finding out what they think rather than in the spirit of judging and blaming.
6. *Tackle the stresses that make you vulnerable.* Anger is more easily triggered when we are exhausted, overburdened, rushed, worried, unwell, etc.
7. *Learn how to calm yourself down.* Think about what you can do to make yourself feel better, other than berating others or lashing out.
8. *Limit your alcohol intake* (see p. 406).

The Red, Orange, and Green Skills

Taking responsibility for your anger puts you in a good position to take constructive action. Three types of skills are described next: *red* skills for use in the heat of the moment, *orange* skills for thinking things through, and *green* skills for the times when you want to take action.

RED SKILLS FOR USE IN THE HEAT OF THE MOMENT

You need your red skills when you are overwhelmed by anger; when, for example, you feel under attack and immediately want to fight back, and to defend yourself. Red lights warn you to stop. When we "see red," blindness, blame, and belligerence dominate, and it is easy to lose control. This is when dangerous and destructive actions do damage to relationships. So this is not the time to act. It is the time to make the space to cool down: to redirect the energy that is in your anger, and use it to generate a cool-down system, just as you would turn up the fridge on a hot day. At these moments it is best to bottle up your feelings and to shut your mouth so that you do not do or say anything that you will regret. Perhaps you can reduce the pressure by diverting your energy into something harmless. Cooling down is not being a pushover, or being passive, or a wimp. On the contrary, cooling down helps you to take responsibility and to act assertively so that you will be more likely to achieve a constructive outcome.

Some of the techniques for developing red skills are shown in the box below. The aim is simple: to limit, and ideally to avoid, any damage that might be caused by an explosion. It is unlikely that losing your temper will lead to constructive change.

Techniques for Improving Red Skills

- Invent your own stop signal. Imagine a large stop sign, or flashing red light, or barrier in the road with **STOP** written on it, or someone shouting **STOP**, or an alarm bell. Or imagine shutting your mouth.
- Get out of harm's way: take yourself out of the situation, even for a short time.
- Try to steady yourself down. Focus on your breathing, and take a deep breath in. Let it out slowly, and tell yourself to stay calm (see also pp. 106–115).
- Count before you speak or act: up to 10 or 200, depending on how long it takes to feel calmer.
- Try to relax, to undo the bad effects of the rigidity and the unpleasant physical sensations that go with anger.

The earlier you can take action the better. Think back over a time when you lost your temper and see if you can recognize your personal early warning signals of entering the red zone. Much pain, misery, and damage can be averted if you learn to:

- Recognize that you are about to lose your temper before this has become obvious to others.

- Avoid showing your anger—or at least the extent of it—so that you can take care over what you say and do.

ORANGE SKILLS FOR THINKING THINGS THROUGH

Once you are no longer in its grip, make yourself think about your anger—not about what someone else did that made you angry, but the more difficult part that many people do not like, of facing up to the whole experience, including your own unpleasant thoughts, feelings, and actions. Orange skills enable you to understand your anger, to think in new ways about the things that make you angry, and to develop new ways of behaving so as to turn your anger to constructive use.

Many orange skills take some time to develop and some effort to carry out. If anger has become problematic you will need to set aside time for the rethinking and planning that will provide the basis for constructive change. In addition to the ideas in this chapter there are many others in this book that could be useful. Use the chapter headings and the index to look for those that fit you personally.

FOUR TYPES OF ORANGE SKILLS

1. Identifying personal triggers
2. Understanding the underlying pain
3. Seeing things differently
4. Working on assumptions and rules

1. Identifying personal triggers.   Sometimes irritating behavior leads to explosions, and sometimes it is like water off a duck's back. If you have had a bad day, then minor irritations (terrible traffic, a noisy family) will be more likely to make you angry. Stop and think about what makes you irritable. The more tired, hungry, stressed, or worried you are, the more likely it is that you will get angry. Alcohol is a particularly potent precipitant of anger and it quickly multiplies the effects of other worries or stresses. It reduces inhibitions about what you say and what you do, and makes it harder to bring things back under control and into perspective.

Anger is a response to a provocation, but what counts as a provocation (or trigger) depends on how you see it, which helps to explain why different things make different people angry. The main triggers are *perceived* insults, put-downs, and unfairness. So it is not only the trigger that produces the anger, it is what goes through the person's mind at the time (often so quickly and automatically that it just seems obvious). To identify your personal flashpoints and your personal rules, keep in mind a specific time when you were angry, and use the box below as a prompt. Doing this for more than one specific episode of anger will give you a broader picture.

Factors That Contribute to Triggering Anger

The external setting:
- heat, noise
- crowds, traffic, hustle and bustle

Your internal state:
- fatigue, stress, worry, disturbed sleep
- feeling frustrated, miserable, hurt, moody, depressed
- hunger, illness, heat, cold, excitement, high arousal
- effects of alcohol and other addictive substances

Your personal flashpoints:
- being exploited, or asked to do too much, or being unfairly treated
- someone taking advantage of you, someone telling you how you feel
- being shouted at, criticized, put down in public, interrupted
- being ignored, passed over, not taken account of, threatened

---

Some people are quick to respond emotionally in all sorts of ways and others are slower. Those who are quick to respond usually also subside quickly too, unless the feelings are kept going by their thoughts, attitudes, and beliefs. Ruminating about the wrongdoing keeps the anger going. So does the attitude of blaming others, and so does the habit of trying to punish them. Thinking about giving people what they deserve (or a piece of your mind), or paying them back provides the fuel that feeds the angry reaction. Such habits may have been learned from others during childhood (see *Chapter 14, Recognizing Voices from the Past*), or they may have developed later. In either case, when such habits are strong it takes a smaller provocation, and a slightly vulnerable state of mind, to make you angry.

2. Understanding the underlying pain. Anger can so dominate the mind that it is hard to think about anything else, including the underlying pain, anxiety, fear, or misery. Robert was furious when his family kept pushing him to get out more, and to stop sitting in front of the TV doing nothing. He focused on trying to get them off his back. He argued with them, and called them bossy. He thought: "they don't have any right to tell me how to live my life," and "anyway, it's not as if any of them are perfect." He refused to turn the TV down one evening, and everyone's anger flared up. Underneath his anger Robert was feeling miserable. He could not find work, his friends had moved on, and he hated having to rely on his parents for somewhere to live. Underneath his parents' anger was their worry about him, and the fear that he had given up looking for work. Acknowledging these feelings, and seeking to understand them, takes everyone involved in different directions: away from the attack-defense cycle, toward something more constructive. Understanding provides an antidote to anger as it opens the way to respect, empathy, compassion, and humor—toward oneself and toward others—all of which help when looking for new ways of seeing things. Anger rapidly closes the door on cooler thinking processes, and on kinder ones, and people end up saying things that fit well with how they feel: "you're a complete idiot," "that's typical of you. You always disregard my feelings," but which may not fit well with the facts.

If you think about, and try to understand your personal triggers, your habits, and the pain behind the anger, you will be in a better position to use ideas from cognitive therapy to search for new perspectives on the things that make you angry. You may also feel more interested in doing so.

3. Seeing things differently.   Stand back from your perspective so as to take another look. Shifting your ground, even by a small amount, can have a large effect on the way you see things. It can, as it were, put you in a boat on the stormy sea rather than leaving you wading in deep water with the risk of being engulfed by the waves. There are many types of crooked thinking that prevent us from seeing straight, and some of these are strongly linked with anger (see also p. 78; and Chapters 9 and 37):

Black and white thinking: "If someone disagrees with me they must be against me."

Emotional reasoning: You feel accused and you think the other person is accusing you.

Taking things personally: Your partner feels ill and does not want to make love. You feel rejected and get angry.

Mind-reading: Someone puts you down in front of people you respect and you think he or she couldn't care less about you.

When crooked thinking contributes to your problems, it can help to remember that patterns of thinking may make sense in terms of the past. For example, in some families children are encouraged to see everything in terms of winning and losing, or of relative strength, or to be especially sensitive to signs of unfairness, or disrespect. Such patterns can leave these children, when they have grown up, vulnerable to anger. Rethinking them can make a big difference.

4. Working on assumptions and rules.   It is especially easy to get angry when someone else has broken the rules, and done something that they should not have done, such as told a lie, or been unfaithful; or when they have not done something that, as the angry person sees it, they should have done, like cleaned up the mess they made, or provided support at a difficult time.

Behind angry reactions lie sets of rules, most of which are unwritten. We all have ideas about the ways other people *should* behave, and we get angry when these rules are broken. Such rules indicate what each of us thinks people should or should not do. Some of these rules are built on the values of the culture we live in: what counts as being polite; how we show affection or consideration for others; what you *should* be able to expect from a partner, or daughter, or colleague. Others are quite personal, and are never precisely put into words. But we get angry when someone crosses the boundaries set by these rules. Common examples of rules relevant to personal relationships are: "I should be able to relax and be myself at home"; "You should understand how I feel without my having to explain"; "I should be able to talk about what I want, when I want"; "This should be a cooperative enterprise—and you're not doing your part." Given that we all have different unspoken rules, it is hardly surprising that conflicts arise.

People have reasons for their rules. The reasons reflect the boundaries with which they feel comfortable: the boundaries that seem necessary to keep the peace. Boundaries protect you. If observed, they prevent people from hurting each other; if crossed people feel hurt and angry. So, it is helpful to reflect on the things that make you angry. Write some of them down, and then, with a specific example in mind, start working on your rules using the following strategy.

1. Identify your rules.   What "shoulds" and "shouldn'ts," "musts," "oughts," or "have tos" are involved? These words provide a good starting point for identifying your rules (see p. 344). Try and put your rules into words, for example: People *should* be reasonable; children *must* show respect; people *ought not* to tell me what to do.

2. Identify the transgression.   How has your rule been broken or violated? What has the person you are angry with done wrong? The more important the rule and the greater the violation, the more it matters—and the angrier you will be likely to feel.

3. Think about the meaning of the behavior that made you angry.   This helps to define how you were hurt or threatened. What do you think the behavior means? For example, that you are not respected? Or cared for? Later, you can ask yourself how you know what was meant. Was it intended that way? For instance, is being ignored a sign of disrespect? Or could it be something else?

4. Find out whether you and the other person disagree about the rules or about the way they are applied.   A disagreement about rules may be resolved by clarifying the rules and negotiating differences (or by agreeing to differ). A disagreement about how rules are applied is more likely to be resolved by thinking about the meaning of the provocative action, for example, when both of you believe respect is important, but you show it in different ways.

Not all rules are good rules. Some lead to inappropriate and unrealistic expectations: "People shouldn't get in my way—or criticize me—or be rude." Anger is less likely to flare up if we adopt rules that work for others as well as for ourselves. The following box provides a guide to questioning your rules.

Questioning Your Rules

Write down one of your rules.

With this rule in mind, answer the following questions:

1. *Is this a rule you want to live by?* Does it reflect your values (see p. 32)? If others lived by this rule too, would that be alright for you?

2. *Where does this rule come from? Where have you heard it before?* Did you decide to adopt this rule? If so, when? At what age?

   Is it an echo of a voice from the past (p. 150), such as "You *should* always do what I say," or "People *shouldn't* make trouble for others"?

   Is it a childhood relic or legacy, such as "I *should* be able to do what I want," or "People *shouldn't* be rude"?

   Is it accepted wisdom? "You *should* always respect your parents," or "Your first loyalty *should* be to your family"?

3. *Decide whether you want to keep this rule,* or whether it could usefully be updated. If you decide to change the old rule, then reword it so that it would work for others as well as for yourself. Write your new wording down.

4. *Practice using the new version of your rule.*

Old rules die hard. To help you keep new rules in mind, write them down. When old habits reemerge, as they will from time to time, think through what went wrong. Would your new rule have kept you out of difficulties?

How would you have behaved if you had been able to keep it in mind at the time?

GREEN SKILLS FOR GOING AHEAD: EXPRESSING YOUR ANGER SKILLFULLY

> I was angry with my friend:
> I told my wrath, my wrath did end.
> I was angry with my foe
> I hid my wrath, my wrath did grow.
> William Blake

Showing someone you are angry with them can lead to resolutions, and hiding your anger can make it grow—but showing anger to enemies may be dangerous. Telling friends may be easier than telling enemies. So, having used your red skills for calming down, and your orange skills for thinking things through, the green skills are for putting your thoughts into action when dealing directly with those with whom you are angry—friend or foe—without doing damage. They are for learning how to express anger without hostility, aggression, violence, or exaggeration. The surprising message is that it takes much less anger than you expect to resolve a difference, provided that you address the right target. Angry behavior does not help. Nor does standing on principle. It's no good saying: "That's obvious," or "That's just the way it is" and brooking no argument. Instead it helps to ask clearly for what you want; to listen to other points of view, to negotiate differences, and to acknowledge diversity. Relationship skills are the most useful ones to practice here, especially those of assertiveness and negotiation. These are summarized in the box below, and more fully discussed in Chapters 13 and 15.

Applying the Skills of Assertiveness to Anger

State what has upset you
- Clearly
- To the person concerned
- Soon: e.g., within 24 hours
- Own the problem: say how you feel
- Ask for what you want
- Find out what the other person is feeling and thinking
- Listen to the other person with 100% of your attention; put reservations on hold
- Move into problem-solving mode—with assertiveness

Applying the Skills of Assertiveness to Anger—cont'd

Refrain from
- Accusation and recrimination; shouting and yelling
- Criticizing the person, rather than their behavior
- Labeling people or calling them names
- Moaning and groaning to others
- Bringing other things in

If the person you are angry with is not available, or if it feels too dangerous to say what has upset you (you have previously been attacked; everyone has been drinking), or if it would be unwise at the moment (just before a family wedding), then it can be helpful to express your anger in another way. You could

- Write about it; let it all out on paper
- Draw a picture to express how you feel
- Play some music that fits with your feelings
- Tell it to the bees
- Confide in a friend

Be careful not to use these techniques just for ventilation of your feelings. Green skills are for expressing the products of your thoughtfulness, and reaching out for a source of resolution. When ventilating you are still in the red zone, and the hot air you produce keeps the flames dangerously high. Instead, acknowledge your anger and the reasons for it, but beware of taking it out on others or on yourself. Focus on building up the life you want—a life that reflects your values and in which you "treat yourself right" (see Chapter 7).

On the Receiving End of Anger

People on the receiving end of other people's anger are likely to feel hurt and angry too, and sometimes frightened as well. If you are being seriously hurt or scared by someone else's anger or by their violent behavior, you should seek help, support, and, if necessary, protection. Domestic violence is a crime, and it occurs in all sections of society, irrespective of age, social class, gender, culture, ethnicity, sexuality, or level of education. Fear of making the situation worse makes it hard to seek help, and so does blaming yourself for things that are not your fault. People you could approach include the police, doctors, members of the mental health or legal professions, and friends, family, or neighbors. Help may also be available in your community.

In less dangerous situations, the following principles can be added to the skills discussed already in this chapter.

- Try not to retaliate, which increases anger and spins the cycle round.
- Try to tune in to the angry person's pain, or fear or distress. Understanding helps, while a cold shoulder, silence, and disapproval make it worse.
- Listen to what the other person has to say. Listen with 100% of your attention, keeping your own reactions and demands to yourself.
- Take the person seriously. If they are very angry, it is because something matters a lot to them, whether or not they are right.
- Try to understand the other person's point of view.
- Use assertiveness skills, and your ability to reframe ideas and look for new perspectives.
- Face up to uncomfortable facts: sometimes people don't care, and do want to hurt you. You may have to choose whether to continue with this relationship.

Making Constructive Use of Anger

At the start of this chapter we said that anger can be constructive. The red, orange, and green skills are intended to help you to steer away from escalation, from doing damage (especially to relationships), from rigidity and from the distress that goes with anger. Seven characteristics that go with constructive anger are shown in the following box.

Seven Characteristics of Constructive Anger

- It is in proportion to what precipitates it
- It is addressed to the appropriate person
- It is focused on the specific problem and does not range beyond this
- It has a clear goal in mind
- It does not spread into blame and accusation
- It is "owned" by the person who expresses it
- It does not shift responsibility for the anger to others

THE POWER OF APOLOGY

Apology can be a powerful constructive force, and it is often appropriate to apologize for what you have said when angry, or to apologize for the anger itself. Apologizing appropriately is another assertiveness skill (p. 130), which has four key elements:

1. *First, clarify exactly what you are apologizing for.* To be comfortable with your apology you should genuinely believe that you have reason to apologize for what you did. Suppose that you believe you were right to be annoyed with the other person but on reflection you believe that you went over the top when you were angry. If that is your genuine view then apologize for the extent and vehemence of your anger but not for being annoyed and showing it.

2. *Decide what you are going to say.* It may be something like: "I am sorry that I got so angry yesterday. I did go over the top. I am sorry." Do not say: "I am sorry I got angry yesterday, I should not have done so" unless you honestly believe that to be true. Otherwise you will find yourself either correcting or qualifying your apology, and this will just reignite the anger on both sides.

3. *Make your apology sincerely.* Half-hearted apologies, apologies made through (metaphorical) clenched teeth or tight lips, will aggravate the situation.

4. *Expect nothing in return.* Do not make an apology in order to seek a particular response from the other person. It is easy to fall into the trap of expecting—or hoping that the other person will respond by saying something you would like to hear, like: "I'm the one who was wrong. You were completely justified to react as you did." Such hopes suggest that you probably do not really think that you should be apologizing in the first place. When the other person fails to take the blame—and simply accepts your apology—you will be left feeling angry or resentful, and will probably want to push for the apology you think you deserve. In short, when apologizing, give your apology without hope or expectation of anything in return.

Making an apology with these four elements in mind is not showing weakness nor does it involve loss of face. It is a mature and assertive thing to do.

Chapter Summary

Feeling angry is normal, and it can have useful effects, but too much anger damages relationships. It hurts the angry person, and the person on the receiving end of the anger.

- Four key facts help us to understand anger: it makes you blind, it escalates, it is painful, and it is not just the words that count.
- Six myths about how to deal with anger tend to lead people astray. There is a grain of truth in each of the myths, but only a grain.

Learning how to deal better with your own anger first involves accepting some of the responsibility and then using "red, orange, and green" skills. Red skills help you to stop when you are firing on all cylinders; orange ones prepare you for action; and green ones help you to proceed safely. Combining these skills helps you to express your anger in the right way, at the right time, and to the right person.

Assertiveness skills help angry people deal with their anger better and also help those on the receiving end of anger.

If you are seriously at risk from someone else's anger you should seek help. Assertiveness skills may also help you to do this.

17

Sexuality and Intimate Relationships

This chapter is about the sexual aspects of relationships and the difficulties that commonly arise within them. In it you will find some principles and strategies that help people to navigate through difficult times in their sexual and intimate relationships. The chapter does not provide information about common sexual problems such as impotence or being unable to reach orgasm. It is not about sexually transmitted diseases or the practicalities of contraception. Books about these subjects are included in the *Further Reading* section on page 515. Instead we focus here on the special part that sex plays in relationships, and on ways of reducing the confusion and distress that are often linked with difficulties in sexual relationships. This chapter also provides an opportunity to think about your own sexual expectations and habits, and about the influences on you of the conventions that surround sexuality in your family and your wider culture.

These are complex matters, in which your personal views play an important part. Sexual feelings are powerful and can be difficult to manage, and sexual relationships are among the most important—the most pleasurable and the most painful—personal relationships in all societies. The continuation of our species depends on them. So it is not surprising that people everywhere have developed ways of regulating them, nor is it surprising that difficulties arise within them. Examples of the kinds of difficulties we are thinking about are shown in the box on page 191.

Examples of Difficulties Arising from Sexual Aspects of Relationships

---

Vulnerability to being hurt, for example if the relationship ends

Fluctuations in sexual interest; losing interest

Mismatches between partners, for example in degree of interest or in preferences

Wanting to be the only one; dependency, possessiveness, jealousy

Not having your feelings returned (unrequited love)

Worries: for example about being "normal," or about your performance

Fear of the consequences, such as pregnancy or sexually transmitted diseases

Expressions of frustration, anger, or aggression

Differences of opinion between sexual partners regarding moral or religious views about sexuality and about what is permissible

Conflicts between what you want and your own ideas about what is right (from a social, moral, religious, or personal point of view)

Power imbalance: use of persuasion or force; patterns of submission

---

Despite what one might think from some of the attitudes expressed on television and in advertisements, few people sail through life without experiencing sexual difficulties of one kind or another, and for some, such problems are of major importance. Yet we are surrounded by images of beautiful people, mostly young and glowing with health, at ease with their sexuality and apparently able to make relationships as naturally as breathing. These images create a pressure that can make it hard to admit to having difficulties, and even harder to seek help for them. It can seem as if everyone else is enjoying exciting, orgasmic, mutually satisfying sex. It may even seem as if you cannot open a magazine, use public transportation, or watch a video without receiving messages about how your sex life should be. It is easy to assume—wrongly—that you are the only one left behind.

First we will consider some general attitudes and the principles that lie behind the views expressed in this chapter. Then we will describe some ways of dealing with difficulties in practice.

Attitudes and Principles

Attitudes toward sexuality and toward sexual behavior vary widely among people and among cultures. They are affected by scientific developments, which make effective methods of contraception readily available; by cultural developments, such as changing attitudes toward homosexuality or to being a single parent; and by economic growth, which has both increased the financial independence of young people, and, through better nutrition, decreased the age of sexual maturity. Attitudes are reflected in our laws: in most countries some types of sexual behavior are illegal. They are strongly influenced by what people believe is right or wrong, and by personal, moral, and religious beliefs. They are often a focus of disagreements between parents and children: the clashes have been going on for generations.

Sexual behavior is partly biologically driven and instinctive ("doing what comes naturally"), and it is partly learned. With practice, confidence, and a willing partner people are able to develop their skills both for giving and for getting sexual pleasure. However a number of myths interfere with this message. One of these is that you should be able to do it right the first time: that it is as easy as falling off a log. Another is that your first sexual relationship "marks you for life." On the contrary, first sexual relationships are often somewhat clumsy and unsatisfactory, and may even be physically or emotionally painful. After a bad experience you may need time to recover, but you can still continue learning, and first impressions can be corrected as you go. Learn from sexual mistakes just as you might from any other kind of mistake. Couples often develop sexual habits, involving, for example, the order in which they do things, or the fantasies they use, or the times and places that feel right for sex. These may serve them well, but they may also become stale or ritualistic and interfere with sexual pleasure. A habit developed with one partner may not match well with another partner. Like all habits, sexual habits can be altered, though this may be difficult and may cause some anxiety and insecurity at first.

Despite being one of the most important sources of pleasure, sex can be taken too seriously. Anxiety and worry on the one hand, or routine dullness on the other, can take the fun away. Some problems in a sexual relationship can be solved by taking a more relaxed, light-hearted, and playful approach to sex, where your mistakes, or clumsiness, or those of your partner, are not taken seriously. In any learning it helps to be relaxed about making mistakes.

THREE PRINCIPLES

This chapter is based on three principles that we believe can be applied in most cultures and by most people. So whatever your views about sexuality and sexual behavior, it will be useful to understand these principles and to think about how to apply them when in a difficulty. If they make sense to you, then using them can help you to deal with difficulties and problems in a way that fits with your own preferences and inclinations.

1. The principle of self-determination. We all have a right to determine what happens to our bodies. In sexual relationships this means that nobody has the right to engage with you in sexual behavior without your willing and voluntary agreement. It works both ways of course: you have no right to engage someone else in sexual behavior without their willing and voluntary agreement.

2. The principle of not causing harm. You should not cause harm, or risk causing harm to yourself or to others. If you recognize the risk of harm, you should take steps to minimize it. You have the right to protect yourself. Risks can be physical, for example of pregnancy, or sexually transmitted disease, or of physical injury; they can be emotional, causing intense, even long-lasting pain and interfering with the ability to carry on normally with life; or they can be legal.

3. The principle of seeking happiness. You have a right to seek out what you enjoy: to go for what you want, provided that it is legal, not likely to cause harm, and involves no one in acting against their will. You can be creative and playful; you can experiment and do things that others may think of as strange.

Dealing with Difficulties

Four ways of dealing with difficulties will be described next:

1. Considering your principles and attitudes
2. Finding out about normality
3. Using good communication skills
4. Living with uncertainties

Considering Your Principles and Attitudes

If you agree with our three principles then it is likely that you will find the ideas put forward in this chapter useful. If you do not agree then you may still find them useful but you may also need to add to them so that they fit with your attitudes and beliefs.

To clarify your attitudes, think about what feels right or wrong to you. Your feelings are a good guide to your attitudes even when they conflict. For example, you might do something that you feel is wrong (like having oral sex, exploring bisexual or homosexual feelings, using "sex toys") and then feel guilty. Even if you do not do the thing you would like to do, but just think, or fantasize, about doing it, you might feel guilty. Your feelings tell you about your attitudes. There is nothing in the principles above to suggest that any of these behaviors are wrong, provided that they are acted on without hurting anyone, with the voluntary agreement of those involved, and in ways that do not break the law. If this position makes you feel uncomfortable then you can of course apply your own personal, moral, or religious beliefs as well.

Finding Out about Normality

A common concern for both men and women is: "Am I normal?" Am I normal in the amount of sex I want, the types of desires I have, the types of fantasies I have? The vast majority of people who have these concerns are normal, and they are greatly reassured when they find out more about what normality includes. If, after reading this chapter, you continue to be dogged by the worry that there is something wrong, talk to a good friend, or to your doctor.

UNDERSTANDING THE RANGE OF NORMALITY AND NORMAL VARIATIONS

A woman comes to her doctor distressed because her breasts are wrong—the wrong shape and size; one is bigger than the other. Her doctor examines her breasts: they are quite normal. "What are you worried about?" the doctor asks. "My breasts are different from my friends'." "Your breasts are perfectly normal," reiterates the doctor. "Breasts come in all shapes and sizes. There is no one shape or size that is normal."

The worry, "am I normal?" is one of the most common reasons for people seeing their doctors for what they think may be a sexual problem.

The worry may be about any aspect of sexuality: your body, your sexual desires or fantasies, your sexual responses and behaviors, changes in your sexual feelings, and so on.

A great deal of guilt and worry surround these questions—our culture seems to generate such concerns. The fact is that people differ widely in all these respects, and there is no single way of being normal. Indeed, most of the time the question of normality is not very helpful. With regard to behavior, or fantasies, for example, it is more useful to ask whether it is a problem, not whether it is normal. Some of the ways in which sexual behavior might be a problem include:

- Forcing or persuading others to do what they do not want to do
- Abusing others, or taking advantage of them; exploiting them
- Hurting others, psychologically or physically
- Damaging or endangering yourself by, for instance, drinking too much or taking drugs that might be harmful; risking infection
- Creating problems within a relationship

There is another side to this coin: if what you are doing sexually is causing difficulties in your relationship, it may be a problem even if it is "normal."

IS MY BODY NORMAL? THE HOLLYWOOD CONSPIRACY

The woman who went to her doctor worried that her breasts were the wrong shape (p. 194) was a victim of the "Hollywood conspiracy" that puts before us stereotyped ideals of perfect bodies, as if these set the standards of acceptability. This view leads to all kinds of unhelpful comparisons with others, and to unfounded worries about one's body, and they usually end by reducing the sense of being sexually desirable. They ignore the fact that it takes all shapes and sizes to make a world—and to keep it going. But the celebrities put before us in the media generally fit within a narrow range of stereotypes. They have been chosen with an ideal of attractiveness in mind, and a combination of plastic surgery, make-up, and the "airbrushing" of images has removed the "imperfections" that mark even these paragons of beauty. The end result is to present an unrealistic picture of perfection.

What are the facts? First, that the human body varies enormously. The main role that doctors have in helping people worried about some aspect of their bodies is to tell them about the huge range of normality: to explain to them that normality includes enormous differences among people. Second, that most variations and "blemishes" have little effect on the possibilities of sexual relationships and pleasure. Third, the main problem with worries about one's body is not in the body but in the mind; in the effects of the worry and loss of confidence in how you think about yourself and how you behave.

IS WHAT I DO NORMAL?

Often people use the word "sex" to mean intercourse, and this then becomes the focus of their attention and behavior. But there are many ways of enjoying sex other than through intercourse, some of which are listed in the box below. There are also many ways of showing sexual interest from a distance: using the telephone, text messages, email contact, Internet sites, old-fashioned notes and letters, sending gifts, and so on.

Some Varieties of Sexual Behavior, Or Ways of Expressing Yourself Sexually

Flirting—without physical contact

Hugging, touching, kissing

Touching—while clothed or unclothed

Stroking

Mutual bathing

Massaging—with or without genital stimulation

Sexual stimulation by hand

Oral stimulation

Sexual interest and attraction can be shown—and provide a current of attraction between people—at almost any time. It can be shown when walking, sitting, dancing, talking, or eating together, for instance

---

Many specific sexual problems, for example impotence, performance anxiety, or fear of sex, result from thinking that sex is almost exclusively about intercourse. The ways of overcoming such problems involve, by and large, an initial change of focus from intercourse to other types of sexual behavior. This is because a focus on intercourse as the only way of relating sexually, or the only purpose of sexual activity, can cause problems.

Imagine that one person in a relationship wants sex, but the other does not feel ready for intercourse. Their disagreement can put intolerable strain on the relationship. But if the couple thinks beyond the question: intercourse or not? and asks: in what ways can we enjoy sex that both of us are happy with, then there can be many possible answers. Exploring these answers can help to bring the couple together emotionally. Understanding the range of sexual behavior is often important when you are trying to find a solution to a problem in a sexual relationship.

Even for people without problems in their sexual relationships, understanding and making use of the varieties of sexual behavior can enhance their lives. Showing your partner how you feel in different ways can help to develop and deepen the relationship, and can help to overcome those times, inevitable in any longer-term relationship, when you feel less close, or are more irritable with each other.

ARE MY SEXUAL FANTASIES ABNORMAL?

Sexual fantasies vary enormously and there are general differences between men and women. The extent to which people fantasize also varies considerably. Many fantasies would be quite outrageous, wrong, and criminal if actually carried out—but of course for the vast majority of people they are not. What you fantasize about is your own affair. The question, as we suggested earlier, is not: "is it normal?" but "is it a problem?" There is the world of difference between thinking and doing.

IS MY DEGREE OF SEXUAL INTEREST NORMAL?

Most people have a sexual drive that can persist, much to the surprise of the young, into old age. But not everyone, male or female, has a strong sex drive. They can still form normal relationships.

Sophie is 28 years old. She has never had strong sexual feelings. She has had a miserable ten years being chased by men, wondering why she felt nothing for them: wondering whether she was lesbian—and even trying to find out if she could discover any sexual feelings for women. She met Ben on a group hiking trip. She liked Ben and he seemed to like her. They just clicked—they enjoyed talking to each other and found they had many things in common. But there seemed no issue about sex. Ben sought out her company but he did not make any move of a sexual kind. Sophie felt comfortable with Ben; and he felt comfortable with her. Can this last? Sophie wondered. As their relationship developed there came a time when Sophie thought that she could not avoid the issue of sex: she had to know why Ben seemed uninterested in that side of the relationship, but she was frightened to raise the question in case it meant that this comfortable "platonic" relationship would come to an end. When she summoned up her courage to talk about it this turned out to be a relief for both of them. They found that they both enjoyed being with each other, and they both enjoyed being physically close, but did not want sex. They got married—and people stopped bothering them about why they were still single. They had no children; they had no sex, and they were content: enjoying their own kind of deep, affectionate, and satisfying relationship.

Sophie and Ben are at one end of a spectrum. Some couples enjoy a degree of sexual contact, but for them it is not very important, while for those at the other end of the spectrum sexual intercourse is the most important part of their relationship. There is no right amount of sexual interest but problems can occur in a relationship when there is a marked difference in the amount of sex that each person wants. To some extent there is almost always a degree of mismatch: nobody's sexual interest or desire remains static. The desire for sex also tends to vary differently between men and women. Most women experience an increase in sexual interest around the middle of their cycle (at the time of ovulation when they are at their most fertile) and a loss of interest around the time of their period. This variation may be suppressed by taking the oral contraceptive pill. A man's sexual interest tends to be related to the time since his last orgasm. But couples are also likely to differ in their overall desire for sex.

IS IT NORMAL TO LOSE INTEREST IN SEX?

Everyone goes off sex at times, and those times can be prolonged. This too is normal. There are many common causes of loss of sexual drive, although sometimes there seems to be no cause at all. Some of the most common causes are shown in the box on page 199.

In most cases sexual interest will return and this can be helped by having an understanding partner, and by showing affection in other ways. However, sometimes this loss of interest interacts with the partners' own worries, and this may make things worse. A partner may, for instance, misinterpret it as a sign of no longer being attractive, or feel that they have done something wrong, or worry that the person who has apparently lost interest in them is more interested in someone else. Talking about what is happening to you and how you feel can lessen the risk of misunderstandings that might otherwise add to the stress.

Causes of Loss of Sexual Interest

Emotional causes:

Stress, worry and anxiety. The preoccupations that come with high pressure

Low mood and more severe bouts of depression

Situational causes:

Tiredness and exhaustion

Lack of privacy: a child might come in; staying with parents

No longer caring for the other person; recognizing that the initial sexual excitement has died down and that you now have little in common

Physical causes:

Excess alcohol use

Medication: e.g., sedatives and sleeping pills, antidepressants, blood pressure pills

Illness: Any illness, acute or chronic, can have its effect on sexual interest, as may the medications used in treatment. Illnesses that affect how we feel about our bodies are particularly likely to reduce sexual interest, for example, breast cancer, and operations such as mastectomy, prostate surgery, hernia repair, and coronary artery bypass grafts

After childbirth: reasons might include physical effects of the birth; hormonal changes; physical effects of caring for the baby; exhaustion. Men can also be affected by the exhaustion and by the changes that follow having a new baby

Menopause: the hormonal changes at menopause can reduce women's sexual interest and this can go on for a long time—months or even years

---

AM I NORMAL FOR MY AGE?

Riaja was 18 years old and in her first year of college. She thought that she was the only girl in the whole university without a boyfriend, and the only person not having sex. What is wrong with me? she continually thought. Am I the laughingstock of the whole university? Am I a freak? Will I never be happy?

Riaja decided that, come hell or high water, she would find a boyfriend and have sex. So at a party, her inhibitions and anxiety dulled with alcohol, she allowed a man, whom she did not particularly like, to take her back to his place. A few days later, feeling used and upset, she went to the campus health center with the symptoms of a sexually transmitted disease.

Riaja's behavior was driven not by the pleasure of sex, nor by her feelings for the man she went with, but by the fear that she was abnormal. She was "coerced" by her own insecurity and lack of knowledge about the range of normality. But Riaja's lack of sexual experience is by no means abnormal. There is no need to rush into a sexual relationship before you want it; and there is nothing abnormal or wrong with you just because you have not had sex.

WORRIES ABOUT SEXUAL ORIENTATION AND IDENTITY

Am I homosexual, or a lesbian? Same-sex attraction is common, and fears about it even more common. The fact that you like, or fancy, someone of the same sex as you is not enough to show that you are gay. Sexual orientation is distributed more on a continuum than as discrete categories. If exclusively heterosexual attraction is at one end of this spectrum, and exclusively homosexual attraction at the other end, then all the way between these two extremes there will be some degree of attraction to both sexes. Many, perhaps most, people who are heterosexual find some people of the same sex as themselves attractive. Sexual orientation also develops over time and there can be a period in adolescence when the degree of same-sex attraction is greater than it subsequently becomes. So you may not be gay even if you have found yourself attracted to a person of the same sex as yourself.

Some people are quite sure that their (main) orientation is homosexual or lesbian, but if you are not sure, one way to find out is to ask yourself the following questions:

1. When you fantasize sexually is the content usually about people of the same or the opposite sex?
2. Have you been in love with someone of the same sex? School crushes, particularly at single-sex schools are not very informative. Indeed teenagers often have crushes on people of the same sex but then go on to have exclusively heterosexual relationships.
3. Do you feel different from your same-sex friends, for example when they are talking about the opposite sex?

Answering these questions may help you to understand more about your sexual orientation. If you believe, or know, that your predominant orientation is homosexual, then whether this is a problem will depend on your attitude, on that of your family and friends, and on your culture.

As in other areas of life, exploring the options open to you helps when making decisions about how to live your life, for example as exclusively heterosexual, or homosexual, or bisexual, and what is right for you at one stage of life may not be right for you later on. It is common for younger people to try things out before settling down, but it also happens the other way around, and a conventional path taken earlier in life comes later to feel too restricting. In the following example of transsexual, not homosexual, feelings we have illustrated how reactions to a more unusual situation can also be perfectly normal.

An example of transsexual feelings: Normal reactions to an unusual situation. Joe is 32 years old; married with three children. He works as a car mechanic. Their friends see Joe and his wife as happily married: as a normal family with the usual stresses concerning their children and jobs, and the normal money worries. But Joe has always felt that he is really a woman in a man's body. He did not want to marry and have children, but he got to know Stephanie and liked her, and she seemed to like him. Then there came a time when it was expected that they would marry, and he felt pressured to do so by the expectations of others: his friends and parents, and also Stephanie's parents. At this time he was confused by his feelings of really being a woman, but he could not speak to anyone about them. He thought that he was a freak. He thought that no one else in the world could have feelings like his. They were so bizarre.

But now at 32 he feels his life rushing by and he feels trapped in a relationship and a role that he can no longer go on with. How can he live this lie for the rest of his life? But what can he do? To whom could he turn? What is going on? He loves his children. He loves Stephanie in a way—but not, he thinks, in the way that a husband is supposed to love a wife. He has taken to fantasizing about being Josephine and making a new life with a new identity.

Transsexual feelings—either of being a woman trapped in a man's body, or a man trapped in a woman's body, are not common, but a minority of people do experience them. They are not the same as homosexual or lesbian feelings, as transsexuals literally feel at odds with their bodies. Part of the problem for those who are transsexual is that relatively few people can help or have an understanding of their difficulties. If you feel this way about yourself, you may need to seek specialist help and advice, as some doctors are knowledgeable, but many are not. Advice can also be sought from The Gender Trust (www.gendertrust.org.uk).

Using Good Communication Skills

The key to many of the problems that arise in a sexual relationship, as with other relationships, is establishing good communication, so this chapter should be read in combination with the other chapters in this section of the book. Good communication depends on being able to say honestly how you feel or what you think, and on being able to listen to what your partner says without being overwhelmed by feelings that interfere with the communication, such as fear or anger or resentment. But talking about sex can be difficult, and many feelings get in the way such as embarrassment, shame, fear of being ridiculed or humiliated, and so on. Many people have little chance to talk openly about sex until they are already involved, and many people think that the talking gets in the way of the doing, which can be altogether easier and more straightforward. Sexual instincts may be natural, but it does not follow that everything will fall into place instinctively, by guesswork. So we need to learn how to talk about sex: which words to use, how to ask for something, how to talk about what you do not like; we need to find out what the other person likes or wants more or less of, how he or she likes to be touched, or what he or she would really like to do if it was not so difficult to ask.

The following example shows how poor communication can threaten an otherwise good relationship.

Jane and Darren had been together for three years. They had liked each other and been attracted to each other right from the beginning. Darren still loved Jane, but he no longer told her so or made a fuss of her, and Jane had begun to doubt it. Their lives fitted well together and Darren felt able to relax and do his own thing when neither of them were working, and he felt understood without having to explain himself. Then Jane started to go out more frequently with her girlfriends; they seemed to appreciate her more. She also became more snappy with Darren, who then decided to go out on his own too. So Darren and Jane found themselves seeing less and less of each other and their arguments became more frequent and more bitter. In those arguments they said hurtful things—things they did not really believe—but it left both of them with the impression that their relationship was falling apart. Then

Darren, on the advice of a friend, told Jane that he really cared about her and did not want to lose the relationship. Jane was angry, and told him that she had felt ignored and taken for granted, but she agreed to give it another try.

The vicious cycle of poor communication can be reversed when one partner starts to talk honestly about his or her feelings and worries. Sometimes all that is needed is communication about how you feel and what you think, and the ability to listen to the other person in an open way, even when they are angry and upset. It may not be necessary to say a lot, if like Darren you are not (yet) a good communicator, and doing so can be hard. But whether or not talking openly will help the relationship onto a better path will also depend upon whether both of you can follow the talking with the kinds of changes that prevent you from reverting to the same old pattern.

Good communication, as explained in Chapters 13 and 15, starts the process of solving problems in all sorts of relationships, but then it needs to be followed through, and negotiation skills are particularly useful when there are disagreements between people. These skills help people to come to solutions that suit them both, and they prevent people from focusing too much on the business of winning or losing, and ending up in the polarized positions that often leave one person feeling defeated. In Chapter 15 (pp. 161–166) we summarized the four steps involved in good negotiation skills: finding out what each of you wants, looking for common ground, broadening the basis of the negotiation, and looking for opportunities to trade. Here we will provide an example of how two people who were having difficulty in their sexual relationship used these four steps. As in other relationships, the bottom line in all negotiations is that there is a possibility of no deal, and it may become clear at any stage in the process that one or both of you is unable to make the changes needed for the relationship to give you both what you want.

NEGOTIATING IN PRACTICE

Negotiation skills help people to resolve all sorts of differences between them in their sexual relationships. For example, these might concern when, where, and how often they have sex, whether they want to start a family, whether to keep their relationship secret, and so on. Kate and Steve's relationship is relatively new, and Kate thinks she is in love with Steve. She wants the relationship to continue, but she is scared she will mess things up because she does not feel it would be right to have full sexual intercourse yet. For her this feels like a big step. Steve thinks otherwise and is trying to overcome Kate's resistance. What should Kate do?

The starting point for Kate is principle 1: the right to self-determination (p. 193). Kate has a right to be in control of what happens to her body, and if she does not want intercourse then she has the right to say "no." But knowing that Steve has no right to try and force anything on her that she does not want does not reduce her difficulties. This is where negotiation skills can be useful.

Step 1: Find out what each of you wants.   The best place to start is with oneself. So what did Kate want? Kate wanted the relationship with Steve to remain close and to develop, and her fear was that if she did not agree to have intercourse, then Steve would break it off. Kate's reasons were moral and religious, and knowing her reasons helped her to decide what to do. Steve had no problem making it clear what he wanted. It seemed perfectly natural for him to have sex at this stage, and he had no moral or religious reservations to hold him back.

Many of the problems that occur in sexual relationships are because of a difference in what each person in the partnerships wants, for example, how much of your leisure time you spend together, and what you do when you are together; or the hundred and one things that are relevant to a close sexual relationship. Whatever the issues, it helps if you can be clear about your views and let your partner know what you think or want. You can help your partner to be honest by showing that you want to find a solution that suits you both, and that you will not blame them for holding the views that he or she does hold. Sometimes, of course, we are not sure what it is that we want or think or feel, and it is only through discussion with others that we start to find out. Being open about uncertainties, even though it may feel risky, is also part of good communication.

Often, in solving dilemmas or considering moral problems we weigh up the pros and cons, and it would be wise for Kate to think carefully before giving up a moral or religious principle that is important to her. But weighing the wrong, as Kate sees it, of having intercourse at this stage against the probability that the relationship will break up if she continues to refuse, is like comparing apples and bananas. When beliefs and attitudes conflict it is useful to step back a bit, so as to think more clearly about what you think is right. Beliefs adopted unthinkingly may or may not be the ones you want to live your life by later. Three questions you might find it helpful to consider are:

1. How important to you is it to hold onto your beliefs right now?
2. What are your reasons for feeling as you do (in this example, for not wanting sex at this stage)?

3. If someone is not prepared to accept your reasons how does this affect your feelings for them? How might it affect the future of your relationship?

Answers to these questions clarify what is and what is not up for negotiation. In Kate's case she was not willing to have sex yet, but she was willing to do everything she could to keep the relationship.

Step 2: Look for common ground.   For Kate and Steve there is an important area of agreement: they both want the relationship to continue. It would be a serious loss to both of them if the relationship broke up as a result of their disagreement over the question of intercourse. There are further areas of common ground: they find each other attractive, both of them enjoy sex, and there are many other things they like doing together, with and without their friends. With no common ground there may be no deal: either you end the relationship or you continue to feel unhappy within it. Keeping the common ground clear will help you in your negotiation.

Step 3: Broaden the basis of the negotiation.   The aim of this step is to build on the common ground, using whatever means you can. Kate and Steve may be able to find ways of enjoying themselves sexually that do not conflict with Kate's morality and that Steve finds more satisfying. As we saw earlier there are many aspects and varieties of sexual behavior. In this case Steve wanted to put a time limit on this stage of their relationship and Kate wanted to expand the range of things they did together (so as to find out more about their long-term compatibility). An important point here is that what sounds difficult in theory may be easier in practice. As part of the negotiation process you can both try things out and come back to talk about it if you do not feel comfortable. While doing this it helps if you can turn down the heat of disagreements between you.

If there is only one thing over which you are negotiating, then someone has to "win" the negotiation and someone has to "lose." So it is important to generate many things to negotiate about. That makes it easier for you both to find solutions that work for you. At this stage you are putting things on the table, asking "What's the deal here?" You can broaden the base for your negotiation to include any other issues over which you disagree: eating habits, what to do when out together, who does which chores and pays which bills, how you arrange or decorate your home, if you share one, and so on.

Step 4: Look for "opportunities to trade."   Within a close personal relationship the idea of trading may seem too commercial. The point is that through broadening the areas of negotiation Kate and Steve get away from arguing over the single issue and talk about many aspects of their relationship where they might each have a different perspective. In this case Kate accepted Steve's timetable, and he agreed not to bring up the subject of full sexual intercourse for a month. Steve agreed to do all sorts of things together provided Kate fixed them up (concerts, seeing friends, visiting each others' relatives); Kate also agreed to more frequent and (for her) more exploratory kinds of sexual activity and found that, as she trusted Steve not to pressure her to do things that she did not wish to do, she was able to be more relaxed and demonstrative generally in the ways in which she expressed herself sexually.

What you are looking for is to "win" on those things which are more important to you than to the other person; and for them to win on those things that are more important to them than to you. Using negotiation skillfully—which takes practice—can in this way turn an initial disagreement into a way of strengthening, rather than weakening, a relationship. Showing someone that you are willing to accommodate the wishes that are important to them is another way of demonstrating your respect and love.

ASSERTIVE COMMUNICATION

In some situations it is not negotiation that is the key, but the ability to be more assertive in the way you communicate. This is not always easy.

Breaking up kindly.   India and Tom's relationship was stagnating—they both felt that at some level. Then Tom precipitated the break up. Ending a relationship is often difficult, and in this case Tom knew that India would be very upset—as indeed he was also. He summoned up his courage to make the break by reminding himself of things that had irritated him about India. He convinced himself that there never had been much in the relationship for him and cruelly told India exactly what he thought was wrong with her. She ended feeling trashed, and as if the good times they had enjoyed had been an illusion. Tom's behavior was aggressive and not assertive, and it caused India a great deal of pain. Assertiveness, as explained in Chapter 13, pages 128–133, is about being fair to yourself and to others at the same time.

Saying "no" gently.   Not long after the break, India texts one of Tom's best friends, Sam, asking if she can come around and see him. Sam and India know each other quite well and Sam was upset about the messy way the relationship had ended. He arranged to meet India, expecting her to talk to him about how she can get back together with Tom. Instead she tells Sam that she has always liked him—even more than she did Tom. Sam is flattered but he is not interested in starting a relationship with India. He likes her but that is as far as it goes. Gently but firmly he tells her this, only to find that India becomes increasingly angry and miserable. Sam is bemused and starts to feel guilty. He feels sorry for India, but he knows that he does not want a sexual relationship with her.

Sam's ability to continue being assertive in this situation was based on realizing that if he started a relationship with India in order to avoid hurting her he would almost certainly end up by hurting her more. Hiding the fact that he is not attracted to her would be leading India on, and possibly it would also prevent her finding a more satisfactory relationship. Fear of causing pain to others is a common reason for not being assertive and honest in a situation like Sam's. Usually the pain is not avoided but delayed, and the delay often adds to the pain. It would clearly not be good for India, who has already received quite an emotional battering, to get close to Sam only to discover that he was never really interested in her.

Difficult times such as those experienced by India cause much pain, and can also undermine people's self-esteem. India's confidence was greatly shaken, and as might be expected this affected her thoughts, her feelings, and her behavior. She felt miserable; she thought "I'm no good at relationships," and "nobody's going to want me again," and she hid herself away, drinking too much if and when she did go out. Gradually, with the help of her friends, she was able to think about things a bit differently and the pain started to dissipate. She remembered that there had been genuine affection between herself and Tom. To her this meant that people could find her attractive, and that she could make more relationships in the future, when she felt ready. If such pain is intense and persists despite your best efforts, then counseling or therapy can help the recovery process along.

Much of the advice given to people today is based on the assumption that everyone benefits from talking—and good communication is an important ingredient of lasting intimate relationships. However, people differ greatly in their reactions to the pain that problems and disagreements in relationships can cause. There are those who like to retreat into silence as well as those who like to talk. The silence can be healing, and the talking can also become repetitive, or complaining. As well as finding your own way it is important to accept that others may choose a different one.

Patterns of submission.   Good communication, negotiation, and assertiveness provide us with a set of tools that can help to resolve many problems arising within sexual relationships, but sometimes old habits and patterns of thinking make this difficult. In many cultures, both in the West and in the East, women are brought up not to be assertive, but rather to be accommodating and flexible. They learn to pay attention to other people's feelings and to do what they can to resolve other people's distress. Or they learn that they should try to meet the wishes and demands of people older than them, particularly if male. Habits of submissiveness can work well much of the time, and they can keep you out of trouble, for instance at school, so it is no wonder that they persist. If it looks as if you are "doing as you should" people are more likely to leave you alone. But such habits die hard, and therefore work against the need to be assertive later on, and make it difficult to apply the three principles mentioned earlier (p. 193) concerning self-determination, preventing harm, and seeking happiness. This can be dangerous if a relationship has aggressive or violent aspects. Patterns of submission make it particularly difficult to stand up for oneself when treated badly or when physically abused. In such situations you should seek help: from friends, neighbors, relatives, doctors, therapists, or the police. Local information about protection from domestic violence is much more readily available now than it used to be.

Jealousy and trust.   Good communication can start the process of resolving problems even when they are complex. Kylie and Kevin are both good looking and they have been going out with each other for six months. Kevin was attracted to Kylie's outgoing, bubbly personality. He is quieter than she is: quietly confident, with many practical skills, and people respect him. Kylie is attractive and popular. Their relationship developed rapidly and was exciting for both of them, right from the start. It was the best relationship either of them had had. They could not believe their luck.

But Kevin had difficulty trusting others, and he readily became jealous. Kylie had a wide circle of friends and many of these friends were other men. None of these relationships was sexual but Kevin started to worry. Kevin's previous girlfriend had dumped him after six months for another man, and this had hurt his pride, but he had also had few chances during his childhood to learn how to trust people. He had been left with the feeling that as soon as you get close to people they leave you. Kylie meant more to him than had his previous girlfriend, and perhaps this made him especially vulnerable. In any case, his jealousy began to grow. He started to accuse Kylie—or at least question her carefully about all her meetings with other men. Even if they were together in a group, Kevin became sullen if Kylie laughed at other men's jokes. He was tormented by worries that at first he kept to himself, but in the end he began to accuse Kylie, unjustly, of having affairs behind his back.

Kylie became more and more upset and angry, and told a girlfriend that she could not stand any more of Kevin's jealousy. Kevin's continual mistrust of her was, as Kylie said: "Driving her crazy; and driving her to have other relationships." She was beginning to doubt whether she and Kevin would be able to stay together.

Few relationships can withstand continual misplaced jealousy, and if Kylie does not want to split up with Kevin she will need to be open with him about how his jealousy is affecting her. It would also help if Kevin could tell Kylie about his difficulties trusting people. He probably had good reasons for mistrusting people in the past (see Chapter 26) and he may need to talk about these further with a counselor or therapist. One of the difficulties about learning to trust people is that it involves learning how to live with uncertainty.

Living with Uncertainties

Relationships are full of uncertainties. You can never know exactly what is going on in someone else's mind, or what they do when you are not there. So many of these uncertainties cannot be resolved and instead we have either to accept them or remain vulnerable to feeling frequently troubled. In this section we will consider a few questions that tend to raise uncertainties.

WHERE IS THIS RELATIONSHIP GOING?

Most people have several fairly brief relationships with different people, and some of these are wonderful while they last, but some of them were never going to work out. Sex and love may or may not go together. It is possible to love someone very much and never to have sex, of any kind, with them. It is also possible to have sex with someone you do not love, and to have sex with someone to whom you are extremely attracted, but with whom you have little else in common. Many people want different kinds of relationships at different stages in their lives, and they may be quite clear about what they are looking for, but often people are uncertain, both about what they want and about how a particular relationship might develop.

Levi and Zara were both experienced lovers, and they quickly developed an adventurous sexual relationship which they found quite compelling. The sexual part of their relationship was the thing that held them together. When the initial excitement began to wear off, Levi was unusually distressed at the possibility of losing Zara, and started to worry about his sexual performance. He visited his doctor, who advised him, if he felt strongly about Zara, to try to give the relationship a stronger foundation: to find out if there were other things that they enjoyed doing together, to talk to each other so as to discover if they shared interests and opinions, to meet each others' friends, and so on.

Relationships are unlikely to work in the longer term if their only basis is sexual. If problems in a relationship are beginning and you want to think about the longer-term possibilities, try to work out how compatible you are overall. The main categories to think about are shown in the box below.

Five Areas of Compatibility

Physical: your degree of mutual attraction

Emotional: whether you feel strongly about the same sorts of things, or share a sense of humor, or feel comfortable talking about your feelings

Intellectual: do you have similar interests, concerns, and opinions? Do you like to read the same newspapers or books? Are you curious about similar things?

Social: do you enjoy the same sorts of activities and like the same sorts of people? Do you like each others' friends? How do you react to each others' backgrounds and families?

Moral and spiritual: do you have similar values and principles? Do you understand each others' beliefs?

Working out how compatible you are is not just about predicting whether the relationship can last. It is also helpful in identifying aspects of your relationship that you might want to change, or develop. Most people at the time they are forming close relationships have some interests or hobbies that they share, and some that they do not share. When each person pursues his or her hobbies to the exclusion of the other person they are likely to drift apart.

Of course people from different social backgrounds or ages can form close long-term relationships, and it is not necessary to share religious or other beliefs. But a disagreement over fundamental values—what you think is right and wrong in your everyday dealings with people—can be more serious. For a relationship to last, it helps if you:

* Respect each other and each other's views, even when you disagree. If one of you treats the other with contempt then the relationship will suffer
* Like each other, and find each other interesting, over and above any physical attraction
* Enjoy some leisure activities together
* Talk to each other about problems, including problems in the relationship

Trying to solve problems in a relationship is often the appropriate thing to do, but not always. The problems may be telling you that there is no future in this relationship, at least not as a special sexual relationship.

CAN YOU TRUST THIS PERSON?

Intimacy of any kind makes people vulnerable. The better someone knows you the more likely they will know your weaknesses. The more you care about someone, the more likely that you will be hurt if something goes wrong. Often—but by no means always—people in sexual relationships hope that their partner will be faithful, both sexually and in other ways. It is hardly surprising that trust is often an issue, and losing trust can have destructive effects.

Many people think of trust in all or nothing terms: as if either you can trust someone or you cannot trust them. But trust is not one thing, it is many. Trusting someone to turn up when they say they will, or not to drink too much at the next party, can be important, but it is different from trusting them with your innermost secrets and deepest feelings. If you are uncertain about whether to trust your partner then you can find out more by separating one kind of trust from another. Of course some kinds of trust matter more than others, and reliability does not come as a self-contained package. Someone who is emotionally trustworthy may still be completely unreliable when it comes to doing chores. So you will have to decide what kinds of trust matter to you, and if your trust has been shaken then recognize that the process of rebuilding it will be slow. In the meantime your relationship is likely to be less close, and you may need to do something to bolster your self-esteem (see Chapter 10). Reservations about trust can trigger self-doubts, and they also interfere with the feeling of being emotionally at ease with someone, and with good communication.

WHAT IS GOING ON?

Sometimes a relationship feels odd, or different, as if something has changed but you cannot be certain what that is. This can be worrying, and it is possible that voicing your fears will provide an answer: there is a problem at work, or your partner has been worrying about getting older, or about signs of possible illness. Such uncertainties are usually better voiced than brooded on, provided that the questioning does not turn into repetitive reassurance-seeking or become aggressive.

There are, of course, many reasons for changes in a relationship—indeed no relationship is completely static, and they all change as people get older—usually at different rates—and all the changes demand adaptation. Some changes have a more hidden cause. An increasingly common problem comes from use of the Internet—by women as well as by men. The world wide web has provided much valuable information for people seeking relationships, and many opportunities for exploring ideas and possibilities that are not otherwise available, and for forging links that sometimes develop into real-life relationships. But surfing the net is, literally, a seductive occupation. It sometimes becomes increasingly compelling, taking up hours of time—which alone may disrupt and interfere with other relationships. Sexual behavior connected with the Internet, or "cyber sex," can involve almost anything: sharing information, watching sexual activity, downloading pornographic material, and so on. Some of these activities are clearly illegal or may lead to dangerous practices, and there are many unscrupulous people around who know how to exploit vulnerable people, of whatever age. One effect of Internet use on intimate relationships is the distress caused by "virtual" relationships that become increasingly intimate and sexually open, and which can take much of the energy, attention, and caring out of real relationships. Virtual relationships also encourage conditional types of commitment which run counter to the development of trust and honesty.

AM I LOSING IT?

Difficulty with sexual performance due to anxiety is common, particularly, although not exclusively, for those who have not had sexual experience. The sixteenth-century French essayist Montaigne wrote about male impotence. He tells of a man (perhaps himself) who was impotent "just when he could least afford it." He found that whenever the moment was approaching when he would need to perform, the memory of his former impotence rendered him again impotent; "the ignoble memory of his misadventure taunting him and tyrannizing over him." He overcame this problem, according to Montaigne, by admitting beforehand, to the woman, that he was subject to this problem, "so relieving the tensions within his soul ... [that] his body, ... taking itself by surprise with its partner in the know, clean cured itself of that condition."

Sex involves physical closeness to another that can be daunting, and our culture makes such a lot of sex that it can come to seem a terrifying prospect. For most people who suffer this anxiety the fear is overcome within a trusting relationship. The majority of problems with sexual performance originate in the mind and are driven by anxiety. Some problems are due to physical difficulties and illness. A problem is more likely to have a physical cause if it represents a change and lasts several months: if previously, in similar situations, there was no problem. If this is the case for you then it may be helpful to seek medical advice. A problem in sexual performance may also be the result (and not the cause) of a problem within a relationship. Sexual performance can, for some people, be surprisingly sensitive to the quality of the relationship. If you have such concerns we recommend the books listed in the *Further Reading* at the back of the book as useful starting points.

Chapter Summary

Few people go through life without at some time experiencing difficulties in their sexual relationships. Three general principles are helpful:

1. We have a right to determine what happens to our bodies
2. We should not cause harm, or risk causing harm
3. We have a right to seek out what we enjoy

Four ways of dealing with difficulties are explained:

1. Each person should consider their own principles and attitudes, so as to be able to deal with difficulties in ways that fit for them and their partners.
2. Recognizing the wide range of normality relieves many people from anxiety or worry, and can help people to feel more comfortable with their own kind of sexuality.

3. Good communication skills are essential, including the skills involved in negotiating when differences arise, and being assertive without being either aggressive or submissive.

4. Developing an attitude that allows you to live comfortably with uncertainties is helpful as there is often no way of being sure, and doubts can bring anxiety and unhappiness with them.

PART FOUR

THE TWIN ENEMIES OF GOOD MOOD

Anxiety and Depression

Anxiety and depression are the two most common enemies of feeling happy and fulfilled. They affect us all to different degrees, but it is a mistake to assume that because they are a part of the human condition, there is nothing to be done about them. This part provides information about anxiety and depression, and describes many ways of dealing with them. It explains how you can help yourself, and how you can support someone else. It is for those for whom anxiety or depression, is an occasional problem as well as for those who suffer greatly.

The normal course of progress, as with most things, is not a smooth one but goes through ups and downs. Do not be discouraged if there are times when things seem to be getting worse rather than better.

Overcoming anxiety or depression involves taking STEPs:

S: Select an idea, and work out how it applies to you.
T: Try it out.
E: Evaluate how it went (keep a notebook).
P: Persist until you feel better.

The chapters about anxiety have been divided up to deal separately with tension and worrying (Chapter 18), fears and phobias (Chapter 19), stress (Chapter 20), and panic (Chapter 21). For clarity, we have devoted a separate chapter to each of these aspects of anxiety, even though they sometimes overlap. We suggest reading all four chapters, starting with the one that seems most relevant to you.

Depression is so common and so distressing that we have devoted a whole chapter to understanding the problem (Chapter 22). Strategies for dealing with it have been divided into those that can be immediately useful (Chapter 23) and those that can prevent a recurrence of the problem (Chapter 24). You will gain most from reading all three chapters.

18

Getting the Better of Anxiety and Worry, or Defeating the Alarmist

> The wind was against them now, and Piglet's ears streamed behind
> him like banners as he fought his way along, and it seemed hours
> before he got them into the shelter of the Hundred Acre Wood and
> they stood up straight again, to listen, a little nervously, to the
> roaring of the gale among the tree-tops.
> "Supposing a tree fell down, Pooh, when we were underneath
> it?"
> "Supposing it didn't," said Pooh after careful thought.

Anxiety and Worry

Many of us have more of Piglet in our makeup than of Pooh. Our minds, apparently spontaneously, come up with a string of alarming possibilities, one worry feeding upon another until, as for Piglet, it becomes impossible to think of anything other than the risks and threats that could lie ahead. The more we worry, the worse we feel; and the worse we feel, the more we think in an anxious and worried way. No wonder Dale Carnegie called his classic book: *How to Stop Worrying and Start Living.* Worry is one of the greatest enemies of a good mood, even though the vast majority of the time worrying turns out to be unnecessary. We cramp our existence worrying about things that never happen, or that turn out not to be as bad as we had imagined, or things that were never that important to begin with. Even on those few occasions when our fears were justified, the worry seldom helped. As Montaigne, the French philosopher, put it: "My life has been full of terrible misfortunes, most of which never happened."

WORRY IS BAD FOR YOU

Worry is not only bad for you, but it also wastes time and energy. In the following box, we list some of the ways in which worry can affect your *thinking,* your *behavior,* your *feelings,* and your *body.* Think about how worry affects you personally and make additions to the list if necessary. This will help you to identify the bad effects that worry has on you and to focus on the aspects of it that you find most disruptive. Not everyone will be affected in all of these ways.

Some of the Ways That Worry Can Affect You

How worry affects your thinking: What is on your mind.
- Keeps you on the lookout for problems, difficulties, or disasters (hypervigilance).
- Interferes with concentration and with your ability to give something your full attention.
- Focuses your attention onto yourself and your own concerns.
- Makes it hard to make decisions.
- Increases your tendency to see threats, risks, and dangers just where they would most matter to you (selective attention).
- Makes you more pessimistic, so you tend to predict the worst.
- Makes you problem-focused, so your mind leaps from one worry to the next.

How worry affects your behavior: The things you do.
- Makes you less efficient (either over-careful, or unwittingly careless).
- Interferes with your performance.
- Makes you rely more on others and less on yourself.
- Leads you to do things less confidently.

How worry affects your feelings: Your emotions.
- Makes you feel muddled or confused.
- Makes you feel apprehensive and fearful.
- Makes you feel out of control.
- Makes you feel overwhelmed, or that you can't cope.

How worry affects your body:
- Reduces your ability to relax and to sleep well.
- Makes you weary and tired.
- Makes you tense.
- Gives you headaches.

WHAT'S THE USE OF WORRYING?

Worry is so common that it is tempting to ask whether it serves a useful function. One reason why it is so difficult to stop worrying is because one has a sneaking suspicion that some good may come of it, and this sneaking suspicion is hard to ignore. Even though we might say to ourselves and to others, "Stop worrying. It's pointless. It won't do any good," or "Worrying will get you nowhere," there is still something compelling about the process that makes it hard to give up.

Worry: The danger signal. Worry could alert you to the possibility that something is wrong: "That cough of yours has gone on much too long." "The steering on this car feels odd." Ignoring these things could be unwise. Worry is useful if it makes you sit up and take notice. It is not useful to be paralyzed with fear, as you might be if you got carried away by your imagination. It is useful to have a red light that flashes—but only if you do something to turn it off.

Worry: The action trigger. Worry can goad you into action. It makes you feel bad until you do something about it, like starting to study before an exam, or getting the cough or the steering checked. You feel better when these things are done. Once again, worry is useful, provided it is turned into a strategy for action.

Worry: The coping rehearsal. Worry can oil the coping machinery. It can provoke you into thinking about "What you could do if . . . ," or "What would happen if," and so it can prepare you for appropriate action or adjustment. Prompted by feeling worried, you may be more likely to develop better studying skills, stop smoking, or make arrangements to get your car regularly serviced.

Worry: The lesser of two evils. Worrying about something is often rather a vague and unfocused process compared with having vivid and alarming images. It is like asking yourself, "What if they have had an accident," when someone is late rather than imagining the horrors of the accident you fear. The things one can see with one's mind's eye can literally make one shudder and quake. But worrying can prevent the images from coming, so doing it may be the preferred option, even though it keeps the worst terrors at bay at the cost of continued anxiety.

Worry is therefore *sometimes* helpful; *sometimes* it makes you feel better or *starts* you thinking about how to cope. This may be what lies behind the superstitious aspects of worry: the feeling that "unless I worry something bad will happen," or that "worrying will prevent things going wrong." The grain of truth behind the superstitions lies in the potential value, or helpfulness, of a *certain degree* of worry in provoking strategies for action. *Useful worry prompts action. All other worry is pointless.*

WORRY: THE SELF-PERPETUATING PROCESS

Angela described herself as a "born worrier." She had worried about exams when she was at school, about what other people thought of her, and about starting her career in a small department store. She was sure that others could see how anxious or nervous she was and that none of them had similar worries. Even when she realized that everyone worries from time to time, this was of no help to her. Her own worries tended to dominate her life to such an extent that she was never free from worry. She worried about whether she was doing her job right, whether she would be promoted, whether others would recognize her abilities or ignore them, whether she would sleep well, and whether she would be too tired to work properly the next day. She worried about aches and pains, about her health, and whether she might be doing herself serious damage by her worrying. She worried about whether her partner Andrew was fed up with her, whether she might one day have to move to a new place, and whether someone in her family might get ill. No sooner was one worry laid to rest than another rose to fill its place, and just occasionally—for example, if she woke up in the middle of the night—all her worries crowded in on her at once. Angela was exhausted by her worries.

What was keeping the worry going? Was Angela just born that way? Research evidence suggests that there is a genetic component that affects our vulnerability to worry. It is also widely believed, by experts in the field, that experiences in childhood affect our tendency to worry, although firm evidence for this is lacking. We know that many people to whom alarming or frightening things happened in their childhoods cope extremely well as adults, but of course we hear less about these people than about those who remain troubled later on, and so we do not yet know exactly how many of them there are. So Angela may to some extent be a "born worrier," but this does not mean that she cannot change. On the contrary, Angela was able to change even though, for her, worry was a major problem. If you recognize yourself in even some of her worries, then you too can benefit from the methods that she found helpful.

How to Get Rid of 90% of Your Worries

There are three things which are not worth worrying about but which account for the majority of all worries: *the unimportant, the unlikely,* and *the unresolved.* Ban these from your life, and you will waste little time in worrying.

THE UNIMPORTANT

It is easy to fill one's life with worries about completely trivial things, and even when a worry is not trivial it is often essentially unimportant. When you catch yourself worrying, start to question yourself instead. Ask immediately: *"How important is the thing that I am worrying about?"* Here are three strategies to help you to answer this question.

1. *The 100-year rule.* Ask yourself, as Samuel Johnson asked his biographer James Boswell, "Will this matter 100 years from now?" This is a way of putting your worry into a long-term perspective. Perhaps 100 years seems too long a perspective—very little is worth worrying about when looked at from a distance of 100 years. But this is partly the point. We tend to adopt such short-term perspectives that molehills appear to us like mountains. One hundred years gives us a distance on life from which most of our worries become trivial. There is, of course, nothing special about 100 years. View your worries from various perspectives: a week, a year, a decade. Ask yourself just how important is your worry—and how long from now will it cease to matter.

   Angela found that asking herself "Will this matter at all in five years' time?" was particularly helpful when she was at work worrying about how much she had to do in a short time. It helped her to work more calmly as well as to disentangle the important from the unimportant things on her list.

2. *The measuring rod.* Ask yourself: Where, on the spectrum of bad experiences, is the outcome I'm worried about? In 1926, Philip Wakeham was a fledgling seaman onboard the *Snapdragon*.[2] Forty years later he gave a graphic account of one terrifying night. During naval exercises after World War I, the *Snapdragon* towed the practice target for the big battleships' night firing exercise. The target was "just a floating base upon which, at close intervals, masts or poles thirty feet high were stepped. Running across these poles for the whole length of the target were wooden slats, the whole making a huge lattice framework. This lattice-work carried two strips of canvas each ten feet wide. Before the firing was to begin, the canvas strips had to be set out like sails, a task which was carried out by seamen from the *Snapdragon*, including Philip Wakeham. He was the last to finish. He walked along the target's deck hanging on to the stays and slats. Suddenly, he stopped dead in his tracks. The small boat which had brought him and the other seamen to the target had gone. It was

pitch dark; he was stranded, alone, on the target, and four British battleships were set, ready for their nocturnal target practice.

Out there in the blackness four grey shapes were even then moving slowly towards me, the men in them preparing to come suddenly upon the target to blast it out of the water. . . . Any moment now . . . the order to fire would be given and a mass of metal would come screaming towards me. My arms were numb with cold, but I took off my black silk handkerchief and my lanyard and tied them together. Then I passed them round my waist and one of the battens—at least I would not fall into the sea by failing to hang on. . . . I must not panic. . . . Thoughts of my mother came to me. . . . I felt sick, empty, and very very cold. . . . Fear had taken possession of my whole body. . . . I have very little recollection of what followed. A large orange flame that seemed so close that I imagined it to be warm; more star shells overhead; and the noise . . . four one-ton shells passed overhead with the shriek of a thousand furies and dropped into the sea beyond.

Shortly afterward, Philip Wakeham lost consciousness, not from an exploding shell but from sheer terror. It was fortunate that the British Navy needed the practice. Not one shell hit the target that night, and in the morning, Philip Wakeham was discovered, alive and unhurt.

This terrifying experience provides another perspective on daily worries. Beside such an experience, their significance pales. Fortunately, it is not necessary to have an experience like Philip Wakeharn's in order to learn the important lesson. Using his experience or a terrifying experience of your own, as a yardstick, ask, of any worry that you have: How does it compare? *How dreadful, really, is the thing that you are worrying about?* When Angela had a disagreement with Andrew, she immediately jumped to the conclusion that they would split up, and predicted that she would soon have a major catastrophe to deal with. Of course, she might well have felt devastated to lose her relationship, but it would not have been catastrophic in the life-threatening sense. Looking at the problem more coolly she realized that the disagreement that made her worry about losing it was more like a molehill than a mountain.

3. *The calculator.* Ask yourself: "Just how much worry is this worth?" Our resources are limited. We only have so much time, so much energy, so much life. But it is very easy to put too many of these limited resources into the wrong things. William had a car crash. In fact, he had been stationary and a car had backed into his front-end. It was a minor crash and resulted in a relatively small amount of damage

to his car. The driver of the other car was profusely apologetic, and said she would pay, but there were no witnesses, and her insurance refused to pay for the damage. William was furious. He sought legal advice. He was in a black humor for weeks and decided to take the other driver to court. The whole process threatened to go on for months and months and become increasingly expensive. There is no doubt that William had been wronged; the other driver ought to have paid. But the way he was behaving was going to cost more than the original damage to the car, the results were uncertain, and he was making himself ill with anger and worry.

Whenever you find yourself worrying, ask yourself; *"Just how much worry is this worth?"*—and make sure that you do not spend more worry on it than it is worth. You need your energy for more important things.

THE UNLIKELY

Piglet was suffering from the very essence of worry. His mind was filled with all manner of possible horrors and disasters. "Supposing that . . . ," "What if . . . ," and their variants are the hallmark of worry and anxiety. "Supposing a tree fell down, Pooh, when we were underneath it?" Of course it is possible. All kinds of dreadful things could happen today, or tomorrow. But most of them are very unlikely. Once you allow yourself to worry about the unlikely, there is no end to worrying. Imagine looking back on a life of worry about the unlikely. It would be a life spoiled by anxiety about things, the vast majority of which never happened. Whenever you catch yourself worrying that something dreadful might happen, answer the Piglet in yourself with Pooh's reply: *"Supposing it didn't."* Tackling existing problems is quite enough; do not waste energy and happiness on problems which do not exist.

THE UNRESOLVED

Madame de Sévigné, in one of her letters describing seventeenth-century life around the French Court,[3] relates the sad story of Vatel, chief cook to the prince. One day the prince and his large retinue entertained the king. Vatel laid on a splendid feast in the evening, and then had to turn his attention to the morning's meal.

By four in the morning Vatel was rushing round everywhere and finding everything wrapped in slumber. He found a small supplier who only had two loads of fish. "Is that all?" he asked. "Yes, Sir." The supplier did not know that Vatel had sent round to all the seaports. Vatel waited a short time, the other suppliers did not turn up, he lost his head and thought that there would be no more fish. He went and found Gourville (the Prince's Chamberlain) and said, "Sir, I shall never survive this disgrace, my honor and my reputation are at stake." Gourville laughed at him. Vatel went to his room, put his sword up against the door and ran it through his heart. . . . Meanwhile the fish was coming in from all quarters. They looked for Vatel to allocate it, went to his room, broke in the door and found him lying in his own blood. . . . Gourville tried to make up for the loss of Vatel. He did so and there was a very good dinner, light refreshments later, and then supper, a walk, cards, hunting, everything scented with daffodils, everything magical.

This tragic story emphasizes, in somewhat graphic form, the dangers of premature worrying. Even if the outcome that you are worried about is quite likely, like Angela's worry that someone close to her might get ill, there is no point in worrying prematurely.

Dealing with Persistent Worries

If you were able to rid yourself of worries about the unimportant, the unlikely, and the unresolved, 90% of your worries would disappear. But of course this is easier said than done. Some worries are remarkably resistant to reasoning, and continue to weigh on your mind despite your efforts to keep them in their place. And a few worries really are significant and realistic. There are two kinds of strategies for dealing with persistent and significant worries: strategies for letting them go and strategies for examining them.

1 STRATEGIES FOR LETTING WORRIES GO

Turn worries into actions. *There are two types of things not worth worrying about: those that you can do something about; and those that you can't.* This summarizes a simple but very powerful way of approaching persistent worries. Worry is useful when it pushes you to tackle and solve problems which need solving. But you can tackle and solve problems without the unpleasant effect of worry. So the first step is to turn your worries into problems and then develop strategies for solving them (see also Chapter 8). If nothing can be done, then, in the words of Dale Carnegie: *cooperate with the inevitable.*

The worry decision tree. The worry decision tree is a structured way of solving the worry problem. It is a way of asking yourself a branching series of questions that help to let the worry drop, and it is summarized in the figure on page 226. There are three questions to ask yourself. The first one—*"What am I worrying about?"*—helps you to pinpoint your worry clearly. When you have clearly identified your worry, ask the second question—*"Is there anything I can do about this?"* The honest answer may be "No." If it is, you can be certain that you will gain nothing from continuing to worry. Cooperate with the inevitable. Distract yourself by finding something absorbing to do instead. If there is something you can do about the worry, however, think about the possibilities. Make a list if necessary. Then ask yourself the third question—*"Is there anything I can do right now?"* If there is something you can do straight away, then do it before occupying yourself with an absorbing activity to prevent further worry. If there is nothing you can do now, then plan a time to take appropriate action, write yourself a reminder if that would help, and allow yourself to stop worrying—it cannot possibly serve any useful purpose. Finding out clearly that further worry is unproductive makes it easier to let it drop. After each step is complete, distract yourself by finding something absorbing to do instead.

Sometimes you can work down a decision tree in your head, without extra help. At other times it is useful to write it down or to get help from friends—help in clarifying the worry, in brainstorming solutions (p. 65), or in simple support.

Crowd your worries out. The mind has a limited capacity: you can only pay full attention to one thing at a time. Keeping yourself busy, keeping the mind fully occupied, will leave no room for worry. Your attention will drift from time to time, and you will need to redirect it when this happens, but the busier you are the easier this will be. For more ideas on how to distract yourself, see pages 281 and 301–303.

Do not, however, misuse distraction as a way of avoiding the task of thinking about problems. Angela came home from work worried about the number of things she had left undone that day. She distracted herself by cooking a meal and felt better for a while, until the worries returned to plague her and threatened to prevent her sleeping. So later the same evening, she asked herself: "What am I worrying about?" She was worrying that she might forget something important. So she listed all the things she had to do. As the list grew she started to feel overwhelmed, and she realized there was a "real" problem to be solved, and not just an "imagined" one that could be swept under the carpet. She decided to talk to her manager, and started the process of problem-solving that in the end had a much more far-reaching effect on her worry than distraction alone would have done.

Worry decision tree.

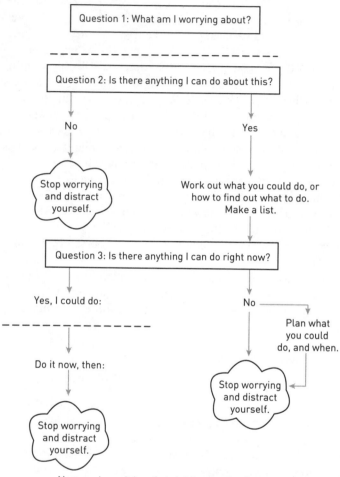

Now you know it is safe to let the worries drop.

Ban nighttime worrying. Worries tend to attack when you are at your most defenseless, especially in the middle of the night. If there is one time not to worry, it is at night when worries get out of all proportion, and it is not possible to tackle them effectively. As soon as a worry pops into your head at night, say *"This is not the time"* (see p. 430 for more on this). Worries like to crawl into bed with you and pinch and squirm so that you cannot sleep. Don't let them in. They can be trained to stay out of your bedroom, but as when training a dog to keep out of the kitchen, you need to be firm and consistent. You may find it helpful to imagine a pleasant image—a place perhaps where you felt particularly happy—in order to crowd your worries out of your mind. The technique of mental relaxation is described on pages 431 and 109.

Boxing your worries. Imagine putting all your worries, one by one, in a box and closing the lid; or hang them on a tree and allow the wind to blow them away. Cast them in handfuls into a river and watch them float away, or put them on the bonfire and send them up in smoke. If you are worried you might forget something important, write the worry down. Get it out of your head and onto paper, where it cannot get lost and can be properly dealt with later. It can be tempting to go on worrying because in the back of one's mind it feels as if some good may come of it, and of course, from time to time, a good idea does come to mind when worrying. But this is not because the process of worrying is useful, except as a trigger toward more effective problem-solving. The occasional solution found by worrying is a side effect that is unlikely to happen often enough to be worth the bad feelings that go with it.

Build a wall around your worries. If you are beset by worries, set aside a regular half hour every day to worry. If you start to worry at other times, postpone the worry to the "worry time" and focus on what you are doing, or what is happening around you instead. When the "worry time" comes around, tackle each worry as a problem to solve. This strategy hits the worry in two ways: it builds a wall around the process, which stops it from spreading, and it turns the worry into something more constructive. Some people even find that they are unable to worry to order, so the worry time turns out to be trouble free. Then worry has found its own level, and you need not worry that it will sink too low: the alarm bells will ring automatically when you need them.

2 STRATEGIES FOR EXAMINING NEBULOUS FEARS

When fears and worries remain nameless, it seems impossible to work out how to deal with them. At an almost unconscious level, we may be too frightened to face the worry directly. In the end this will cause more problems than it solves. Our deep fear will keep returning as intractable worry. When faced directly, the underlying fear can be tackled; when hidden it can grow to grotesque proportions and undermine the foundations of our happiness.

Unpacking the fear. A child who was frightened there was a bogeyman under his bed took a running jump to the safety of the stuffed menagerie he kept by his pillow, and then settled down to listen to a story and fell asleep perfectly calmly. Helped by others, he was able to overcome the fear.

An elderly woman who lived alone kept an orange by her bed. Every night before she climbed in, she rolled the orange underneath the bed, and when it came out the other side, she was able to settle down feeling safe.

Sometimes fears are nameless, and we like to be reassured by others, or by doing quite irrational things. The trouble is that if you *always* take a running jump over the fear, or find something irrelevant to do that makes you feel better, the worries cannot be laid to rest, and the bad feelings become overwhelming when comfort is not available.

Angela had two worries that she found particularly hard to face: worries about headaches, which she tried to ignore, declaring that a headache was nothing to complain about; and worries about the times when Andrew seemed fed up with hearing about her problems, when she went into a paroxysm of apologies. Either of these things set off a bad bout of worry that spread from one thing to another and kept her awake for nights on end. The underlying fears, which she found hard to face, concerned the possibility that the headaches were a sign of serious illness, and that her worrying would interfere with her relationship with Andrew. She learned to face her fears by answering three sets of questions:

1. When did the worry start? What triggered it this time?
2. What's so bad about that? What does it mean to me?
3. What's the worst that could possibly happen?

Angela had learned to take out the fears from under the bed and look them full in the face. When she did so, she discovered two things: that the catastrophes she feared were unlikely to happen; but if they did, she had resources that would help her cope. Excessive worry did not help her develop such resources: on the contrary, it stopped her from even acknowledging what her fears were about.

What is the worst that can happen? Imagine a child, playing on the beach below a cliff. He finds a cave, and full of excitement, goes in. Suddenly fear seizes him. In the deep dark of the cave, he cannot see the way ahead. What is frightening him is the sense of the unknown stretching into the black distance. Worries can be like this. Our anxiety is not about something specific, but more of a sense that unknown and uncertain possibilities may be out of sight far ahead. We can place a limit on these worries. A powerful flashlight could have shown the child the limits of the cave. We can place limits on our worries by asking: "What is the worst that can happen?" More often than not, the worst that we fear is much less terrible than our vague, unarticulated fear. Once we know the worst, we can face it directly and work out more sensibly what to do.

CLARIFY YOUR UNCERTAINTIES ABOUT THE FUTURE

Worry and anxiety are about the future—about things that have not yet happened, so there is bound to be something unknowable and uncertain about them. It is not possible to walk around the mountain and discover it is only a molehill before you have reached it. Worries may seem to be about the past, but this is largely an illusion.

Although people say "I'm worried about what I might have said," or "I'm bothered about having lost my passport," their worry is about the future effects of past events. If I have said something offensive, then I *will* be rejected or disliked. If I have lost my passport, then I *will* have to go through a lot of hassle to get another one. Worry refers in this way to some "unfinished business"; otherwise, the matter would either be forgotten or be a cause for feelings associated with the past, such as regret or sadness, rather than the future, such as worry and anxiety.

It follows that worry conceals hidden predictions: for example, about the awful things that might happen, or about one's own inability to cope with them, or both. It is therefore useful to identify and think about the predictions being made, which are often exaggerated or concern hidden guesses of the mind-reading variety about what others are thinking (Chapter 9 has more to say about this).

Ask yourself some questions:

- What am I predicting? Or expecting? Or supposing will happen?
- How can I find out whether my prediction is right?

Angela was anxious about preparing a report in time for a deadline at work. She predicted she would not be able to get it done in time, and also that she would not be able to handle the argument that would ensue. It turned out that her first prediction was right. Facing it helped her to think seriously about what to do. She drafted most of the report, indicating parts that would need to be filled in later. She took her notes about these along to the meeting. She explained why there was a delay. She estimated, as realistically as she could, when the final report would be available. She was surprised to find how many things she could do to alleviate the difficulty she was in, and her second prediction, that she would not be able to handle an argument, was shown to be completely irrelevant, as no such thing occurred. Having made the specific predictions beforehand, when in the throes of the anxiety and worry, Angela was finally able to reassess her worries with the facts at her fingertips. She had to conclude that she was more resourceful than she had feared.

If you write your predictions down, then you will be able to check out later whether you were right, and to think more clearly about problems you may have to deal with. The next time you will be able to challenge your predictions more effectively. Worry and anxiety die away as your confidence builds.

Question your assumptions. Sometimes it seems impossible to put your finger on exactly what you are anxious or worried about. The worry seems to come in vague terms: "What did they think of me?" "What if I get in a muddle?" "Suppose something goes wrong?" "Something dreadful might happen." The root of the problem in this case may be in underlying beliefs or meanings that are rather hard to put into words. Angela expressed her sense of vulnerability by saying that she was not sure she was "any good at managing by herself." Deep down she believed that being bad at managing on her own meant that she would never be confident. Her sense of inadequacy made her feel especially at risk and vulnerable. In her case this was a longstanding attitude. She made the assumption, without even realizing it, that she would not be able to cope, accepting the anxiety and worry that ensued as familiar and inevitable. What she discovered, as she learned to deal with her anxiety and worry more effectively, was that her assumption had prevented her from building up self-reliance and from using the resources, which she certainly had, more effectively.

Living with Uncertainty

Uncertainty about something important is a major cause of anxiety and worry. Many different situations create uncertainty: the threat of being fired, finding a lump in your groin, being told that someone close to you might have a serious illness, waiting for a mortgage to come through, selling your house, and so on. Uncertainty is especially difficult to handle when:

- The situation is *uncontrollable*
- You cannot *predict* what might happen

It is like being faced with an insoluble problem.

FIRST, DO WHAT YOU CAN

Try not to let uncertainty paralyze you. If there is something you can use-fully do, then do it. Once you have done what you can—for example, fill-ing in the right forms, or talking to someone such as a friend or the doctor—then resist the temptation to continue searching for something else to do. Try to accept that you have done what you can, and start think-ing about yourself and your reactions to uncertainty instead. Stop and think now: *Have you done what you usefully can?*

THEN, DEAL WITH YOUR REACTIONS TO UNCERTAINTY

Some common reactions include worry, anxiety, disturbed sleep, feeling agitated and preoccupied, difficulty concentrating; and seeking reassur-ance. Everyone reacts differently, so your reactions will depend both on you and on the sort of situation that you are uncertain about.

Recognize the uncertainty for what it is. Uncertainty is an unpleasant and distressing feeling that can interfere with daily life. The difficulty is worth thinking about.

Limit the problem. Find some certainties to hang on to. A routine of go-ing to work, or eating meals in the usual way, can provide the building blocks of basic certainty. Or you may turn to your most reliable sources of support, such as music or your friends.

Normalize your life. So far as possible, keep doing the things that you usually do, in the way that you usually do them. This is especially impor-tant if you are preoccupied or distressed about somebody else. If you run out of clean clothes, for example, because you were too worried to notice the hamper filling up, you will feel worse.

Be reasonably selfish. Treat yourself to something nice. Look after your-self well when you are going through a difficult time—just as you would look after someone else.

Do not withdraw from activities that you usually enjoy. Pleasures, relax-ations, or recreations often feel like an effort when you are preoccupied with an uncertainty. You may feel too tired or too worried to bother. But withdrawing from activities you used to enjoy can leave you brooding, un-productively, on your worries. Enjoyable activities will provide useful dis-traction, even if you enjoy them less than you usually would.

Talk to someone else about the problem. Most people feel worse if they isolate themselves with a worry. Try to find the balance between retreating silently into yourself and repeatedly seeking reassurance or talking about nothing other than your problems. Allowing your feelings to show helps you, and others, to understand them and to find ways of coping with them.

Do not cross too many bridges—keep the problem in perspective. It is only too easy to jump to the conclusion that the worst possible thing will happen. The more one thinks about the bad things that might happen, the more likely they seem, and the harder it is to see how to cope with them. So recognize that the worst has not yet happened. You notice a lump in your breast, or your groin, and immediately you imagine yourself dying from cancer. In your mind you have crossed too many bridges. Most lumps are not cancer; many cancers are curable. Take problems one at a time and keep your mind focused on the present.

Turn your mind to something else. Distraction is a very useful strategy, provided it is not the only one you use. If you always keep busy instead of facing your difficulties, you may find it hard to face them later. But if you have first considered carefully what constructive steps you can take, it is then extremely helpful to give yourself something to do, especially if it prevents you from turning the problem over and over in your mind. Methods of distraction are described on page 301.

Take the pressure off. Living with uncertainty is tiring. It can deplete your resources. So this is not the time to take on an extra commitment, if you can help it. On the contrary, make sure that you are eating well, getting as much sleep as you can (see Chapter 30), and exercising enough to keep up your strength and stamina.

Ask: "What good might come of this in the end?" Uncertainty is unsettling, but old patterns of living may have become stale or sterile. Being swept along with the current of life can help people to adapt in creative ways, to develop new skills, or to overcome old anxieties. It is not always a bad thing to have one's foundations shaken up by uncertainties, even though the period of adjustment may be painful and difficult.

Turning to Others for Help

Other people can provide an enormously useful sounding board when you are feeling anxious or worried. They can ask the questions that help you work out what the worry is about, and they can keep you in touch with reality, so the fears do not get exaggerated. They can ask, just like Pooh, questions that challenge you to think about the situation from a different angle. Pooh's question, and his refusal to think about Piglet's worry about a tree falling down, helped Piglet to think again for himself.

Asking for reassurance, however, can become a bad habit, just like "getting a fix." It makes you feel better but the feeling does not last, and so the more you have the more you want. Reassurance becomes unhelpful when it subtracts from self-reliance. If you find yourself constantly or repeatedly asking for reassurance from others, use a *"questioning strategy"* instead: Ask yourself the question you want to ask someone else, and then try to answer it yourself. Work out if there is a problem that you might be able to solve some other way. Angela wanted to ask Andrew (repeatedly) "Do you think I'm really ill?" "Am I getting on your nerves?" You can imagine how he felt the third time she asked in one evening.

If someone is repeatedly asking you for reassurance, then take their fears and worries seriously: answer them once, and then ask them to try to answer their own questions. Repeatedly reassuring someone is not helpful. Andrew repeatedly reassured Angela, both by his actions and his words, in an effort to help that proved to be counterproductive. He learned not to do this when Angela explained to him what else he could do instead.

Related Chapters in This Book

Very often anxiety and worry go hand in hand with a sense of vulnerability or lack of confidence, as if the ability to cope was precariously balanced between a sense of all the things that might go wrong and all the difficulties one would have in dealing with them. The specific strategies described in this chapter have helped many people deal with worry, but they are not the only ones available. The following chapters also contain helpful strategies.

Chapter 7, Treating Yourself Right. When you have a problem, and worry about it, it can easily dominate how you feel, and make you feel tired. There is less time or energy left for doing things that you normally enjoy, or that you are good at. Learning how to be kind to yourself when you have a problem helps to keep the problem itself in perspective.

Chapter 8, Problem-Solving. This chapter will help you define problems, think of solutions to them, and try them out in order to see which ones work for you.

Chapter 10, Building Self-Confidence and Self-Esteem. The skills and strategies described here fit well with those described in this chapter.

Chapter 11, Learning How to Relax. Physical tension is painful and exhausting. Physical relaxation is not something that happens automatically, but something that you can learn to do. Feeling more relaxed can help you in many ways: it reduces feelings of anxiety, gives you more energy, makes you feel calmer, and so on. Using meditation (a mental method of relaxation) is also helpful since it focuses your attention on the present moment, teaching you how to recognize the fears and worries, but allowing them to flow harmlessly by.

Chapter 20, Stress: How to Live with the Right Amount of It. Anxiety, stress, and worry often go hand in hand. These chapters are a complement to each other.

Chapters 28, Breaking Habits and Overcoming Addiction, and *31, Good Eating Habits.* The better you feel, the more confident you will become. Think about your diet, getting enough exercise, and the amount that you smoke or drink (especially alcohol and caffeine).

Chapter 30, Overcoming Sleep Problems. Worry is exhausting and often interferes with sleep patterns. Give yourself a good night's rest and you will also feel less anxious and worried.

Chapter Summary

Worry makes you feel bad, but most of it is unnecessary. Worrying can be helpful if it prompts you to take action, so the first step is to work out what action you should take.

You can get rid of 90% of your worries by sifting out:

1. The unimportant
2. The unlikely
3. The unresolved

More persistent worries can be dealt with by:

1. *Learning how to let them go.* Holding on to the worries keeps you feeling vulnerable. Life will feel calmer when you let them flow by.
2. *Learning how to look them in the face.* Exploring and examining the worries keeps them in proper perspective.

Living with uncertainty is especially worrying, but there are many things you can do to reduce the strain.

Other people can be a great help when you are feeling worried. Do not be reluctant to turn to them, but try not to fall into the habit of repeatedly asking for reassurance.

19

Overcoming Fears and Phobias

About Phobias

Why some people have fears that seem, even to them, to be irrational is not known. Such irrational fears are known technically as *phobias*. Occasionally a phobia has its origin in some specific experience: a child bitten by a terrier may grow up to be excessively wary of dogs, but often no such event can be recalled. Many people have a phobia of spiders, even in countries such as Britain, where no poisonous spiders exist. Perhaps this fear goes back to a time in our evolution when dangerous spiders were common enough for those who feared them to survive better than those who did not.

None of this would matter if phobias did not interfere with the enjoyment of life. Ellie was frightened of being in small spaces, such as an elevator or a shower stall. She found it impossible to remain in a room without a window and felt panicky if unable to reach the door quickly, for example, if two or three people came into her kitchen and stood between her and the door. She was unable to go to the theater or the movies, could not travel by bus or train, and had not been in an airplane since she was a child.

Rob was terrified of dogs. He traveled everywhere by car, avoided walks in parks and in the country, and had given up playing football. He was convinced that dogs could sense his fear and would come for him even when they might leave others in peace.

Pauline hated supermarkets. Crowds of any kind made her break out in a sweat. Even going to her local newsstand worried her, so she avoided doing any shopping at all. Gradually she became almost completely housebound.

Some of these fears have a grounding in reality: dogs *can* be dangerous. But in all these examples the sufferers knew that their fear was excessive. They were embarrassed and felt stupid because their fear, and the way this fear interfered with their lives, was grossly in excess of any real danger. The attitude of their families and friends did not help. Pauline's husband was so considerate that he made it easy for her to place herself under house arrest by doing all the shopping. Ellie's husband could not believe her fear was real, and either teased her about it or became irritated. Rob's friends increasingly went their own way without him.

Phobias are the opposite of horror movies or suspense thrillers. The thriller frightens you, but deep down you know that you are safe. When the phobia frightens you, however irrational you know it is, deep down inside you feel unsafe.

THE FEAR IS REAL: THE DANGER IS NOT

The fear felt by Ellie, Rob, and Pauline was real. It was as distressing and frightening as true danger. It affected their bodies, feelings, thoughts, and behavior just as any other fear would. When Rob saw a dog, he would feel afraid and his heart would pound against his chest. His mind would be filled with worrying thoughts—for example, that the dog would suddenly break from its leash and go straight for his throat. He would walk rapidly away, down a side road if necessary, to get as far away from the dog as possible.

Dogs are not that dangerous. What Rob needs to take seriously is the fear, not the dogs. Instead of berating himself and feeling ashamed, he needs to accept that *this is fear,* and that overcoming it requires *strategic planning.* Anyone trying to overcome fear is doing something courageous because it means facing a genuine fear. It is just as terrifying as it would be for most of us if we were asked to walk along a tightrope strung high up in a circus tent. The difference between facing a phobia and walking the tightrope lies not in the amount of fear, but in the amount of danger. Fortunately, with strategic planning and sensible training, you can learn to master irrational fears and stop them from interfering with your life.

Types of Phobia

One of the interesting things about phobias is that there are relatively few kinds of them. Perhaps the best known is the kind that Pauline had: the fear of being away from a safe place, or *agoraphobia*. The Greek *Agora* was the marketplace, and supermarkets seem to be the modern equivalent.

The Most Common Phobias

Fears of insects or animals:
Spiders, snakes, mice, birds, moths, dogs

Fears of being away from a safe place:
Driving
Leaving the house or going out alone
Going to crowded stores, or to open areas (supermarkets)
Traveling by bus, car, airplane, subway, or train

This and the next type of phobia often go together:

Fears of being trapped or confined:
Meetings, cinemas or theaters; lines, escalators, elevators, showers

Social fears:
Meeting new people, socializing
Doing things in front of others like writing, speaking, eating, or using the telephone

Fears of natural phenomena:
Thunder, lightening or storms, water, heights, darkness

Fears of illness or injury:
Seeing blood, needles, vomiting, hospitals

Vicious Circles Perpetuate the Problem

Fear usually dies away of its own accord, as if it had a natural life span. When it does not die away, it is probably because vicious circles keep it going. These vicious circles develop out of a natural reaction to fear: the wish to keep safe. Rob used a number of "safety-seeking behaviors" in an attempt to keep his fear of dogs at bay. Whenever he went out he took a stick with him. He avoided walking near parks and going to other people's homes in case they had dogs. The more he tried to keep himself safe, the more fearful he became. He thought of each successful expedition as a near miss or a lucky escape from possible danger. These were some of the vicious circles that kept his problem going:

ROB'S FIRST CIRCLE

Rob thought constantly about how to keep himself safe. As well as carrying a stick, his "safety behaviors" included keeping an eye out for signs of dogs and asking someone to go with him when he went out. These safety behaviors made him feel better and so he came to rely on them. Then he felt even more unprotected and nervous without them. Eventually it became second nature to him to do something to keep himself safe, and harder and harder to venture out without some form of protection.

ROB'S SECOND CIRCLE

When Rob succeeded in avoiding a dog he experienced an immediate sense of relief. Whenever he arrived home safely his fear vanished. He learned he could stop the fear by restricting his activities, but his avoidance spread from one thing to another and his fear increased in step with his avoidance.

ROB'S THIRD CIRCLE

As Rob's fear continued to grow and his activities became increasingly restricted, he felt more and more embarrassed about his difficulties and ashamed of being so fearful and "cowardly." His confidence also began to dwindle, and the less confident he felt, the more susceptible he was to his fears, and so on, around and around.

You can see that Rob's reactions to his fear created vicious circles that kept his phobia going. All kinds of safety-seeking behaviors, both safety behaviors like preparing to make a quick getaway, and avoiding things, like not going out and about, work in the short run because they make you feel safer. Then it can be tempting to think (even if you have never put it into words) that you have to do these things in order to protect yourself. Because you do them you never discover that they may not be necessary. In the long run the safety-seeking behaviors also undermine your confidence.

If you suffer from a phobia, try to work out how your own vicious circles work.

Rob's vicious circles.

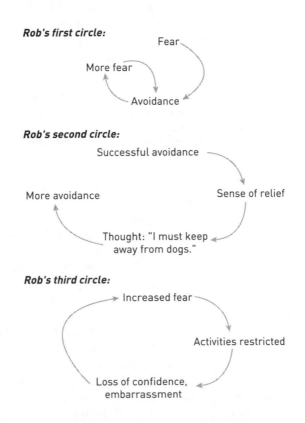

Rob's first circle:

Fear

More fear

Avoidance

Rob's second circle:

Successful avoidance

More avoidance

Sense of relief

Thought: "I must keep away from dogs."

Rob's third circle:

Increased fear

Activities restricted

Loss of confidence, embarrassment

Overcoming the Fear: Strategic Planning for Action

Strategic planning is needed to break the vicious circles that keep the problem going, and to help you to learn, in a way that you find convincing, that there is no real need to be fearful. Then the fear will die away of its own accord. Four helpful steps are shown in the box on page 240 and some of the many different ways of taking these four steps are described next.

A Four-Step Strategy for Overcoming a Phobia

1. *Work out what you do to protect yourself.* Make a list of your "safety-seeking behaviors." Include both the things that you do to keep yourself safe, and the ways in which you try to avoid the things that frighten you.

2. *Make a prediction.* Ask yourself: What would happen if I did nothing to keep myself safe? If I went ahead without my safety behaviors? If I faced something that I fear instead of avoiding it?

3. *Carry out an experiment.* Decide what you will do to test out your prediction, then go ahead and do it.

4. *Think carefully about what happened.* Was your prediction right? Or partly right? Or was it wrong? Think about what you have found out from your experiment and about what that means.

Using this strategy helps to reduce fears and phobias even if they have lasted for a long time. Sometimes, but not always, you can nip a phobia in the bud if you notice that a fear is creeping up on you and catch it early on. Taking action early can prevent you from developing the self-protective habits that keep the fear going. But using the experimental approach, and turning yourself into a "scientific" observer of what really happens by using the four-step strategy, can help you to overcome a phobia even if it is well entrenched and you feel stuck. Using the four separate steps helps you to make plans that you will find manageable. You will have to work hard to face your fears and you will have to do things that might feel truly dangerous before you start, but this does not mean that you will have to suffer intensely while you do the things that help to reduce your fear. The preparation that you will do in steps one and two lays the groundwork for venturing into the world of changing your behavior, and if you spend time on this, and do it carefully, then starting to change can be more like exploring a new way of approaching the world than entering the lion's den.

STEP 1: WORK OUT WHAT YOU DO TO PROTECT YOURSELF

Seeking to protect yourself is a natural reaction to fear, and it is tempting because in the short run it makes you feel more confident and less fearful. However if you always protect yourself you can never discover that your protective devices were not necessary. There are two ways of trying to protect yourself: *doing something* to keep yourself safe, or using a "safety behavior," and *not doing something* for fear of what might happen if you did, or avoidance. Make a list of your safety behaviors, and of what you avoid. They work in the same way to keep the fear going, so you will have to stop both to overcome your phobia. But you will not be able to stop them unless you know exactly what they are, and notice when you use them.

Safety behaviors. Some safety behaviors are easy to identify: things like asking someone to come with you when you feel nervous. Others may be so habitual that you no longer notice them, like taking a set of emergency phone numbers with you when you go out, or not saying very much about yourself. When identifying your safety behaviors give yourself a prompt by thinking about a recent situation that you found difficult, and ask yourself the following key questions:

1. What did you do to prevent bad things from happening?
2. How did you protect yourself from the things that you fear?
3. What is the first thing that you do when you feel at risk?

Write down all the safety behaviors you can think of, and keep adding to the list as you become more aware of what you do. Here are some examples to help you tune in to what we mean by safety behaviors.

Putting things off. Rob put off making plans for his summer vacation. Somehow he always seemed too busy to think about it. He did not want to admit how much this fear of dogs was interfering with his life.

Making sure that safety is close at hand. Ellie knew that she was perfectly safe in her own home, but nevertheless only took a shower when her husband was at home.

Hiding your feelings. Rob tried so hard to hide his fear from his friends that they could not understand what was happening and began to think he was avoiding them.

Keeping busy so you do not have to think about the problem. Pauline busied herself with housework, cooking, and knitting for all the family. She invited friends and neighbors in so often she had no time to go out.

Using others to hide behind, or using them as a prop. Pauline relied on other people to do things that made her feel nervous and Ellie arranged to have a "safe" person nearby if ever she did something "risky."

Creating your own props. Pauline bought herself a shopping basket on wheels to give her something to lean on if she felt shaky, and Rob went everywhere in his car.

Some of these safety behaviors, such as Pauline's dependence on a shopping cart, feel like good ways of coping with the anxiety, and indeed they might make it possible to do something that would otherwise be too difficult. Using a temporary prop or support system can help you to start making changes. But once they become habits, they create the vicious circles that keep the fears going.

Avoidance. Simple avoidance is the obvious kind: avoiding crowded places, or meeting new people, or cliff-top walks, or places where you think you could come into contact with moths, birds, or dogs. There is no doubt what you are avoiding, and it is relatively easy to ensure that you will not come across the situation unawares.

More subtle kinds of avoidance are easier to miss. Pauline avoided thinking about her phobia. Instead she turned her mind to other things and kept herself busy. Rob avoided thinking ahead and making plans for his future. Ellie avoided quiet and silent places, and this made her feel doubly protected as keeping talking was one of her safety behaviors.

Avoidance and safety behaviors are closely linked, and the links between them strengthen the sense that it would be risky to do things differently. For example, Pauline developed a weekly routine to make her feel safe, and she avoided changing it in case that triggered her fears again. These behaviors make it hard to discover that the dangers and threats from which you are trying to protect yourself are exaggerated out of all proportion. So you will have to face your fears, and drop the safety behaviors in order to overcome the phobia. But first you need to think about what you expect to happen when you start to do this.

STEP 2: MAKE A PREDICTION

There would be no need to think about how to protect yourself if you did not think you were at risk in some way. Making a prediction helps you to work out what you fear would happen if you stopped protecting yourself, and here it is important to remember that each person is different. Only you know what is in your mind, and it is highly likely that what is in your mind gives you "good reason" to feel afraid. If you think that dogs will go for the jugular, or that you will collapse when out on your own, or that you could become so anxious that you would lose control of your bladder, then it is only sensible to try to protect yourself. The predictions make sense of the whole set of safety-seeking behaviors. That does not make the predictions right, which is why you need to test them out, but first you need to think about your own personal fears and expectations, and to turn them into predictions that you can test.

You need a specific frightening situation to start from. Think about a recent situation that made you feel bad, or think about something that might happen quite soon, and then ask yourself what you fear might happen to you. There are many questions you could ask yourself at this stage: for example, *"What am I predicting will happen? What might go wrong for me? What would happen if I went ahead without trying to keep safe? Or if I faced the fear instead of avoiding it?"* But the most important, key question is this one:

"What is the worst thing that could happen to me in this situation?"

Let yourself "look into the abyss." Put into words the catastrophe that you fear, even if while doing so you realize that it is unlikely to happen. Sometimes your worst fear is almost too frightening to think about, and putting it into words brings intense feelings of fear—or of embarrassment—with it. Sometimes it seems not too bad when it is brought out into the open, and sometimes it sounds quite absurd: so extreme that you can immediately see that it is not likely to be correct. Other predictions have more reality behind them: people do get lost, or bitten by a dog, or have accidents of one kind or another, but these events are relatively rare.

There are two main sources of the fears that lie behind the predictions: the threats and the rescue factors. First, there are the threats and dangers linked to the phobia, such as Rob's fear that he would be attacked and badly bitten. Second there are fears about not being able to cope—or not being able to cope on your own, without help. Ellie feared that she would become uncontrollably frightened, and start crying or screaming if she felt trapped, and that she would not be able to make contact with anyone who would be able to support her. Her worst fear was even more extreme: that the anxiety would be so overwhelming and uncontrollable that she would "crack" and go mad. To her this meant that she would never be able to cope again as an independent adult and would have to be looked after in a hospital for the rest of her life. The point of exploring your predictions in depth is that they help to make sense of the safety seeking.

STEP 3: CARRY OUT AN EXPERIMENT

The next step is usually the hardest. The idea is to change your behavior: to do something different, or to do something in a different way, so as to test your prediction. Plan your experiment carefully. The aim is to face a feared situation without protecting yourself: to drop your armor and see if the disaster you fear comes to pass. Rob decided to walk past the park on his own, without rushing and without carrying a stick. He predicted that any dogs he saw would attempt to bite him. He predicted that the owners of dogs on leads would have difficulty restraining them and that if a dog were not on a lead it would come for him as soon as it saw him.

By definition, a phobia is an exaggerated fear, and the predictions reflect this exaggeration. But it may not feel like an exaggeration before doing the experiment. In his heart of hearts Rob knew that other people walked by the park without being bitten or chased. He knew that he was suffering from a phobia. But until he started experimenting he still *felt as if* his predictions were true. Once he found the courage to carry out his experiment, and to pay careful attention to what happened, his phobia started to decrease. His worst moment, and this is often true for people working to overcome their phobias, came shortly before he did his first experiment.

Ellie's first experiment was a little different. When she was not afraid she knew perfectly well that her anxiety would not drive her "to breaking point." She only believed this prediction when she felt trapped and the fear had begun to grow. So she knew that she would have to make herself feel the fear in order to test the prediction. She decided to shut herself in the cupboard under the stairs and to stay there for two minutes when her husband was at home. He agreed to be the time keeper.

STEP 4: THINK CAREFULLY ABOUT WHAT HAPPENED

This is when you need to think about exactly what happened, and about what that tells you about your prediction. Make sure you stick to the facts rather than jumping to conclusions. When Rob walked past the park he saw quite a few dogs, one of which was bounding around everywhere. His heart leapt into his mouth, but he kept walking and he kept watching. The dog appeared not to notice him. At home again he thought carefully about what this meant. Clearly the dog had seen him, but had not rushed up to attack. He had not seen any dogs on leads, so he would need to go out again to test the prediction that their owners would have difficulty restraining them if they tried to attack him. He realized that he had missed out on one of his predictions: that dogs could sense his fear of them, and so they would recognize his weakness and take advantage of it. They would bite him even if they did not bite others. So Rob had more experiments to do.

Ellie stayed in the cupboard for two whole minutes and then her husband opened the door. She had felt terrified as soon as the cupboard door was shut. Her anxiety increased rapidly, she felt hot and sweaty, and her heart was pounding in her chest. She paid close attention to her symptoms, watching for signs that she was losing control. But she did not call out, or scream, or lose control in any way. Talking about the experiment immediately afterward, she realized that she had been able to notice her symptoms and to describe them well. She noticed that they rapidly declined when the door was opened. Her belief in the destructive powers of high anxiety was greatly reduced. She was able from then on to take a shower whenever she wished, but had to plan more experiments before she felt ready to use an elevator or go traveling.

ANSWERS TO SOME QUESTIONS ABOUT DOING EXPERIMENTS

What if all the experiments I can think of seem too hard to do? This is when you need to think about how to introduce something into the experiment that would make it easier, like asking someone to accompany you the first time you try. Of course this is rather like using a safety behavior, but a safety behavior that provides a step on the road to recovery. As long as you do not make a habit of it, and give the safety behavior up as soon as possible, it can help you to make progress. Rob found a friend to run with, and together they took more adventurous routes than he had been able to manage on his own. He carried a stout stick with him the first time he tested his prediction that dogs would sense his fear and attack him. Carrying the stick enabled him to stay out in the park for much longer than he would have been able to do without it, and it helped him to hold his ground when a dog ran toward him—and then past him. His experiments convinced him that dogs were no more interested in him than in others, and the new conviction enabled him to leave the stick behind.

Pauline's anxiety in the supermarket never seemed to be far below the surface. She learned how to relax (see Chapter 11) and found this helped her to feel less anxious. She had struggled at first to find the courage to test any of her predictions, and found that if she did each new thing with a companion first this helped her to do the same thing on her own later on.

The first time Ellie went on a train, predicting that her anxiety would shoot up when the train started, she listened to music and took a newspaper with her. After an anxious start she began to settle down. Then she turned the music off, put the earphones away, and dared herself to look around to take in her surroundings. She was trying to make sure that she was avoiding nothing, and that she was not using any safety behaviors. She wanted to realize fully where she was and what she was doing. The more interested she became the better she felt.

Should you start with easy things and work up to harder ones? When you face your fears by doing experiments it is not usually necessary to work slowly through numerous practice steps before you start to feel better. The experiments help you to find out whether your ideas about the thing that you fear were right. You may have to do quite a few experiments to be sure of your conclusions, and for the real meaning of them to sink in so that you no longer feel as if you are in danger. You should also think carefully about what you have done, as this often suggests other predictions to test.

Supposing I do many experiments but still feel anxious? One common reason for this is that you are holding back in some way, or still using safety behaviors, possibly in such a subtle way that you are hardly aware of doing so. Could you still be protecting yourself in some way? Examples of safety behaviors that are easily missed include not really giving the "dangerous" situation your full attention, or seeking reassurance from others, or watching other people to see how they react, and taking your cue from them.

Overcoming the Fear: Investigating the Facts

Fear fills the mind with horrors. Rob was convinced that if dogs "smelled his fear" they would set upon him, and as we have already seen, the dire predictions he made increased his fear. In addition to the strategic plan for changing behaviors, he was helped by investigating the facts. This strategy is part of cognitive therapy (which we have described in more detail in Chapter 9). Rob asked himself questions about reality, as described on page 80 in order find out more facts about dogs and the ways in which they behave.

Rob started doing some research, looking for evidence for and against his belief that dogs spontaneously attack people, and he made a big effort to keep closely in touch with reality. He read about pit bull terriers, and occasions when someone had been badly bitten. He knew that police dogs can be trained to attack and that postmen sometimes feel as if they are in extreme danger when they open the garden gate and walk up to the front door. But he also found out that these were rare or special situations. Most dogs kept as pets are either kept under reasonable control or are harmless. The *probability* that he would be bitten was far lower than his fears had led him to believe. To check this out he asked a number of friends whether they had ever been bitten, and he was also interested in whether any of these friends were fearful of dogs. He wanted to find out whether dogs really do bite people who are frightened of them. Although most of his friends had not been bitten, a few of them had. However, nobody he knew had been spontaneously set upon or mauled, not even those who were themselves nervous of dogs. A few friends had been bitten, but those had been no more than nips received when playing with a dog or tripping over one. Rob thought he was unlikely to be involved in either of these situations against his will.

Rob had been doing what many people with phobias do: *overestimating the likelihood* that his fears would be realized, and *overestimating how bad it would* be if they were. At the same time, he *underestimated* his ability to cope, to take action to improve the situation and get rid of the phobia. Reexamining his predictions and investigating the facts brought him back in touch with reality, and helped him feel more confident.

The Course of Progress

People make progress at different rates, so it is not possible to provide a general guide to how long it should take. Ellie improved fast, and quickly felt comfortable when taking a shower, when other people crowded into her kitchen, and when traveling locally. It was a month before Rob noticed that he felt more confident and another couple of months before he was able to take a friend's dog for a walk. Pauline spent about three weeks testing out her ideas about shopping on her own while her husband waited nearby before she felt able to do some local shopping entirely alone. Having successfully done these things she set her sights on going to the supermarket again, and used what she had learned already to make a new set of predictions to test in supermarkets. It does not matter how slowly you go. As long as you keep working at it you will keep progressing. However we also know that the more time you can devote to working at it the faster you will improve, and leaving long gaps between experiments can allow the fear to creep back again, which can feel discouraging and make it hard to keep trying.

SETBACKS ARE PART OF PROGRESS

Everybody has good days and bad days, whether they have a phobia or not. This means that sometimes it is hard to do today what you could easily do yesterday. Your confidence is bound to fluctuate, so apparent setbacks are normal. They are disappointing and frustrating, but they are not a sign of failure. So try not to be discouraged by them, and think perhaps of making fewer demands on yourself when you are not feeling your best, and more when you feel better.

DEVELOPING AN "EVER-READY" ATTITUDE

The unwritten message you give yourself when you seek out safety, whether you do this in an obvious or in a subtle way, is "this is dangerous." Your attitude builds up an expectation that cannot easily be disconfirmed because your safety behaviors and avoidance prevent you from finding out that it is not really dangerous. Adopting an "ever-ready" attitude breaks this circle by helping you to face your fears without bothering to protect yourself from imagined dangers. One new message is: "When you feel like avoiding something, try to work out how you can approach it instead." Instead of saying to yourself: "I can't," ask yourself: "How could I . . . ?" This is the attitude which helps you to nip fears in the bud, and to start the strategic planning that will make you feel better.

Adapting the Strategies to Different Types of Phobias

FEARS THAT MAKE IT HARD TO PRACTICE

It is difficult to find practical ways of facing fears of flying, snakes, or thunderstorms on a regular daily basis. But you can practice in your imagination instead of in reality, and this is known to be remarkably effective. Make your strategic plan for action in exactly the same way as we have described earlier in this chapter; try to find a peaceful and relaxing place to practice; then imagine yourself in the situation that you fear, providing all the realistic detail you can muster to make yourself feel fearful. Use this exercise to identify the ways in which you protect yourself: your safety behaviors and avoidance. Make your prediction about what would happen if you did not protect yourself, and allow yourself to "look into the abyss." Then imagine yourself back in the situation "wearing the hat" of an experimenter or explorer: facing all the fears and difficulties without seeking to protect yourself in any way.

FEARS THAT INDUCE FAINTING

Some people faint at the sight of blood, or when faced with things associated with illness or injury. If this is a problem for you, you should start by learning the method of "applied tension" to overcome the problem of fainting. Fainting is associated with a sudden drop in blood pressure, and this can be prevented by tensing up your muscles instead of trying to relax. Practice doing this at home first. The aim is to tighten all the major muscles in your arms, legs, and torso at once, and to hold this tension for about five seconds. Then, let it go briefly before tensing up again. You should practice doing this for ten minutes twice a day, to where you feel comfortable at home before you try to apply it in situations you find difficult. Learn to apply the tension sitting down first, and then try it standing up. When you can do this, use the method whenever you face a situation that is difficult for you, for example if you have to have an injection, or have a blood sample taken—or even looking at pictures of such things. Many people who have practiced this method are able to become regular blood donors, and this commitment seems to help them maintain their new-found confidence.

SOCIAL FEARS

One of the most common phobias is social phobia—fear of situations involving contact with other people in which you fear that you will do something embarrassing, or even humiliating. People with a social phobia tend to think that others are always judging, or criticizing them. They fear being rejected, and tend to think of themselves as less acceptable than others. The situations that trigger their fears include meeting new people, going to a meeting at work or to a bar or social event, and speaking in front of a group of people. Since you cannot control what other people do, and can only guess at what they are thinking (most of the time), it can be difficult to plan strategies for action.

Social phobia makes people self-conscious, and self-consciousness interferes with social interactions as it fills your mind with the sense that you are not doing things right. It makes you painfully aware of all your personal signs and symptoms of anxiety (such as blushing, or stumbling over your words), and of the ways in which you assume others are judging you ("they think I'm stupid"; "they don't like me"). So first it is important to become less self-aware, and to focus your attention outside yourself: onto other people or onto what they are saying or doing. Otherwise you remain at the mercy of your own imagination—which easily conjures up all the horrors you most fear. Attention always wanders, so just redirect it outward again if the self-awareness creeps back in. Second, a social phobia goes with numerous ways of trying to protect yourself, such as keeping quiet, not letting people get to know you, avoiding eye contact, and so on. As we know, safety behaviors will keep the problem going, and they can be changed using the four-step strategic plan for action. Third, the thoughts about being continually evaluated and judged by others can be examined and tested using the methods of cognitive therapy. If you suffer from a social phobia read Chapter 9 (and also see *Further Reading*, page 515).

You will also find other ideas that help to build the confidence to interact comfortably with others in Part 3 of this book, which focuses on relationships, particularly in Chapter 13.

Helping Someone Else to Overcome a Phobia

It can be enormously helpful in overcoming a phobia to have the support of someone else: a partner, friend, or relative. This section describes how to help someone to overcome their phobia. Both of you should read the whole chapter, and of course it is vital that the person with the phobia wants your help.

THE FEAR IS REAL

Sometimes other people's irrational fears and phobias can seem ridiculous, and be difficult to sympathize with. Or they can seem to be trivial matters that should be easy to change. But they look, and feel, different from the inside. It is important to realize that the fear is real, even though the danger is not, if you are going to be able to help someone overcome their phobia.

One summer, many years ago, Josh was on vacation with two friends. They had lunch under the shade of a large umbrella in the garden of a bar on the English coast. It was not long before a wasp came to investigate their food. It flew away, but a few minutes later there were half a dozen wasps sipping their beer and munching from their plates. Josh had never worried much about wasps, but his two friends were in a great state of anxiety. They thrashed uselessly in the air in an attempt to chase the wasps away. Josh laughed at these vain attempts and at their fear, bathed in the smugness of his own indifference. After this lunch the three friends continued their walk along a cliff. The path became narrower and narrower, and the cliff edge steeper and steeper. Although indifferent to wasps Josh had a definite fear of heights. He came to a part of the path where he simply froze: ahead the path came close to a steep drop straight down to the sea, and as his courage evaporated, he could not face returning along the vertiginous path he had been walking along with increasing difficulty. His companions did not laugh at him. They saw how fearful he really was, and they helped him along until he came to a part of the path where he felt safe. For them the fear of the wasps around their food was like the fear of the steep cliff for Josh; he never laughed at their fear of wasps again.

GIVE SUPPORT, BUT AVOID BECOMING OVERPROTECTIVE

The first way in which you can help people suffering from fears or phobias is to give them your support; to show that you accept their fear and that you want to help them to overcome it. They are going to need courage, and you can help to give them this courage, but you should not protect them from facing their difficulties. Such protection is "overprotection" because it will prevent them from doing the things that they need to do in order to discover that there is no need to be afraid. This is what Pauline's husband did. He overprotected his wife by doing all the shopping so that, until he understood better how to help her, she never had to leave the house without him, and consequently never faced her fear.

CLARIFY WHAT ROLE YOU ARE GOING TO TAKE

If you want to help, then talk this over with the person who has the phobia, and ask them what they would like from you. Their efforts will be more successful if they feel in charge of the work they are doing. They will need encouragement and support, and they may need a good listener, but it would probably be sensible not to offer advice unless you are asked for it. If you allow yourself to be guided by them it is less likely that adopting the helping role will cause friction between you.

HELP TO PLAN THE STRATEGY FOR ACTION

A further way in which you may be able to help is in planning the strategy for action. Some people are embarrassed to talk about the ways in which they protect themselves, and also about the predictions they make about what would happen if they gave up doing so. You can help them by being accepting and understanding. Often it is hard to think of experiments, and two heads may well be better than one. When it comes to thinking carefully about what actually happened during an experiment then you can help by asking questions about what they noticed, and also by thinking about what this really means. Does it mean (as the person with the phobia often supposes when things go well for them) that they have just had a lucky escape, or does it mean that the situation was not as dangerous as they thought? Again, two heads may be better than one, but remember that different people are convinced by different things. If someone remains fearful even when you are sure they need not be, then it is probably because they are still thinking that there is a risk from which they would only be sensible to protect themselves. You may be able to help here by encouraging them to investigate the facts further, or by helping with the investigation yourself. You can also be someone to whom to report. Then your job might be to receive the progress report while understanding just how much courage is involved in attempting to face things that provoke fear.

Helping someone else overcome their phobia involves committing yourself without knowing how big that commitment might be. But some help can be better than none at all. Be careful not to commit yourself to more than you have time for.

HELPING TO PLAN REWARDS

Finally you can help to plan rewards. People with phobias often feel that they should not have the phobia in the first place, and so they do not feel that they deserve to reward themselves for making progress. This is quite wrong. They need a great deal of courage to tackle their phobia, and finding that courage can be exhausting. Each step on the way is an achievement and marking these achievements with a reward provides the kind of encouragement that helps people to keep working at it. You will find more ideas in Chapter 7.

Chapter Summary

Phobias are irrational fears that can interfere seriously with your life. The fear experienced by someone with a phobia is real, even though the danger is either imaginary or greatly exaggerated.

Overcoming phobias involves *strategic planning for action,* and a realistic investigation of the facts. It helps to think of yourself as a kind of explorer or scientist when overcoming a phobia: your job is to find out whether the situation you fear is really as dangerous as you think it is.

The four-step strategy:

1. Work out what you do to protect yourself
2. Make a prediction
3. Carry out an experiment
4. Think carefully about what happened

Overcoming a phobia involves doing things differently. Confidence comes from facing difficulties without (unnecessary) protection, so that in your heart of hearts you come to know that there is no real risk. It also involves working on your thoughts, as people with phobias tend to overestimate the risks they face and to underestimate their ability to cope. If you learn to recognize the exaggerations and distortions in your thinking, you will overcome your fear more easily.

Progress will have its ups and downs, so go at your own pace and try not to be discouraged by occasional setbacks.

20

Stress: How to Live with the Right Amount of It

Some Facts about Stress

We could all be experts on stress. Everyone of us has experienced it at some time, and few people manage to keep it under control all the time. The problem is so common that learning how to deal with stress should be part of the national curriculum! This chapter starts by looking at stress from several angles and then suggests ways of dealing with it.

THE UPSIDE AND THE DOWNSIDE

One of the difficulties about stress is that it can work for you or against you, just like a car tire. When the pressure in the tire is right, you can drive smoothly along the road: if it is too low, you feel all the bumps and the controls feel sluggish. If it is too high, you bounce over the potholes, and easily swing out of control.

The effects of stress are illustrated in the figure on page 255. This figure shows the results of different levels of stress on performance—for example, on the ability to understand instructions or to concentrate on what you are doing. For low levels of stress, for example at point A, increasing stress can improve performance. High levels of stress, however,

The effects of stress on performance.

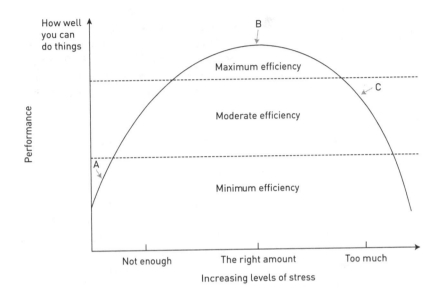

impede performance. Susceptibility to stress varies from person to person, and in a single person it also varies from time to time. In general, as the stress increases beyond the level at B, performance gets worse. Once point C is reached, performance rapidly deteriorates with increasing stress. The difficulty is that many people, when they notice the strain, react by re-doubling their efforts. What this tends to do is to increase stress at just the time when such an increase leads to a worsening performance. Then problems come thick and fast; it gets harder to think ahead and tempting to adopt the first solution that comes to mind: reaching for the bottle, asking for sleeping tablets, or hiding your head in the sand.

THE OUTSIDE AND THE INSIDE

Stress comes both from outside and from inside. Outside stresses reflect the pressure you are under or the burden you are carrying: your job, the demands your children or parents make on you, your mortgage, and a myriad other things. Inside sources of stress reflect your reactions to these things. If the demands seem many and your resources seem few, you will feel stressed: "There's far too much to do." "There's no way I can cope." Internal sources of stress also include wants, feelings, and attitudes. Wanting to do your job well, to succeed, to be liked, or to make other people happy puts pressure on you. Feeling worried, angry, or jealous saps your energy. If you have the attitude that things should always be done quickly and efficiently, for example, you will feel more stressed than someone who is able to take a more "laid back" attitude. If you value the sense of being stimulated, interested, and useful, then you will find boredom stressful. None of these attitudes is, of itself, either better or worse than the others. But sometimes these internal sources combine with external sources to produce too much stress. When this is the case, stress can be reduced either by reducing the external stresses, or by reducing internal stresses (for example, by changing attitudes), or both.

Annie was able to cope with three children, a part-time job, most of the household chores, and worrying about her elderly mother. She fell apart one day when the washing machine broke down. Martin started his own business, was facing a shrinking economy, volunteered to help out at the local youth club, and was involved in a turbulent relationship. He exploded when his assistant was late for work.

THE PHYSICAL EFFECTS OF STRESS

The results of scientific research strongly suggest that stress can be bad for our health. Evidence comes from two types of studies: the first is the investigation of physiological responses to stress in both people and animals; the second is the study of psychological factors associated with physical illness. The single most important effect of stress is that it, almost certainly, increases the chance of a heart attack. There is further evidence that psychological techniques that reduce the effects of stress in those who have had one heart attack reduce the chance of a second heart attack.

Stress can also cause bowel problems, notably diarrhea and tummy pain, as well as headaches; and it probably makes asthma attacks more frequent and severe in those already prone to asthma. Many people with chronic problems, ranging from skin rashes to arthritis to epilepsy, report that their problems are much worsened at times of stress.

Physiological research shows that stress can affect hormone levels, and the immune system (the system that helps fight against infection and some cancers), but whether these effects lead to disease is not known.

Are You Becoming Too Stressed?

One of the keys to managing stress is to recognize early when you are becoming too stressed. Go through the following *four* steps to help you decide whether this is happening to you.

STEP 1: LEARN TO RECOGNIZE YOUR OWN SIGNS

Everyone responds in their own way to increasing stress. Some people become progressively more frantic and impetuous, others drag their feet and avoid making decisions. In both cases, stress makes them less efficient. The important thing is to know how *you* react. The better you know your own signs, the better you will be able to cope with the problem. Learn about yourself by focusing on situations and times when you know you were stressed in the past. You can then learn to recognize your signs early in order, in the future, to take action before the stresses get out of hand. The following questions will help you to recognize your reactions.

1. What does it feel like when you are stressed?
2. How does it show?
3. What thoughts run through your mind?
4. What do you do?
5. How does it affect others?
6. How do their reactions affect you?

In order to help you to detect stress in your life, we have listed some common changes in the following box. Read the list carefully, marking those which apply to you when you are stressed, and adding others as appropriate. Look for your personal signs of stress, and remember that the things on the list normally fluctuate as you negotiate everyday ups and downs.

The list is divided into four sections. Most people who suffer from stress find that it affects them in all four ways, so if you mark nothing in one of the sections, you should probably think again.

STEP 2: WEIGH THE SIZE OF THE LOAD

Take an objective look at the stresses you face, and write them down if you can. Stress is cumulative, so the small things (the chores) count as well as the big ones (your job, your finances, and friendships). Beware of discounting the load in the way that many people do, thinking, for example, *"everyone else* copes with at least as much," or "I *should* be able to manage. I could last year." A heavy load, carried for a long time, wears you down in the end, and different people find different things stressful. Discounting your load only adds internal stress to the external load and puts you under more pressure.

Changes That May Be Signs of Stress

Feelings
Irritability; you become short-tempered, or easily flare up
Anxiety or feelings of panic
Fear—e.g., of being out of control
Feeling worried—e.g., about your health, or anything else
Feeling miserable or tearful
Apathy or agitation
Lowered self-esteem

Thoughts
Forgetting things; making mistakes
Finding it hard to concentrate
Becoming indecisive
Getting muddled or confused
Procrastinating
Being unable to think far ahead
Worrying or ruminating rather than solving problems
Becoming rigid and inflexible in an effort to keep control
Predicting the worst

Behaviors
Getting worse at managing your time
Getting worse at organizing yourself, and others
Rushing hither and thither
Finding it hard to delegate or ask for help
Working longer and longer hours
Bringing work home; working on weekends
Avoiding tackling problems, or doing things you dislike
Cutting down on the things you do for pleasure
Losing touch with your friends

Changes That May Be Signs of Stress—cont'd

Blaming others for the problem
Taking it out on others ("kicking the cat")
Finding there's no time to enjoy yourself
Needing a drink; turning to drugs
Needing tranquilizers or sleeping tablets

Sensations
Aches and pains, especially headaches or stomachaches
Tension—e.g., in your neck and shoulders
Frequent minor ailments
Disrupted sleep patterns
Appetite for food increased or decreased
Appetite for sex increased or decreased
Ulcers
Flare up of stress-related illness, such as asthma or psoriasis

---

STEP 3: THINK ABOUT RECENT CHANGES IN YOUR LIFE

Changes demand that you adapt, so all of them, even if they are for the better, contribute to your level of stress. The demand is obvious if the stress is an illness like arthritis or losing your job, and less obvious if it comes from being promoted or getting married. Changes that can lessen your load, like retirement or readjusting after your children leave home, can also be stressful. Changes of all kinds use up energy, leaving you less to spare until you have adjusted to the changes. Moving is the most underestimated of major changes, and can take months to adapt to completely. Add to your list any changes that have happened to you in the last year. In the box on page 260, you will find some examples of the types of event which research has shown commonly contribute to stress.

STEP 4: THINK ABOUT RECENT CHANGES IN YOURSELF

Having thought about how you respond to stress, the pressures on you, and recent events in your life, do you think that you are becoming too stressed now? Look again at the box on page 258, "Changes That May Be Signs of Stress." Have you noticed any recent changes in yourself that might be due to excess stress?

Examples of Stressful Events

Major changes
Changing jobs
Getting married, separated, or divorced
Business readjustments
Pregnancy
Moving
Leaving school, or changing schools
Outstanding achievement
Getting or losing a mortgage
Retirement

Losses
A friend or relative dies
People you are close to move away
Children leaving home
Stopping work
Giving up work to have children

Disruptions to routine
Vacations, Christmas, bank holidays
Someone new in the home (e.g., a friend or a new baby)
Stopping smoking or drinking
Dieting
No opportunity for exercise

Trouble and strife
Arguments, especially with a partner
Brushes with the law
Illness
Injury
Financial problems

Note: These are not in order of severity. That depends on you.

Dealing with Stress

Most people who suffer from stress manage the problem sensibly themselves, and many succeed. If you catch the problem early, your own ways of dealing with it are likely to work, because you have probably developed effective strategies over the years. There are, however, two cautionary notes to bear in mind.

TWO NOTES OF CAUTION

1. *Make sure that the solutions you use will be helpful in the long term as well as in the short term.* As the demands upon him increased, Martin began to drink more. It helped him to relax, to find the energy for his extra commitments, and to deal more calmly with his difficult relation ship. However, the stress continued and he found himself reaching for the bottle at ever-increasing intervals. As he drank more, he became more argumentative and slept less well. The more stressed he became the more he wanted to drink. This apparent solution became another of his problems.

2. *Beware of caffeine.* Caffeine winds you up, and could undo the good work you are doing in other ways. Annie's efforts to fulfill all her commitments left her little time for herself. She forced herself to stop by making a cup of tea or coffee, by joining in the coffee breaks at work, and by chatting to a friend over coffee while the children were at swimming classes. She started to suffer from tension headaches, felt more frantic rather than less, and had difficulty falling asleep. After limiting the number of caffeine drinks she had in a day (including tea and cola as well as coffee) to about four, and cutting them out altogether after 6 P.M., she began to feel more in control.

When you are not able to get your stress under control, try these five steps.

STEP 1: TAKE STOCK OF THE SITUATION

The more you push yourself when you are stressed, the less you are likely to achieve, because trying harder increases the pressure—and also the inefficiency. Striving not to strive can also be counterproductive and add to the tension.

The first step is therefore the hardest of all: find a moment to stop and think. When stress builds to high levels, you need a breathing space. However pressured you feel, give yourself time to take stock. It is time well spent because it helps you put things in perspective and plan the next move. Have a brief rest if you can, and assess your level of stress in the ways already described. Think about the four main aspects of your life: work, play, health, and relationships (both family and friends). Are these equally important to you? Are some more important than others?

Ask yourself: to which do you devote most time and energy? Does the way you fill your time fit with what matters to you? Devoting all your time to one aspect of life—work or family, for instance—will create stress if you also value the others. Besides, if you put all your eggs in one basket, there is nothing to fall back on when things go badly awry.

STEP 2: START WITH THE END IN MIND

Stress makes it hard to give priority to the most important things. Indeed, the choice of what to do next often becomes so haphazard that you find yourself thoughtlessly taking up the first thing that comes along, and worrying about not having enough time for everything else. If you have clarified your major priorities, you will find it easier to interrupt this process, and make decisions that lead to a more balanced, and less stressful, life. Martin learned how to stop work in time to play squash or eat with friends; Annie learned how to share the family chores more fairly and joined an evening class with the idea of finding a more interesting job.

Use your priorities to guide small decisions, like how to spend the evening, as well as big ones like changing your job. If you know what is "vital" to you, it becomes easier to "cut your losses" when stress builds to high levels. You can then consider, for instance, whether someone else might like to take on a task that you could drop. The central importance of being guided by your priorities is explained in Chapter 5.

Putting your priorities into practice. The ideas discussed so far are easy to understand but hard to put into practice. Once you have thought about the basics, and about your priorities, start by dealing with the effects of stress. Here are some ideas about how to do this.

1. *Stress affects your memory and concentration.* Relieve yourself of this extra strain by writing things down—for example, in diaries, on wallcharts, or on lists.
2. *Stress makes planning and decisions difficult.* Give yourself planning time every day (first thing in the morning may be best).

3. *Stress makes you tired.* Give yourself proper breaks—for meals, refreshments, exercise, and on weekends.
4. *Stress slows down your speed of recovery, and lowers your resistance to illness.* Learn to stop before you are completely worn out. Take regular exercise, and eat a balanced diet.
5. *Stress makes you feel pressured.* Think about how to take the urgency out of your life (see Chapter 5).
6. *Stress tempts you to avoid difficulties or put off dealing with them, so that they do not get resolved.* Try to face them instead. It is often best to do your least favorite, or hardest, task first (see Chapter 6).
7. *Stress reduces your efficiency.* Find out how you use your time—for example, by thinking back or keeping a diary. Does the way you spend your time accord with your values and goals?

Keeping your values and priorities clearly in mind makes all of these easier.

STEP 3: REDUCE THE "OUTSIDE" LOAD: THE LESSON OF THE CAMEL'S BACK

Stress is cumulative. Deal, therefore, with small problems (the mess in your room, answering letters) particularly when there seems to be little you can do about the big ones (someone's illness, or the amount of traffic on the roads). Identify all the stresses on you; none is too small to consider. Which of these stresses can you reduce? Problem-solving strategies are explained in detail in Chapter 8.

STEP 4: REDUCE THE "INSIDE" LOAD: CHANGING ATTITUDES

Stress comes from the inside as well as from the outside. For each of us, it is determined partly by the way we see the world, or by our attitudes. Many of our attitudes originate in our childhood. Some, no doubt, are absorbed from authority figures, in particular from parents or parent substitutes and from teachers; others are derived from our experience, for example, from having grown up with a competitive brother or sister. Such early experiences probably determine to a great extent whether we are driven by a desire to please, or a wish to win, or whatever. And these different drives and desires affect what causes us stress (see also Chapter 14). Those men who believe that success in life is measured by success at work are especially stressed by being unemployed. Those women brought up to believe that they should devote the major part of their energies to their children are especially stressed by the demands of combining a career and a family. *Such attitudes are not in themselves right or wrong, but they can be more or less helpful.* Unhelpful attitudes of any kind make difficulties and increase your burden, while more helpful ones take the pressure off, so it is worth examining your attitudes and looking for alternatives that create less pressure. Some of the ways of doing this are explained in Chapter 9, and some common examples of attitudes that can contribute to feeling stressed are listed here, together with some more helpful alternatives.

Putting the pressure on	*Taking the pressure off*
I have to get this done.	I will do as much as I can in the time I've got.
I shouldn't ask for help.	Everyone asks for help sometimes. I would happily help someone else.
This is really important.	In five years this won't matter at all. When I'm on my deathbed, I won't be saying "I wish I'd spent more time in the office."
I must do things well.	I can only do my best.
Others cope far better than I.	Everyone is susceptible to stress. I am not alone in this.
There's nothing I can do.	Try solving the small problems first.
I'll crack up completely.	I need a break, so I'll take a break.
I can't let anyone see how I feel.	There's nothing to lose by talking to someone about my feelings.

STEP 5: LAY THE RIGHT FOUNDATION

Feeling stressed is a danger signal: a sign that you are reaching the limits of your resources. Stress is bad for your physical health as well as a cause of increasing inefficiency and worsening relationships. The danger is that when under stress you ignore your health, and put your relationships under increasing strain. This sets up a vicious cycle because poor health and poor relationships then add to the stress. It is important, therefore, to focus not only directly on the stresses but also to look after your health and your relationships.

Diet and exercise. Regularity is the key. You need regular meals and you need regular exercise—always, and not just when you are young and growing. If you feel stressed, now is the time to build up your stamina by keeping fit.

Martin regularly rushed out of the house without breakfast, skipped lunch or grabbed a sandwich on the way from one appointment to the next, and filled himself up with cookies, chocolate, and coffee when he noticed he was flagging. Annie tried to eat at regular times and to provide a varied and balanced diet for the family, but at mealtimes she constantly leaped up and down to fetch and carry for her children. Because she put her own needs last, her children learned to expect her to be constantly serving them. She hardly knew what it felt like to sit comfortably throughout a meal. Eating "properly" not only means eating the right things, but eating them in the right way. Eating properly would help both Annie and Martin cope better with their stressful lives, and encouraging Annie's children to look after their own needs, or to help at mealtimes, would be especially helpful to Annie.

The same idea applies to regular exercise. Even ten minutes of daily exercise makes a difference. So does walking more and using the car less. Ideally, you should take at least an hour of exercise twice a week, building up the strenuousness gradually. It is time well spent, even if at first you feel too tired to change your clothes. Surprisingly perhaps, exercising when you are stressed is more invigorating than exhausting, and often leaves you with more energy than you started with. Of course, it improves your physical state, but it also marks an important shift in attitude, away from neglect and toward caring for yourself.

The Three Rs: Rest, recreation, and relationships. Being stressed adds its own pressures. To prevent being caught up in the vicious cycle of stress, which leads to even higher levels of stress, you need: *rest*, to renew your energy; *recreation*, to provide you with pleasure and fulfillment; and *relationships*, as a source of support, perspective, and fun.

1. *Rest.* Stress is associated with tension and poor sleeping patterns. It makes it hard to switch off and to take advantage of opportunities

to rest, especially brief ones. Good quality rest restores your good mood as well as your capacity to function well. So schedule regular rest periods, both brief ones and more substantial rest periods. Examples of brief periods of rest are: soaking in the bath; having a coffee break with a friend; spending 30 minutes in formal relaxation. Examples of longer periods of rest are: a week's vacation; a day out with the family (unless the family is a source of stress); a weekend break. If you are sleeping badly, read Chapter 30. If you are unable to relax, read Chapter 11. If worry prevents you from getting rest, read Chapter 18.

Rest means not working. It does *not* mean doing your work sitting on the sofa while listening to music. Nor does it necessarily mean doing nothing. Almost everyone finds it hard to do nothing, except for rather short or rare periods, like when lying in the bath. It is even harder to do nothing when you feel stressed, when worries pile up ready to grab your attention whenever it is free.

2. *Recreation.* Recreation makes you feel better about yourself—more fulfilled, more satisfied, more interested, and more engaged in the world outside that of your own personal concerns. Recreations come in infinite varieties. They are often not restful in that they can be quite demanding and even exhausting (playing football or squash; cooking for friends), but they are a source of pleasure and satisfaction and a chance to extend your skills. If they are to be truly recreational, they should be markedly different from your work routine or from the source of your stress. If the stresses come mostly from your office, then cooking on the weekend could be recreational, but not if constantly providing for the family is itself a source of stress.

Hobbies are usually recreational. They give you an added interest and often bring you into contact with like-minded people (dog-breeders, gardeners, bridge players), and if they are to serve their purpose, they should be kept free from trouble and strife. Everybody needs recreations, which may be creative or contemplative, social or solitary.

3. *Relationships.* Relationships are a common source of stress. You may have problems with family members, colleagues, friends, or lovers. People who are stressed may also be irritable and argumentative with those to whom they are closest and to whom they would like to be able to turn for support and comfort. Stress easily affects relationships: disappointment, sadness, or anger

about a relationship may add to your burden, but if it cuts you off from others, you will lose a major source of "restoration." The following box suggests ways you can gain support from your relationships.

Other Can Help When You Are Stressed

- Do not cut yourself off from other people.
- Talk to someone both about your difficulties and your feelings.
- Seek out companionship of the kind that you usually enjoy.
- Keep in touch with friends.
- Explain what is happening if you are irritable—others may take it personally when that was not what you intended.
- If you need time for yourself, say so.
- Think about how to help others when they, too, are stressed.

There is far more to be gained than lost from talking to others about how to cope with your stress, because although everyone reacts differently, the process is normal. Everyone would eventually suffer from it if their burden was continually increasing. Both Annie and Martin discovered that two heads were better than one when it came to looking for solutions, although, perhaps because he is a man, Martin found it particularly difficult to talk about how he was feeling. Annie talked to her women friends and neighbors and heard about some volunteers able to visit and help with her mother. Martin's bout of anger with his assistant when he was late led, after some strong words had been said on both sides, to a discussion that surprised Martin. He discovered his assistant was bored and frustrated at not having more responsibilities. With a mixture of trepidation and relief, Martin shed some of the load he was carrying. Ways of sharing a load include delegating more of your tasks, unburdening yourself to a close friend, or asking someone to help you out.

Relationships with others are also an important source of pleasure. They are a resource when you feel stressed, but often an underused resource: because some of them contribute to the problem, because stress absorbs every ounce of energy, or because of a natural, but unhelpful, reticence and reluctance to talk about difficulties. Furthermore, when we are stressed we may inadvertently put a strain on our relationships, too, by "taking it out on others" or "passing on the bad news." In order to make constructive use of your close relationships, consider carefully who is likely to be able to give you support. This might be just one person, your special partner perhaps, or several people. Then think about whether you have explained clearly to this person, or persons, how you are feeling, and under how much stress you are. Have you been expecting them to make the first move? Finally, has your stress meant that you have been particularly irritable with those close to you? If you have, it may be helpful to apologize and explain that your irritability is not because of them, but because of the stresses you feel.

When tension runs high, most people need their relationships more, not less, and so it is in their own best interest to think about how to look after them. It may be important to let off steam in ways that do not run the risk of upsetting others and damaging relationships—for example, by going for a run, thumping a pillow, or expressing feelings of frustration and anger forcibly on paper. Ensuring that you continue to do things you enjoy with the people around you will both help you feel less stressed and keep the relationship in good working order. You will find many more ideas about how to foster good relationships in Part Three of this book.

Chapter Summary

1. Everyone gets stressed from time to time.
2. A moderate amount of stress can be helpful and make you function more efficiently. A lot of stress is not only unpleasant: it is counterproductive.
3. Try to recognize the signs of stress, as early as possible, by following these four steps:
   • Tune in to the early signs of stress.
   • Take an objective look at the pressures on you.
   • Identify recent changes in your load at work and at home.
   • Identify recent changes in how you feel.
4. Most problems with stress can be dealt with using a systematic approach.
   • Make a little time to take stock of your situation.
   • Review your values and goals: start with the end in mind.

- The camel's back: throw away some of the load.
- Restructure your attitudes: many pressures are stressful only because we make them stressful.
- Look after the basics: diet, exercise, and the three Rs of rest, recreation, and relationships.

21

Dealing with Panic:
Controlling the Alarm System

When the Alarm Bell Rings

Liz was sitting at her desk, staring out of the window. By her side she had an empty coffee mug and a blank sheet of paper. The report was not due until next week and she was finding it hard to concentrate. She allowed her mind to wander among a familiar mixture of feelings, worries, and preoccupations, becoming increasingly irritated and frustrated with her inability to keep focused. The sun was shining directly onto the desk, and feeling hot she stood up to open the window. Suddenly she felt dizzy and light-headed. She felt apprehensive, just as if her internal alarm bell had started to ring. A confusing number of things then happened in quick succession. She grabbed the chair for fear of falling, started to tremble and sweat, noticed her heart was pounding, and wondered if something was seriously wrong. She felt a terrifying feeling of breathlessness and tried to gasp for more air. The papers on the desk seemed to recede to a great distance, and when she put out her hand to touch them, her fingers tingled even though they felt numb. By now she was seriously frightened, certain that something terrible was happening to her. She rushed to the bathroom and held onto the basin while she splashed some water onto her face. Then she sat down cradling her head in her hands. Slowly her body began to return to normal. The worst seemed to be over as the dizziness and heart-pounding gradually subsided. Still feeling frightened and shaky, she sat in a comfortable chair for half an hour before trying to get back to work again. The first thing she did when she reached her desk was telephone the doctor to make an appointment as soon as possible. She thought she might be ill, but was also puzzled about what sort of illness it could be, and she dreaded being labeled as yet another neurotic woman, unable to cope with both work and family life. Whatever the cause, the terrifying experience seemed to have come upon her with absolutely no warning: completely out of the blue. She no longer felt safe sitting at her desk.

Liz's terrifying experience was a panic attack—or as she came to call it, a "Satanic attack." Panic attacks are common. More than 10% of all people, men and women, experience at least one panic attack during their lifetime, and often the first one happens during early adulthood. They are more likely to occur at times of stress or strain, or after unpleasant or traumatic experiences, but they also occur at other times.

A panic attack is a terrifying experience. The physical sensations of fear escalate with amazing speed until it feels as if something catastrophic might happen, like collapsing, losing control, having a heart attack, or dying. The panic usually peaks within the first few minutes, and the sensations then subside, but more slowly than they started. It is not surprising, given how terrifying panic attacks can be, that they tend to shake people's confidence. Some people live in dread of further attacks, searching for ways of ensuring they will not happen again. A panic attack is a version of the normal alarm reaction, except that it occurs in the absence of real danger. If you were threatened by a mugger, or slipped in front of a car as you crossed the road, you might react in a similar way, and the alarm reaction would die down soon after you were safe again. Panic attacks are harder to come to terms with, and their effects may persist, partly because it is hard to understand what precipitated them. Even people who can recognize the situations that make them susceptible to panic, such as lining up in busy shops or speaking to a large group of people, are often at a loss to explain exactly what triggered a particular attack— "It seemed to come out of the blue"—and it is hard to believe that such a dramatic event could happen without there being something seriously wrong.

Dealing with panic involves understanding what happens during panic attacks, learning how to control them, and how to deal with their consequences. Recurrent panic attacks can now be treated successfully using psychological methods, and in the majority of cases people learn what to do quite quickly and can soon regain their confidence.

UNDERSTANDING PANIC

Panic affects all systems: sensations, actions, emotions, and thoughts. The main symptoms of panic are shown in the box on page 273. Read carefully through the list. If you have had even one panic attack, you may already have experienced a large number of these symptoms, and you may want to add some more of your own to the list. Not everyone reacts in exactly the same way.

Some people may find that reading through this list itself makes them feel quite panicky. If this should happen to you, think of it as a demonstration of the power of the mind. Thinking about the symptoms can be enough to trigger them off. Do not avoid reading through the list, but read the rest of the chapter first if you find it particularly difficult.

The bodily symptoms of panic are all part of the normal reaction to fear. They are useful, adaptive reactions for use in an emergency. They show that your body is preparing itself for action by, for example, pumping the blood faster or increasing the supply of oxygen to the muscles in case you need to take quick evading action. These reactions are protective in times of danger. They are normal and not harmful. Even when they occur in the absence of real danger, as in a panic attack, the symptoms themselves cannot harm you. They will do no physical damage, and they will not make you lose control or go mad. As soon as the danger is past, they will die down of their own accord. The heart beats faster during exercise (playing tennis, aerobics, climbing a mountain) than during a panic attack, so there is no danger of a heart attack.

Many people who have had panic attacks are particularly alarmed by the speed at which symptoms increase. They suppose that if the symptoms went on increasing at this rate "something dreadful would happen"—as if they might explode or burst. It is easy to assume that the symptoms would have gone on increasing if they had not taken action, such as sitting down, or running away. But they are wrong. The symptoms will reach a peak of their own accord and then start to decline. The fear reaction is designed to keep the body ready for action, and to protect it in case of need, not to blow a fuse at exactly the wrong moment.

TRIGGERING THE FEAR REACTION

The setting. It is, at first sight, strange that an extreme fear reaction, or panic, can be triggered in the absence of danger, but, like other kinds of alarm systems, the setting varies. If the setting is too low, it can scare you by producing false alarms, and if it is too high, the alarm may fail you in

---

Symptoms of Panic

Sensations
Palpitations: heart-thumping
Smothering or choking sensations
Feeling faint, dizzy, or unsteady
Sweating or hot flushes
Numbness or tingling—in the hands or feet
Breathlessness; shortness of breath; gulping for air
Trembling or shaking

Nausea
Feelings of unreality, as if things that are close at hand are at a distance
Tightness in the chest or chest pain

Actions
Shouting for help
Hanging on to furniture, or to people nearby
Running away; escaping from the situation
Sitting or lying down
Stopping ongoing activities
Seeking safety

Emotions
Apprehension
Dread
Fear
Terror
Panic

Thoughts
Something dreadful is happening.
I shall collapse.
This is a heart attack.
I can't breathe.
I'm going to die.
I might lose control.
I'm going mad.
I'm trapped; I can't get out.

---

the hour of need. It is certainly possible that some people are naturally more sensitive than others, or react more quickly than others, and at times of stress or strain, when tension levels are already high, it is easier to trip the switch than at other times. But for everyone there is some level at which their alarm system will be triggered, and the ease with which this happens is changeable. For example, the more you dread having an attack, the more anxious you become and the more likely you are to trigger one off. As you learn to understand panic, and to control the processes involved, the easier it is to reset the system at a more comfortable level.

The triggers. It appears that thoughts, and in particular *misinterpretations of normal events*, play a crucial part in triggering false alarms. The first thing that Liz noticed when she stood up to open the window was feeling dizzy and light-headed. The panic reaction followed quickly after these sensations, which, understandably, made her feel apprehensive. Talking about it later she said that the speed of her reactions (the efficiency of her alarm system) made it hard to sort out what happened first. However, with help, she was able to disentangle the thoughts and the feelings and to pick out the elements of a chain reaction: first, she felt dizzy and thought she might faint. Then, she felt apprehensive, more unsteady (grabbed the chair), and thought something must be seriously wrong. This thought frightened her, and her heart started pounding. That suggested something was definitely going wrong. Even more alarmed, she gasped for breath, her fingers tingled, the papers before her receded, and she became convinced that something terrible was happening to her. At each stage, she interpreted the changes in her feelings as "danger signals." Each time she made such an interpretation, she boosted the fear reaction into the next gear until she suffered a full-blown panic attack. Although at the time her thoughts were not put into words, later Liz said that these were the things that were in her mind: "I might faint"; "Something must be seriously wrong"; "Something is definitely going wrong"; and "Something terrible is going to happen to me right now."

This illustrates the standard pattern of panic. The trigger is usually a harmless or normal occurrence, which sets off the alarm system because it is interpreted as dangerous. In Liz's case the trigger was an internal one: feeling dizzy. She may have been particularly vulnerable to feeling dizzy because she was hot, had been drinking coffee, and suddenly stood up after sitting at her desk for a while. Or it may have been an effect of the stage she had reached in her menstrual cycle. But she ignored these "harmless" explanations of the dizziness and thought instead that something must be wrong. The more alarming her thoughts, the worse she felt; and the worse she felt, the more she believed she really was in serious danger—of what kind she could not be sure.

The range of triggers. There is a vast range of potential triggers for fear reactions. Whenever something is interpreted as a danger signal, the fear may escalate into panic. Catastrophic misinterpretations of harmless events are the main triggers of panic, and the fact that they cannot be explained makes them even more distressing. Imagine you were walking home alone in the dark late at night when you heard footsteps close behind you. If you thought someone was creeping up on you, your alarm system might well "blow." The same thing might happen if you narrowly missed having a car crash. You might also feel highly anxious and "panicky" before an important, challenging, and demanding event such as an interview, examination, or golf match. The threshold of panic gets nearer in many such situations. However, the difference between these examples and Liz's experience is that the trigger can be understood.

When we can understand our fear and the sensations that accompany it, it is easier to accept what is happening. But when a panic attack comes "out of the blue," or in a situation which should not be stressful or dangerous, another dimension is added to the fear reaction: it feels unreasonable, inexcusable, or unacceptable. The feeling of panic is a profoundly disturbing and undermining experience when the fear is not associated with a real threat.

In searching for a cause, or trigger, people who have panic attacks often latch on to *internal* events. They may truly believe, at the time, that they are having a heart attack; or that they will suffocate or choke, collapse or die; or that they are losing control and going mad. The evidence for these beliefs comes from their feelings: the sense of panic feels *as if* one of these things might happen. Common internal triggers of panic include missed heart beats, changes in heart rate or breathing, temperature changes (particularly feeling hot), hunger and low blood sugar, visual anomalies such as occasional blurring, tension or chest pain, the effects of having a hangover or of taking strenuous exercise. Indeed, *any* physiological change in body state can be misinterpreted. It is the misinterpretation, the conviction that a normal, harmless event is potentially dangerous, that turns these events into panic triggers.

Changes in one's state of mind can also be misinterpreted and can therefore trigger panic attacks—for example, being unable to think clearly; having alarming images, thoughts, or memories; the mind racing or suddenly going blank. Particular situations like having an argument, being criticized, or being alone can trigger panic attacks because of the fear that these events might have personally or socially disastrous outcomes. Again, it is the interpretation—the meaning of the event—that can trigger the alarm.

Nocturnal panics. Waking suddenly in a state of panic can be very frightening, but is quite a common experience. During sleep the mind does not switch off completely—it can still produce alarming dreams—and it can also respond to normal bodily changes, for example, in breathing and heart rate, that can be misinterpreted as danger signals. So it is possible to wake in fear from a nightmare or to be frightened by unusual but harmless physical sensations caused, for example, by an episode of very slow breathing or by a missed heart beat, and to wake feeling terrified or gasping for air. The speed of the alarm reaction and its capacity to operate when you are asleep reflect its efficiency—not an impending disaster. Of course, panic triggers that occur during sleep can only be guessed at, so it is important to learn how to calm yourself down and not to add alarming thoughts to the fear.

Resetting the Alarm System

WORK ON THE THOUGHTS THAT FEED THE PANIC

A panic attack is analogous to a burglar alarm which goes off when the wind rattles the window panes. The key to overcoming panic, therefore, is to reset your alarm system so that it does not go off when there is no real danger. In order to reset your alarm you need to focus on four things: the thoughts that trigger the panic; your breathing; your responses to the attack; and your general level of anxiety. But even the best set burglar alarm can go off at the wrong moment, so you need also to learn some strategies for coping with the attack itself.

Clarify your thinking. If panic follows after the misinterpretation of harmless events, then the thoughts, the misinterpretations, will be your first targets for change. The best way to sort these out is to think in detail about a recent panic attack. Try to cue yourself in by remembering what was happening and how you were feeling before the panic began. Then tell someone, or write down, all the things that happened to you, moment by moment. Pay particular attention to the meaning of the events, to the way you reacted to what happened to you, as well as to the sensations of panic. See if you can disentangle a chain reaction of thoughts and feelings in the same way as we did with Liz. Separate the thoughts, including images, suppositions, beliefs, and assumptions, from all the rest. Try to put into words the thoughts that alarmed and frightened you. Ask yourself, *"What is the worst thing that could have happened?"*

The most common difficulty people have when they try to disentangle the panic reaction is missing the trigger. The panic grabs your attention in a way that the harmless trigger does not, and until you know, and believe, that ordinary, harmless events *can* trigger panic you will not know what to look out for. Remember that mild and completely ordinary sensations, such as those of hunger, or the after-effects of too much coffee, can be sufficient to start you off, and the process of panic, once started, gathers speed alarmingly quickly.

Pinpoint the misinterpretation. After the event you know that nothing dreadful happened. It might have been embarrassing or distressing, but you are still here to tell the tale, so you know that it must have been wrong to believe that something catastrophic was going to happen. Beware of being tempted into thinking that you just had a near miss—of thinking that if you had not sat down, or kept still, or kept completely silent you really would have suffered a disaster. Remember that the panic reaction is a self-limiting process. To be effective when you need it, it has to get off to a fast start, but it also reaches a peak and then slowly subsides.

So reexamine your understanding of what happened to you. Try and pick out what it was that alarmed or frightened you, and think about it again. Take another look at it and ask yourself now whether your alarm and fear were justified. Maybe the disaster you feared (e.g., having a heart attack) would actually feel different from the sensation that set off your panic. The most useful question to ask yourself is this: *Is what happened more like a real catastrophe, or is it more like being frightened and worried about that real catastrophe?* You will find more strategies for answering these questions, and more useful questions to ask yourself, on pages 80 to 82 (see *Chapter 9, Keeping Things in Perspective: Help from Cognitive Therapy*).

Some of the most common misinterpretations made by people who have panic attacks are shown in the following list.

Dealing with Panic	
Sensations	**Interpretations**
Heart-thumping or racing	This is a heart attack. I have serious heart disease.
	I will lose control.
Breathlessness	I can't breathe. I shall choke and die.
Dizziness	I will collapse or faint.
Confusion, lack of concentration	I am going mad. I'm losing my senses.

In a panic attack, blood pressure rises. When you faint, blood pressure falls. It is therefore most unlikely that you will faint during a panic attack.

CONTROLLING YOUR BREATHING

For some people overbreathing, or hyperventilation, contributes to their panic attacks. It is natural to breathe more quickly and more deeply when afraid because this prepares the body for appropriate action. However, hyperventilation is breathing in excess of what your body needs, and this produces mildly unpleasant sensations (associated with reduced levels of carbon dioxide). These new sensations are of course ripe for misinterpretation, and so they contribute to the chain reaction. One of the paradoxical sensations produced by hyperventilation is a sensation of breathlessness, as if one was short of air rather than *over*breathing, making the person who is panicking want to gasp or gulp to get more air. This only makes the sensations stronger.

Overbreathing and its effects can be controlled by learning how to breathe calmly. You should practice this many times when you are not anxious before using it to control the symptoms of panic. You may find that it takes much practice, and many attempts, before you are able to breathe calmly when you feel panicky, so it would be sensible to practice at least twice a day for a week before using the method during a real panic attack.

Calm breathing (see also p. 107). Breathe in through your nose and out through your mouth. Put a hand on your stomach while you do this, and see if it moves up and down when you breathe. You are aiming for diaphragmatic breathing, during which your stomach rather than your chest moves. Keep practicing even if you find it difficult to breathe naturally when focusing on your breathing. Just be patient, and repeat the exercise frequently until you can do it more easily. Once you are breathing in the right way, try to slow your breathing to a calm rate It may help to count to yourself as you breathe ("one hundred, two hundred, three hundred"). Find out how much to count for each breath by doing it when you know you are breathing calmly and using this as your standard. Breathing out usually takes a little longer than breathing in.

Breathing into a paper bag. If you are troubled by hyperventilation during panic attacks, and you have not been able to overcome this through control of your breathing, you may be helped by using a paper bag. The idea is that you need to increase the level of carbon dioxide that has fallen because of the overbreathing, and that you can do this by rebreathing the air you have just breathed out. The technique, which you should use during the panic attack, involves holding an empty paper bag (*do not use a plastic bag*) tightly over your nose and mouth with both hands. Be sure there are no holes in the bag, and breathe in and out into it for a maximum of ten breaths; the unpleasant sensations caused by overbreathing should rapidly disappear.

DEALING WITH YOUR RESPONSES TO THE PANIC ATTACK

A panic is an alarming experience, and because of this it leads to a variety of responses that can maintain the problem and make you more susceptible to further panics.

1. *Anticipatory anxiety.* If you are expecting to panic, the expectation works like a self-fulfilling prophecy. Try to give yourself the benefit of the doubt. If you start to feel anxious, recognize consciously that this is *anxiety,* caused by misinterpretation of something harmless. Remind yourself that the feelings of anxiety are not due to physical illness, and are not signs of imminent collapse, insanity, or any other disaster—personal, physical, or social.
2. *Avoidance.* It is easy to avoid facing the situations that could provoke another attack or to take protective action. But the trouble is that if you do this you will undermine your confidence and you will not learn that the situations in which the panic occurred, and the sensations it provoked, are in fact harmless. Of course, heart attacks do happen, airplanes crash, and elevators get stuck between floors. But these are relatively rare events which come to seem much more likely—even quite certain—when one is frightened. It is essential to face the situations or sensations associated with your panic. You should keep going to shops, traveling alone, running upstairs, or taking other forms of exercise even if this makes you apprehensive at first. Facing the difficulties gives you the opportunity to recognize your

misinterpretations and to learn how to cope with them calmly once more. In Chapters 6 and 19 we deal with these issues in more detail.

3. *Self-monitoring and hypervigilance.* Because panic attacks are so unpleasant, you keep on the lookout for symptoms and sensations that could be "dangerous." Too much checking is counterproductive. If you sit perfectly still and think of nothing else but your heart for five minutes, you will become oversensitive to what it is doing. The normal beating will feel like thumping, and you will start to notice the small irregularities, missed heart beats, and changes in strength or speed that are quite normal. The more you focus on your sensations, the more changes you will notice, and the more opportunities you will have to misinterpret them and trigger another panic. A similar thing happens if you start to worry that the person sitting next to you has head lice; your scalp will start to tingle and itch and the desire to scratch becomes overwhelming. The imagination is a powerful instrument.

4. *Fear of fear.* The fear of the panic attack itself—the worry that the symptoms themselves could be harmful—helps to precipitate the next attack. This is why it is important to understand that a panic attack is not dangerous, and to tell yourself this whenever you start to worry.

LOWERING YOUR GENERAL LEVEL OF ANXIETY

Panic attacks are like mountain peaks that arise from the foothills. Most people who suffer from panic attacks tend to be more generally anxious. Reducing this general level of anxiety will reduce the chance of a panic attack. So the other chapters in this book which deal with general levels of anxiety will help in overcoming panic. The chapters which are likely to be particularly helpful are:

Chapter 7   *Treating Yourself Right*
Chapter 10   *Building Self-Confidence and Self-Esteem*
Chapter 11   *Learning How to Relax*
Chapter 18   *Getting the Better of Anxiety and Worry, or Defeating the Alarmist*
Chapter 20   *Stress: How to Live with the Right Amount of It*

Keeping yourself physically fit by exercising regularly, eating sensibly, getting a good night's sleep, and avoiding excess caffeine and alcohol will also help to reduce the chance of panic attacks.

COPING WITH THE ATTACK ITSELF

1. Try to learn more about the sorts of things that trigger your panic. It helps greatly to catch the panic early, before the chain reaction has gathered speed and the sensations and fears have escalated.

2. Try to stay where you are. If you run away, or sit or lie down, or take other evasive action, it makes it harder to learn that the panic will peak and then subside of its own accord. You do not need to do something to prevent a disaster occurring, as no disaster will occur.

3. Once you have sorted out the kinds of interpretations that frighten you, write down a reminder to yourself that shows how mistaken they were. Try to pinpoint the mistakes you tend to make, and to remember that panic attacks, although they seem frightening, are in fact harmless. When your heart thuds, or the train slows down in the tunnel, the cause of the problem is almost certainly benign. Write these on a small card to carry with you and read if you feel at risk.

4. Instead of focusing on what is happening to you, on the things that you fear, turn your attention to something else instead. Try to distract yourself. Keep busy, move about, talk to someone, or think of something else. Set yourself a mathematical problem to force yourself to concentrate on something else. Remember the birthdays of members of your family. Try to put something other than fearsome thoughts into your mind. The mind has a limited capacity. If you occupy it with something else, it will not be able to work overtime on alarming possiblities.

THE VALUE OF MEDICATION

Many drugs have been used to help people who suffer from panic attacks. Some of these are tranquilizers, which help relaxation in the short term but which become less effective over time and are addictive. Others are antidepressants—which can help with panic even in the absence of depression. Addiction is not such a problem with antidepressants, but the symptoms of panic tend to return when the drugs are stopped.

Reminders for an Emergency

You could copy the following list, or photocopy it, to carry with you in case of need.

When you feel panicky, remind yourself:

1. The bodily sensations are normal, not harmful or dangerous.
2. There is no real danger. This is only a panic attack.
3. Do not run away. The fear will start to subside quite soon.
4. Practice breathing slowly.
5. Use distraction, and pay attention to something else.
6. What was the trigger? What was the first thing you noticed?
7. What made that happen then?
8. Make use of relaxation techniques.

Add to this list any ideas that you have found helpful. In the heat of the moment it is easy to forget the things that seem obvious later.

Chapter Summary

A panic attack is a terrifying experience during which it *feels as if* something dreadful, and probably catastrophic, is about to happen to you. The sensations of panic are normal reactions to danger, triggered by something harmless such as an odd sensation or change in heart rate. Interpreting the sensations as dangerous triggers your alarm system and can also produce more false alarms. At least one in ten people have had, or will have, a panic attack.

You can build your confidence again by resetting the alarm system. There are four main ways of doing this:

1. Deal with the thoughts that trigger the panic.
2. Learn how to control your breathing.
3. Keep your reactions to the panic under control, so that they do not keep the problem going.
4. Lower your general level of anxiety.

22

Depression—The Common Cold
of the Mind

The distinguished psychologist Martin Seligman described depression as "the common cold" of psychiatry. About 12% of the population experience a depression severe enough to require treatment at some time in their lives, although the vast majority of episodes of depression end within three to six months even without treatment. This does not mean that there is nothing you need to do when you feel depressed. There are things you can do to help yourself, things that friends and family can do, and ways in which professionals can help. We will show you how you can overcome your low moods more quickly, how you can recognize them early in order to nip them in the bud, and how to prevent a low mood from attacking you in the first place.

Nobody likes depression, either within themselves or in those around them. The result is that we often get little support when we are depressed. Friends and relations may tell us to pull ourselves together, if not directly then in subtle ways, or they may draw away from us to avoid the icy fingers of our low mood. This usually makes us feel even worse: on top of feeling depressed we come to feel guilty and weak. When depression has us in its thrall, we can rarely throw it off with the ease that those around us would like. There are ways of gradually freeing yourself from depression, but these will not be like "pulling yourself together."

It requires more kindness, more understanding, and in a way, more indulgence.

Many parts of this book are relevant to depression. Together with anxiety, it is the main enemy of "good mood." There is no single way of releasing everyone from their depression. It will be necessary to pick and choose from the ideas in this part and throughout the book, and to select those which seem relevant and helpful. Be wary of offers of a miraculous cure. There are many ways in which you can help yourself, some of which take time and persistence: but there are no quick and easy answers.

The Experience of Depression

We all know what it is like to be sad and miserable. It is normal for moods to go up and down from day to day, and the downward sweep of these fluctuations is usually not severe enough to make you depressed. However, if you can recognize problems before they become severe, then you can deal with them more easily and more effectively. So it is important to understand what depression is, and how to recognize when these bouts of low mood are slipping into depression.

Many people mark this difference by using the term "clinical depression" to describe the low mood that goes deeper than usual, or feels as if it has got stuck and gives you no respite. This is a useful term because it helps people to take the problem seriously, to think about how to get help, and to find out what they can do to help themselves feel better. Using the term also helps them to understand that it is not their fault that they feel depressed. Blaming yourself for feeling depressed only makes the problem worse. However, the term has no absolute and clear definition. There is no way of drawing a hard and fast line between low mood and "clinical depression" because the two shade into each other by degrees, just as shades of blue, as they darken, turn into black.

It is important to get to know more about the effects of depression and to think about what the early signs of depression are for you. If you observe yourself or ask those close to you what they first notice, then you will be able to learn what you can do when you start to slip. Make note of your early signs of low mood (a written note is better than a mental note), and read this and the following chapters again as soon as you feel you are getting depressed.

Effects of Depression on the Way You Function

You may be surprised by the effects of depression on your general functioning. Depression can take away your energy and interests. It can feel like you are wading through mud: everything becomes an effort. Things which you used to do easily are now impossible to face. Sexual interest often disappears relatively early, as the mind turns inward and focuses on the self. Disturbances of all of the body's daily rhythms can be expected: appetites, activity levels, and sleep patterns may all change. Sleep is often disrupted and no longer refreshing.

The feeling of depression normally varies to some extent over the course of the day. If the depression is closely related to daily problems, then it may get steadily worse during the day, and make it particularly difficult to fall asleep, as you are racked with worry, tossing and turning with all your problems crowding in on you. But often, if the depression pervades the whole of your being, the worst time is the early morning. Then the sufferer may wake much earlier than usual, feeling in the depths of despair. Gradually as the day wears on, these feelings may start to lift.

These changes in mood emphasize the episodic nature of depression: the periods of depression tend to have their own cycles that vary immensely, and within an episode of depression mood can vary considerably. Only in the deepest stages will there be no glimpse of the possibility of a lifting of the darkness.

Some of the main signs and symptoms of depression are given in the box on page 286. These illustrate how depression affects thinking, feelings, behavior, and bodily functions. Read through the list looking for the signs that are yours, but remember at the same time that normal low mood shades gradually into depression, so if you have some of these signs and symptoms, you may not be "clinically" depressed.

Not everyone who is depressed has all of these symptoms, and for some people their depression will show in other ways. The list is given here to show the range of ways depression can affect you. When you have other symptoms as well as the depressed mood, it is important to recognize that this could be part and parcel of the same thing. Often it is not that there are many problems. There is one problem—and that is being depressed. There is no more point in blaming yourself, or others, if things like tiredness, irritability, and tension go with the depression than there would be for blaming yourself for feeling weak and lethargic when you have a fever.

Some of the Signs and Symptoms of Depression

Thinking

Inability to concentrate

Inability to make decisions

Loss of interest in the things going on around you, and in other people

Self-criticism: "I've made a mess of everything"

Self-blame: "It's all my fault"

Self-loathing: "I'm utterly useless"

Activities seem pointless

Pessimism: "This will never change," "there's nothing I can do"

Preoccupation with problems, failures, and bad feelings

Believing you deserve to be punished

Thinking about harming yourself

Feelings

Sadness, misery, unhappiness

Feeling overwhelmed by everyday demands, feeling burdened

Low confidence and poor self-esteem

Loss of pleasure, satisfaction, and enjoyment

Apathy, numbness

Feeling disappointed, discouraged, or hopeless

Feeling unattractive, or ugly

Helplessness

Irritability, tension, anxiety, and worry

Guilt

Behavior

Reduced activity levels: doing less than usual

Everything feels like an effort

Difficulty getting out of bed in the morning

Withdrawal—from people, work, relaxations, or pleasures

Bouts of restlessness

Sighing, groaning, crying

Bodily changes

Loss of appetite, or occasionally increased appetite

Disturbed sleep, especially waking early in the morning

Loss of interest in sex

Fatigue, lack of energy, or exhaustion

Inertia: inability to get going, dragging oneself around

Understanding Depression

There is no single simple theory that explains and accounts for all aspects of depression. Some experts favor explanations that take into account fluctuations in the biochemistry of the brain: others account for depression in terms of early childhood experiences. Countless other theories have been proposed. Some of these theories are of academic interest only given the present state of knowledge. However, there are some ideas that might be helpful to you in overcoming your depression.

DEPRESSION IS LOSS

Sigmund Freud saw depression as a reaction to *loss*. The idea that anxiety is a reaction to *threat* and depression a reaction to *loss* is one that has proved to be useful over the years. Freud was led to the idea of depression as loss through observing the similarities between mourning—the normal reaction to the loss of someone close to you—and depression. But in the case of many people, when they are depressed, there is no obvious loss in their lives. This led Freud to consider other less obvious losses that people with depression might be suffering.

The usefulness of this idea is that it helps you to think about what losses might be important in causing and sustaining the depression. The losses are not necessarily bereavements; they may be losses of status or hope or self-image. Ken became depressed after he suffered a small heart attack at the age of 52 years. He had always prided himself on his fitness. His depression was "mourning" the loss of his self-image as 100% fit and healthy.

Simon was a 65-year-old man who retired from his job as managing director of a chemical company. Eighteen months later he came to the clinic suffering from depression. He had never before been seriously depressed. The root of his depression stemmed from his loss of status. His sense of self-worth had been closely connected with his high status within the organization, and without his job he lost sight of his self-worth.

DEPRESSION AS AGGRESSION TURNED AGAINST YOURSELF

Laura was a mild-mannered woman, 35 years old, who was regularly plagued by feelings of depression. She hated arguments. When her husband shouted at the children, she would become quiet and leave the room. She described herself as the snail who would withdraw into the inner security of her shell. When she became depressed, she would say how useless and valueless she was, and how wonderful everyone around her seemed. Her mind at these times was full of thoughts about how worthless and bad she felt, and everything that happened only seemed to confirm that she was right. It appeared as though she never had a negative thought about anyone but herself. Her friends saw her as the kindest and gentlest of people, but also as something of a doormat.

Her husband really did not do his share of caring for the children, and would go out for a drink with his friends when his wife could have done with some help at home. Surely she sometimes felt angry with her husband? The answer was that she did, but it took her months of being seen regularly in the clinic before she admitted even a single negative thought about him. One day she came to the clinic feeling more than usually depressed. Her husband had been out with his friends three evenings in a row. Her therapist commented to her that this seemed unreasonable of him, and suddenly the dam burst. She launched into a tirade against her husband. Her anger surprised both herself and her therapist, and it marked the beginning of her journey out of depression. Her depression had masked her anger with her husband, concentrating the bad feelings inward on herself.

DEPRESSION AS A DARK FILTER

Being depressed is like seeing everything through a glass darkly: This is the theory behind cognitive therapy. Whether you are thinking about yourself, the world, or the future, everything appears in the same gloomy and depressing light. "Nothing ever goes right"; "I've been such a failure"; "I can't change anything, so there's no point in trying." People call "only out of a sense of obligation." When you make a mistake, or your mind wanders, it's "because I have lost the ability to do things properly"—and it seems to have gone for good. Thinking back, your memory is filled with a trail of failures, miseries, and losses and those things you once recognized as achievements or successes, your affections and friendships, seem to count for nothing at all. The memories are tinged with the color of depression.

Once the dark filter is there, you can no longer see anything in any other light. Negative thinking and depression go together: the low mood leads to negative thoughts and memories; the negative thoughts and memories lead to lower mood, and so on, in a cycle of sustained or worsening depression (see also Chapter 9).

DEPRESSION AS A BIOCHEMICAL CHANGE IN THE BRAIN

There is a danger that you will be too hard on yourself about getting depressed. This is a question of balance. To some extent you need to take responsibility for your depression as there are many changes you can make which can help you to bring it under control. But nevertheless, people differ in the extent to which they are prone to get depressed. Each of us has swings in mood, and it seems likely that this is partly due to differences between us in the precise biochemical makeup within our brains. Not all of this can be under voluntary control. It is sometimes helpful to treat your depression as if it were outside your control, and to treat yourself kindly just as you would if you had a bout of flu. Treating yourself kindly in this way can help you out of the depression and stop it from taking hold even when its cause is partly biological.

There has been a great deal of scientific work that attempts to understand the biochemical basis of depression. The evidence suggests that some kinds of depression can be caused by an abnormally low amount of two brain chemicals: noradrenaline and serotonin. These chemicals play an important part in the transmission of nerve impulses within the brain. The medication used to overcome depression ("antidepressants") helps to correct the abnormality by increasing these chemicals. Just as insulin is used to treat diabetes (which can be caused by a lack of insulin), so antidepressants *can* be used to treat severe depression.

SEASONAL AFFECTIVE DISORDER OR SAD

Some people feel depressed regularly during the winter months. There is some evidence that this is caused by a combination of genetic factors and the effect of sunlight on brain chemistry. It has been suggested that exposure to bright light, or to specific types of rays, can help to improve the mood of people affected by SAD, but the evidence on this point is not yet conclusive.

Perhaps There Are Payoffs for Your Depression

It may seem inappropriate, perhaps even cruel, to suggest that you may be gaining something from your depression. But there are advantages to depression, and if you fail to recognize these, you may get stuck when, in fact, you are able to help yourself out of the prison. A clue to the fact that you are gaining something important from the depression is that you find yourself giving reasons for not adopting the suggestions which others make. This is what Dorothy Rowe in her book *The Way Out of Your Prison* calls the "yes, but . . ." response. Every time someone makes a suggestion about something you might do that could help you reply, "yes, but . . . ," and your doubts prevent you from trying. So what possible advantages could there be to depression?

One possible advantage is that it could get you out of facing some of the things you are frightened about. Being depressed can save you from facing responsibilities which worry you; it can save you from carrying out tasks which you find stressful; it can block your need to make important changes—for example, in a relationship or at work. Your depression becomes the reason for not doing things that, for one reason or another, you do not want to do.

Although this could be one advantage of depression, in the long term it causes more problems than it solves. Failing to face these problems and responsibilities gradually deepens the depression because it leaves these problems and responsibilities unresolved.

Underlying the resistance to helping yourself out of your depression there is likely to be a *fear of change*. This is especially likely if the depression is long-standing and if this low mood has come both to determine what you can and cannot do—in effect, suffusing all aspects of your life including your relationships. So you could be holding the key to unlocking yourself from the prison of your depression. For example, your depression could be helping you to avoid certain problems, and holding you back from change. You may be less helpless, and the situation may be less hopeless, than it seems when you are under the influence of depression.

Kim was 27 years old, and a low mood had become the rule rather than the exception for her. She had been married for three years and as yet had no children. When she got married, Kim gave up her job as a personal assistant, because she and her husband planned to have a baby. But when, after a year, there was no sign of a pregnancy she became depressed. They decided that they should stop trying for a baby until she felt better. After another year her husband, Howard, again wanted them to try for a baby, but Kim felt that she was still too depressed. The question arose as to whether she should get a job in the meantime to help with the mortgage payments. Howard suggested that it might help with the loneliness Kim felt during the day. "Yes, but. . . ." The problem was that the kind of people she was likely to meet at work would not be the kind of people who would, she thought, supply her with the support and friendship she needed.

Kim had not worked for three years and the truth was that she was frightened that she could no longer be an effective secretary. And she was frightened of trying for children, because the first year of their marriage had been so stressful every time that her period proved yet again that she was not pregnant. She was frightened to go through all that again. She had vague but deep-seated worries that they might not be able to have a baby at all, and she was nervous of what would happen if she and her husband went to a doctor to ask for help.

So, the easiest thing was to go on being depressed and not to face the worries either about work or about having a baby. The key to unlock the prison of her depression was to confront at least one of these fears (see also Chapter 6).

The Time Course of Depression

When you are feeling depressed it is important to remember that moods swing up as well as down for psychological as well as for biological reasons. It is easy to lose sight of this fact when the walls of the prison press in, or when there seems to be no light at the end of the tunnel. The speed with which the upswings start is so variable that no two people are quite the same, and the same person may experience more than one kind of pattern at different times.

Before John found his feet in the building trade he spent ten years constantly changing jobs, feeling disillusioned about the choices he had made. Each spring he suffered a renewed bout of hopelessness, feeling that things would never improve. It was as if lost opportunities were accumulating and new beginnings were leaving him behind, and he began to dread the spring in anticipation of the start of the downward spiral. This expectation became almost self-fulfilling, but it completely changed when his career started to take off. Although he still had periods of low mood, these were no longer so regular, nor were they at their worst in the spring.

Helen's pattern was completely different. She had hardly known what the word depression meant, at least from the inside, until she was 47 and the children had all left home. Then suddenly her life seemed purposeless and empty. All the activities she used to become involved in now seemed pointless. The color of life was unremittingly gray, and occasional bursts of sunlight were so brief and unpredictable that sometimes she despaired of ever getting back to her old self. In her case the first episode of depression was the worst, like a dark and unfamiliar beast that she had no idea how to harness or tame. Gradually, helped by her family and by her doctor too, her mood lifted, and the darker periods grew shorter while the lighter ones grew longer.

So do not assume, when the roller coaster has taken you down once more, that each cycle will be like the last.

A Two-Part Strategy for Change

Whatever your pattern, there are two types of steps you can take to help yourself out of your depression: *long-term strategies* (p. 315) and *short-term strategies* (p. 294).

The long-term strategies involve thinking about how to make changes in a range of aspects of your life, which will make it less likely that you become depressed. These will put in place structures in your life that will help when you are depressed. The short-term strategies help you to dig yourself out of the slough of despond.

If, at the moment, you are in one of your deep depressions, then you will not be able to work on the longer-term strategies. You need to do some of the digging out before you can get to grips with the long term. But if, at the moment, your mood is not profoundly depressed, then this is a good time to work on the long term.

You should read both the following chapters, and pick those suggestions that seem the most helpful to you. It is our experience that different people are helped by different things. You may find further helpful suggestions in the first two parts of the book. We suggest that you scan through the headings looking for those parts to read more carefully.

Chapter Summary

It is normal for moods to swing up and down, and most people experience relatively severe depression from time to time. There is no need to feel helpless in the face of depression. There is much you can do to help yourself out of a trough.

No single theory explains everything about depression. Four main ideas can be helpful:

1. Depression is a reaction to loss.
2. Depression results from aggression turned inward.
3. Depression is seeing everything through a dark filter.
4. Depression is linked with biochemical changes in the brain.

Sometimes depression has advantages, and overcoming it may involve facing fears or difficulties. There are ways of doing this, step by step.

The cycles of depression have many different patterns, even when they afflict the same person.

Short-term strategies for change will help you out of depression. Long-term strategies will reduce your chances of future depression.

23

Digging Yourself Out of Depression

It's not easy facing up when your whole world is black.
—*Paint It Black*, The Rolling Stones

When you feel depressed, it can seem as if you will be stuck in the dark tunnel forever. Pessimism is the order of the day, and it colors your attempts to overcome the problem, just as it colors everything else. But this is an illusion wrought by the lens through which you see the world when you are depressed. We know that moods swing up as well as down, even though we lose sight of this fact when feeling at our worst, and there are many things you can do to speed the depression on its way. There are also things you can do to make it less likely that the depression will come back to plague you. So we have divided the ways of tackling depression into two sets of strategies: things that can be done immediately (described in this chapter) and things that are more helpful in the long term (described in the following chapter). Many of these suggestions are likely to be helpful to you, but probably not all. Each person's depression is to some extent individual, so pick and choose among these ideas, making use of those which help you most. Suggestions specifically for people who are feeling deeply depressed can be found on pages 310 to 311. Turn to these pages straight away if you think this applies to you, and then turn back to read the rest of this chapter.

Short-Term Strategies: Dealing with Depressive Episodes

There are three areas on which to work to help pull yourself out of the pit: your *activities*, your *thoughts*, and your *support systems*. Depression will try and undermine you as you help yourself to get better, and you need to be on the lookout for this. When you plan to do something helpful, the depressive thinking will throw blocks in the way of change, filling your mind with bleak thoughts: "There's no point in trying"; "It won't make any difference"; "I'm feeling too bad even to try." This kind of thinking blocks you from using your own resources and gets in the way of change.

The best way of helping yourself out of your depression is to focus on small changes that take you in the right direction. Do not look at the distant horizon; look toward the next bend in the road. Aim to put down your burden. Aim to feel *better* than you feel now, but don't think you will feel well again all at once. If you concentrate on making small changes, you will find the rest will take care of itself. To start with, adopt one strategy at a time. Work on each for about a week, before adding another, and develop ways of using them that suit yourself.

Work on Your Activities

Depression makes us sluggish and takes away our energy. It can be just as potent as the flu in making us withdraw into inactivity and this inactivity can get in the way of the healing process. The first way of helping yourself out of the slough of despond is to involve yourself once more in daily activities.

SET YOURSELF SIMPLE TASKS

Set yourself some simple tasks which, because of your depression, you are no longer doing. Do not worry if these tasks would normally seem simple, like writing a letter or making a telephone call, doing the shopping or ironing, fetching children from school or meeting with your colleagues. The fact that you are finding them difficult means that they are difficult for you at the moment, in just the same way that someone who has the flu may find it difficult to do things which would normally be straightforward. Be kind and realistic to yourself; acknowledge that you are depressed and that this makes a difference.

Those who are not much troubled by depression can adopt a rather unhelpful attitude: "Pull yourself together. Stop moaning and groaning, and get on with it." There is an element of value in this although the fundamental attitude is completely wrong. It is right to say that pushing yourself to do some of the things you dread or feel too tired to do will help to lift the depression. It is wrong to suggest that it is simple to do this, or that failing to do so is due to weakness of will. The attitude that is most helpful is to accept that you are suffering from depression, in rather the same way that you might accept that you are suffering from a bad cold, but then try and push yourself to doing a little more than you are doing at the moment.

Do not expect to find the activities you attempt to be enjoyable, even if you really like doing them when you are well. For example, because of your depression, you may have stopped meeting with friends over lunch, which is an activity you normally enjoy. When you are depressed it will probably feel somewhat pointless, you may not want people to see you feeling low, and you may tell yourself that you will be more of a liability than an asset. It is important to do it nonetheless, because it will be a first step in helping you out of your depression. As you reengage in the activities you have given up, the grip that the depression has over you will weaken. But this *is a* gradual process and the depression will not lift overnight.

THE DIARY OF DAILY ACTIVITIES

Keeping a diary of daily activities is especially useful when you are feeling depressed because it helps you to focus on how you are spending your time. It can be used in a variety of ways to counteract the inactivity and loss of energy that accompany depression. This is a method that was invented by Dr. Aaron Beck in the 1970s and has been successfully used by thousands of people. There are four main steps in using the diary of daily activities.

Step 1: Use the diary to find out how you spend your time. Divide up your diary so that you have a slot for each hour of the waking day, and for a few days fill in everything that you do. This is one way of counteracting the sabotaging effect of depressive thinking, which, when you look back over the day, tends to make you think that you did nothing much of anything. An example of such a diary of daily activities is shown on page 297.

Diary of daily activities. This is an example of an activity schedule which has been partly completed.

How do you spend your time?

	Friday, Oct 3	Saturday, Oct 4	Sunday, Oct 5
7-8 A.M.	Lying in bed awake	Made tea	
8-9	Get up late—no breakfast	Back to bed	
9-10	Bus to work	Wash, had breakfast	
10-11	Short meeting	Breakfast	
11-12	Letters and phone calls	Shopping	
12-1 P.M.	Letters and phone calls	Shopping	
1-2	Lunch in cafeteria	Shopping	
2-3	Started monthly report, minutes from meeting	Sandwich lunch	
3-4	Sorting out desk		
4-5	Left work early		
5-6	Watched TV news, had a drink		
6-7	Brother telephoned, started supper		
7-8	Supper		
8-9	Watched video, had a cup of coffee		
9-10	Video		
10-11	Put clothes in washer, washed up, did chores		
11-12	Detective story in bed		

Step 2: Rate your activities every day for *mastery* and *pleasure*. Go back over the diary at the end of each day and focus on two aspects. First, pick out those things you found particularly difficult to do, such as dragging yourself out of bed to get ready for work. If this was difficult and yet you did it, then you should give yourself credit, even if you got to work later than usual. Give yourself a *mastery* credit rating, using a 0 to 10 scale, to acknowledge that you overcame the difficulty. The rating should be a measure of how difficult the thing is for you to do *at the moment,* not how difficult it would be if you were not depressed. A rating of 8 to 10 is for very difficult things. A rating of 4 to 7 for moderately difficult things. Anything that was difficult needs a rating even if you rate it at 1 to 3. Ordinary activities are *much* harder when you are depressed. This is not your fault. It is a fact about depression.

When you have done this, go through the diary once more, picking out those activities or times when you were engaged in something that you found relatively enjoyable or pleasurable, and give these activities a rating for *pleasure*. Again, use a 0 to 10 scale. Even small amounts of pleasure should be rated. You might write P=4 beside watching an absorbing television program or P=6 for the time you escaped from the family and soaked in the bath. Looking back from the depressed perspective, it is easy to forget completely that anything remotely pleasurable happened. Do not agonize over the precise rating for *mastery* and *pleasure*. Put down the number that seems most appropriate.

Step 3: Troubleshoot. Think about how to increase the amount of mastery and pleasure in your day. The things that you find difficult and the things that you enjoy will be particular to you. Use the questions in the following box to help you think about how to increase these things for yourself.

Questions to ask yourself about mastery:

How do I feel if I make no effort to do the things that are difficult?
How do I feel if I do them, and give myself credit for doing them?
Which are the major trouble spots in my day?
What could I do to make it easier to master these difficult times?

Questions to ask yourself about pleasure:

What things are most enjoyable at the moment?
How could I do more of these things?
What could I do to increase the amount of pleasure I have each day?
What sorts of things used to give me pleasure?
Are there things I have stopped doing that I used to enjoy?
Copy these questions out, and keep them where you can find them when you need them.

Step 4: Plan. Use the diary of daily activities to help you plan ahead. Now you have the facts in front of you, you cannot be misled by the fantasies induced by feeling depressed. Use the facts to guide your future activities. Here are five ideas about how to do this:

1. Schedule more pleasant events: big ones such as an outing with a friend, and small ones such as taking a leisurely bath. If you find this difficult, turn to Chapter 7. Depressed people sometimes think they

do not deserve to enjoy themselves, or feel guilty about doing things they enjoy, especially after a day when they have found it difficult to do as much as they used to do. Use your diary to help you sidestep the guilt trap.

2. Schedule those activities that increase your energy level, like walking to the store, cutting the grass, or taking the dog out. The sense of fatigue that goes with depression can increase the less you do, and the more you withdraw. Becoming involved in daily activities can help to energize you, and so can regular exercise.

3. Look for activities that you find relatively absorbing. Being absorbed in something can bring much relief from a depressed mood. This is worth having, and building on, even if the relief is temporary at first. If concentration is hard for you, reading may not be absorbing, but looking at a magazine or watching a video might be.

4. Look at your diary and think about how you are using your time. Some people lose their sense of direction when they become depressed, and their activities become progressively more disorganized. If this happens to you, it could help to establish a daily routine for yourself. Other people become depressed when they feel completely stuck in a rut, and they can benefit from shaking up the routine a bit, even if this sounds somewhat alarming at first.

5. Think about the balance between duties and pleasures in your daily activities. Good moods are almost certain to ebb away if you live on a diet of pure duty without pleasure. This is counterproductive because depression interferes with your ability to carry out duties while feeling better makes it easier to do them better.

Work on Your Thoughts

Valerie was a 20-year-old university student. Like most students she did some of her work assignments better than others. She came to the clinic because of depression. She had had several bouts of low mood over the previous two years, and these episodes were getting longer and worse. When her mood was low, she always had good reasons for being depressed. For example, she would say that her work was going badly, and would cite as proof a low mark which she had received for one of her assignments. Even the vacation times were bad: when she had arranged to meet a friend for a meal before going to a film, the friend had turned up so late that there was no time to eat; and the film had been dull anyway. The examples which she gave were accurate in themselves, but they were highly selective. The fact was that she had also done some work assignments which had gone well, and she had recently had a hiking vacation during which she had made a new friend.

The story of Valerie illustrates something you may well have noticed about yourself and that has been found, in research studies, again and again: that being depressed affects what we remember. And it affects memory in a way that maintains the depressed mood. When we are depressed, we tend to remember the bad things that have happened to us, and these memories confirm our depression.

It is not only memory that is affected in this way. Our judgments are colored by our mood too. We will blame ourselves out of all proportion for things we have done wrong: one depressed patient felt that she was a wicked person because she forgot to give her son his weekly pocket money.

These psychological facts have led to what is known as the *cognitive model of depression,* which was developed by Aaron Beck.[1] What this says is that there is a very close relationship between feelings and thoughts. When we are in a low mood, our thoughts and memories will be selectively bad. This will have the effect of making our mood even darker. Our thoughts get worse and our mood follows, and so we enter a downward spiral of increasing depression.

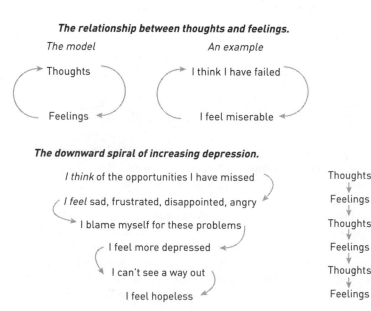

The relationship between thoughts and feelings.

The model   *An example*

Thoughts   I think I have failed

Feelings   I feel miserable

The downward spiral of increasing depression.

I think of the opportunities I have missed   Thoughts
I feel sad, frustrated, disappointed, angry   Feelings
I blame myself for these problems   Thoughts
I feel more depressed   Feelings
I can't see a way out   Thoughts
I feel hopeless   Feelings

This cognitive model leads to a particular kind of treatment called *cognitive therapy*. Essentially, this therapy concentrates on helping people to recognize and to reexamine their thoughts to get rid of the negative, depressive bias. The downward spiral is reversed by working to change the negative patterns of thinking. As thinking becomes more positive, the depression starts to lift, and produces more positive thoughts and feelings, until the downward spiral is converted into an upward spiral.

One of the most valuable aspects of cognitive therapy is that you can learn how to do it yourself. The techniques of cognitive therapy are useful in helping you to achieve a good mood whether you are climbing out of depression, trying to overcome anxiety, or dealing with a mixture of emotions. They provide some of the most useful skills for helping to develop and maintain a good mood. In Chapter 9 we explain how you can make use of the method of cognitive therapy to control your negative thinking patterns. If you want to use this method, you should read Chapter 9 after you have read this one. In this chapter we focus on its use for depression, but ideas in both these chapters will be helpful to you.

Applying Cognitive Therapy to Depression

BREAKING UP PATTERNS OF NEGATIVE THINKING

Ella's depression had become pervasive. She felt on the verge of tears most of the time, and worse at the end of each day when she sat at home, alone, thinking about the relationship that had gone wrong and all the failures and mistakes she had made at work that day. She had also been too tired to bother to shop, so there was nothing much to eat in her home, and everywhere she looked she saw the signs that she had lost her grip. The whole place seemed to her to be a mess—just like her life. The unhappy thoughts churned around and around in her head, leaving her no peace. Ella was stuck in a stream of negative thinking. The longer it continued, the worse she felt. She thought that she "ought to be able to think it through," even though it seemed to her that the same record was playing endlessly, and painfully, inside her head and getting absolutely nowhere.

Distraction is the first line of defense. Ella needed a break from her negative thinking. She needed to interrupt the internal dialogue and to clear a small bit of mental space, and the easiest, quickest way to do this is to use distraction. Fill the mind with something else, and give yourself a rest from dwelling on unhappy thoughts. This will provide some respite from the ruminative pattern, and lift your mood just enough to allow you to start problem-solving instead.

Ella turned on the television. She made herself listen to a program for a short while and then she realized she was thirsty. She made a cup of tea and sat down to drink it. She looked around at all the papers in the room, and wondered how many there were: newspapers, cards, used envelopes, unanswered letters, a shopping list, magazines, and so on. She suddenly realized that she was no longer listening to the television, or to the thoughts about the things that were making her so depressed, but instead was wondering if she could find something to put all the rubbish in.

There are many ways of distracting yourself. Here are five ways that others have found useful:

1. *Try sensory awareness exercises.* What can you see, or hear, or feel, at the moment? Pay attention carefully to each of the senses in turn.
2. *Describe an object.* This is a way of forcing your attention onto the outside world. Pick any object you can see; a window or a table would do. Imagine that your life depended on being able to describe it precisely, in every possible detail, to someone else. Test yourself in as many ways as you can think of (draw it, write down a description, memorize it, and so on).
3. *Involve yourself in an activity.* Choose something undemanding but as absorbing as you can manage. Reading may be too hard to concentrate on if you feel very depressed, so a physical activity like tidying up, knitting, or gardening may be easier. Stop and think: what activities might be the right ones for you?
4. *Recite a poem or sing a song to yourself.* Think of nursery rhymes, or poems you learned in school, or jingles from advertisements, or Christmas carols. Remember songs you enjoyed with friends or songs from a show you have seen. Concentrate on trying to remember the words.
5. *Play counting games.* Count things you can see, or count backward, or say multiplication tables, or remember telephone numbers.

What happened to Ella when she first distracted herself by turning on the television reflects a common pattern. First, she tried to listen to what was being said, but could not concentrate very well. Nevertheless, the TV interrupted her thinking pattern just enough for other things to come to her attention: she noticed she was thirsty. This helped her into a more active mode: she made a cup of tea. Then, as she sat down with it, still not really concentrating on much, she found herself wondering about how to clear up the mess. She was starting to solve problems. Becoming aware of the way in which this process works helped Ella to use it more often, and more effectively.

SWATTING THE "NATs"

Negative Automatic Thoughts (or NATs) buzz around inside the head when you feel low: "It's pointless"; "I'm no good"; "Why bother?" The bites from these NATs can depress your mood even more. It's important to swat these NATs, and strategies for dealing with them are described in more detail on pages 80 to 87. An illustration is given here to show how they can be used when you are feeling depressed.

Step 1: Identifying problematic thoughts. Ella did not find this exercise easy. She was so immersed in her distress that she could not see things clearly. Besides, everything seemed so obviously bad to her that she could not see the point of trying to look for any other points of view. Nevertheless, she asked herself the *"Key Questions"* on page 78:

- What went through my mind at the time?
- How am I seeing things now?
- What is it about this that matters to me?
- What does this situation mean to me?
- What does it mean about me?

This is what she wrote on her Thought Record.
   Situation: Coming home after a day at work
   Feelings: Hopeless and sad
   Thoughts: It's all my fault. There's nothing I can do about it. My whole
       life is a mess.

Step 2: Looking for other perspectives. Ella decided she would try filling out an "Alternative Diary" form (p. 82), and wrote each thought down separately. She then asked herself, "Is there another way of seeing things?" She worked on the last thought first, as this seemed to her to be the central one. This is what she wrote:
Automatic thought: My whole life is a mess.
Alternative points of view: I've still got a job. It's only been like this since the relationship broke up, so I must have been able to hold things together before this. Maybe it's not surprising to feel sad right now, but that doesn't mean the feelings won't ever change. There's certainly a mess in the flat, and I'm not working well, and I've lost the person I cared about

(the facts of the case), but I've still got friends and my music. This certainly is a rough patch, but everyone has rough patches from time to time. If I really take a look at my *whole* life I can see that I am probably exaggerating how bad this is.

When doing this exercise Ella had many doubts and queries. In particular, she found that for every new way of thinking she could also find some reasons for discounting it: that giveaway phrase "Yes, but . . ." kept jumping into her mind. "Yes, but none of that really matters. What matters is how I feel right now." When this happens it is important not to get sidetracked. Write down the reservation, or "yes, but," and come back to it later in exactly the same way. After all, it is only another NAT, or automatic thought, and can be reexamined using the same strategy.

Learning how to reexamine *Negative Automatic Thoughts*—the NATs—when you are depressed is difficult. We recommend that you practice doing this using the two other thoughts that Ella identified: "It's all my fault" and "There's nothing I can do about it." It is often easier to work out where other people are going wrong than to see one's own mistakes and blind spots, so this is an especially useful exercise if you are feeling low.

Key Questions

Questions about thoughts:
What other points of view are there? How would someone else think about this? How else could I think about it? How would I think about this if I were feeling better?

Questions about reality:
What are the facts of the case? How can I find out which way of thinking fits the facts best? What is the evidence?

Questions about crooked thinking:
Could I be making a mistake in the way I am thinking? Am I thinking straight? Am I using one of the thirteen kinds of crooked thinking (pp. 78–80)? Am I pressuring myself? Or using the language of the extremist?

Questions about coping:
What is the worst that could happen? How bad is this going to get? What can I do when that happens? How can I get help?

The *key questions* to ask yourself are in the box above.

Be specific. Depressed people tend to think in a rather vague and general way, as if the shaded, depressed view of the world obscured their detailed vision. It is therefore particularly helpful to focus on specific facts of the case when looking for alternative points of view. For example, instead of saying "I've still got friends," name the people with whom you are friendly, and think of specific things that you have done together in better times, or specific plans that you can make with them for the future.

If you write the key questions for identifying problematic thoughts (p. 78) and for reexamining NATs (p. 80) on opposite sides of a small card (or photocopy pp. 87–88 from Chapter 9), you can keep them at hand for whenever you need them. Answers to the key questions help you keep in touch with the facts, and to avoid some of the distorted perspectives of depressed thinking. The most likely mistake that the depressed person is making is mistaking feelings for facts: supposing that because it feels this bad, everything really is this bad. Bit by bit, start to gather all the information together so that you can take a new look at it.

LOOKING AT BELIEFS AND ATTITUDES—THE HALL OF MIRRORS

Our attitudes to ourselves tend to be distorted, but the distortion is not all in one direction. When Brittany, age six, went to the fair she visited the *Hall of Mirrors*, and she was fascinated by the different ways in which her body was distorted. In one mirror she looked tall and thin; in another short and fat. Other mirrors, however, distorted some parts of her body in one way and others in another way. Her head was made tall and thin; her chest long and wide; and her legs shrunk until her feet seemed almost to spring directly from her hips.

The distorted beliefs we have of ourselves can be very similar. Most of us operate in (at least) two ways: we can be extraordinarily critical of ourselves, or we can give ourselves outrageous leniency. We may do first one and then the other, even though they seem contradictory. We may put our own interests above those of others, and yet place our self-worth well beneath that of others. Indeed, perhaps one distorted view springs from the other. Because of the deep fear that we are inferior to others, we might try and boost our self-image through bragging and attempting to get the better of others.

At the root of depression there is usually a distorted view of oneself. To help you to see yourself more clearly, it may be helpful to think about what you would say about yourself if you were on the outside looking in: as if you could be another person and take a thoroughly objective look at yourself. When Ella did this, she uncovered one of her unwritten assumptions: "I can't be happy if I'm on my own—if I do not have a close relationship."

Here are some other common beliefs: "I must do well at everything I take on"; "Unless I am doing something useful my whole life is worthless"; "I'm no good unless people like me"; "If someone rejects me, it's because I'm not good enough." Beliefs such as these can be questioned and reexamined using the same methods as those used for examining automatic thoughts (pp. 80–87).

Even though it is difficult, it is important that you try to look at yourself with compassion and objectivity. Particularly when depressed, we are inclined to be excessively hard on ourselves. We whip ourselves, saying how useless and worthless we are. Take a *compassionate* view toward yourself, as you would toward someone else, and you will find it easier to develop a sense of ultimate trust in yourself.

THE BLACK DOG: TAMING THE BEAST BY GIVING IT A LABEL

Winston Churchill suffered from recurrent, short-lived depressions. He gave them a name: *the black dog*, a name that had been used by Samuel Johnson before him, and has been used by many others since. Labeling the depression helped him to cope with it and to accept it, knowing that in due course it would go away. Such labeling helps to domesticate the depression so that it becomes, if not a friend, at least an enemy you know and for which, perhaps, you even feel some affection.

When relatively short-lived, recurrent depressions attack you, it may be best to wall them off—to limit or contain them. Then they will take the shortest course. Say to yourself, "Ah, it's my depression again. It will pass away soon as it always does; I've just got to keep going." This is especially helpful for people who tend to get depressed about getting depressed, which is a very common problem and adds insult to injury.

A similar technique is used in mindful meditation (see *Further Reading*, p. 515). Such meditation encourages continual awareness of the present. Your moods and feelings are recognized, acknowledged, and accepted. In mindful meditation your feelings of depression would be quietly acknowledged. It would be as if you nodded acquaintance with your feelings, but your being would not be absorbed by the depression, or by regrets about the past or hopelessness about the future. Rather than being wholly dominated by depression, the aim is to become aware of depression but from a stance which is at one remove, and which helps to keep present feelings in perspective.

Use Your Support Systems

George Brown and Tirrel Harris[2] carried out an important study into the causes of depression in women. They studied almost 1,000 women and looked carefully at their mood and some of the factors which might affect it. A major finding was that a close confiding relationship was the single most effective protection against depression. This central finding probably applies as much to men as to women.

If there is someone with whom you can talk about how you are feeling, then do not shy away from letting them know. If you can't think of anyone in whom you could confide then consider seeing your doctor, or finding a support group.

There are many things that make it difficult to tell someone else you feel depressed—such as feeling embarrassed or worried about bothering them; feeling guilty, as if being depressed was your fault and a sign of weakness; and living in a world in which talking about yourself, and especially about your feelings, is treated as if it were taboo. Nevertheless, "a friend in need is a friend indeed," and if you are depressed, you are in need. A friend can help you, in many ways, to overcome the depression. It is, first of all, very helpful just to have the support: to know that there is someone who realizes how you are feeling and who cares. Talking with a friend also gives you the chance to think about why you are depressed and about what problems in your life have got you down. The friend can help you to find ways of tackling these problems. A friend can also provide you with a different and, probably at the moment, a less distorted perspective, both on your problems and on your views of yourself. A friend can help to encourage you in carrying out the activities that you have chosen to do.

One of the ways which, as therapists, we help people who are depressed is not through any arcane skill but by being essentially a friend—a professional rather than a personal friend—but nevertheless a friend. And the two things we do which are of particular value are to be a sounding board—to listen and reflect various perspectives—and to be someone to whom our client "reports back." Do not underestimate the power of this reporting back. When a depressed person decides, for example, to start meeting friends over lunch once more, something she stopped doing when she became depressed, the chance of her carrying this through is greatly enhanced if she knows that she will be reporting back to her therapist on how she got on.

Friends can fulfill this role as long as they know that you want them to help in this way. Choose one or two friends whom you think are in the best position to help you. This may include your special partner, if you have one, but sometimes a partner is too close to your problems, and perhaps too much a part of them, to be the ideal friend to help you out of your depression. When you have decided who can help you best, let them know that you are depressed and discuss how you feel, and how you see the problems, as freely as you feel able. It might be a good idea to ask them to read this chapter, including the section below (p. 311) "Supporting a Friend Who Is Depressed." But do respect your friend's position. While a good friend will want to help you, your depression may be a burden and the person you would like to have support from may not be able to give you as much support as you would like. If your friends make it clear that this is the case, then you need to respect the limits that they want to place on how much support they give you.

Thoughts of Harming Yourself

When depressed you may have thoughts of harming yourself. This is quite common. It does not mean that you are "going mad"; but you do need to take the thoughts seriously. *Tell someone else about your thoughts:* a friend, or your doctor. Do *not* be afraid of talking these thoughts over with someone else. Many people are reluctant to mention them for fear that others will disapprove, or fail to understand, or for fear that talking about them may actually make it easier to put them into effect. In fact, talking about thoughts of harming yourself usually brings some relief.

If you feel like putting these into effect, or making plans, then seek help at once, and promise yourself that at any time when you really do feel at risk of harming yourself, you will immediately talk to someone about how you feel.

If the thoughts are vaguer—more a feeling that life and its problems are too much for you at present—try to clarify them. The following three questions might help you to do this:

- What would prevent me from putting any plans into effect?
- What would I like to be able to do, supposing that the depression lifts?
- Which of my problems are so bad that no solution could ever be found?

You may find it helpful to discuss these questions with someone else. Throughout these low periods, hang on to the fact that it is your depression that is talking, and your depression will eventually lift.

When to See Your Doctor

Do not be shy of sharing your feelings with others whom you trust, and sometimes you will find it helpful to discuss these feelings with your doctor. If you feel you are seriously depressed, or have regular bouts of depression, and you would like to talk about how you are with your doctor, then do not hesitate to do so: you have nothing to lose and may gain a lot. To some extent this depends on how you feel, the other supports that you have, and the relationship you have with your doctor. But there are times when it is wise to see your doctor even if your first inclination is not to go. Professional help and medication can sometimes be of great benefit. Here are some guidelines that can help you decide whether it is time to see a doctor:

1. If you are so profoundly depressed that it is seriously interfering with your work or family life.
2. If those close to you think that you should see your doctor. It is a feature of depression that you cannot judge objectively how you are. If those around you are sufficiently worried to think that you might be helped by a professional, then they are more likely to be right than you are at the moment.
3. If you are consistently waking more than an hour earlier than usual and feeling particularly miserable at that time. Disturbances in physiological functioning (e.g., sleep and appetite) are good indications that medication might help you.
4. See a doctor if you are having some bizarre experiences, such as hearing voices when there is no one there.
5. If you are seriously considering harming yourself or doing away with yourself, see a doctor immediately.
6. If your mood swings both up and down, so that in addition to becoming very depressed you sometimes become very "high," doing things which others consider excessively extravagant, and which when your mood is normal you realize were excessive, it is important to see a doctor. This is called "manic-depressive" illness, or "bipolar depression," because it has two poles: a depressed, underactive pole

and a manic, overactive pole. Medications can be particularly useful in helping to prevent both the deep depression and the excessive highs.

Your doctor may prescribe antidepressant medication for you, and this is very likely to be helpful. It is also useful to think of yourself as working at the problem from two angles: the biochemical one, which is helped by taking medication, and the psychological one, which is helped by working on your activities, your thoughts, and your support systems. The two approaches go well hand in hand. You should not think that, because you have approached the problem in one way, the other way will not also be helpful. Combined methods of treatment for depression can be very effective.

Deep Depression

If you are currently suffering a deep depression, you may not be able to make use of all of the techniques described. They may be too complex for you at the moment. The purpose of this section is to help you focus on the essentials. When you are a little better, read or reread this chapter and make use of the more complex techniques. It is a part of depression to feel hopeless about the future. That means that severely depressed people feel that they will never get better. If this is how you feel at the moment, then *hold onto the fact that your depression will eventually lift.* If you are in one of the troughs, you will in time come out of it. We do not want to trivialize the depression in any way, and we do not underestimate the utter despair that you may feel. Glib reassurance is banal; but time is a healer.

If you are currently imprisoned within a deep depression, there are several things you can do to help yourself.

- *Seek professional help.* Trying to defeat the depression on your own may be taking on too much. Medication and professional therapy are likely to be great value.
- *Do simple things and give yourself credit.* If you are severely depressed, nothing that you do at the moment will be pleasurable. Indeed, you are probably finding it a struggle to do almost anything. Even the simple chores of everyday life—preparing meals, getting washed and dressed, getting up in the morning—can seem like hard work. This is all part of the depression. Do not blame yourself for

these feelings. Instead, *set yourself simple tasks and give yourself credit when you do them.* This is the stage to start using a diary of daily activities (p. 296).

- *Reduce tasks to manageable proportions.* If you approach the things you have set yourself to do with the same standards that you would use when feeling good, you will run the risk of failing at your set task, and blame yourself for not being able to function in the way that you usually would. But would you blame someone with bronchitis for not being able to sing a song? When very depressed, it can feel as if you are shouldering all the burdens of the world. Everything is an effort. Everything takes more time and an amount of energy far greater than seems available. No wonder you think: "I won't be able to do this"—and are tempted to give up trying. Set yourself much smaller tasks instead. What matters is that you do *something,* rather than nothing. Set your objectives low enough to be sure you can succeed.
- *Do not try to do too much.* To some extent you must let yourself, as it were, be carried along by the depression and float along with it until you reach shallower waters. If you try too hard to defeat it, you will become dismayed and will blame yourself for what you will then see as your failure. This will only make you feel worse about yourself and deepen the depression. Deep depression is like quicksand: if you struggle too much, you will only dig yourself in further.

Supporting a Friend Who Is Depressed

If a close friend is suffering with depression, then your support, if given in the right way, can be particularly helpful. If that friend is very close, your partner for example, you may be finding it especially difficult. Living close to a depressed person engenders ambiguous and complex feelings. Part of you will feel sympathy and a desire to help; part of you is likely to feel frustrated and irritated. You may make what seem perfectly sensible and straightforward suggestions which are resisted on what seem to be totally inadequate grounds, and you may get your head bitten off for trying to be helpful. Yet despite this, you can see that your friend is deeply unhappy and needs help and support.

When helping someone else, you may yourself need some support: someone with whom you can talk. But make sure that you do not break any confidences. Depressed people who open up to others will need to know that they can talk in confidence about these things that they would not like anyone else to know.

One of the most difficult things in trying to help is that it is easy to become increasingly unsympathetic. Depressed friends and relatives may seem alternately pathetic and unreasonably irritable. They may be quite hard to be with, different from their normal selves and even quite unlikeable. It is because of this that it is vitally important to understand the effects of depression, and the differences in personality that seem to accompany it. Hang onto the fact that, underneath the mask of depression, people you have known and liked remain unchanged. Sooner or later, the depression will pass and they will once again return to their former selves.

You may have been trying to help but finding that all your help appears to be rejected. What, you may be wondering, is the point of giving support? This is when it is important to know just how valuable is the fact that you are there, that despite the apparent rejection of all your attempts to help, you have not, emotionally, run away. It may not be obvious now, but in the long run the support you are giving by simply tolerating the person when depressed is providing the framework within which recovery can grow. Try not to overestimate the speed of recovery, even when you can see clearly that it has started. There will be intermittent breaks in the clouds and black patches to go through before the sky clears again.

Encourage your friend to read this and the previous chapter, if they have not already done so, and possibly the books recommended in the *Further Reading* at the end of the book. This will help you both to clarify your role, and will give your friend some ideas about what action to take. The two main ways in which you can help, in addition to simply being there and not rejecting your friend, are: to act as a sounding board; and to act as a listener to whom your friend can report.

You cannot expect to be an expert counselor, but you can use some of the well-known principles of counseling. We have used the words "sounding board" to emphasize one of the important points: your role is not to solve other people's problems for them; not, on the whole, to give advice. Your role is to listen, and to reflect honestly on what you have understood. It is to help clarify what has been said, to help establish the various options. Try and help people when they are depressed to decide what specific activities they want to set themselves and then act as someone to whom they can bring a progress report. Give encouragement to carry out these activities. However, it is not your role to use persuasion. Often when trying to help someone who is depressed, one feels helpless because one cannot solve the problems. But solving problems is *their* responsibility. Your role is to act as a sounding board. Do not think that you are failing because you are not solving problems. Indeed, if you imposed your solutions, it would be unlikely to work in the long term.

Do not try and force people to talk to you. Everyone has a right to privacy and a right not to tell, just as you too have the right not to be used as a support. If you are finding that trying to give support is too painful, or if *you* are not able to give it, for whatever reason, then you have the right to say so.

Related Chapters in This Book

Chapter 9, Keeping Things in Perspective. It is important to read this as well if you are working on your thoughts.

Chapter 10, Building Self-Confidence and Self-Esteem. Many people who are depressed think badly about themselves and can be helped by learning how to build up their confidence and self- esteem.

Chapter 18, Getting the Better of Anxiety and Worry. Sometimes anxiety and depression go together, and sometimes when depression lifts, it leaves you feeling worried about how to take up the reigns again, so this chapter may also be helpful.

Chapter 25, Loss and Bereavement. Depression and loss, even without bereavement, may go hand in hand. Some of the ideas in this chapter might be helpful to anyone with depression.

Chapter Summary

When you feel depressed, hold on to the idea that moods swing up as well as down, and focus on the short-term strategies that can make you feel better:

1. *Work on your activities.* Keeping active is helpful, even though it is harder to do when you are depressed.
2. *Work on your thoughts.* Depressed thinking keeps you stuck. Learning how to look at things differently helps you to get moving again.
3. *Work on your support systems.* Try not to be reluctant to ask others for help and support. Depression is so common that many of them will understand.

If you feel seriously depressed, start working on your activities first. The chapter also contains important guidelines concerning:

1. Thoughts of harming yourself
2. When to see your doctor
3. Deep depression
4. Supporting a friend who is depressed

24

How to Become Less Vulnerable to Depression

The Fundamental Importance of Long-Term Strategies

It is normal and natural to miss people when they are not there, or occasionally to feel melancholy or sad. Experiencing the full range of emotions is a normal part of life. People often use the word "depression" to describe these sad episodes, but serious depression, as we explain in Chapter 22, is different. It weighs you down and diverts you from the mainstream of life. The aims of this chapter are to help you to reduce the depth of your depressive swings, and to help to protect you from serious depression. If at the moment you are in a seriously depressive phase, then you need to focus on helping to restore yourself to normal (Chapter 23). But it is unwise to ignore your depression during the good periods because this is precisely when you can work most effectively on those things that make you vulnerable to further episodes.

Low mood has both *physical* and *psychological* causes, and for most people there will be several contributory causes of each type. These can add up, so tackle any which can be affected, even those which you do not think are of major importance. As with stress, it can be the straw that breaks the camel's back and attention to detail pays off. There are *five strategies* that help to prevent future depression.

Strategy 1: Attend to the Basics of Sleep, Diet, and Exercise

Do not ignore the fundamental physiological factors that can contribute to low mood. If you sleep badly, fail to eat well, and allow yourself to fall into poor shape physically, you become more susceptible to low mood because daily activities drain away your resources and more quickly get you down. Poor *sleep* is a common consequence of low mood, but it can also contribute to making you vulnerable. During periods of depression there may be little that you can do about poor sleep directly: you may need to focus instead on overcoming the depression. But at times when your mood is relatively good, make sure that you develop sensible sleeping habits. In Chapter 30 we describe many ways in which you can improve your sleep.

Be careful, too, about *alcohol.* This can be a particular problem for those who are prone to depression. In the short term alcohol can help to hide problems and worries. The relaxation and warm glow of confidence which alcohol can activate are, however, skin deep. Below the surface the problems lie, developing and growing in the dark. Eventually they burst forth, bringing with them a depression that is deeper and more intractable than it would otherwise have been. If alcohol could be a problem for you, turn to Chapter 29.

Excessive *dieting* can make you irritable, depressed, tired, and weak. It is common, in our culture, for women to feel better about themselves when they feel happy about their weight and shape, and are able to control what they eat. For some, however, self-esteem can become much too closely bound up with physical appearance and with diet. If this is the case for you, then read Chapter 31.

Exercise protects against episodes of depression and can help to build up physical stamina and energy. It can also temporarily lift your mood and provide a brief respite from depression.

Strategy 2: Clarify Your Values and Goals

If you are prone to depression, then you need to look at your goals and values and at how you spend your time. One of the major reasons for recurrent low mood is that there is a mismatch between what you really value and what you do. Instead of this mismatch making itself obvious, it becomes manifest as general depression.

Derek was apparently very successful. He had done well in his university studies, and after his degree he trained as an investment adviser, working in a major city. He earned a great deal of money, but still he suffered from recurrent depression. He sought professional help. During the therapy it became clear that he did not value the kind of success he had attained. He castigated himself for being selfish and wanted to feel that his work was more directly of benefit to others. That is what he valued. He started to look for other jobs. A position was advertised which would make use of his financial skills working for a housing association. Although the salary was very much less than he was making at the time, he applied for the job because he was convinced that happiness in his work depended on doing work which he valued. He got the job, and two years later, although his moods continued to go up and down, he did not experience anything like the depth of depression that had previously been his frequent experience.

You might think that Derek was lucky, and also that he had many advantages that others do not have, which, of course, is true. But thinking about your values if you are stuck and feeling depressed is not just a luxury. Janet was working as an office cleaner when she found herself in a similar situation. What she valued in her work was the opportunity to meet people and to talk to them, but arriving as others left to work on her own made her feel like a drudge at work as well as at home. She found a new job at a local bakery which suited her much better, and as her depression lifted her confidence and her self-esteem grew.

If you have not yet written out your own personal statement of values and goals (described on p. 33 in Chapter 5), we recommend that you do this. It will help you to evaluate whether what you are doing in your work and in your personal life is in tune with your values, and if it is not, then it may help you to work out which sorts of changes are likely to help you move away from depression.

Strategy 3: Put Pleasures into Life

Depression goes hand in hand with low self-esteem and even self-loathing. People prone to depression are often kind, thoughtful, and altruistic but yet do not value themselves highly, and they frequently downgrade themselves by denying themselves pleasures. Even when their mood is normal, they often feel that they do not deserve to do enjoyable things. They are not worth it, and other people's needs always come first.

Some parents can be like this. They put their children's needs so much above their own that they give themselves no personal time and space. Ron and Miriam used to enjoy going out once a week dancing and meeting with a couple of friends for a drink. Then they had a baby girl. For three years they never had an evening out together. They could have arranged babysitting, at least occasionally. Ron went out to work so he, at least, had some space for himself away from his family. But Miriam felt that it would be wrong to go out and enjoy herself in case her daughter woke up while she was out and needed her. She became increasingly miserable and irritable, and her relationship with Ron became strained. At this point Miriam saw her doctor. He made time to talk with them both and to discuss their situation. It rapidly became clear to them all that Ron and Miriam had lost the time alone with each other that they used to enjoy before their daughter was born. They agreed to go out together once a month, and the space that this gave them greatly improved both her mood and their relationship. This small change in their routine had an enormous impact on the whole family.

Even if at the moment you do not think that you deserve to enjoy yourself, make sure that you do things that you like doing. However busy you are, you need to make some time to indulge yourself: a little of what you fancy does you good. Present pleasure will help to protect you from future depression. Indeed, putting pleasures into life is one of the basic strategies for good mood (Chapter 7).

Strategy 4: Do Not Put All Your Eggs in One Basket

Nothing goes well all the time. Everyone experiences occasions when work, or some aspect of work, is going badly—when there are difficulties with close relationships, when a hobby ceases to be fulfilling, or when life seems to be full of problems. If all our self-esteem, therefore, is bound up in just one aspect of our lives there will be times when we become very vulnerable. Think about your own depression. Is it closely bound up with how things are going in just one aspect of your life? Is it, for example, when your work seems to be going badly that your mood becomes low? If the pattern of your depression suggests a close connection with just one part of your life, then it is likely that you have too many eggs in this one basket.

In order to protect yourself from such dependency, it is wise to have several parts to your life: friends, family, work, hobbies, and interests, both inside and outside the home, both social and solitary. Each part contributes to your self-esteem. At those times when one part of your life does not seem to be going well, you can gain comfort and support from other parts.

Strategy 5: Build Up Supportive Relationships

Being able to confide in someone else, whether a relative, partner, or friend, is one of the most important forms of protection from becoming depressed when something bad happens. If you do not have a close supporting relationship, or if your friends do not provide you with the kind of emotional support which helps to protect you from depression, then it will be useful to look at how you could begin to build up such supports.

Building up supportive relationships takes time and effort. It does not happen overnight, and when it seems difficult, it helps to remember it can be done at any stage of life and there are always many steps on the way. Here are some examples of how you can get started.

Step 1: Meeting new people. Seek out places where you will come across people with similar interests or hobbies. Make contact with neighbors. Get involved with local political or voluntary groups. Join a club.

Step 2: Building a friendship. Friendships flourish on shared experience, especially shared activities and shared pleasures. Think of things you can do together with new friends.

Step 3: Consolidating a friendship. Keep in touch. Regular contact helps, and so does remembering about other people's concerns and becoming a good listener as well as a good talker (see Chapter 13).

Step 4: Keeping your friendships in good working order. Look for ways of showing you care—in good times as well as bad. Do what you can when others are in trouble. Tolerate their moments of bad temper or silence.

Step 5: Using your friendships for support. Do not run away from people when you are depressed. Try to keep in contact even if you feel less outgoing than at other times or embarrassed about imposing yourself on them. Low moments are so common that many other people will know how you feel. Many different kinds of relationships, not just intimate ones, can be supportive.

A supportive relationship must not be a smothering one. We need our own space, our own independence and autonomy, as well as support. Think about your key relationships. Are any "too supportive," giving you too little of your own independent time? If so, you need to negotiate a change (Chapter 15) in order to find the best balance between support and independence. A lack of independence can be a particular problem for elderly people, especially when they are unwell and forced to depend on others. In these circumstances, retrieving as much independence and autonomy as possible may be the best protection against future depression. If you are trying to help a close friend in this situation, be careful not to do too much, and not to take over. Listen and try to understand, but continue to foster a sense of autonomy and a feeling of being in control.

Work on these five strategies and you will become more resilient and better able to resist the slide into depression.

Strategy 6: Recognize the Danger Signs of Depression Early

Depression is often the result of a vicious downward spiral of thoughts and feelings (see previous chapter). For most people who have recurrent bouts of depression there is a pattern. The depression starts with some negative experience, or negative thoughts, or the beginning of feeling down. These thoughts and feelings persist and get steadily worse until the depression has taken hold.

It is much easier to prevent this downward spiral if the problems are dealt with early.

What are the early signs, for you, that you are becoming depressed? It may be waking in the morning earlier than normal, feeling low. Or it may be ruminating on a negative experience earlier in your life, or it may be finding that you no longer seem to enjoy your work, or your leisure as much. Or it may be something else.

Can you identify some of your early warnings signs? If you can then plan how you will take action, and put your plan into action as soon as you notice them. Put into practice the ways of dealing with depression that work best for you, and that have been described in this, and the previous, chapter. Talk with your friends; break up the patterns of negative thinking; look after yourself.

Recent studies have shown that mindfulness meditation, combined with some of the ideas from cognitive therapy, can make a relapse less likely. If this approach attracts you then you may find the books listed in *Further Reading* (at the end of the book) of particular help.

Chapter Summary

If you deal with some of the contributory causes of depression *in between bouts of low mood*, you can do much to help prevent future depressions.

1. Attend to the basics of sleep, diet, and exercise. Do not ignore your body just because the problem is with your mood. The two are inextricably entwined.

2. Think about the direction your life is taking overall and try to live in a way that fits with your values and goals.
3. Put pleasures into life. Everyone deserves pleasures—in fact, no one can function well without them.
4. Do not put all your eggs in one basket. This leaves you vulnerable when something (inevitably) goes wrong.
5. Build up supportive relationships. They provide both a protection and a support.
6. Recognize the warning signs of depression early on. Take action before negative thoughts get a hold on you.

TRAUMATIC EXPERIENCE

Part Five of this book will help you to understand normal reactions to severely distressing events such as bereavements and traumatic experiences, and it will explain how to make use of a wide variety of recovery processes. One of the main ideas is that the normal reactions to such events can be intense and seem strange or bizarre. So it helps to know what to expect, and what to do to help the process of recovery along.

Chapter 25, Loss and Bereavement recognizes the wide variety of losses that can give rise to similar reactions.

Chapter 26, Dealing with the Past explains how traumatic and distressing experiences in childhood can cast a long shadow and interfere with life for a long time. It explains what to do to become free of these shadows.

Chapter 27, Recent Traumatic Events and Their Aftermath provides information about more recent traumatic events, reactions to them, the normal course of recovery, and ways of helping the process along if it has gotten stuck.

This part of the book should be useful both to people who have had such experiences and to their friends and relatives. As many of the ideas are based on those of cognitive therapy, we recommend readers also to read Chapter 9, which introduces these methods. Chapters 16, 18, 20, and 23 explain how to use them when feeling angry, anxious, stressed, or depressed. Any of these could also be useful.

25

Loss and Bereavement

This chapter is about loss, of someone or something. It is about losses that cause you pain and demand that you change or adjust. Losses can stop us in our tracks and may make us feel unable to go on, or they can force us to change direction so abruptly that we do not know what to do. This loss is difficult enough, but adjusting to the loss is also hard, and both aspects are important: both the feelings and the need to change.

Much of this chapter is about the difficult and painful loss of bereavement through the death of someone important to you. However loss strikes us in many forms, so some of the different types of loss are shown in the box on page 326. It may be surprising to read, for instance, that retirement is included in this list. Yet feelings at this time can be most bewildering. Instead of feeling relaxed, or at ease, some people feel gloomy and uncertain, or lose interest, energy, or self-esteem. This is because retirement brings losses as well as gains: for example, loss of productivity, status, a way of life involving routine or respect; loss of daily contact with colleagues; loss of income. Dealing with loss is thus a far more common experience than many people suppose, and the ways in which we have learned in the past to cope with smaller upheavals often provide the pattern for our reactions when subsequently facing larger ones.

The purpose of this chapter is to help you adjust to, and cope with, any loss that you are experiencing as painful. More serious losses, and those that happen at the wrong time (the death of a young person), and more unexpected losses (through accidents, assault, some types of disease, unexpected job loss) are known to have a bigger impact. There is no magic solution that will immediately take away the pain and put you back on your feet. Time is needed. But there are ways in which you can help yourself through this time, ways that will enable you to suffer less, and to reestablish yourself in life once again, despite the loss.

Types of Loss

Losses create an absence or leave a void. They demand that you adjust.

Bereavements:
The death of someone important to you
Miscarriage
The death of a pet

Loss through changes in a relationship:
Separation, divorce, relationship break-up of an affair
Consequences of illness such as Alzheimer's disease
Effects of serious mental illness, such as schizophrenia

Loss of access to people, or contact with them:
A parent moves out of the home, or to live with someone else
Children leave home, marry, or move abroad
Reduced contact with children following separation or divorce
Severed contact following retirement, unemployment, or changing jobs
Leaving your home, or family, or country

Loss of health or of the ability to use your senses, or skills:
Loss of hearing or eyesight
Loss of mobility, for instance through arthritis
Loss of a breast

Loss of possessions:
The theft, or loss, of something you value
Loss or damage to something important, for instance through fire, flood, or accident
Loss of money, or of your home

The bigger, the more untimely, and the more unexpected the loss, the longer it takes to recover

Although there is no single path to follow, it may be useful to have a kind of "road map" to help you as you travel. The road map provided here has five parts:

1. Understanding the experience
2. Journeys through grief
3. Coping with and expressing feelings
4. Starting to adjust
5. Finding sources of support

After the road map, the main dilemmas you will encounter on your way are described, and the chapter ends with guidelines concerning when to seek professional help, and some ideas for those who are helping someone else in their struggle to deal with a loss.

1 UNDERSTANDING THE EXPERIENCE

The pain of grief gnaws at the core of our being. It has many manifestations. First the feelings you might expect, such as sadness and sorrow; despair and desolation. Then the feelings that may come more as a surprise: the numbness that follows a shock, or anger, guilt, helplessness, and fear. Loneliness and depression may follow. The feelings can be so perplexing, so intense, and so horrible that you fear they will overwhelm you, and you may think you are going mad.

The pain of grief also affects thoughts. Odd things may come into your mind. You may have flashes of unexpected images, or hallucinations in which you see or hear the person you have lost, and then find yourself interacting with them. Memories may stab you with a red hot pain. You may find yourself thinking: "I can't go on," "This is unbearable," "Nothing will ever be the same again." You may be haunted by thoughts of things you said, or did not say; by regrets; by "unfinished business" of any kind.

Physically you may feel restless and agitated, unable to stop and rest. Or you may be, quite literally, stopped in your tracks, and find it difficult to move. Sleep is often hard to come by. Exhaustion follows quickly, but still you cannot rest. It is sometimes hard to keep organized. Often people describe starting, out of habit, to do something involving the person who is lost—laying an extra place at the table, turning to ask their opinion—only to be faced with the stark reality of their loss once more.

Thinking about the personal impact of a loss helps us to understand these experiences better, and also to find a way through them. By itself, the list of losses in the box on page 326 tells us only the first part of the story. The effect of a loss also depends on its personal consequences. Some examples are shown in the box below.

Defining the consequences of a loss helps to predict what will be most painful, and thus allows you to prepare yourself ahead of time. It also helps you to think, with compassion, about why the loss is so difficult for you. Many people chastise themselves: "I should be over this by now," and add self-blame or shame to their grief. Understanding the personal consequences of the loss helps to make sense of your pain, and we know that losses that make sense are easier to adjust to, in the end.

What Has Been Lost?

The impact of a loss depends on its personal consequences. These examples may prompt you to add some more of your own

Companionship, friendship, shared memories and experiences

Intimacy, physical closeness, sex

Appreciation and feedback, a counselor or adviser or friend

Security, safety, stability, peace of mind, the ability to rest and to relax

Trust: in others, in yourself, in the world

Confidence and certainty, a sense of continuity

Freedom: to move about, interact, be yourself, be independent

Hopes: of peace, or success; for children or grandchildren

Expectations: of help or support, of sharing responsibilities, of having more time

Pleasure: in another person or thing, laughter, humor

Opportunities: for setting things right, for saying what you thought or felt

Roots: a family, a home, a language, a culture; an ease of communication

Routine, structure, familiarity

Role, or status or position

Self-confidence and self-esteem are often shaken by a loss, and by the demand to adjust that it brings with it

---

2 JOURNEYS THROUGH GRIEF

There is no way of avoiding the pain and the loneliness of grief but it can be helpful to know what others have found useful. Rebecca Abrams, whose father died when she was eighteen, and whose stepfather died two years later, speaks from her experience: "Grieving is less like a smooth wide motorway than a potted, windy, bumpy, dirt track with no lights and signposts. Very often you end up wondering in despair if you are on the right road, having lost all sense of direction and distance." Details of her book, *When Parents Die*, are provided in the *Further Reading* (page 515).

People grieve in their own particular ways, and these are based on a mixture of personal, cultural, and sometimes religious preferences and customs. In some parts of Zimbabwe, for example, a ritual on the first anniversary of a person's death welcomes them back into the family as an ancestor. Some Western textbooks give the impression that people should be over their grief in a matter of months. Such expectations can make people whose pain lasts longer feel inadequate, or afraid of their own reactions, as if they have failed to reach the right destination. But you have a right to grieve in your own way, even if you sometimes behave in ways that you wish you had not, or which seem strange to the people around you. This is a time when it is particularly important to be kind to yourself (see Chapter 7), and better to acknowledge and accept your reactions. It is hard enough to live with a major loss without adding to your burdens by worrying about whether your experiences are peculiar or wrong.

It has been suggested that people progress through stages when they suffer a loss: stages of shock and denial, anger, relief and guilt, sadness and despair, anxiety, and finally acceptance and strength. All these experiences are common but the idea that they form a sequence of events like stations along a railroad line is too simplistic. As Rebecca Abrams writes, "Grief, as I found out, has its own timing and is not averse to going back and doing certain things again. Grief does not have some checklist of stages which are gone through in sequence and neatly ticked off."

Not only may feelings come and go; there is no right amount of time to spend with them. Those around you, and some of what you read, may give the impression that you should be able quickly to recover your former self. But when someone (or something) has helped to define who you are, you can never completely forget. You can come to terms with the loss, and pick up your life again. You can move on, and start to enjoy yourself, both in new ways that suit you now, and in old ways that were part of your former life. As you do this the times of acute pain become less frequent, less insistent. The times when you realize that you are enjoying yourself become, it is to be hoped, more frequent. But the pain, or sadness, may be there after one year, or after two years, and may never go away completely.

Remembering. The task that faces you is not to forget but to remember. It may be tempting to think that if you can block out what has happened and try to forget, then the pain will be less. But this is not usually true. The better aim is to remember, but to adapt and change so that the memories are part of your new life, and help you to be the person you were then, as well as the one that you are now. "Better to turn again to life and smile, than to remember and be sad," Christina Rossetti says at the end of her poem that starts: "Remember me, when I have gone away."

Richard Collin writes fifteen months after the death of his wife, Rima: "where is Rima in all of this new life? Never absent for a moment. I do not miss her because she remains a part of me, not in sentimental memory, but as a presence that is a part of everything I do. She is my context. When I do things she would not have done, I think of her and what she would have missed were she alive. When I do something she would have liked, I know that we did those things many times and I can (momentarily) recall them with pleasure. Rima is with me not in memory (although that too at times) but as a part of the unity of the twenty-eight years together, which nothing can erase." Details of his book, *Travels with Rima*, are provided on page 516.

A person who was important to you remains with you, as they helped to make you who you are. Their presence can be felt in your thoughts, attitudes, reactions, and preferences—good ones and bad ones. Abrams writes: ". . . you will begin to discover that the time you feel so cheated of is there after all."

The journey of change is complex, and it often runs on twin tracks. The first of these involves expressing and attending to the feelings that come with the loss, and the second involves adjusting and adapting to the loss, for example in practical ways required by your present life. These two tracks are described in the next two sections of the road map, and in Western cultures often women pay more attention to expressing their feelings, and men attend more to dealing with practicalities. However, both processes are needed, and people oscillate naturally between them. You may wake feeling wretched, you may weep, then the feelings may dissipate as you engage in your work and daily activities. Later, the sense of loss may hit you when a piece of music brings on a wave of emotion. This oscillation may help the process of recovery from loss. If you focus only on the feelings then it is difficult to start anew. If you focus only on practical activities, then the feelings remain raw, or threaten to overwhelm you, or you end up stifling both the feelings associated with the loss and all other feelings as well. These patterns stop the journey of grief from moving forward.

3 COPING WITH AND EXPRESSING FEELINGS

Feelings of anguish, desolation, and sadness are common experiences after a loss, and they may keep coming with astonishing persistence and intensity. But there is no right amount of time to spend with them. Expressing your feelings helps you to make sense of them, and helps you to assimilate the change in your life, and the implications for how you must change. How you express your feeling is up to you—and nobody can tell you that you are doing it wrong. You may wish to talk to others, or you may prefer to let go in private. There are many ways of expressing feelings, including drawing, writing, painting a picture, and making music, as well as talking to others. If you can find a way of expressing your feelings that suits you, then you will also find that doing so improves both your physical and your psychological health, and helps you to move forward on your personal journey. But some feelings may be harder to acknowledge, to understand, and to accept than others. Some of these are described briefly below.

Guilt. Guilt following a loss can be so strong and overpowering as to be frightening. People can become totally preoccupied with things that they did or did not do; things that they said and now regret, or things that they might have said but never did: "If only . . ." keeps coming to mind. Or they might feel guilty that they survived when someone else (or in the case of a disaster, many other people) did not. Such feelings may be linked to the sense of having done something wrong that it is no longer possible to put right, as if the "bad" things for which you feel responsible have set a final seal on the nature of the relationship that is lost. Such guilt undermines self-esteem, chases away more positive, or balanced, memories, and prevents you keeping in touch with a constructive sense of your personal value and worth. Of course all relationships have difficulties within them, and breaking a relationship, whether through separation, abandonment, or death can leave you focused on its negative aspects, so that the jagged edges remain exposed and are hard to smooth over. If you feel guilty it is likely that the relationship you have lost was important to you, and therefore it matters to you that it was not "better" in some way. Try not to let the guilt complicate your loss, as if you alone were responsible for its imperfections, and recognize it for what it was—an important relationship.

Anger. Anger after a loss can be alarming because of its strength, and also because of the speed with which the feeling comes, making you feel wild and uncontrolled, and then goes, leaving you feeling drained and some-times ashamed. Anger is linked to thoughts such as "Things *should have been* different." "This *should not* have happened," and may be turned in almost any direction: to the person (or thing) you have lost, to someone you blame, reasonably or not, to yourself, to God or fate or the powers that be, or to those around you, who may be trying to help. Being angry with them often adds guilt to the anger.

Although it may seem simplistic, one way to take the sting out of the anger is to replace the "should" with a "could" or a "might": "Things *could* have been different—but they weren't"; "This *might* not have happened—but it did." Anger makes less sense as accepting the loss be-comes more real as the reality of the loss is assimilated.

Helplessness.   Helplessness is hard to bear because it means "There's nothing I can do": you cannot change the past, and you are caught up in a maelstrom of feelings and practical problems that were not of your choos-ing. Initial shock may take away your ability to act, or to control what happens to you, or to take responsibility. Decisions may be taken out of your hands. These are normal reactions, and for a while you may need to accept your helplessness and let it flow through you.

Fear.   When the ground has been taken from under your feet, when you have lost your way, when you no longer know how to go on, or which way to turn, or whether you have the resources to cope with your experiences, then fear creeps in. Uncertainties create fear, and familiarity chases it away. But losses can uproot you, and put you in a new place which is not at all familiar. You may doubt your capacity to cope. Before the journey can continue you will need to explore, learn something about your new position in life, make it familiar again. If and when you can create a sense of safety and security for yourself, maybe with the help of others, the fears will diminish.

There is no magic way of immediately removing painful or problem-atic feelings, but there are ways of lessening or shortening their impact. Many of these have been described in other parts of this book, for ex-ample in Part Two on the seven basic skills; in the chapters on anxiety, and in those on depression. We suggest that you look over the list of chapter titles, or browse through the index to find more ideas. Remem-ber that different methods are useful at different times when you have suffered a loss, and so it makes sense to choose that which is best for you at the moment.

4 STARTING TO ADJUST

It is a tribute to the resilience of the human spirit that the process of adjustment, or readjustment, starts almost immediately after a loss. Our individual cultural conventions and the rituals we have devised for saying goodbye may help with this, as they mark the ending that is also a new beginning. Adjustment is therefore harder if it is not possible or appropriate to say goodbye; when, for example, your ex-partner still has contact with your children, or when someone has disappeared or is out of contact. However, adjustment is also demanded of us by practicalities: by basic needs for warmth, food, clean clothes, company, and by domestic, financial, or other decisions that may have to be made following a loss.

Decision-making. There is a clear message from those who have experienced bereavement: if at all possible, do not make important decisions until at least a year after your bereavement. Be cautious of doing anything irreversible with things associated with or belonging to the person you have lost, and think twice if you are advised quickly to get rid of significant possessions. You may need to use the skills of assertiveness (see Chapter 13) to ensure that you are not steamrolled into decisions that you might later regret, even though others may genuinely be trying to help you. If you need urgently, for example for financial reasons, to make important decisions, then seek the advice of someone you respect and trust. Professional advice is available from lawyers, accountants, and doctors, if you need an independent view from someone who is neither overly involved nor themselves suffering from the loss.

Meeting your basic needs. Dealing with losses takes its toll on our bodies as well as our minds. When mental suffering is great we tend to ignore our bodies, and to forget the huge amounts of energy that readjustment requires. An increase in physical ailments and illnesses is common after bereavement, and possibly also after other types of loss. It is therefore important to eat sensibly and regularly (see Chapter 31), and to avoid the twin problems of comfort eating and not bothering to eat. The same applies to exercise. Losing physical fitness makes adjustment harder, and again people react differently: some lose energy and motivation while others find it hard to stop, possibly because activity tends to keep thoughts, memories, and images at bay.

Discovering how to sleep is perhaps the hardest aspect of adjustment. Sleeping pills and other tranquilizers are only useful for emergency use, and are counterproductive in the long run. One approach is to remove as many barriers to good sleep as possible (see Chapter 30). Another is to devise methods of relaxing and calming yourself, and to remember that it is at night, when you are alone, that you are likely to be beset by memories, by unfinished conversations or arguments. Your mind may run on in surprising ways at night, and things may get out of perspective. You may need to work hard to hold your imagination in check (see pp. 430–432 for some more ideas).

Building self-confidence. A loss, together with the realization of what that means to you, or about you, can reduce self-confidence and introduce self-doubt, even in a normally confident person. If your confidence is fragile at the best of times it can expose all your vulnerabilities. Confidence is built up by doing things, and it may be worth pushing yourself even if this is hard, and even if pleasure does not come with success in the way that it used to. Spending time with friends who make you feel better about yourself and avoiding those who make you feel worse helps. There are more ideas about building confidence and self-esteem in Chapter 10.

Rebuilding your social life. The loss of someone close, particularly your partner, is likely to have a profound effect on your social life. A partner often provides the major component of one's social life. In addition, many of your friends are likely to have been joint friends, and some of them may no longer relate easily to you—or you to them. Besides, you may no longer feel like socializing, and this may create a vicious cycle: because of your grief you no longer socialize, and the lack of social activities exacerbates your grief. Then when you do socialize you may feel guilty for betraying the person you have lost, for example, by enjoying someone's company, conversationally or sexually.

Rebuilding a social life takes effort, and you may need to push yourself; to put yourself in the way of meeting people and doing things with people. Think about which activities to involve yourself in, and ask yourself the following questions:

1. What things did I enjoy before (e.g., going to the movies, watching live sports)?
2. What things might I enjoy now—things that I have not done for a long time or perhaps never done? In partnerships we often spend our time doing things we both enjoy. This means that there may be new ways of spending your time that your partner did not enjoy, and for this reason you hardly ever did them.

It may seem wrong to enjoy some things without the person you have lost, or you may fear that pursuing those activities will only remind you, painfully, of your loss. But ask yourself: would they have wanted you to remain miserable, without pleasures in your life? Enjoying pursuits that you used to share with someone else is no betrayal: it can provide a sense of continuity. Being reminded of the person you have lost is not a bad thing: it is a way of linking your past life with your new one, and of acknowledging more aspects of yourself. So there is no need to carry on the same track as before; if there are things that you enjoy and that you have not done for a long time, then why not enjoy them now? Finding out what you enjoy could be part of the exploration that helps to establish you in your new territory, and perhaps with capacities that you would not previously have thought you had.

Making new relationships. Whether a relationship that is important to you has been broken by death, or divorce, or in some other way, it is likely to be important for you to make new relationships. In Part 3 we consider many aspects of relationships and ways to improve them. Following the loss or breakdown of a relationship, it may be helpful to think about how you are going to develop new relationships. Two steps may be helpful.

1. Meet people—either new people, or spend more time with people whom you already know. This means that you need to put yourself in the way of meeting people. This may need some effort, particularly if you are not the kind of person who normally joins clubs or groups or agencies. Think about your hobbies or interests: are there groups you can join in order to meet others who share these interests? Think about your workplace and colleagues: are there ways you can extend your number of friends? Think about your friends: are there ways they can introduce you to some of their friends? Let your friends know that you would like to meet more people.
2. Be aware of negative thoughts that might be stopping you from meeting people or from building on a relationship. These thoughts might include feelings that you are worthless, or unattractive as a friend and companion or as a person, or unattractive sexually. Your grief may make you feel that you are not fun to be with and this will undermine your confidence in forming new relationships. And you may, quite rightly, be concerned about what the other person, in the case of a new friendship, thinks about the fact that you are bereaved, or divorced, or separated.

One issue will be what you say about your state (the fact that you are divorced, for example). Do you tell a new acquaintance early on or do you keep it a secret? There is no simple answer. It is probably best to approach this question with no preconceived view either that you need to be "honest" from the beginning and tell a person early on, or that it is something that you must hide—something that is private to you. The best guide is whether it seems natural and right to say.

One danger in forging new relationships is attributing to a new person the characteristics of the person you have lost for some rather spurious reason (you are reminded of a habit of their speech, or hairstyle, or a belief or pleasure that they enjoy). You may go further than this and attribute not only a whole set of aspects that remind you of the lost person but also of their feelings toward you. Be cautious of making any longer-term commitments and of becoming too deeply attached too soon. That is not to say that you should entirely hold back from relationships nor that you should not let the relationship develop, but don't be caught on the rebound. McIlwraith, in his book *Coping with Bereavement* (see *Further Reading*), suggests asking yourself two questions if you feel strongly attracted to someone you meet especially in the first few months of a loss:

1. Does this person really have the same values as the person you have lost; and
2. What does this person really want and feel—are you assuming too much?

5 SOURCES OF SUPPORT

In pain or suffering, when feeling desolate or alone or uncared for, most of us need a guide, counselor, or friend. Sometimes no such person is available. So learning to care for yourself, and to show yourself that you care, is the first resource. Harsh thoughts, or internal critical or blaming voices can at times insist on making themselves heard. Ask yourself, is this the way you would talk to someone else in pain? Would it help them? What would a kind, compassionate person, intent on helping you on your way, say to you instead? If this is hard, read *Chapter 3, Valuing Yourself,* and *Chapter 7, Treating Yourself Right*. The titles of these chapters can themselves be read as signs on your road map: signs that prevent you from taking a perilous, wearying, and undermining detour.

Then there are sources of support, such as music, books, videos, your garden or work, a warm fire or meal, and the routines and structures that provide the background or framework of your life. Remind yourself to draw on them, and to put necessary things in place, such as fuel for the fire, the CDs or DVDs. As we grow up, and deal with all manner of upheavals and losses, we may also learn how to comfort ourselves. Think about what has helped you before, and use these coping strategies too.

Of course other people are also an important source of support. But there can be difficulties. Those close to you may be suffering from the same loss that hurt you. You may be able to share your memories and feelings, but it may also mean that none of you has the strength to support the other. It can be especially difficult when two bereaved people prefer different tracks on their journeys. The one who readily expresses feelings may disturb the other, or be labeled as self-indulgent or uncontrolled. The one who gets involved in practicalities and activity may seem detached, or even insensitive. Each person suffers, and gets over that suffering in their own way. Suffering does not have to show to be deeply felt.

Friends who are not deeply affected by the loss may be able to be more helpful, though this too can be difficult. Most people do not know how best to help those who suffer. They are uncertain whether to help you to talk or to encourage you not to dwell on the sadnesses, and to "get out of yourself." They may expect you to be better long before you have recovered. They may be embarrassed by tears, or anger, or other strong feelings. Or they may think it would be best to help you "get in touch with" your feelings. Most of us find it difficult to help a bereaved friend. So try not to resent the mistakes and the clumsiness, and think about whether you can help others to support you by being open about what you would like them to do.

Sometimes people further away from you, acquaintances rather than friends or relatives for example, can provide good support. Someone who has experienced their own loss or bereavement may be able to understand what you are experiencing, and be able to recognize parts of your journey, so they can also provide you with the reassurance that you too will come through.

If you do not find the support you are offered helpful, this is not the time to be too concerned with the feelings of others. You should make your own selection of supporters, and choose what you want even if this means rejecting some offers. Remember you can accept, or ask for, practical help: a meal cooked for you, a lift into town, instead of being landed with a heart-to-heart that makes you feel worse. More formal support groups can be of enormous help too, as can books, and it is worth looking for one by an author who has experienced the same type of loss as yourself (see *Further Reading* at end of the book).

Dilemmas Encountered on the Way

Four dilemmas are particularly common.

1. *Keep memories fresh or avoid thinking about them?* Constantly thinking about your loss can be driven by the fear of letting go; the fear of real, irretrievable loss; or by guilt about not keeping someone's memory alive. Blocking out memories can be driven by the fear of sinking into permanent despair, or of being overwhelmed. In the long run, being driven by avoidance, fear or guilt keeps problems going rather than resolving them. Experimenting with small changes that help you to face your fears is more useful.

2. *Stay as you are or move on?* How do you decide whether it is time to push yourself on, so as to rebuild your life, or whether it is best to stay as you are? In the short term, the decision is not crucial. The best guide is to think whether, over the last six months, you have changed at all. If there has been no change, or if you feel stuck, then you might try to push on, for example, to tackle practical problems, or to try something new. If you have been becoming increasingly depressed, as well as feeling stuck, then consider seeking professional help (see p. 339).

3. *Talk about the loss and your problems, or keep quiet?* Ask yourself: does talking help you? Does it give you some pleasure and support, or help you to make practical decisions? Or does talking make you feel miserable, angry, or helpless? You are the best judge of what is right for you, so if you benefit from talking but your listeners disagree, perhaps you can find others. Another option is to write down your feelings. Turning our emotional experiences into writing has been shown to improve both psychological and physical health, and when you write about major upheavals you begin to organize and make sense of them, and to distill complex experiences into more understandable packages. This makes it easier to move on.

4. *Carry on as normal, or take time out?* What suits one person may not suit another or may not even be possible for them. Some people have no option but to struggle on. For some their thoughts and memories intrude and make it hard, or impossible, to think about anything else, and they need time out, and may need the support of their doctor to get it. Others feel better if they keep to their usual routines and commitments, which may provide a helpful framework to counteract the sense of disruption. Once again, your

decisions should be based on your needs, and should keep you moving on your journey. Decisions should not be based on fear or guilt, and you should take care not to push yourself up to, or beyond, your limits. Use your physical health and ability to sleep and rest as indicators. If these deteriorate, then it could be sensible to retreat for a bit.

When to Seek Professional Help

Needing more help than those around you can provide is not a sign of failure. Many organizations have been founded to help people cope with losses, particularly with bereavement, and professionals such as doctors, therapists, and counselors expect to help when needed. The question for you is: Would you benefit from such help? If you are uncertain, you can always try and see. Some guidelines for deciding when to seek professional help are listed below:

1. If a deep depression has continued over several months, without any sense that it is getting better, a professional may help get you moving forward.
2. If you are seriously considering harming yourself, or doing away with yourself, you should see your doctor, or someone you trust, immediately.
3. If those close to you think you need professional support, then take their views seriously. It can be difficult to judge your own needs.
4. If you feel utterly lonely, and none of your sources of support are helpful, then contact a relevant helping organization.
5. If over a period of six months or more you have been completely stuck, making no progress either with your feelings or with adjusting to your new life, then consult someone who has experience of recovery—either a friend or a professional.

Helping Someone Who Has Suffered a Loss

First, read this chapter, and think about whether you are in a position to help. We know that people who share a loss can provide some of the best kinds of support, but their ability to do so also depends on understanding that there are different, healthy, and effective ways of recovering from a loss.

The most useful thing you may be able to do is to listen, without judgment. The psychoanalyst and writer Anthony Storr titled an essay on counseling: "Don't Just Do Something, Listen." This is important advice. Listen, not with the expectation of coming up with clever solutions to problems, but with empathy, kindness, compassion, and understanding. Your job as a friend is to be kind. Any embarrassment or discomfort you might feel at first will dissipate if you listen with kindness and without running away (see also a pp. 311–313).

Guidelines for helping a friend:
1. Be there when they are feeling in need of support. Do not overstay your welcome. Ask if you are not sure.
2. Listen and be kind, especially when they are on the emotional track.
3. Help them think through problems and possible solutions, especially when they are on the adjusting, practical track.
4. Help your friend to persist and keep motivated if their activities give them little pleasure.
5. Hang in there: many people offer help soon after a loss and forget that it may be needed for longer. Find out what your friend wants, and remember they may not ask.
6. Remember anniversaries, or other important dates when friends may feel especially in need of support.
7. Try not to take offense if your friend treats you unpleasantly, or angrily at times. This may be a reaction to the pain of loss and have nothing to do with you.

Chapter Summary

The pain of grief can show itself in many ways, some of which can be frightening and confusing. People may think they are going mad because their experience is so unusual and bizarre. Others may think that they should be "over" their grief within a certain time. But each of us has to grieve in our particular way. Some of the painful and confusing feelings that follow an important loss are: guilt, anger, helplessness, and fear.

It is a tribute to the resilience of the human spirit that the process of readjustment starts almost immediately after a loss. In coping there are some useful guidelines, such as: do not (if you can help it) make important decisions for at least a year after a major loss and look after your basic needs of sleep, food, and exercise. If your loss has had a major effect on your social life then it will be important to rebuild your network of friends and, perhaps, to make new relationships. Consider your sources of support and make use of them.

The purpose of this chapter is to help those who have suffered an important loss through providing a kind of "road map" based on what others have found helpful.

26

Dealing with the Past

This chapter is written for people to whom bad things happened early in life, and for whom the pain of these bad experiences has left its mark. Here are some examples of the distressing circumstances we are thinking of:

- Being hurt, neglected, or unvalued
- Being criticized, put down, disliked, or treated unfairly
- Being rejected, blamed, or bullied
- Being taken advantage of or abused, physically, emotionally, or sexually

This chapter includes ideas that may also be useful for people who have experienced important losses or suffered serious illness or trauma. *Chapter 25, Loss and Bereavement,* and *Chapter 27, Recent Traumatic Events and Their Aftermath,* deal with these issues in more detail. If you have been affected by either of these, it might be helpful to read the relevant chapter, as well as this one, before deciding which ideas you would like to use first.

It is not easy to come to terms with deeply painful experiences, especially when they happened during childhood. This is true for reactions to experiences which later seem relatively trivial, as well as for those that were unquestionably damaging and harmful. Such experiences may cast their shadows over many aspects of later life, and memories may intrude unexpectedly, bringing the pain to life again as they come.

Almost everyone of course has been hurt, or rejected, or suffered some loss or illness—this is part of normal experience. Sometimes, however, the consequences of these damaging experiences adversely shape the ways in which we relate to others, or approach the world, or express ourselves. Distressing experiences seem to color our approach to things years later. If you had no one to talk to, or if no one was a comfort to you at the time, a bad or sad memory may linger in your mind. The ways that we learned to live with our bad experiences when they were happening help to define how we see the world. The key idea in this chapter is that these perspectives, or frameworks, are powerful and problematic; but they are not unchangeable. You can learn how to step out from under the shadow of the past.

A "problematic framework" is a framework or set of perspectives which determine important aspects of how a person sees the world, and these fixed views often lead to persistent difficulties. Such frameworks usually develop because they help to lessen the pain of the bad experiences at the time. When they persist unchanged even though they are no longer useful—when they have passed their "sell-by date"—they cast shadows that make it hard to judge a situation or a person in a fresh or clear way.

The way to overcome the difficulties is to change the "problematic framework": to update it, and if necessary to replace it with one that is better adapted to your life as it is now. Updating, changing, dismantling, or replacing a much-used framework is hard work. It is worth

---

Outline of a Two-Stage Strategy for Change

Stage 1: Laying the foundations for change

1. *Understand your current frameworks*
   Name the painful experiences and recognize their meaning
   Understand why your frameworks developed
   Identify the problems that your frameworks are giving you now
2. *Create a context for change: a comfort zone*

Stage 2: Changing a problematic framework

1. *Find a focus for change: feelings, beliefs, or behavior*
2. *Start taking steps toward change, and don't worry if the steps are small*
3. *Learn to recognize and deal with stumbling blocks as you go*

trying to change as it helps to resolve persistent problems and to make you feel less stuck. We will look at three case examples to demonstrate how to make some changes. The three people described here had very different problems but the general approach was the same: first, build the foundations for change; second, make the changes themselves. The main details of these two stages are outlined in the box on page 343.

How Our Frameworks for Seeing the World Develop

What do we mean by "frameworks"? Our early experiences shape the ways we see the world and relate to others. If your predominant experience as a child was of being loved and protected, then you are likely to expect good treatment later on. But if you suffered significant hurt or neglect, you are likely to expect more pain and neglect later in life—even though you may hope for something else. Experiences provide us with a framework for understanding our worlds and how they work, and the framework acts like a filter affecting how we process new information. It is like wearing sunglasses and seeing the whole world shaded by their color: everything is filtered through the shadow of an unhappy, powerful past experience. Even when people are not aware of this background force it may shape their choices and reactions as it affects their view of themselves, of other people, and of the world in general.

This framework links and affects three things: our patterns of thinking, our feelings, and our ways of behaving. If you were well cared for you might *think* that others are usually friendly, *feel* comfortable in their company, and generally *behave* in a friendly way yourself. If you were constantly yelled at, abused, and criticized you might *think* that other people are basically hostile, *feel* threatened by them, and *behave* so that you protect yourself and build up your defenses.

These frameworks provide us with basic strategies, or "rules for living," such as: "be open and friendly with others" or "don't let people get close." The frameworks usually developed because at some time in the past they worked: they kept you going when things were bad. They were reasonable responses to experience. Keeping your distance, for example, is one way of reducing the amount of criticism or abuse that comes your way. But if these frameworks, or rules for living, persist when your life has moved on, they cause problems. If the rules do not change, then the same sorts of problems keep coming. You may find that your relationships never develop or that they are strained to the breaking point with arguments, for instance. It is common to feel bad about yourself even if good things happen. If you keep coming up against the same problems, either in your relationships or in your views about yourself; if you find yourself repeating the same unhelpful patterns of feeling, thinking, or behaving; if you feel stuck and powerless to change, unhappy and stressed, then your framework needs updating.

CASE EXAMPLE: DUNCAN'S FRAMEWORK

Duncan was in his early thirties: a tall and rather awkward-looking man whose imposing figure contrasted with his shy, diffident manner. Inside he was anxious, depressed, and lonely, and the root of his problems was a profound difficulty in making friends. Duncan had been bullied throughout his school years. He had learned never to let down his guard, and to remain constantly alert to the possibility of attack. As an adult others found him touchy and distant and thought he was reluctant to make friends. They left him to his own devices, which only convinced Duncan more strongly that he was basically unlikeable. His old "rule" ("Never let your guard down") had protected him at school, but as an adult it stopped him from getting close to people and making friends. Behaving as if he would be rejected (which fit with his old rule) was so automatic that he only recognized it after he began to talk to a therapist, who helped him to see that his loneliness was partly to do with the signals he was giving off. She then helped him gradually to start trying out different, less guarded ways of behaving. It took practice, and it felt quite strange, but it led to his making better friends and in due course to closer, more satisfying relationships. He began by making a decision to sit with his coworkers for coffee, instead of reading his newspaper at his desk, not every day but once or twice a week. After a while, colleagues got in the habit of saying, "You coming with us today, Duncan?" He didn't always say "yes" but it lightened his mood.

Duncan had made the assumption that "this is how I am," and had thought that he was stuck that way forever. He started to change when he realized that his patterns of thinking, feeling, and behaving were based largely on a framework that he had developed as a result of his childhood experiences. This framework had made sense at the time but now it was holding him back and causing him problems.

Stage 1: Laying the Foundations for Change

IS YOUR LIFE AS BAD NOW AS IT WAS THEN?

In encouraging you to work toward changing we are assuming that you are no longer living in an abusive or damaging situation. We hope that your world has moved on, and that you now have a good friend or a partner, or a safe place to live or share. We also hope that the negative or damaging experiences that led to your framework are now in the past. But if this is not so, if you are still with people who are causing you serious harm and distress, it will be difficult to change without changing your situation. You may need first to seek help or advice from others such as a doctor, neighbor, friend, or mental health practitioner. A frequent effect of an abusive past is that you get into a relationship or place that looks different, but makes you feel some, if not all, of the sadness you are used to. To live more happily with less uncertainty and stress can feel strange at first, as if it does not fit for you. If you wish to make changes in where you live or in your relationships, but for various reasons feel unable to do so, you need good support—help and guidance from someone who understands what it will take. There is an increasing quantity of information available on the Internet, as well as places in such as libraries and health centers. But if you have already moved on, even though in one way or another you are still carrying your past with you, then you may be ready, or might at least consider, laying the foundations for change. This means beginning with an understanding of the framework you are using.

UNDERSTANDING YOUR FRAMEWORK

Change begins with understanding. This chapter will help you to understand the consequences of harmful childhood experiences and to use this understanding to change: to start along the road of resolving the difficulties. In our clinics we see many people who have suffered from harmful childhood experiences, and we know that there are many more who have also suffered but who do not come for help. Some may not need help, and some prefer not to seek it. Others struggle on, doing the best they can, and a few suffer without knowing where to turn. If you are seeking to help yourself, focus first on the possibility that you can look at your past life in a new way, and that this can help to make sense of your experiences and your situation. The understanding that comes from making sense of your story, and of how you got to be where you now are, makes a difference. If you want to start the work of resolving some long-standing problems, go at your own pace, and seek extra help if you need it. Sometimes it is not possible to do all this work by yourself.

Naming the painful experiences.   Start by giving a name or label to the bad things that happened to you. Think of something that still hurts you or makes you angry: the worst time you were hit; the day your mother or father left; the day you decided your brother or sister was the favorite. There is no need to rake up the past, exposing all the buried details; at this stage you just need a name for the experiences that hurt you. You are the judge of what you found painful at the time, so think about anything that hurt you badly enough to leave its mark. Do not contradict your thoughts by saying to yourself: "Well, that was nothing really—I can't still be going on about that," or "Worse things have happened to others." Do not disregard the unacceptable behavior of people in your past because it was normal in your experience, and happened all the time, or to everyone in your family. You are older now, and you know those things did not happen to everybody. What matters is what the experience meant to you, how it affected you, and how it is still affecting you.

Recognizing the meaning of what happened to you.   Having named these painful experiences, think about how they have led to your current beliefs: beliefs about other people, about yourself, and about the world. In the box on page 350 we suggest some questions to help you to do this. Look at these questions and then read the following three cases of Jim, Natalie, and Loretta. The answers that these people gave to these questions illustrate how each of them came to understand the relationship between their past experiences and their current beliefs.

Case example 1: Beliefs about other people.   Jim's childhood memories are of being yelled at and hit. After his father lost his job he started drinking and became increasingly violent toward Jim's mother, and also toward Jim. His mother often left home unannounced, sometimes for days on end. As far as he knows, she never stepped in to protect him from the violence of his father, or from his three elder brothers, who took their cue from their dad. They either taunted him or bullied him into doing everything for them when his mother was absent. All through his childhood, Jim was exploited and hurt by the people closest to him.

Jim's belief about others: they can't be trusted—not one of them.
Jim's rules for living: hit before you get hit. Don't let anyone near.
Jim's pattern of behavior: aggressive, distant, and secretive.
The original payoff: it kept others at arms' length.

Jim's problems now: getting into fights, being rejected by others, feeling constantly under attack; loneliness and lack of confidence.

Case example 2: Beliefs about yourself. Natalie felt she was born fighting for attention and failing to get it. She was an only child and knew nothing about her father. Her mother worked long hours and from the age of nine, Natalie had to look after herself and the apartment where she lived with her mother—and occasional boyfriends who never stayed for long—as if she were an adult. All she received for her efforts were complaints, criticism, and verbal abuse. She felt neglected and unvalued, and cannot remember ever being given a hug, except by an uncle who used to keep her company when her mother was out. However, she realized later that his attentions had been inappropriately sexual from the start. Between the ages of 11 and 14, until she refused to have anything more to do with him, he abused her sexually at every opportunity.

Natalie's beliefs about herself: I'm worthless; I'm not a good person; I'm bad.

Natalie's rules for living: Natalie oscillated between two somewhat contradictory rules of living. The first was: try hard to do well and to please people. The second was: don't bother. It's not worth it because you will probably fail.

Natalie's patterns of behavior: Natalie flipped between the two extremes of trying to do things perfectly, and giving up, feeling so unmotivated that she could not even try. She either kept the apartment spotlessly clean or she neglected it totally.

The original payoff: Natalie got attention from her mother both when she did something well and when she sat in a heap doing nothing. Even when the attention was critical, and her mother accused her of being lazy and careless, it felt better than being ignored.

Natalie's problems now: Natalie says: "I'm a complete failure" and that is how she feels. She also says: "However hard I work, nothing I do seems good enough," and this applies at home with her partner and six-year-old son Jason, and at work in the finance department of a local charity. She is often exhausted and when she can do no more she gives up trying and goes to bed at the same time as Jason, feeling depressed as well as a failure.

Case example 3: Beliefs about the world. In Loretta's life so many things had gone wrong that she had come to think of herself as doomed. She had lived in the same town all her life, with her parents and younger sister. They

were part of a strong local community, and had few problems until everything started to go wrong. First, when she was 12, she was injured in a car
accident, and missed nearly a whole year of school. Two years later, when
the family was on vacation, her mother and sister nearly drowned. They
were both shocked and upset, and although they appeared to recover
quickly, the accident had badly shaken her mother's confidence. Then,
when Loretta was 17, her father, who worked for an airline company, was
laid off, and money was so short that Loretta gave up her plans to go to college.

> *Loretta's beliefs about the world:* nothing ever goes right. Good things
> don't last.
> *Loretta's rules for living:* grab whatever comes, and don't think ahead
> too much.
> *Loretta's patterns of behavior:* Loretta is constantly moving on. She
> changes her job, her boyfriend, and her friends every few months.
> There is something in Loretta that makes her unsettled and easily dis-
> satisfied. She gets restless and bored when life settles down. She
> drops a promising boyfriend after a few months. She is thrilled when
> she gets a new job but changes jobs too often.
> *The original payoff:* focusing on new and exciting things kept her pes-
> simism at bay when times were hard.
> *Loretta's problems now:* Loretta says her life feels chaotic and out of con-
> trol. She can't keep a job or a relationship, never makes plans, and feels
> depressed and hopeless if she looks ahead more than a week or two.

The three patterns described here are common ones. We could call Jim's
a pattern of mistrust; Natalie's a problem of extreme reactions, showing "all
or nothing" patterns of thinking, feeling, and behaving; and Loretta's a
problem of control—or lack of control—leading to instability. You may recognize in yourself some of these patterns, or your experiences and beliefs
may be quite different. Your first step is to find a way to look at yourself so
as to be able to see your own patterns, and the questions in the box on page
350 are to help you to do this. Take as much time as you need to think
through your answers, using the examples of Jim, Natalie, and Loretta for
guidance if necessary. This stage of understanding yourself is harder than it
seems, and it may bring with it some painful feelings. Remember that, from
the perspective of the child (or young person) that you were at the time that
you were hurt, it made sense that you developed your particular pattern.
For example it may have been the best way you could find to cope with the
situation you faced. It is not a sign of deficiency to think, feel, and behave

as you do, or to be stuck without knowing how to change. You deserve understanding; you deserve to be treated kindly, with warmth and compassion, rather than with self-blame or self-criticism. Try to treat yourself with kindness, understanding, and acceptance as you do this work.

Questions to Help in Recognizing Your Patterns

Given the bad things that happened to you earlier in life:

1. *What do you believe?* What did your experiences tell you? What conclusions did you draw from them about yourself? About other people? About the world?

2. *What are your rules for living? What should you (always)* do? *What should* you *(never)* do? Other "pressurizing" words linked with rules for living are: *Must, ought, have to, need* (see also p. 80). Try to put into words a rule that you live by, not one that you wish that you lived by

3. *What pattern of behavior fits with this rule?* What does this rule make you do, or want to do? Given your rule, what should you do? Here are some examples: *Never expect a favor; Never trust anyone; Keep myself to myself; Keep trying or I am a bad person; Keep my head down*

4. *What was the original payoff?* How did this rule help in the past? Or how did you hope it would help (even if sometimes it did not help)? Does it still help sometimes?

5. *What problems do you have now that stem from these beliefs, rules, and behaviors?* What difficulties might living according to this rule make for you now? How might it interfere with your relationships? Or get in the way of doing what you want? Or stop you being the way you would like to be? How does it make you feel?

Answering these questions for yourself, and by yourself, is no small task. We suggest that you take your time, and that you make a place to write down your answers so that you can look at them later and think again if you need to. The examples of Jim, Natalie, and Loretta are based on real people but we have stripped away the details to make the main points clear, and changed some of them to protect their privacy. In practice things are likely to be more complicated than we have made them sound. That means that you may need to go back to the main points and to read the ideas in this chapter many times to help you unravel the complexities.

For example, Jim's beliefs were about other people ("They can't be trusted"), Natalie's were about herself ("I'm worthless and bad"), and Loretta's were about the world ("Nothing ever goes right. Good things don't last"). In reality all three kinds of beliefs might be relevant, but like

Jim, Natalie, and Loretta, you should focus first on the one that feels most important.

IDENTIFY THE DISADVANTAGES OF LIVING WITH AN OUTDATED FRAMEWORK

Frameworks are like strong habits: they are hard to change, and it is easy to slip back into old ways of doing things after you have started to change. It is important to work out the disadvantages of going on as you are, and to keep in mind your own reasons for wanting to change. Examples of some of the more common disadvantages of outdated frameworks are listed below, and more than one of these may be important. Updating your framework can help with all of them.

Feeling stuck. The same familiar feelings and difficulties keep coming. Without help, or ideas about what to do, there seems to be no hope for change, so no reason for trying to change.

Thinking badly about yourself. Self-blame, and sometimes a sense of shame as well, often lurk in the background, and with them come low self-confidence and low self-esteem. Taking action to explore and to change in the ways that you wish helps you to think better about yourself

Thinking that you deserve to be punished. If it seems to you that it was your fault that you were treated badly, then you may also think that you did not deserve anything better, or that there is something inherently wrong with you, or bad about you. This leaves out of account the wrong-doing of the people or person who hurt you, and the fact that you were young when this happened. It is also counterproductive because it blocks the will to change. You may feel that you do not want to blame others— that that would get you nowhere. If this is how you feel then getting help is very useful. Someone else might help you to see that you are not bad—bad things have happened to you, and the badness of it became part of your internal framework.

Repeated crises. Sometimes crises seem to come "out of the blue," and sometimes they feel inevitable and even predictable. Trying to change can put you back in charge.

Unsatisfactory relationships. Most of the problematic experiences from childhood involve relationships: loss, neglect, or abuse. As a consequence of this, outdated frameworks often have their destructive and negative effects on later relationships, leading people to avoid getting too close, for instance, or to treat everyone with mistrust.

CREATE A CONTEXT FOR CHANGE: A COMFORT ZONE

In order to lay down firm foundations for change you need both to understand the framework that needs changing and to be kind to yourself; you need to create a "comfort zone." Changing old patterns puts you in unfamiliar territory, which feels risky and frightening. If the ground is taken from under your feet, it is normal to feel scared. If you change, for example, then others may change in response, and you may no longer know what to expect. If you bring about big changes, the consequences can make you feel unsafe, so that you wish to return to your old framework despite the pain and unhappiness. For this reason you need to look after yourself during the period of change. Looking after yourself can be surprisingly difficult, particularly if you are not used to doing it. It involves thinking, feeling, and doing. If you tend to think badly or critically about yourself, try to recognize your inner voice for what it is—an unhelpful voice from the past—and let it fade into the background. Try to think of yourself with kindness. Ask how you would feel toward someone else who had been hurt, and then imagine giving those feelings of kindness and compassion to yourself. What would you then do? How would you look after yourself? Do you need to take the pressure off? Or to find more ways of enjoying yourself? To take more exercise, or to eat better?

Here are some ideas that might encourage you to take care of yourself in small but important ways:

1. Identify a safe place to go to if the disruption of trying to change unsettles you too much. Surround your safe place, for example a comfortable chair in your sitting room, with things that you like to look at. Make this a warm and welcoming place, with a window or blanket, in reach of books or music.
2. Develop ways of calming down, soothing, and comforting yourself if you feel upset. You may want to talk to someone, or get out in the fresh air; to play some sport, or to take a warm bath; to make a warm drink, or play some music. You may want to sleep, or to retreat, or to use relaxation (see Chapter 11).
3. Learn to distract yourself (see pp. 301–303), and to turn your mind to other things, especially if painful memories intrude too much and too often. It is helpful to find ways of anchoring yourself in the pres-

ent, as a reminder that the events of the past are now over. Some people find meditation and mindfulness useful (see *Further Reading*, p. 515).

4. Make good use of the relationships that you find supportive. It helps to feel connected to others, and this feeling grows from doing ordinary things together and from doing things that you both enjoy. Confiding in others is not necessary, though it can bring comfort and give you a feeling of being understood. It can also leave you feeling disappointed and lonely when people do not react in the way that you hoped for or expected that they would.

In Chapter 7 (Treating Yourself Right) we describe more ways in which you can help to give yourself the support you may need in order to change.

Identifying your strengths and resources. None of us would choose to have painful experiences, but they may bring with them benefits as well as harms. Even if you still suffer from the consequences of one or more childhood traumas, you have almost certainly developed some strengths and resources that have helped you get to where you are now, and which are still helpful, for example the ability to persist and keep going when in difficulty. Your experiences may also enable you to understand and help others who have had painful experiences—in ways that those who have not had such experiences never can. This ability to help others may also help you to recognize your value.

Using humor and playfulness. So many people whose childhoods were marked by suffering have missed out on an important source of learning as they grew up: learning that comes from being able to play and to laugh. Many people, as they start to recover, say that they benefit enormously from allowing themselves to play—from doing something as simple as going to a fair, or spending a day on the beach with a friend, or playing card games. Play stimulates creative and constructive capacities; it helps people try out different ways of doing things and become more flexible. Play and laughter in safe situations help to break old links with fear. It may be a revelation to discover that you can laugh when something startles you, especially if this challenges the assumption that surprises can only be bad. Enjoying a game with others can strengthen the links between you, making you feel connected to people rather than disconnected and isolated, and it can also help you to feel that others value your company. Nothing brings relief from suffering so well as laughter, and nothing lightens the load so readily as play.

Stage 2: Changing a Problematic Framework

Change is possible. We know this to be true because we have seen it happen, but many people do not know, or believe, that it is possible to change. If you doubt it, try visualizing what change would be like for you. What would be different? How would other people know you had changed? What might you gain? Old familiar patterns often feel "comfortable," like a worn-out and threadbare coat. Losing it before you have found a new one leaves you feeling exposed. It may take time before you find a new one that fits, and that feels comfortable again.

So there is no way of changing without taking some risks and that is in part why we have devoted so much of this chapter to laying the foundations for change. If the foundations are in place then the risks will be smaller and the benefits larger. The box on page 355 outlines the general approach, but there is no single best way. One size does not fit all. The main idea is that your problematic framework affects your beliefs, your feelings, and your behavior, and makes close links between them. This is illustrated in the model shown in the box. We will put some flesh on this model by explaining how the three people you have already met, Jim, Natalie, and Loretta, used this way of working. Their cases will help to clarify the principles of change and how to put them into practice. Each of them made a personal formulation by drawing out the links between their personal beliefs, feelings, and behaviors to show how their problematic frameworks were operating. Look carefully at the box, then read all three of the examples below and take from them any ideas and methods that fit your situation. Mix and match as you think best.

One of the key issues is to decide what to focus on first. The answer, in general, is that it may not matter where you begin because change in one area often leads to change in another. Your behavior, your beliefs, and your feelings will all link up, as they did for Jim, Natalie, and Loretta. Jim found it easier to start by learning to alter his impulsive *behavior*, and this led to changes in his experience that led, in turn, to changes in his beliefs and feelings. Natalie began by examining, and changing, her *beliefs*. Loretta started to change by first understanding and accepting some of her *feelings*—feelings which she had previously been running away from. After reading through these cases think about the best starting point for bringing about the changes that you want to make. Drawing out your own *"personal formulation"* will make this easier, so do this first. Then choose something relatively straightforward to start with: something that you think is likely to make an important difference to you once the problematic framework starts to change.

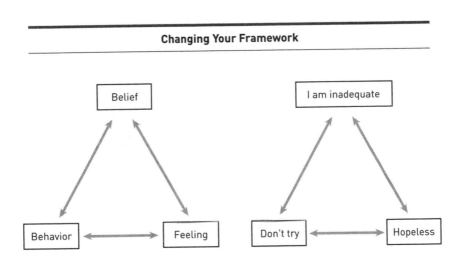

Changing Your Framework

How do your beliefs, feelings, and behavior link up? The answers to the questions you asked when identifying your problematic framework (see box on p. 350) will help you to fill in the model above for yourself. It is often useful to draw out several examples.

Decide what to change first. In order to start the process of change it is best to start with one clear and specific change. Use your personal formulation to guide your choice of which belief, feeling, or behavior to focus on. Two considerations should guide your choice. First, start with something that is connected to an important problem for you, so that the change you make is likely, eventually, to have a positive effect on the problem. Second, identify a clear and specific way of changing that would start you moving along that road.

JIM: CHANGING THE BELIEF THAT PEOPLE CAN'T BE TRUSTED

Jim's old pattern of behavior was aggressive, distant, and secretive. This is a lot to change all at once, especially if you still believe, as Jim did, that people cannot be trusted. But his habit of getting into fights was getting worse, and his problems of loneliness and feeling rejected cannot be resolved by keeping people at arms' length. What should he do instead? Jim wanted to overcome his loneliness, but it was clear that he could do little about that

Jim's Personal Formulation

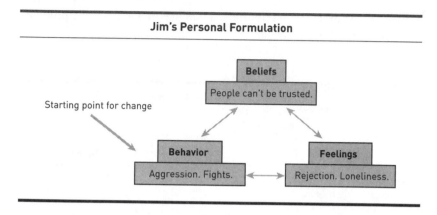

until he was able to sustain longer relationships and to stop pushing people away through his aggressive behavior, as shown in the box above.

The starting point for Jim was to learn a new skill: how to control his aggressive impulses. Then he decided what kinds of people he would like to spend time with, and then he started to go to places where he was likely to meet more of them. Eventually he found ways of joining in with activities that he enjoyed (mostly musical, and at the local bar). Only when he started to get to know people better did he begin to disclose personal things about himself. So the process of change for Jim involved first learning a new skill (impulse control) and then a gradual move into new territory as he changed his old behavior for something new.

If there is a specific behavioral pattern that contributes to your problems (as there was with Jim), then making this behavioral pattern the target for change is a good place to start. Experiment with doing something differently to find out whether your old framework needs rethinking. The process of behavior change has four steps.

1. Identify the old behavior.
2. Ask what kind of new behavior you need instead, so as to find out whether the old framework can be updated. You might need new skills as well as new behaviors, such as those involved in meeting people, talking to them more openly, or sticking up for yourself assertively without being aggressive.
3. Decide what to do differently. For some people it is best to start with small changes and then build up; others prefer to take the plunge. Be guided by your intuition, and if you are uncertain, experiment. Try to be clear about exactly what you will do differently, and

try not to be put off if you feel apprehensive and anxious. The difficulty in doing this can be that new ways of behaving, such as telling people about yourself, or letting them get close to you, can feel completely wrong, and out of character at first. They can make you feel anxious and fearful, or as if you have lost your way and no longer have firm ground beneath your feet. Then you need to take small steps first and build up your confidence gradually. You will need to persist, and to be prepared to resist a strong internal pressure to go back to old, and sometimes damaging, ways. For most of us it is pretty scary to try out something new and break away from old patterns of behavior. Every part of your mind and body, it may seem, is screaming at you to go back to your old ways of behaving. Expect this. Use your reason to help you to see that this comes from a real fear of change, not from real danger.

4. The last step is to think about what happened when you changed your behavior. How did it affect your feelings? How did it affect the behavior of those about you? How might it affect your relationships? Or your beliefs?

Jim's conclusion, after reducing his impulsive behavior over several months (with ups and downs along the way), was: "maybe some people can be trusted after all, at least in some ways." He began to learn whom he could trust to turn up when they said they would. Trust turned out to be far more complicated than he thought it would be. He accepted that most things are not "black and white." Natalie, on the other hand, was very much a black-and-white thinker. For her there were no shades of gray. It was on this way of thinking, rather than on her behavior, that she started to work.

NATALIE: CHANGING A PROBLEM OF EXTREMISM AND A SENSE OF WORTHLESSNESS

Natalie's old behavior involved flipping from one extreme to the other. She operated either at 110% and wore herself out, or she gave up and did nothing. In both cases she felt she had failed again, which only confirmed her beliefs about being worthless and bad. What changes did she need to make? Something that would help her to feel less of a failure, and also something that would allow her to update her self-opinion—the negative framework that slips into place only too readily. The trouble was that Natalie thought that she had to try her best to please others, and that it would be selfish to put herself first. This way of thinking made her feel worse rather than better when she thought about doing something for herself (like taking a rest)—as if this would prove what a bad person she was. It was Natalie's thinking, and her low self-esteem, that were getting in the way of change, and for her the best way of starting was to look carefully at these negative thoughts and then begin to change them. Her *"personal formulation"* showing the starting point for change that she chose is shown in the box below. Natalie began by answering these three questions about her belief that she was worthless and bad.

1. *How long have I believed this?* When did I start to think this way? Her answer was: "Too long ago to fix with a definite date."
2. *How did I come to think this way?* Is it because I am so bad and worthless that it was obvious to everyone even when I was small? Or is it a result of what happened to me? This is what she realized when answering these questions: "I was treated as if I was of no importance; as if I had so little worth that I could be used, and abused, as others wished—and ignored too, when it suited them."

No one is born with ready-made opinions about themselves. Opinions about yourself, and hence self-esteem and self-confidence, are built up through experience, and especially through relationships. Being cared for, loved, and appreciated tells you that you are worth caring for, loving, and appreciating. From the way that she had been treated, Natalie felt worthless and bad about herself. She had never questioned this feeling. Instead she struggled to do things

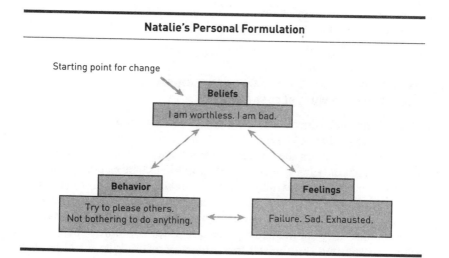

Natalie's Personal Formulation

Starting point for change

Beliefs

I am worthless. I am bad.

Behavior

Try to please others.
Not bothering to do anything.

Feelings

Failure. Sad. Exhausted.

well so as to earn some sort of recognition from people who otherwise neglected or abused her. So her beliefs made sense in terms of her experience, but that does not make them right. Natalie moved on to the next question.

3. *Could my belief be wrong?* Could it be based on conclusions I drew when I was young on the basis of what happened to me at the time? Natalie could see the logic of her answer to this: yes, it could be wrong. Her new understanding lifted her cloud of negative beliefs enough for her to see how her patterns worked: how, for example, they kept her at work long after others had gone home, making another extra effort to compensate for her badness by doing something extra well.

Natalie understood intellectually—in her head—that her old beliefs were wrong, but in her heart she still felt that she was a bad person. However, this does not mean that her intellectual understanding was useless: quite the contrary. This "knowing in her head" provided her with the motivation, and the insight, to begin to change. Working on her beliefs was the first step—and an important one. For her, the second step was to start to change her behavior. Thinking about her answers to the three questions enabled her to see the point of trying, and opened the door to change. Now she had to decide how, whether, and when to walk through it.

So, the next stage—making some changes in her behavior—was bound to be difficult. It was bound to make her anxious and even terrified. Natalie followed the same principles as those described for Jim. She wrote down a few examples of her old, extremist pattern of behavior, to make sure that she kept them in mind. Her task was to find the middle ground between all and nothing. For example, instead of trying to please others, she would have to stop working while she still had energy to spare. So she would have to focus on herself and pay close attention to how she felt—to her needs. She knew with her head that this was not being selfish and bad. She also knew that it would make her feel guilty and fearful, as if she was doing something wrong.

At home she decided to clean up less thoroughly. At work she decided to work calmly and steadily during the day, matching what she did with what others did, and to leave when they left rather than staying late. At first she felt miserable and guilty at the end of each day, and fearful at the start of the next one, as if she was about to be discovered doing something seriously wrong. It was quite a long while before she began to sense a glimmer of hope that she would be able to stop herself flipping from one extreme to the other—a glimmer that contrasted greatly with her former depressed view of things.

Over time Natalie learned to recognize the signs of doing too much: the sense of gritting her teeth and not wanting to let go until she had finished. She took the risk of leaving things unfinished, even though she still felt anxious about it. The payoff was that she no longer became so exhausted. The swings from overwork, on the one hand, to giving up in despair, on the other, had slowed down. By degrees she began to feel less of a failure, and less driven by an overpowering need to please other people. The sense that she could take charge of her life and make choices that she wanted (underneath) to make started to take root, and then to grow.

How did other people react to the changes she had made? They had come to expect 110% from Natalie when she was well, and so they too had to adjust. But mostly they took this in stride and could understand why Natalie had changed, and their attitude started to contribute to Natalie's sense of being acceptable. Having recognized her negative thoughts about herself, and her black-and-white thinking, Natalie chose to adapt her behavior—behavior that had been driven by her problematic thoughts. Her self-understanding—what she knew "in her head"—enabled her to weather the anxiety and guilt that were caused by her changes in behavior, for example. She reminded herself to expect these feelings, and she also reminded herself of the conclusion that she had no real reason to feel bad, worthless, or guilty. She did not need to compensate for her badness by making excessive efforts to please others. Her change in behavior led to improvements in her thinking and self-esteem, and also prevented the wild swings in behavior (excessive work followed by idleness, exhaustion, and despair) that had previously dominated her life.

Extremist ways of thinking, like those of Natalie, and all or nothing ways of behaving, are like bad habits that keep problems going. Seeing things as black or white also makes it hard to understand the behavior of others. For instance, if you have not experienced close relationships that worked well in the past, then when something goes wrong between you and your partner you might, for example, alternate between demanding total devotion and wanting to push them away. It can seem that "Either you love me or you don't," or "Either you're for me or against me," with no room for anything in between. We all need to learn how to find out what someone else's behavior really means, rather than jumping to conclusions based on what we feel it means, and then feeling (unnecessarily) devastated and rejected when something small goes wrong. For Natalie, moving away from extremist positions made life much less clear—much less black and white, but it also made her less vulnerable to mistakes and misunderstandings, and better able to adapt to others and to new situations. Changing behavior, even in small ways, helps to change patterns of black-and-white thinking, and to feel less stuck.

LORETTA: CHANGING THE FEELING OF BEING OUT OF CONTROL

Jim worked first on changing his behavior. For Natalie it was important to start with changing her thinking. Loretta began with her feelings.

Loretta's pattern of behavior was of constantly moving on. After a series of unpredictable, traumatic, and distressing events, she believed that nothing would ever go right for her and that good things would never last. Her life was chaotic and unsatisfying, but feelings of fear, guilt, and anger were calling the tune. Focusing on new and exciting things kept bad thoughts out of her mind. As long as she was engaged in something new—a new job, a new relationship, a new project—she could avoid thinking about the awful things that had happened to her in the past. She feared that if she turned to look them in the face she would start crying and never stop; or that she would get angry, but without being able to express that anger in an acceptable way. Loretta felt that she was like a small boat in a storm: entirely at the mercy of the wind and the waves. She decided that the best place to begin was to change her feelings; but how can that be done? She started by thinking about how her feelings, beliefs, and behavior were connected. That is, she started by making her "personal formulation" as shown below.

It is not helpful to pretend that you have no feelings, or to be told to snap out of it. In the long run, trying to blot out feelings or using alcohol

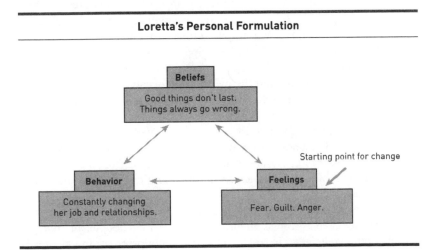

Loretta's Personal Formulation

Beliefs
Good things don't last.
Things always go wrong.

Starting point for change

Behavior
Constantly changing
her job and relationships.

Feelings
Fear. Guilt. Anger.

or recreational drugs so as to forget about them for a while only makes things worse. The starting point for Loretta was not to try and change things but to try and understand.

Understanding how feelings work. Feelings provide you with important information, for example they tell you what you want, or what you want to do. Feeling scared makes you want to get away. Feeling angry makes you want to hit out, or to do something to put things right and so on. Feelings motivate us, and prompt us into action, and without feelings we would be lost. But if you take no action when you have strong feelings, if you do not even acknowledge that the feelings are there, then you can get stuck in unhelpful ways of being. When people become locked into responding to the same feelings in the same unhelpful ways, it may be that only by acting "out of character" that they can make changes that bring a positive difference.

Responding to feelings with understanding. The first step for dealing with problematic feelings is to treat them with understanding. If a child is distressed, for example by a nightmare, it helps to be kind and understanding. Being calm and showing that you accept the feelings are more helpful than trying to reason away the tears. It is the same with yourself: first accept your feelings with a kindly understanding. The thinking comes later.

Instead of running away from feelings, or denying they are there, or trying to bury the bad and painful ones under a heap of distractions, we should acknowledge and accept them—even when they are confusing and difficult to name. Feelings come in many curious mixtures. We may be fond of people who have hurt us. We may feel resentful, disappointed, and hopeless all at once. We may be cross with ourselves for worrying about something that could not be helped. Whatever your feelings are, meet them with understanding and acceptance. Acceptance helps you to acknowledge their power and the pain that they cause. It reduces the tendency to blame yourself for having them, or to be ashamed of them.

Expressing feelings. Many things are to be gained from expressing feelings: greater understanding of why you feel as you do, and why the feelings make sense; relief; sympathy and understanding from a listener; and new discoveries, for example about the meaning of the experiences that troubled you.

In saying that it is valuable to express your feelings we do not mean that you need always to express them directly to other people, or that you should completely let go in order to express them properly. In Chapter 16

(Anger in Relationships) we explain how showing anger directly sometimes makes situations worse. We are referring here to being explicit about
your feelings. One way of doing this is to talk about your feelings to someone you trust, although sometimes talking about your negative feelings can
reinforce them and leave you feeling low. Some people, in any case, prefer
not to talk, and some have no opportunity to do so, unless they seek counseling or therapy. Other ways of expressing feelings include writing and
drawing pictures. Expressing feelings in any way that suits you can help to
lay them to rest. It contributes to the process of getting unstuck.

Overcoming fear of feelings.   Loretta was scared of her feelings: of their
overwhelming strength, and of the things she might want to do if she acknowledged them. Some people fear that if they open up the box of
demons, like Pandora in the myth, they will never be able to stuff them
back in again. Indeed, when bad things have happened to you, turning
your attention toward your memories, rather than ignoring them or blocking them out, can at first bring with it strong and upsetting feelings—hence
the need for creating a safe place and good support systems before you begin. But it can also be a step on the road toward finishing the unfinished
business.

How did Loretta use these ideas?   Thinking first about how feelings
work, Loretta realized that much of the time she was running away from
them: chasing an exciting possibility or a chance of something new so that
her underlying feelings could be kept at bay. She knew that she had some
unresolved problems from the past, but she had never given time to them,
nor spoken about them or thought them through.

The idea that feelings are understandable made her wonder whether
this was true of hers. Loretta had picked up this idea from a magazine and
had been turning it over in the back of her mind for some time when a
friend asked her why she always seemed to have a new boyfriend. Trying to
answer the question made her realize that underneath she was scared and
confused. Gradually it dawned on her that she still felt scared by her memories of the time when her mother and sister nearly drowned, and that she
also felt guilty, as if she had done something wrong. Again she was confused by her feelings, and did not understand the reasons behind them, but
she tried to acknowledge them, and to accept that they were still there.

She decided she would take up one of the suggestions in the magazine
and write about the things that her feelings brought to mind. Loretta
wrote, without thinking too hard, about the story of the swimming accident on vacation. She had been for a walk along the cliffs and came back

to find the beach in an uproar. A freak wave had pounded onto the rocks where some people, including her mother and sister, were sunbathing, and swept them into the sea. Rescuers were pulling frightened people out of the water, and she was told that two people had drowned. In the few minutes that it took to find that her mother and sister were alive and well, she became frantic with distress, and in her memory quite incoherent. After the accident, her mother and sister were comforted and cared for, and encouraged to talk about what had happened. Loretta was haunted by what she had seen, and for months suffered from vivid, terrifying nightmares. But she felt she had no right to talk about it. The accident had happened to them not to her, and the message she received at home was: "You've got nothing to worry about. They're the ones who need help. You ought to know that, after being injured in a car accident yourself." So she tried to stifle her feelings, and felt guilty for having them, and even more guilty for bothering people with them.

Loretta had to overcome a good deal of fear to face up to the degree of guilt that she felt, and to the sense that her feelings were wrong. She realized that she also felt angry about her father having been laid off, and about giving up her plans to go to college. She felt guilty about her anger, but had suppressed both feelings. It was working on these feelings that started the process of unraveling the old framework for Loretta, and set her on a more constructive path. It was not wrong to have the feelings that she had; nor was it wrong for her to need help after the accident. Her angry feelings about having to change her plans were also quite natural. Realizing these things provided Loretta with a route into changing her thinking.

Loretta then turned her attention to doing things differently. Again her feelings interfered with her plans. Loretta wanted her life to be less chaotic, and to give it some direction, but thinking ahead frightened her. "What if . . . ?" was the first thing that came to mind, and her imagination filled in the blanks only too readily. If she built up her life more coherently then she would be vulnerable once more to accidents. It could all come tumbling down again. These fears had the potential to stop her from making any changes. In order to change she had to keep in mind the realization that if she made no changes she would continue to lead an unhappy and chaotic life. Although bad things might happen to her in the future, they would not be any less bad if she remained as she was, and they could possibly become worse.

Loretta turned back to her friend for help, and she also started to talk quite casually to other people about what made them take up with a new boyfriend, or give up on a job. She had been reluctant even to mention such topics before as she assumed other people were able to run their lives better than she was, and that she would only feel inferior, and out of control, compared with them. After listening to them she decided she would try to be less impulsive and to make more considered decisions. She realized that changing the old pattern would make her worry that she was tempting providence, and inviting more disasters into her life, but nevertheless she resolved to talk things through with others before making sudden changes. It was a less exciting and a more difficult way to live at first, and many times she made mistakes or gave up the struggle, feeling tearful and frustrated. But she had started along the road that made her feel better about herself, and she had no doubt that it made her feel more in control.

COMMON PITFALLS ON THE ROAD TO CHANGE

Making changes rarely goes completely smoothly, particularly when the old ways of thinking—the old frameworks—are deeply engrained. So be alert to common pitfalls and do not let the bumpy road to life stop your resolve to carry on, step by step, making the changes that you hope will give you more contentment and more fulfillment in your life.

Setbacks. Setbacks occur on almost every path to overcoming problems. When childhood trauma is part of the problem, setbacks can feel dramatic: not just stubbing your toe, but piercing an old wound (see pp. 375–385).

Blaming others. It is important not to spend too much time and energy blaming others. They may be at fault. They may have caused pain and damage. You may be quite right to blame them. The difficulty is that you can only change *your* life, and the ways that *you* think, feel, and behave. When you make changes others may follow suit, and you may then be able to adjust in ways that you find helpful. They too (probably) have their own, relatively rigid and fixed frameworks for approaching the world, so it may take more than a prompt from you to make them change. Some people who have got stuck blaming others, their parents for example, have found it useful to imagine the childhood and youth of the person or people who hurt them in as much detail as possible. The purpose of this is to see and understand how they became what they were, and to use this understanding as a basis for moving on and leaving the blame behind.

It can feel lonely. Harmful experiences during childhood can lead to difficulties in forming supportive and close relationships. If this is the case for you then you may be feeling lonely and unsupported on your road to change. Part Three of this book is about relationships, and in Chapter 25

(Loss and Bereavement) we discuss the problem that most, or all, of your friends may shy away from talking to you about your difficulties, and we also discuss practical ways of finding new friends.

Intrusions, memories, and flashbacks. These are common following trauma and are not a sign that you are going mad. Ways of dealing with them are described in Chapter 27 *(Recent Traumatic Events and Their Aftermath)*. It can also help to label them for what they are (see p. 376), to use distraction techniques (pp. 225, 301–303), and to develop your skills for keeping yourself safe.

Dealing with urges to self-harm. See *Further Reading*, and p. 308. The book by Schmidt and Davidson, *Life After Self-Harm: A Guide to the Future*, contains many useful and practical ideas.

Eating habits. These are sometimes disturbed as a result of distressing childhood experiences. See Chapter 31.

Chapter Summary

Bad experiences early in life help to define the perspectives from which we view the world. These frameworks affect what we think, feel, and do, and they developed because at the time they were useful. If the frameworks persist when they are no longer needed they can cause problems. Then it helps to update them.

1. Lay the foundations for change by understanding your current frameworks. This involves thinking about the painful things that happened to you and recognizing their meaning, and the problems that arise from them.
2. Create a comfort zone. Change can feel risky, and it can trigger bad memories. Look after yourself well as you change.
3. Draw out your personal formulation, to make sense of your problems and what keeps them going, then decide where to start. There are many routes to change, starting with behaviors, beliefs, or feelings. Once you are clear about what to focus on then you can mix and match the ideas as you wish.
4. Old habits die hard, so try not to be discouraged if the changes you first make seem small, and bad old habits reemerge from time to time, even though you have started to change. It is cumulative: one small success leads to another and gradually you find yourself moving forward to a place that feels better.

27

Recent Traumatic Events
and Their Aftermath

Intensely frightening or traumatic experiences often produce extreme reactions, and some of these can be strange and very alarming. Some people, for instance, repeatedly feel or behave as if the awful event is still happening, and cry out or become rooted to the spot in terror. These reactions may perpetuate the horror of the trauma, and sometimes they can interfere with the process of recovery. This chapter is for people who have suffered a traumatic experience, and also for those who wish to help them. It describes the common and normal reactions to traumatic experiences, and then provides a framework for recovery explaining the main coping strategies that are known to be useful.

What Is a Trauma?

The word trauma is loosely used to describe the horrific things that happen in the world. However it also has a technical definition, and this is the one that we will use here. According to this definition a traumatic event involves the threat of death or of serious injury to oneself or to others, and the event may involve real serious injury or the death of one or more people. People can be traumatized by experiencing events which provoke intense fear, horror, or feelings of helplessness, or by witnessing such events, for example as an uninvolved observer, as a rescuer, or as a member of one of the emergency services. Examples of traumatic events include automobile and other accidents, assault, violent crime, rape, fires, natural disasters such as earthquakes, man-made disasters such as industrial accidents, and many of the products of terrorism and war, including torture or threat of torture. If you add all the possibilities together, traumatic events are surprisingly common. A recent American study found that 81% of men and 74% of women had been exposed to at least one traumatic event in their lives.

Common Reactions Following a Traumatic Experience

Many people recover well from a traumatic event, and they do so in their own ways and frequently without professional help. Nevertheless, there is much to be gained from knowing more about what to expect and what to do to help the recovery process along.

Common experiences following a trauma include feelings of intense distress, nightmares, memories, or images of the trauma repeatedly forcing themselves into consciousness accompanied by distressing thoughts, feelings, and sensations similar to those experienced at the time. Bouts of intense feelings other than fear or terror are also common, for example guilt; over failing either to prevent the traumatic event or to lessen its impact. Some people feel ashamed of something that they did, or did not do, at the time. Some feel miserable or hopeless about the future, or believe that the traumatic experience has damaged them irretrievably, or that they will never be the same again. Some people feel so hopeless that they wonder whether they can carry on with life. These experiences do not always happen immediately after the trauma. Sometimes people feel numb and detached at first, the more intense feelings starting only after a delay.

All of these experiences are normal reactions to abnormal events. Knowing they are normal does not lessen the pain, but it can be reassuring to know that you are not going mad and that you are on a path that leads to recovery. In the box on page 369 we have listed the most common responses to trauma, organized into three groups: reexperiencing the trauma; avoidance and numbing; and increased arousal.

Feelings and signs of distress following a trauma often fluctuate. They tend to be worse around the time of the anniversary of the event, and to be better during periods of full engagement in present-day activities and relationships. They sometimes worsen at times of major life changes (e.g., during physical illness, or after retirement), and very rarely people who had previously had no symptoms develop a full blown syndrome much later when new information becomes available to them. This happened, for example, to a woman who was assaulted and later discovered that her assailant killed his next victim.

Common Reactions Following a Traumatic Experience

Most people experience some, but not all, of these reactions

1. *Reexperiencing the trauma, or aspects of it:*
   - Repetitive and intrusive thoughts, images, and memories
   - Flashbacks in which you feel (or act) as if the trauma was happening again and you were still in danger. This may include a sense of reliving the experience
   - Intense sensations
   - Distress triggered by reminders of the trauma
   - Nightmares

2. *Avoidance and numbing:*
   - Trying to avoid activities, people, or places that bring the trauma to mind
   - Trying not to think or talk about the trauma, or to have similar feelings
   - Trying to keep safe from similar threats, risks, or dangers
   - Feeling emotionally numb, distanced, detached, or estranged from others
   - Restrictions in the range of emotions experienced, and loss of interest
   - Reduced ability to think about the future or to plan ahead

3. *Increased arousal:*
   - Difficulty falling or staying asleep
   - Irritability or outbursts of anger
   - Difficulty concentrating
   - An exaggerated response to being startled; symptoms of panic
   - Hypervigilance: being constantly on the lookout for threats or dangers

---

1 REEXPERIENCING THE TRAUMA

Reliving the trauma is a common and painful experience. Intrusive thoughts, images, memories, and sensations come unbidden into the mind just as if the event was happening right now and you were still in danger or facing a serious threat. These may be provoked by obvious reminders of the event such as seeing a newspaper report, or they may come apparently out of the blue.

Flashbacks can be as vivid and as "real" as the original experiences, and bring the same feelings with them. When this happens something is likely to have triggered the reaction even though the connecting link may be hard to pinpoint—and may never be certainly known.

2 AVOIDANCE AND NUMBING REACTIONS

Avoidance and numbing reactions involve withdrawing so as to protect yourself from danger, or shutting down so as to reduce the pain and suffering, with the result that the ability to feel positive emotions such as affection, pleasure, or interest is also reduced. It may be difficult or impossible to remember some parts of the traumatic experience. Your story of the event may have gaps in it even if you did not have a head injury. More extreme reactions lead to feeling disconnected from your surroundings, from others, or even from your body, as if you were unreal. Some people feel alienated from others after a trauma, and become preoccupied with mistrustful thoughts about them.

3 INCREASED AROUSAL

Increased arousal makes people jumpy and quick to react, producing physiological changes such as a racing heart, sweating, or trembling, and interfering with sleep, appetite, and sexual responsiveness. Irritability and anger are easily provoked, and it is difficult to unwind or to concentrate. Reminders of the trauma such as a sudden noise or being unexpectedly touched (even by someone you are fond of and know to be harmless) can produce immediate panic reactions.

Three Common Questions

1 HOW LONG DO TRAUMATIC REACTIONS LAST?

Traumatic events often occur suddenly, so they hit people unawares and take some time—weeks or months—to adjust to. Most people feel better within about three months, but it is not possible to predict exactly how long the distress will last. Ongoing traumatic events such as those encountered by soldiers or civilians in a war zone, or by people living with domestic violence, produce more prolonged reactions because of continual reminders that the danger is not over. Usually, in spite of intense trauma reactions, most people are able to carry on relatively well with their lives even during the first month following the event.

2 WHAT MAKES SOME PEOPLES' TRAUMA REACTIONS WORSE THAN OTHERS?

We know only some of the answers to this question at present. In general, reactions will be worse the "higher the dose" of trauma and the more severe the symptoms immediately after the traumatic event. People suffer more if they are not able to draw on the support of others, if they have experienced previous trauma (including sexual abuse as a child or young person), and if they have previously suffered from serious psychological difficulties.

3 WHAT IS DEBRIEFING, AND DOES IT HELP?

Debriefing involves encouraging people to talk in detail about their experiences soon after the trauma is over, and encouraging them to develop a complete and coherent story about what happened. There is no evidence that debriefing helps, and it may even make things worse for those who find the trauma especially distressing. Being told what to expect, receiving support from others, and talking with people who suffered the same experience can be useful. If you want to offer support to someone who has suffered a trauma, provide opportunities for the person to talk about what happened and to express any of the feelings or concerns that may follow. Try to listen with understanding and compassion, but do not probe for more information than you are offered.

A Framework for Recovery

Most people who experience a trauma recover without professional help within a few months, although different people recover in different ways and at different rates. Each of us is different and your most reliable guide is yourself: following your instincts and doing what feels right for you. There is no single road to recovery, no one right way of going about it, but sometimes we get stuck, or overwhelmed. If this happens it is helpful to have a framework for recovery to help you along the way. The framework described below has two parts. The first part consists of some principles to bear in mind. The second part involves understanding how memory works. This understanding helps to make sense of the reactions to a trauma, and to recognize that some of them are part of a normal adjustment to a major upheaval.

**PART ONE: SEVEN PRINCIPLES FOR A PERSONAL
RECOVERY FRAMEWORK**

1. *Establish a routine for your daily life.* This helps to make things feel predictable, under control, and more secure.
2. *Turn to others for help and support.* This is known to be helpful and may even protect you from the worst effects of trauma. Talking or meeting with people who have had similar experiences can be especially helpful, but if you are not one for talking you may just need company, or an opportunity to take part in joint activities, or to be around people at home or at work. It can feel good to let someone know how you are feeling even without any further discussion, and indirect contact with others, for example through email or Internet sites, can also provide valuable help and support.

   The fatigue and irritability that follow a trauma can produce conflicts which add to the strain. Try to find a way of resolving such conflicts or arguments as soon as you can, especially with those close to you. Otherwise these may add to your difficulties.

   If possible, ask someone who knows you well to read this chapter, so that they understand more about what is happening to you. If they know what to expect and what you are trying to do, they will be better able to understand your struggles and achievements, and to offer effective encouragement without pressure.
3. *Be kind to yourself.* Read *Chapter 7, Treating Yourself Right,* and try not to add self-blame or self-criticism to your other difficulties. You may feel unstable, or overwhelmed, or out of control. You may feel that you acted badly at the time, or failed to do something that you should or could have done. Such thoughts are understandable, but often they fail to take account of the realities of the situation or the precise circumstances surrounding the trauma. Often people later think of things they could have done differently without realizing how fast things happened at the time, and how little time there was for making decisions or for the consideration that comes later.
4. *A degree of acceptance can make a big difference.* Try to accept that none of us can protect ourselves totally from risk. We can take sensible precautions but we cannot control everything—and we have to accept a measure of risk in order to live healthy lives. Try to accept that you will have painful thoughts, images, and memories without making an effort to suppress them. Trying to suppress such things is counterproductive: the more you do it the stronger they

become. Instead think of them as you would think of express trains thundering through a station. Stand back a bit so that you can watch them come, recognize their power, and watch them go.

Try to accept all of the thoughts and feelings that come to you, and find a way of expressing them if you can. If you do not wish to talk about your feelings you may prefer to express them in some other way, for instance by writing about what happened, through painting and drawing, through activity and exercise, or by making something. Expressing them, sometimes repeatedly, helps you to reflect on them, to understand them better and to feel less overwhelmed by them. So do not struggle to keep them under control, or try to stop having them.

5. *Find time for relaxing and recreational activities.* It may be hard to enjoy yourself at first, or you may feel bad about doing so at a time of pain and loss, but distracting yourself in this way, including joining in playful activities, is good for your mental health. It breaks up the pattern of distress and helps to reestablish some normality and a full range of feelings. It also helps you to feel less tired.

6. *When you are ready, try to face the situations, people, and places that remind you of the trauma, in your own way and in your own time.* This may make you more anxious at first, so you should judge what you are ready for and make use of any people or strategies that make this easier for you. Putting too much energy into protecting yourself from possible danger, or keeping yourself safe, can interfere with your ability to carry on with normal life again.

7. *Make use of prescribed medication as advised by a medical practitioner, but do not make a habit of using alcohol or street drugs* to lessen your pain, or in an attempt to help you to sleep. In the long run this will add to your difficulties rather than reducing them.

These ideas are easy to lose sight of when feeling distressed, overwhelmed, or chaotic. Use the summary to help you to think of ways in which you could apply each of the seven principles to your own life and circumstances. Write down your ideas and put your list somewhere easy to find. Look at the list if you feel especially bad, and use it to plan what you could do and when you will do it. It may also help to tell someone about these ideas so that they can make suggestions or prompt you into action if you feel stuck.

Summary of Principles to Guide Recovery

Seven principles for the recovery framework
1. Establish a routine for daily life
2. Seek support from others. Talk as much as you wish. Resolve conflicts quickly
3. Treat yourself with kindness and compassion
4. Accept your feelings rather than fighting against them
5. Face what you are ready to face
6. Make time to relax and play
7. Beware of dependence on alcohol or street drugs

PART TWO: MAKING SENSE OF TRAUMA MEMORIES

A traumatic experience bombards the mind with a huge quantity of intensely distressing information—so much so that the mind cannot make sense of it all at once. Some of the after-effects of a traumatic experience reflect this struggle to assimilate, and digest, what has happened. Two kinds of memory are involved.

Two kinds of memory.   In normal circumstances memories of past events enable us to tell a (more or less) coherent story about what happened. We know that we are talking about something that is in the past (for example a summer vacation a few years ago), and it is possible to think and to talk about it relatively dispassionately. You might remember how irritated you were when you lost your camera, or how much you enjoyed an adventurous or relaxing day, but such memories are unlikely to make you particularly irritated, or relaxed, now. Such memories have been successfully processed and stored: you can bring them to mind if someone asks you, but otherwise they are unlikely to come back to you without the help of a specific reminder, such as finding the old photographs. Even then the memory is experienced as a memory, as though there is some distance between you now, and you then. There is not that vivid sense that accompanies current experience.

Trauma memories are different. Trauma memories are often muddled, patchy, and intrusive. Fragments of memory may unexpectedly grab your attention, bringing with them intense feelings and sensory details (the smell of gas; the sound of a voice). These fragments of memory are often vivid and detailed, and when they occur it is as if the event is happening all over again, right now in the present moment. Sometimes the fragments do not fit with the whole story, but seem distressingly disconnected: for example, you may have the sense all over again of being unable to move or call for help, even though you now know that this moment only lasted a few seconds; or you may truly believe for a moment that someone close to you has been killed even though you know they are still alive. You may remember some things in excruciatingly fine detail even though your memory for the whole event is full of gaps, and these gaps can obscure important parts of what happened. Remembering in this way is triggered by reminders of the trauma, even if you cannot pinpoint exactly what these are.

Current understanding of these phenomena suggests that the intense feelings associated with the trauma make it hard to process the memory and lay it to rest, as if the brain is overloaded with details and sensations, and not as yet able to make sense of what has happened, nor label it as a past, rather than a current, event. Normally the intense feelings (good or bad) that follow an important experience (the making or breaking of a relationship for instance) gradually fade. Following a trauma the memories can be so distressing and vivid that we are unable to stand back from them. Not surprisingly, we may try to prevent such memories from coming into our mind, and when they do, we try to shut them out. But, paradoxically, such attempts are likely to make the memories all the more intrusive by slowing down or preventing the processing that is needed for the memory to be stored, like the memory of the summer vacation, as a past event that no longer intrudes, and that can be brought to mind appropriately without the accompanying sensory and emotional detail that is so disturbing.

Coping Strategies

The three cornerstones to recovery following a traumatic event are:

1. Trust yourself and your intuitions, for example about how much to talk to others about the experience.
2. Make use of the seven principles summarized on page 374, and of your own ideas about how to apply them to yourself.
3. Use your understanding of the two memory systems to make sense of the ways in which you reexperience the trauma.

In addition you can make use of the wisdom and experience of others for coping with some of the more disruptive and unpleasant reactions that are so disturbing.

When to Seek Professional Help

You should seek professional help at once if:

1. You feel at risk of harming yourself.
2. You have become so depressed that there seems to be no point in going on.
3. Your outbursts of anger and irritation put you at risk of harming others.

You should also seek help and advice if your symptoms have persisted for several months without changing, or if you feel you want the help of a professional. At any point in the process professional advice may be useful and you should not hesitate to seek it out, from medical practitioners, mental health workers, websites, leaflets, and books. Such support can speed you on the road to recovery, and there are a number of research-based treatments that are known to be effective.

Medication can help you sleep or feel less panicky, for instance, but it is generally helpful only for brief periods, and can cause problems if taken on a long-term basis.

Coping with Flashbacks

A flashback is a memory that comes suddenly to mind, apparently unbidden, bringing with it the sense of living through the trauma once more with all of the same distress. Flashbacks can involve sights, sounds, or any other sensations or feelings, and they can be momentary or can last for more than a few seconds. Sometimes the same fragment of memory comes over and over again, each time bringing with it the sense that the horror is still going on right now, in the present.

Flashbacks are often profoundly upsetting, and it is natural to try to suppress them or to stop them from happening, or to find ways of detaching oneself from the pain and distress. Such detachment can lead to feelings of being disconnected from the surroundings. Extreme forms of detachment are called dissociation—a state in which people may be so cut off from reality that they are apparently unable to hear or respond to the things that are going on around them. But trying to suppress memories from intruding does not work. Consider the following example. If you were told, out of the blue, to make sure that you did not think of a giraffe in the next few minutes you would immediately think of—a giraffe. Telling yourself not to think something works against you as it brings that thing straight to mind. Instead of trying to suppress a flashback it is important to try to accept what is happening to you. Try to anchor yourself in the present as it really is now: for instance, look at and feel the chair you are sitting in; remind yourself of the date and time; say something out loud so that you can hear yourself talking; look out of the window; turn the light on. Such activities help to mark the difference between the time of the trauma and your current experience. They assist in the process of extracting yourself from the sense of reliving the trauma by forcing present reality into mind. Sensory experiences are especially useful for making you feel grounded in the present, especially if your flashbacks contain their own sensory elements. Finding different smells, sounds, tastes, or sensations helps to interrupt the flashback and brings you back to the here and now. Some examples of what you might do are: smell a lavender bag; suck a mint; say today's date or your name and age, or "it's over now," out loud; engage in a physical activity such as swinging your arms about.

You can prepare for future flashbacks by making a list of some ways in which your current situation differs from the events surrounding the trauma. For example the time and date will be different; you may be in a different place or have moved to a new place, or be surrounded by different people. It may help to put photographs up as reminders: photographs of your life as it is now to contrast with the actual time of the trauma.

Dealing with Nightmares

It is common to have occasional nightmares following a trauma, and some people repeatedly have the same one, or a series of them, many times during the night and also if they fall asleep during the day. Often the feelings that come with the nightmares linger during the day even when the details of the nightmare fade. Sometimes the nightmares clearly reflect details of the traumatic incident, and sometimes they reflect its implications or personal significance: feeling helpless, or bereft, or damaged, or threatened, and so on. Persistent nightmares are especially distressing and debilitating. They do usually subside, but two sets of strategies can help to get rid of them.

1. *Sleep-related strategies.* When you wake from a nightmare wake yourself fully and try to ground yourself in the present (as described above for dealing with flashbacks). It may help to use a nightlight so that you can quickly find your bearings when you wake. Stay awake

until you feel sleepy again. You could read, listen to music, or get up and engage in some distracting but gentle activity, so as to clear your mind of the shadows (images) left by the nightmare. Try not to compensate for the loss of sleep at night by allowing yourself to doze during the day (even though you may feel exhausted), and avoid drinking caffeine or too much alcohol at any time. You will find further ideas about how to improve your sleep in Chapter 30.

2. *Strategies for dealing with the content of the nightmares.* The purpose of these strategies is to help you adjust to the emotional impact of the trauma as it is reflected in your nightmares by crystallizing their meaning for you, and reexamining that meaning just as one might reexamine the meaning of other thoughts (e.g., p. 80). During the daytime, when you feel as comfortable as possible, ask yourself what the nightmares are about. What feelings do they bring with them? What is the personal significance to you of the things that happen in your nightmares? What kind of an impact do they have on you? What are their implications, for yourself and for your future, for instance? The aim is to focus on the meanings reflected in the nightmares, not on the details of what happened.

Then think again about both the feelings you have and about those personal meanings. Your feelings tell you something about what you need, and this will differ depending on whether you feel, for example, terrified, victimized, guilty, or angry. The meanings tell you more about what matters to you, and they help to make sense of your feelings, but this does not mean that they reflect the only way of seeing things. They define your perspective and it can be helpful to search for other perspectives.

For nightmares that always end in the same way it can be helpful, during the daytime when you feel comfortable and safe, to imagine that the nightmare was like a video or film to which you could provide the ending. Imagine the ending you would like: an ending that resolves your feelings of distress. Try to picture that ending, and, if you feel strong enough, try to watch, in imagination, your whole new video again, this time with your ending attached. The purpose of the ending is to reflect the emotional resolution that would be helpful to you, and it can be quite unrealistic if you wish. Some people like to try out different endings until they find one that resolves as much of their distress as possible. If this feels comfortable at the time, then go through it many times, and when you next are woken by a nightmare see if it helps to imagine your new ending.

Facing Your Memories

Facing your memories, with all their associated pain and sometimes horror, helps you to lay them to rest; it makes them less emotionally disturbing and less likely to intrude unexpectedly in the way that flashbacks and nightmares do. Begin by facing them deliberately, and bit by bit, in the easiest possible way. Work at this slowly, in a gentle and compassionate way if your progress has been stuck for a couple of months or more.

Because facing the memories is hard to do, therapists have developed a method called "reliving," in which they guide people through this part of their recovery and help them to describe the details of what happened to them, and to pinpoint which were the worst moments for them. Reliving has been shown to be extremely useful but we do not advise you to try to do this on your own if you think that it would provoke too much distress.

Returning to the Site of the Trauma

If it is practically possible to return to the site of the trauma, and if it is physically safe, it can be useful to do so because it helps to anchor the trauma firmly in the past, and sometimes helps people to discover that their original memories were faulty in some way. However, you should not force yourself to do this unless you think it would be useful and unless you feel sufficiently strong. It is generally best not to do this until your recovery is well advanced. Think about taking someone with you who can help you to decide what you would like to get out of such a visit, and what you would need to do, or see, in order to achieve your aim. The prospect of returning to the site of the trauma is often so alarming that people do not think of making it possible. In some cases it can, however, be enormously helpful, for example for someone who kept blaming herself for not avoiding an attack and then discovered that there was no way she could have seen her assailant coming.

Building the Confidence to Take Risks

Following a traumatic experience many people are driven by the need to reestablish a sense of security. A traumatic experience forces us to recognize that there are serious threats and dangers in our worlds, and we need a safe base from which to face them, and to deal with them when we have to. Our homes, our relationships, our jobs, our routines, and all manner of familiar activities and surroundings contribute to making us feel safe. So it can be helpful to reestablish familiar activities in familiar places following a trauma. However the need to feel safe can also be carried too far, and then our safety-seeking behaviors may prevent us from becoming confident again. For instance driving very slowly, or never going out after dark, or sleeping with the light on, are safety behaviors which keep the idea of possible danger in mind and interfere with ordinary activities. Such safety behaviors may feel sensible at first, but in the long run they tend to make the likelihood of another traumatic experience feel greater: they stop us from taking to heart how unlikely this is. Safety behaviors can add to the problems that follow a trauma when they lead you to take unnecessary precautions, interfere with ordinary activities, and keep you alert to possible signs of danger. You can build the confidence to give up the safety behaviors by starting to take small risks and moving on to bigger ones as your confidence grows.

Rethinking Your First Impressions

There is hardly a moment in our lives when our brains are not trying to make sense of what is happening to us—but it is often hard to make sense of traumatic experiences and our reactions to them. The interpretations we make at the time are sometimes correct, but often they are not. They are often emotional, and quite unreasonable, partly because we leap to conclusions before we have all the information, and partly because they are influenced by our feelings at the time, and by our habitual ways of seeing things. The frameworks that reflect our thinking habits, and the way they develop and later influence us are described in *Chapter 26, Dealing with the Past.* Examples of unhelpful interpretations are thinking, "This must be my fault," or "I should have been able to prevent this happening," when in fact there was either nothing you could have done, or it is only with hindsight that you can see that you could have acted differently. Interpretations of reactions to the trauma may also be mistaken: "I must be weak—or mad," "I will never be safe again," "This shows that I can't trust myself to do the right thing in a crisis," "I will never be able to cope with difficulties again," and so on.

A central message of this book is that the ways we think have a big influence on the ways we feel. So the conclusions we come to when trying to make sense of a traumatic experience will influence the way we feel.

If these conclusions are wrong, or if they are colored by a habit of self-blame, for instance, then they will contribute to our distress. Taking another look at them can open up unexpected routes to change. The main ways of doing this are described in *Chapter 9, Keeping Things in Perspective: Help from Cognitive Therapy.*

Searching for Meaning

The first reactions to a traumatic event are those of intense shock and distress. Once these reactions have subsided, many others emerge, including reactions that are influenced by the meaning given to the event—for good or for bad. This is particularly clear after traumatic events that affect large numbers of people at once. People try to make sense of what has happened in different ways, and in doing so they tend to give the event the kind of meaning that makes sense to them and that reflects their ways of seeing things. For example, the same disaster may be seen by different people as resulting from different causes: as a product of political, or economic, or natural forces, or as a punishment for misbehavior and immorality, or as an opportunity to reevaluate what matters in life and to clarify values. There are bound to be many different opinions after traumatic and unsettling events which threaten our sense of security and which often leave us feeling confused.

Recent research has found that those who are able to find a positive meaning in their traumatic experience, or in some aspects of it, are more likely to recover quickly, and some examples of positive meanings are provided below. Of course these are personal meanings, and they cannot be put on, and others taken off, like a winter coat. But all of us can attempt, when we are ready, to stand back from our traumatic experiences and make contact with the values that matter to us. From these we may be able to find more hopeful meanings that may help to guide our recovery.

Some of the more positive meanings others have found come from discovering how much they cared about others, or how much others cared about them. They could also come from realizing what matters to you and what is unimportant, so that you can decide how not to waste your life on trivialities; or from the feeling that you have been lucky, or rescued for a purpose which then directs your energies into a particular direction, such as helping others, or working to prevent such things happening again. Some people survive with renewed faith, or discover a spiritual belief for the first time. Some are able to let go of former fears and worries, including the fear of death.

Recognizing Echoes of Previous Traumatic or Unpleasant Events

For some people a traumatic experience brings with it echoes of previous events in their lives: for instance an assault makes you feel hurt or victimized as you were during your childhood; being cared for after an injury reminds you of previous neglect; being questioned by police or emergency service personnel makes you feel accused or criticized. Recovery from a traumatic event is less straightforward when such complicating factors are also present. If the new traumatic event revives memories and intrusive thoughts about earlier traumatic experiences, you should consider seeking professional advice. You will also find in *Chapter 26, Dealing with the Past,* some ideas to help you to cope when echoes from the past are causing present difficulties.

Difficult Feelings Often Associated with Trauma

ANXIETY, FEAR, AND PANIC

Traumas are unusual and terrifying events which tend to shake people's underlying sense of security or safeness. It is not surprising that anxiety, fear, and panic often result. The symptoms of increased arousal listed in the box on page 369 are often exaggerated for a time afterward, and may also lead to panic attacks (see Chapter 21), frequent, intense bouts of worrying, and to more specific fears clearly linked to the trauma, such as fear of driving on freeways, or of going out alone at night, or of traveling on the subway. In Chapters 18–21 you will find many ideas for dealing with the different ways in which anxiety can affect you.

DEPRESSION AND LOSS

A profound sense of despair can follow a trauma, especially one in which the person felt helpless at the time. Chapters 22–24 are focused on ways of dealing with depression. Traumas are also often linked with major losses such as bereavements, and with important but sometimes less obvious losses such as loss of physical health or integrity, of the ability to work, of self-confidence, or pleasure, or of a sense of security. Chapter 25 focuses on loss and bereavement.

ANGER

Anger is a common reaction to traumatic experiences: anger with those who hurt or victimized you, for instance, or anger at the interruption to your life, or with yourself for being unable to snap back into action. In the period following a trauma, frustrations may build up if you are unable to carry on with your life as before; or you may feel angry about the arbitrariness or unfairness of what happened. Distress and exhaustion may leave you with a short fuse, feeling constantly irritable, aggressive, or explosive. Others may be unable to understand or to help, and when you are irritable they may respond in kind and the anger may escalate. The ways in which anger interferes with relationships, and ways of dealing with it, are described in Chapter 16.

GUILT AND SHAME

People may feel guilty or ashamed about things that they did during the traumatic experience—even when they had no other options at the time. Or they may feel that their distress is a sign of weakness or lack of moral fiber, or worry about the effects on others of their distress. They may feel bad about being persistently unable to function as they had in the past. Such feelings are often rooted in earlier beliefs about what one should or should not do, or should be able to do, and link with long-standing attitudes and expectations which may not have been put into words before. The methods of cognitive therapy (see Chapter 9) have been developed to help people stand back from such thoughts, assumptions, and beliefs, and to search for new, realistic, but also more helpful and consoling perspectives.

FEELING PHYSICALLY UNWELL

Traumas provide a major shock to the whole person, and often upset the immune system, making people vulnerable to infection and disease. Disrupted sleep patterns, worry, and distress are exhausting and can deplete your resources as they take their toll. Headaches, gastrointestinal problems, chest pain, dizziness, and many minor infectious illnesses often increase for a period following a trauma. Be aware of your vulnerability, and take especially good care of yourself for several months. Allow yourself more rest than usual, and give yourself a healthy diet.

Effects of Injury

Some people have to endure a prolonged period of recovery after a traumatic incident, and others have to adapt to living with the kind of chronic pain or disability that interferes with their lifestyle and relationships, or that demands permanent changes from them and those around them. Persistent pain and disability can serve as a constant reminder of the trauma, making it hard to move on. The time, energy, and flexibility demanded by the need to make major adjustments should not be underestimated. Talking to others who are further down the road to recovery is often helpful.

Overuse of Alcohol and Street Drugs

Many people use alcohol or street drugs when seeking relief from intrusive memories and other distressing symptoms. These may bring with them a temporary respite, but in the long run they will make the symptoms worse, for example by further disrupting sleep patterns or lowering your mood. It is important to be very careful not to change your alcohol intake following trauma. If your intake has increased and you are finding it difficult to cut down, then seek professional help. The sooner you can nip any increase in alcohol or drug use in the bud, the easier it will be to prevent longer-term problems.

Post-Traumatic Stress Disorder

The common reactions to a traumatic event described above are called post-traumatic stress disorder (PTSD) when they have continued in a severe form for more than a month, and when they cause sufficient distress to interfere with or impair the ability to function at home or at work. The idea behind this definition is that these normal reactions to an abnormal event start to resolve in most people within about a month. About half of the people whose symptoms are sufficiently severe to count as PTSD continue to improve, and a year later they too have recovered. The number of people who suffer from PTSD varies, depending significantly on the nature and severity of the trauma. Generally speaking, man-made trauma carries a higher risk than natural disasters, and physical and sexual assault are most likely to cause PTSD. In one study 46% of women and 65% of men who were raped were found to have developed PTSD. However, over a lifetime, the chance of developing PTSD after a trauma is much lower: around 5% for men and 10% for women.

Chapter Summary

1. Traumas are horrific, threatening events which cause a large amount of distress. Most people recover well from them, and often without professional help. This chapter describes a framework that can help to keep the normal recovery process on track, and it lists some ways of coping that others have found useful.

2. The framework has two parts:
   - Seven principles to guide recovery. Make your personal version of these.
   - Information about memory that helps you to make sense of the reactions to a traumatic experience.

3. Coping strategies are described for dealing with flashbacks, nightmares, and avoidance of thoughts, feelings, and places associated with the trauma; for building confidence; and for thinking again about the personal impact and significance of the trauma. Select the strategies you need.

4. A wide range of feelings, such as guilt, shame, and anger, follow a trauma. This book contains many ideas that could be useful at this time. Use the index, or thumb through the chapter headings on the contents page, to help you find what you need.

PART SIX

MIND AND BODY

How the mind and body work together is a question to which no one has found a complete answer, but one thing is clear: the mind affects the body and the body affects the mind. In order to keep fit mentally, therefore, you need to attend to your body. The purpose of this section is to help you to overcome problems that affect your body, such as difficulties with sleeping, eating, drinking, or smoking. Many of these problems involve bad habits, so the first chapter on breaking habits is a key to the others. Here are the main themes that recur throughout these chapters:

1. *Make a definite decision to change.*
2. *Be systematic in the way you go about it.*
3. *Tackle other problems as well.*

If your bad habit makes you feel (temporarily) better, it is easy to lose sight of how short-lived these feelings are. There are longer lasting solutions to problems such as worry, shyness, loneliness, and unhappiness.

General Strategy

Read the chapter on breaking habits first, then choose which chapter you want to work on. Read it through once, then go back to the beginning and start to take STEPs.

S: Select an idea and work out how it applies to you.
T: Try it out.
E: Evaluate how it went (keep a diary in your notebook).
P: Persist until you feel better.

Work at your own pace, without hurrying. The right pace is the one that works for you. Buy yourself a notebook in which to keep track.

If you have not already done so, read Part Two of the book (The Seven Basic Skills). Several of the skills will help you deal with physical problems—provided you do not try to work on too many things at once.

28

Breaking Habits and Stopping Smoking

Habits are automatic routines of behavior that are repeated regularly, without thinking, and most of them are very useful. Without them you would not be able to do things nearly so efficiently. If you had to consciously direct and control every action each time you dressed in the morning, or drove a car, it would take as much effort as it did when you learned to do these things in the first place. Most complex skills—for example, writing or playing a musical instrument—require the development of well-learned habits. Once you can rely on your fingers to play the tune, you can turn your attention to more important things, like what the conductor is doing, and the sounds coming from the rest of the orchestra. The more you can do automatically, the more attention you will have leftover for other more important and interesting things. Habits, therefore, are very useful to you. However, most of us also develop *bad* habits—habits which can be harmful or unpleasant, like scratching or nail-biting; habits which irritate others, like criticizing or nagging; or habits which get in the way of other things we want to do, like losing things. The purpose of this chapter is to explain how to break the habits which you want to get rid of.

The Varieties of Habits

There are many different kinds of habit which you may want to break or change.

SO-CALLED "BAD" HABITS

These include bad physical habits such as nail-biting, thumbsucking, pulling or plucking out hair, scratching, and so on, which have the potential for doing harm to the person who has them. They also include bad interpersonal, social, and emotional habits like interrupting, "comfort" eating, leaving your shoes where others fall over them, saying "no" without thinking about the demands of children, crying when criticized, or hitting out before you get hit. These habits can potentially damage your relationships.

ROUTINES OF DAILY LIVING

Do you put your clothes on a chair when you take them off? Or do they land on the floor and stay there? How do you make sure that you do not lose your keys? Each of us carries out regular routines in a standard way, but these routines do not always work well for us. You may wish to replace some of these routine habits with other more helpful or less irritating ones.

CHARACTERISTICS

Many aspects of what we think of as essential characteristics of a person are routines or habits—untidiness, for example, or reaching for the cookies when you feel upset. Others might reach for the telephone or the box of tissues instead. "Characteristic habits" can be changed in just the same way as other habits.

INTERPERSONAL ROLES

People living close to each other usually divide up their responsibilities in ways which suit them—and then develop habits which go with those responsibilities. Some of these habits, however, can become a cause for irritation. For example, if one person takes total responsibility for cleaning the kitchen, others may develop messy kitchen habits. Or habits may clash. One person may use the telephone pad to write down shopping lists, while another may doodle over the shopping list, making it unreadable. Such clashes of habit are trivial, even funny, but over time they can wreak havoc in a relationship.

ADDICTIONS

Some habits are addictive—for example, smoking (see this chapter), drinking excessive amounts of alcohol (see Chapter 29), and becoming dependent on tranquilizers (see p. 404) or dangerous drugs. The ideas in the first part of this chapter will also be useful when trying to break addictive habits.

How to Break a Habit

We learn our habits, and therefore we can unlearn them. The point about habits is that we have learned them so well that we have to take active steps to break them. Just as a stream will cut deeper and deeper into the rock, so the repeated performance of our habits results in their becoming more and more entrenched. If a stream is diverted, temporarily, into a shallow channel, it will readily revert to its old course. But if it is repeatedly diverted, it will cut out a new path and, in time, naturally flow this way. So it is with habits. Each time you perform your old habit, it is strengthened; each time you replace the old habit with a new way of behaving, the old habit is weakened and the new one strengthened. The way to break habits is to replace the old way of behaving with a new way. When this is done repeatedly, new channels of behavior are created, and then the new way becomes automatic.

Do not be beguiled by those who say that breaking a habit is easy. It can be done, but it involves adopting a structured, step-by-step approach and it involves persistence. In order to travel from Oxford to London by train, you have to go through Didcot and Reading. In order to break your habits, you have to go through the steps explained below; if you skip some of the stages, you may not reach your destination.

WHY DO YOU WANT TO BREAK THE HABIT?

You will only break the habit if you are motivated to do so, and this means becoming absolutely clear about whether you really do want to change. You will need to be motivated not only to break the habit, but in order to be able to persist. Think carefully about the following questions, and then decide: Do you really want to put in the effort needed to break the habit? What do you stand to gain?

1. Is the habit harmful to me? Am I likely to hurt myself if I go on doing it—by, for example, scratching myself raw or chewing my nails down to the quick?
2. Is the habit dangerous, either to myself or to others? For example, forgetting to turn off the iron or the cooker, smoking in bed, or not using the rearview mirror when driving.
3. Is the habit embarrassing, irritating, or upsetting to me? For example, sniffing, sucking my teeth, pulling out patches of hair or an eyebrow, crying or losing my temper easily, talking with my mouth full.
4. Is the habit my problem, or someone else's problem? Is it a problem about how I live or work together with others around me? If so, it may also help to learn more about negotiating change (see Chapter 15).
5. If I persist with the habit, what are the three worst possible consequences?
6. If I break the habit, what are the three most important gains?

Six Steps for Breaking Habits

Step 1: Decide to change.
Step 2: Use awareness training.
Step 3: Devise strategies to help in stopping the habit.
Step 4: Replace the habit with an alternative behavior.
Step 5: Persist by being consistent and keeping track of progress.
Step 6: Learn to manage lapses.

STEP 1: DECIDE TO CHANGE

The most usual reason for failing to break a habit is going about it halfheartedly. You must be certain that you want to change. *To increase your resolve, think about the disadvantages of the habit* and about the advantages if you break it.

Imagine the habit clearly, then ask yourself "What's wrong with doing this?" What are the disadvantages, both immediately (the pain, making your fingers bleed), and in the longer term (losing your job as a hairdresser). Or imagine someone else doing what you do (complaining, giggling), and think what the disadvantages might be for them. Do they apply to you too? What are the worst possible consequences of going on with the habit? Describe them to yourself in detail and face up to them squarely. Now think about the advantages of breaking the habit. Finally, ask yourself "Why should I bother to stop?" *Make a list of reasons for stopping the habit* and put it where you will read it often (use it as a bookmark, or stick it in your wallet or handbag). It may help to take a photograph (if the effects of your habit are visible) to demonstrate to yourself the reasons why you want to break the habit.

We have labored the importance of getting clear why you want to break the habit because it is *the single most important step*. Without it you will fail. By itself it may well be sufficient to break the habit that you want to break. Gary came to the clinic because he was getting into the habit of checking everything he did. As soon as he stepped out of the house in the morning, he would go back inside to check that he had switched the stove off. As soon as he got to work, he would return to his car to check that he had locked it. He was starting to develop obsessional habits, and his doctor referred him immediately to a specialist. We asked him to answer the six questions we posed above and to come to a clear decision. He needed no more help. It was enough, for him, to get clear that he did not want to become enslaved by repeated checking. He nipped his bad habit in the bud.

STEP 2: USE AWARENESS TRAINING

Because the habit is automatic, you may not be aware of when you do it, or of exactly what it is that you do, so you need to become aware of it in order to stop it. If this is the case, the next step involves studying the habit. You will need to do two things: first, to *describe* it; and then to *monitor* it.

Describing the habit. You need to know the details, from the first move to the last. If you bite your nails, find out whether you bite all of them and whether you bite your fingers as well. What makes you move your hands up to your mouth? Which teeth do you use? What happens to the bits you bite off? On which side of the nail do you start? You may find it helpful to enlist someone's help at this stage.

Monitoring the habit. The only effective way of monitoring the habit is to keep a record. An example of a self-monitoring sheet is shown on page 395. The precise form of the record depends on you and on the habit. Use the monitoring sheet to answer *three* questions:

1. How *often* does the habit occur over a particular time, such as a week, day, or hour? If you cannot carry your monitoring sheet with you, keep count by using a knitting or golf counter or by moving small objects (e.g., paper clips) from one pocket to another.
2. *When* does the habit occur? Note the time of day on the monitoring sheet.
3. *What* is going on when you start doing it, and *where* are you at the time? For example, do you pull out your hair, absentmindedly, when on the telephone, or only at work? Do you criticize others when you feel attacked? Or cry when you feel undervalued? The situations in which you tend to perform the habit are known as the *setting conditions*.

Study your habit record. Self-monitoring, or keeping a habit record, helps you to detect relevant patterns and influences. So examine your record carefully after about a week, and work out how often you performed the habit, at what times, and in what situations. When are you most at risk? What triggers the habit? You may find it happens after meals, or when you are bored, embarrassed, or upset. For you it may be a sign that you are under stress or tired.

A note of caution. Self-monitoring often changes the habit you are trying to record. This is largely because it makes you more aware of what you were previously doing unawares, and so gives you a chance to interrupt it before it starts. If so, then remember that your record will underestimate how bad the habit really is. Do not be tempted to stop there: if you do, you will forget all about the habit once again and it will come back precisely because it *is* automatic.

Example of a monitoring record for studying a nail-biting habit. The person with this habit used the form as a brief diary to remind herself of things that she thought might be relevant. She did not keep a record of how long she went on biting her nails each time, because either she stopped as soon as she noticed, or she did not notice when she started, so could only guess.

Nail-Biting Record

When?	How often?	Situation	Feelings
Aug 12 7:30 A.M.	3	Waiting for coffee to brew	Nothing—sleepy?
8:45	1	Caught in traffic	Worried and late, also angry with myself
10:30	2	Coffee break, alone	Bored
2:15	5 or 6	Waiting to see boss	Afraid she noticed I was late
4:25	1	Learning new job	Interested, concentrating hard
6:00	5	Watching TV	Nothing much
9:00–11:00	12+	In bar: met Jeff	Embarrassed, couldn't think of anything to say

Note: There may have been more than this. Probably did not notice every time I did it.

STEP 3: DEVISE STRATEGIES FOR STOPPING THE HABIT

You are now in a position to bring Steps 1 and 2 to bear in breaking the habit.

Prepare yourself. To make the effort, you will need repeatedly to remind yourself why you want to break the habit (Step 1). Keep a list of the reasons so that you can look at them at least every day—more frequently if need be.

Develop an early-warning system. To catch the habit before it starts, learn to be on your guard at the times when you are most likely to carry it out. You can then make a special effort at these times. The "warning lights" should go on when you are in those situations in which the habit commonly occurs (the *setting conditions* for the habit); and when you find yourself performing an early part of the habit, think about what you are doing. For example, suppose that you tend to pull your hair out, with your left hand, when speaking on the telephone. Your warning bells should ring both when you are on the telephone and when your left hand goes up to your head. If you raise your voice and start shouting as soon as your ideas are questioned, you should be on your guard whenever faced with a possible questioner.

Develop a STOP strategy. If you catch yourself carrying out the habit, it is not too late to do anything. Stop doing it straight away. You could say "STOP" to yourself, out loud at first and later under your breath. Or write "STOP" in big colored letters on a card that you can look at, or imagine a "STOP" barrier coming down in front of you. Some people find it helpful to have a "stop routine." This might include: looking at your list of reasons for stopping the habit, or shocking yourself out of the habit by wearing a *loose* elastic band round your wrist and snapping it hard whenever you catch yourself doing it.

Enlist the support of others. Other people can be extremely helpful when you are trying to break a habit. They can help you notice when the automatic behavior has come back, and they can encourage you when the going gets tough. Showing your monitoring sheets to someone else can help you persist. Of course, it does not help to be nagged, so if you want someone else's help, you should tell them exactly what you need them to do, and possibly ask them to read this chapter.

Monitor. Continue to fill in your monitoring sheets so that you are keeping a record of how frequently you are carrying out the automatic behavior.

Reward yourself for success. Set yourself targets for reducing the frequency of the habit, and reward yourself when you reach these targets. A celebration with someone else at each target point can be particularly effective (see also Chapter 7).

A second note of caution. Sometimes when people try to break a habit, it seems to get worse before it gets better. This may be because trying to keep track of something you tend to do automatically reminds you of doing it. Or it can be because the effort to stop makes you more tense and your habit is triggered by feelings of tension. This stage is usually short-lived, so do not get discouraged and give up trying.

STEP 4: REPLACE THE HABIT WITH AN ALTERNATIVE BEHAVIOR

Most people experience urges when trying to break a habit and these can be hard to resist unless you find something else to do instead, and best of all, something that uses the same part of the body—even the same muscles. If the habit involves your hands, as when pulling out hair, then try to occupy them in some other way. Playing with a toy or Play-doh might be the answer. Or you could clench your fists for a couple of minutes. People who pull out their hair could use a comb instead, or put on gloves. The habit of scratching can be replaced with rubbing in some lotion or patting with the palm of the hand. Nail-biting can be replaced with using hand-cream or a manicure set. One 35-year-old woman who used to rub her eyes with the heel of her hand until they became sore and often infected found it helpful to put on makeup when she was tempted to rub.

If the habit is triggered by upsetting feelings such as tension, worry, or boredom, then it may be necessary to resolve these feelings. What is making you feel tense, worried, or bored? What could you do to make yourself feel better? (See Chapter 18.)

Untidiness is best tackled by developing a "habit of organization." Relatively simple measures, like buying a set of coat hangers for your shirts or picking up a ring binder for your statements from the bank, can dramatically reduce the amount of hassle caused by losing things. This alternative behavior can then become the focus for self-monitoring to ensure that you carry it out regularly.

Interrupting people can be stopped by developing better listening skills (p. 136), and many of the habits that affect relationships (arguing, making excuses, telling fibs) can be changed by learning how to be fair both to yourself and to others (Chapter 13), and by learning negotiation skills (pp. 161–166).

STEP 5: PERSIST BY BEING CONSISTENT AND KEEPING TRACK OF PROGRESS

It is important to be consistent when working to break a habit. Trying hard one week but giving yourself a break from trying the next will change nothing, and could be counterproductive. You could, for example, bite one nail and immediately feel better without doing yourself much harm because the urge has gone. So you might be tempted to conclude that biting your nails just once makes no difference. This is the "beginning of the end." Once leads to twice, and before you know where you are, the habit is reestablished in full force.

In order to be consistent you will also have to persist. It is not easy to break a habit. There will be times when you want to give up altogether and times when you feel discouraged despite making a big effort. You may also get tired of trying. You have made an enormous effort to be tidier, but still the place looks a mess, and you keep losing things. This is the time to think of the *advantages of stopping your habit* (as opposed to the disadvantages of going on with it). Keep the list you made earlier and read it regularly. Think about the gains you have made so far, even if they seem ridiculously small.

At this stage make sure that you reward yourself for the effort you are making. Rewards are a better way of helping yourself than punishment.

The carrot is better than the stick, and you deserve to be rewarded for your progress in breaking the habit (see Chapter 7).

Finally, make sure you continue to keep your habit record. Write down, as close to the time as you can, each time you catch yourself "in the act." It may help, once the habit has diminished, to keep a record of the urges to perform the habit and to rate their strength. Make your record form simple, and fill it in at the same time every day. At the end of each week look back over the seven days and work out how you are changing.

STEP 6: LEARN TO MANAGE LAPSES

The problem with habits is that they are automatic, which means that until they are fully broken they can easily come back. It can be disheartening to have made progress in breaking a habit and then to find that it is back, possibly in full force. It is easy to think that you are back to square one even though you are not. If you have made progress once, you can make progress again, and the second time it will be easier because you have trodden the path before. It is helpful to think about why the lapse occurred so that you can learn from this, but the most important thing is to repeat the steps that helped to reduce the habit before. The key to success is to see the present setback as a *lapse* not a *relapse*. The lapse is like falling off your bike: if you pick yourself up and dust yourself off, you can continue cycling along.

Applying These Principles to an Addiction: The Example of Smoking

Smoking is both a habit and an addiction. The methods for stopping smoking are the same as for breaking any other habit; and the key to stopping is motivation. *If you really want to stop, you can.* Most people who are diagnosed as having lung cancer stop smoking immediately, however much they smoked before. They simply stop because they feel highly motivated. It is a great pity that they did not feel so highly motivated earlier.

The Key Facts about Smoking

WHY STOP SMOKING?

The reasons for stopping smoking, in two words, are *health* and *wealth*. The connection between smoking and serious ill health is stronger than any other environmental cause of disease, and it is not lung cancer which is the biggest killer. If you smoke 20 or more cigarettes a day, you are five times more likely to suffer a stroke than if you do not smoke, and three times more likely to have a heart attack. This is because smoking accelerates the formation of atherosclerosis—the narrowing of arteries. This narrowing leads to poor blood flow. Poor blood flow to the brain can cause stroke; poor blood flow to heart muscle can cause a heart attack. Look at the list of major diseases in the following box which are strongly associated with smoking.

Major Health Problems Exacerbated by Smoking

Stroke
Heart attack
Severe chronic bronchitis
Poor circulation leading to leg amputation
Lung cancer
Stomach cancer
Cervical cancer
Miscarriages
Low birth weight babies
Secondary effects of smoking on your children: increase in chest problems—
for example, asthma, pneumonia, bronchitis—and increase in infant mortality.

Heavy smokers, of pipes as well as cigarettes, are twice as likely to die in middle age than nonsmokers. In broad terms, your chance of dying, if you are a heavy smoker, is the same as that of a nonsmoker ten years older than you.

All these dangers and risks of smoking are proportional to how much you smoke. The more the worse, but any amount of smoking is harmful, and so-called mild, or low tar, cigarettes are also harmful—there is no such thing as a safe cigarette. All these problems become less likely once you have stopped smoking, and dramatically so. The chance of heart attack, for example, has halved a year after stopping smoking, and after five years it is almost the same as if you had you never smoked.

THE BENEFITS OF GIVING UP SMOKING

It is helpful to turn the question around and to focus not only on the dangers of carrying on with smoking but the benefits of giving up smoking. The main benefits are listed in the following box. Think about how these benefits will affect your life in specific ways. Stopping smoking will improve your health not only in the sense of lowering the risk of death and serious disease, but also in improving your everyday health and fitness: increasing the amount of energy you have and your ability to get things done efficiently. Work out just how much money you will save over a year if you stopped smoking. What else could you do with this money?

Some Benefits of Stopping Smoking

A longer life
Improved physical fitness
Better skin (fewer wrinkles)
Better appearance (no nicotine stains)
Smell better to others
Taste food better
More money

ARE THERE DISADVANTAGES TO STOPPING SMOKING?

Not really, except for the unpleasantness just after stopping. Some people are worried that they will put on weight if they stop, often because this has happened when they have tried stopping before. The most common reason you gain weight is because you replace cigarettes with high-calorie foods, such as snacks, potato chips, and sweets. But whatever the reason for the weight gain, it is a problem that can also be dealt with: first by eating a sensible diet and increasing your intake of fruit and vegetables, and second by increasing your exercise (see also Chapter 31). Some people, especially those with chronic bronchitis, find that immediately after stopping smoking their chest feels "tighter," and they conclude that the smoking is good for their chest because it helps them cough up the phlegm. This is a very dangerous and false conclusion. It is the smoking that has caused, and is causing the chest problem, and continuing smoking will cause gradual but steady worsening of the chest problem. Immediately after stopping smoking, there may be a short-lived change in the way in which secretions are cleared from the chest; but the important fact is that your chest will get *better* if you stop smoking and *worse* if you continue to smoke.

How to Stop Smoking

APPLYING THE SIX STEPS TO STOPPING SMOKING

Step 1: Decide to change: Be clear in your mind about why you want to stop. Motivation: that is the key, so be sure you are quite clear about why you want to stop and what the advantages of stopping will be. Write down these advantages and keep the list at hand.

Step 2: Use awareness training: Assess your smoking (study your habit). As with breaking any habit, it is most helpful to have a clear idea of exactly what you are doing. A "smoking diary" will show you not only how much you smoke, but in what circumstances, when, and with whom. This is invaluable information when planning to make it as easy as possible for you to stop.

Assess also why you smoke. In the box below there are listed seven major reasons why people smoke. What are your reasons? You may think of one which is not on the list. If you understand which reasons are important for you—and there may be more than one reason for your smoking—you will be better able to plan how to stop.

Step 3: Devise strategies to help: Develop your personal strategy. You can stop all at once, or you can cut down and stop over five or so days. It doesn't much matter which you do as long as you do two things: decide exactly which day you are going to stop (or start the process of cutting down); and do exactly what you planned. If you choose to stop over several days the best plan is to smoke fewer cigarettes each day. For example, if you currently smoke 20 cigarettes a day, plan to decrease each day by four, so that

---

Seven Major Reasons for Smoking

It helps you to relax.
Handling cigarettes feels good.
You like the taste.
It gives you confidence, particularly in company.
You think it helps you to concentrate, and gives you energy.
You just automatically light one up.
You are addicted, and feel ill if you don't have a cigarette.

---

on the fifth day you have stopped smoking. One of the easiest ways of doing that might be to have the first cigarette of the day later and later.

Step 4: Replace the habit with an alternative behavior: Find something else to do instead. Go back to your smoking diary and think about what the dangerous situations are for you. How are you going to reduce the temptation to smoke? How can you make it easier to give up? One important way is to make sure that there are no cigarettes around. But there are also other ways. For example, you may tend to smoke when in the car, in which case this will be a situation in which you should take special care not to have cigarettes available, and in which you should find a substitute for smoking (chew gum or listen to music). Or you may tend to smoke after meals, especially if you also have coffee, in which case consider leaving out the coffee as well and occupying yourself in some other way at this time. The craving for the cigarette will pass once you are out of the situation which normally prompts you to smoke, and once you are well past the time at which you habitually lit up.

Think too about your reasons for smoking and use this insight to help you. If you like the feel of the cigarette in your mouth then what else could you put in your mouth? A pencil when at work? Sticks of carrot when cooking or waiting for a meal? If you smoke to help relax, look for less harmful ways of relaxing (see Chapter 11). If you smoke to boost confidence, read Chapters 10 and 13. If smoking makes you less anxious, read Chapter 18.

Steps 5 and 6: Ideas to help you to persist, keep track of progress, and manage lapses: Enlist support. To keep the momentum going, enlist support from friends and family. Other people can help, and if they do not know that you have given up smoking, they may offer you cigarettes and thus tempt you. So let key people know that you no longer smoke, and discuss ways in which they can help you. If you know other people who also want to give up smoking, it can be helpful to everyone to form a group to help each other quit. Plan together, and use the group to report on progress. Some groups plan treats as a way of marking successes, and they may also use "punishments" or demand a "forfeit" for continued smoking. Each member of one successful group put a "deposit" into a kitty. If someone smoked, the deposit would be paid to that person's *least* favorite charity (a hated political party, for example) as punishment.

Start a "ciggy bank." When you stop smoking, you will have more money. It is easy for this money to be "hidden" in your day-to-day living expenses. In order to see just how much you are saving, put the money you would have spent on cigarettes into a "ciggy bank." You can then use this money for something special.

Freshen up. Ask your dentist to clean all the stains off your teeth, and air your clothes and your house. Throw away all ashtrays. You will soon dislike the stale smell of smoke and this dislike will help you to keep off cigarettes. Taking up exercise will also help because you will feel and enjoy the fitness which smoking otherwise takes away.

Be assertive. You will be offered cigarettes, particularly by those who know you as a smoker and do not know that you have given up. Simply say: *"No thanks, I don't smoke."* If they say that you did smoke, reply: *"I did smoke, but now I don't."* Practice saying these phrases until they feel right. There is no need for further explanation (see Chapter 13).

When you feel a great desire to smoke. The feeling of craving will pass shortly. So when it comes over you, remind yourself that it will pass. Take a few slow deep breaths; do something to distract yourself; and take a drink of water to occupy both you and your mouth.

If Addiction Is a Problem

If you have smoked heavily for a long time, you are likely to be addicted. The addiction will show in cravings for a cigarette, and in some withdrawal symptoms on occasions when you have not had a cigarette for several hours. If, on the other hand, you regularly go 12 hours without a cigarette, then you are unlikely to have a significant physical addiction. The following box lists typical withdrawal symptoms which indicate addiction.

Common Symptoms of Withdrawal

Becoming irritable and snappy
Gasping for a drag
Feeling jittery and clammy
Feeling dizzy
Tingling feeling
Headache
Feeling nauseated

These withdrawal symptoms are worst in the early days when you have just stopped and may last a few weeks if you have been a very heavy smoker. Although they can be unpleasant, they are not dangerous or overwhelming. You have a lot to gain if you can persist and beat the habit, and this is the hardest time.

NICOTINE CHEWING GUM OR NICOTINE SKIN PATCHES

You can separate the problems of physical addiction from the difficulties in breaking the habit by replacing the nicotine using either patches, which stick on your skin and from which the nicotine is slowly absorbed, or by chewing nicotine gum. If you replace the nicotine in this way, then you will not experience the withdrawal problems, and so you will not have to deal with these while coping with the difficulties of breaking the habit. Two or three months after stopping, you can wean yourself off the nicotine by using a lower dose patch or chewing less gum (your pharmacist can advise you). *Do not smoke on the same day* that you use one of these methods. If you do, you will have a *nicotine overdose* which may give you severe stomach pains.

Obtaining Help

It helps to get support. If you cannot form your own support group and are finding it hard to stop smoking on your own, contact your doctor and find out if your local hospital or community center has a chest clinic which organizes support groups. In the United Kingdom, find your nearest *withdrawal clinic* (the local library of the Citizen's Advice Bureau should know the number); or contact *ASH* (Action on Smoking and Health) which publishes self-help guides to help you stop smoking. In the United States, contact your local chapter of the American Lung Association, or call your local Smokenders or Smokenders International. You are not alone, and if you really want to stop, then take whatever measures are needed.

Other Addictions

Many people come to depend on sleeping tablets or other tranquilizers. The "six steps" described in this chapter are as relevant to coming off tranquilizers as they are to stopping smoking. Attempts to stop taking these tablets may lead to withdrawal symptoms, and these withdrawal symptoms can feel just like the problems that caused you to take the tablets in the first place, such as anxiety or poor sleep. So you may, wrongly, think that these problems will persist. Coming off tranquilizers and sedatives should be done slowly, as stopping them suddenly can cause problems. If in doubt ask your doctor for advice.

Chapter Summary

Habits are hard to change because they have become automatic. Nevertheless they can be changed by following these six steps:

1. Make a positive decision to change; do not be half-hearted about it.
2. Study the habit until you are aware of exactly what you do.
3. Develop a personal strategy for stopping.
4. Find something else to do instead.
5. Once you have started, keep the momentum going.
6. "If you don't at first succeed, try and try again."

These steps can be used to break any habit—from smoking to nail-biting.

29

Averting Problems with Alcohol

Alcohol can give great pleasure. We use it to mark celebrations, like weddings and birthdays, and other important occasions like homecomings, departures, or funerals. Alcohol is available at most social gatherings, and it would be flying in the face of reality to deny that having a drink has its uses. It can oil the wheels of communication or dampen down fears and sorrows. But it can only do this when used in moderation—in a controlled way—because alcohol is a dangerous, addictive, and depressant drug. In large quantities, or when not carefully controlled, it can also destroy life. The passage from pleasure to destruction is so insidious that a person can be dependent on alcohol for years before realizing that there is even a problem. The purpose of this chapter is to help you to drink alcohol with safety and pleasure, and to give you some guidelines if you already have a problem. The first part of the chapter explains how to assess your drinking, and the second part explains how to manage your drinking.

Assessing Your Drinking

THE ASSESSMENT TREE

There are three questions to ask yourself, which can be illustrated as shown in the tree diagram on page 407.

Assessment tree for deciding whether your drinking could be problematic.

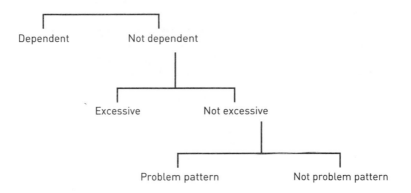

1. *Are you dependent on alcohol?* If you are, then the dependence needs to be tackled whether it is physical or psychological. If you are not dependent,
2. *Are you drinking too much alcohol?* Even if you are not dependent, you could be drinking enough to cause you serious health problems in the future. If you are not drinking excessive amounts, then
3. *Is your drinking pattern potentially dangerous?* Some patterns of drinking are likely to lead to problems with alcohol even if you are neither dependent nor drinking excessive amounts.

Question 1: Are You Dependent on Alcohol?

If you are dependent on alcohol, you may find it difficult to be honest, even with yourself, about your drinking. You may, at some level of thinking, have a sense that all is not well with your drinking but resist confronting yourself with exactly what this sense of unease is about. If so, you have a great deal to gain from being straight with yourself. You may not want to be honest with anyone else, but if you are fooling yourself, you are certainly on a dangerous path.

In order to assess whether you are dependent on alcohol, answer the questions in the box on page 408. Think carefully about each, and answer each honestly. If you cannot be honest with yourself, this itself will tell you that you do have a problem with alcohol.

If you have answered *yes* to four or more of these questions, you are probably dependent on alcohol. Even a single answer of *yes* should cause you to think carefully about the level of your control over drinking and the harm it might be storing up for you.

The Dependence Questionnaire

Answer yes or no to each of the following questions:

- Does one drink tend not to satisfy you?
- Do you almost prefer to drink alone?
- Do you tend to have a drink at night to help you sleep?
- Do you tend to drink in such a way that others are not aware of how much you drink?
- When expecting to drink, would you have something you do not normally like, if that was all that was available?
- Would it feel strange to leave your glass half full?
- Do you have an absolute rule not to drink before a certain time of day?
- Do you often drink significantly more than you intend?
- Have you committed two or more driving offenses?
- Have you ever lost a job because of drinking?
- Has anyone else ever been seriously concerned about your drinking?
- Are you worried about your drinking?

Source: Adapted from B. Colcough, *Tomorrow Will Be Different* (London: Viking, 1993).

THE DANGERS OF DEPENDENCE ON ALCOHOL

Dependence on alcohol has two aspects: physical dependence and psychological dependence.

The key point about *physical dependence* is that if you stop drinking you may experience physical *withdrawal.* This is a potentially dangerous condition which usually starts from a few hours to a few days after the last drink. The first signs of withdrawal are "the shakes," followed by a feeling of acute anxiety and restlessness. As the withdrawal progresses, there may be disorientation (not knowing the time or place where one is); hallucinations (either seeing things or hearing voices which are not really there); and delirium tremens (the DTs), in which the person feels completely terrified with vivid hallucinations and marked shaking. Occasionally, if not treated under proper medical supervision, withdrawal can lead to seizures, coma, and death. There is no absolute rule about who will experience withdrawal symptoms, but it generally takes several years of heavy drinking—fifty units (see p. 412) a week or more. If you get "the shakes" in the morning, needing a drink to steady you, then you are physically dependent—the shakes are the beginning of the withdrawal. If this happens, then you *should seek medical help.* Your drinking is likely to seriously damage your health, but it is also *dangerous to cease drinking without medical supervision* because this could precipitate a full-blown withdrawal.

The key point about *psychological dependence* is that alcohol comes to feel as if it is essential. You need it, rely on it, and feel bad without it even though you do not suffer the effects of physical withdrawal when you do not have a drink. Many people who are psychologically dependent drink as a way of coping with problems, and they may do this because they cannot find, or do not know, a more effective way of managing them. There is no doubt that alcohol, which is a *depressant* drug, can dull psychological as well as physical pain.

Although psychological dependence on alcohol can start at any stage of life, people are especially vulnerable at moments of stress and difficulty—for example, when coping with a baby who cries a lot at night; when feeling anxious or lonely in a new place; when stressed or overworked; when the children have all left home or when life seems empty; when facing apparently insoluble housing, financial, or employment problems. People who spend a lot of time with other people who drink heavily, and to whom having a good time means having a lot to drink, are also more vulnerable than others.

People who have seen their families, friends, or colleagues use alcohol to help them cope with problems may also be more at risk than others of becoming psychologically dependent. They have firsthand evidence that this is an acceptable way of behaving *in the short term,* and they may not have learned many other ways of behaving that are likely to be more effective—as well as being a lot less dangerous—*in the long term.*

Both physical and psychological dependence are dangerous and are likely to cause, not solve, serious problems. Heavy drinkers are three times more likely than others to die in a car crash and six times more likely to commit suicide. The number of arguments and fights they have with their families and close friends is enormously increased. They frequently have problems at work sufficient to disrupt their careers and are often troubled by unhappy relationships. In Chapter 16 we say more about the links between problems in relationships, anger, and alcohol.

Question 2: Are You Drinking Too Much Alcohol?

Even if you are not dependent on alcohol, you may be drinking an excessive amount: that is, an amount that will cause problems for you in the future if it continues. In the long run this might cause you serious health problems, and it will also increase the chance that you will become dependent (physically and psychologically) on alcohol.

THE DANGERS OF ALCOHOL TO HEALTH

Medical students are taught always to think of the possibility of alcohol as a cause of a patient's health problems. This is because alcohol can cause a very wide number of problems. The following box summarizes some of the more common ones seen by doctors.

Some of the Physical Dangers of Alcohol

- Irritation of the stomach, leading to bleeding and stomach ulcers
- Liver damage, leading to liver failure or dangerous internal bleeding
- Brain damage, leading to very poor memory
- Heart failure
- High blood pressure
- Impotence
- Poor sleep
- Peripheral nerve damage
- Pancreatitis
- Diabetes
- Anemia
- Injury from falls and poor driving

Alcohol is also a common cause of problems in daily living because it affects your mind, your feelings, your actions, and the workings of your body, as shown in the next box. As you read through this box, ask yourself whether any of these problems have happened to you as a result of drinking. Add on any other problems you have noticed.

HOW MUCH ALCOHOL IS SAFE?

There is no clear-cut answer to this question because people differ markedly in how much alcohol is needed to damage their health, and it is very difficult to collect the research evidence to pinpoint just what problems are caused by just how much drinking. The simple, but not very helpful, answer is that any amount of alcohol *could* cause a problem. One drink might cause someone to fall, or crash the car, and a single binge on alcohol could cause dangerous bleeding from the stomach. Most of us, however, enjoy having a drink, and either deny there is any risk at all, or think that it is worth taking such a small risk.

Common Problems Caused by Alcohol

Effects on your mind
Poor concentration
Forgetfulness
Permanent, severe damage to memory following very heavy drinking
Slow reaction times
Muddled thinking

Effects on your feelings
Unhappiness and apathy
Depression
Frustration
Irritability
Hostility
Hopelessness
Despair

Effects on your actions
Disagreements and arguments
Difficulty doing your work, inside or outside the home
Carelessness, leading to more frequent accidents or mistakes
Difficulty getting up and going to work
Secretive behaviors and suspicious behaviors
Telling lies, to yourself as well as to others

Effects on your body
Loss of appetite
Feeling thirsty for some hours afterward
Disturbed sleep in the later part of the night, having initially slept quite well
Loss of interest in sex and inability to get sexually aroused (this is a problem for both men and women)
Headaches
Nausea (and vomiting)
Reduced motor coordination, clumsiness
Blurred vision
Dizziness
Feeling shaky or wobbly

This lack of clarity is reflected in the conflicting advice being given by various authorities over the years. However, a guideline is useful, and we suggest the one provided by The Royal Colleges of Psychiatrists, Physicians, and General Practitioners and by the Health Education Council. This says that each week *men should drink no more than 21 units* and *women should drink no more than 14 units*. The different recommendations reflect differences in metabolism. If you drink less than these recommended amounts, there is little danger of causing yourself physical harm or of becoming psychologically dependent. Many people may be able safely to drink more than these quantities, but the risks of harm increase if they do.

HOW MUCH ARE YOU DRINKING?

The standard way of measuring how much alcohol you drink is in terms of *units (or "drinks") per week*. One unit represents 8-10 grams of pure alcohol. The following box gives the unit equivalents of various drinks.

A DRINKING DIARY

The best way to work out how much alcohol you drink is to keep a drinking diary. This should be filled in using a diary, cards, or small notebook which you can carry around with you throughout the week. In order to calculate your intake, you need to write down every single drink you have (including "refills"), giving the type of drink and the quantity. Work out the number of units using the information in the box. It is im-

---

Number of Alcohol Units in Various Drinks

• One pint of beer (many bottled beers are much stronger)	2 units
• One small glass of wine	1 unit
• One bottle table wine	8 units
• One bottle of sherry	12 units
• One measure of spirits (whiskey, gin, vodka)	1 unit
• One double measure	2 units
• One bottle of spirits	30 units

Note: Drinks poured at home are nearly always much bigger than standard measures.

---

portant to fill in the diary very close to the time you drink, and if you have several drinks in an evening, you should make a note of each one. Trying to guess how much you had later that night or in the morning is not likely to be accurate. If you want to keep the diary private, you might be able to go off to the restroom to fill it in, or you might be able to find another way of keeping a tally—for example, by putting one coin, or match, or bit of paper in whichever pocket you have empty for each unit of alcohol you drink.

A drinking diary can also be used to find out about other factors that affect your drinking, like where you were, who you were with, and what else you were doing at the time. This is very helpful if you want to cut down. In order to keep a *full drinking diary,* write down the headings as shown in the following example, and always fill the diary in whenever you drink, or it will inevitably be inaccurate.

Example of a Drinking Diary

Questions	Answers	
	6:00 P.M.	8:30 P.M.
Where?	Home	Home
With whom?	Alone	With Ben
What?	Sherry after work	Wine
How much?	2 large glasses	2 glasses
Units?	3	2
With food?	No	Yes
Why?	Tired and strained	Usually do

You are now in a position to answer the question about whether you are drinking too much. The recommended guideline for men (21 units a week) works out to an *average* of three units a day, or one and a half pints or three glasses of wine: in a week, this would add up to 10½ pints or 2 ½ bottles of wine. The recommended maximum for women (14 units a week) works out to 2 glasses of wine a day. The message is that *if you drink almost every day, you do not need to drink very much for it to add up to more than the recommended amount.* If you are drinking more than these guidelines, then you should seriously consider whether to cut down. Your long-term health might be at risk.

Question 3: Is Your Drinking Pattern Potentially Dangerous?

Even if you are drinking less, at the moment, than the recommended maximum, your pattern of drinking may be potentially dangerous because it may lead to serious problems in the future. There are two danger signs to look out for. The first is turning to alcohol when you are stressed, when you feel as though you *must* have a drink. The danger is that the more stressed you are, the more you will drink, and the more dependent you will become. Try to break the habit now, before it becomes deeply entrenched, by dealing with the stress instead. Read Chapter 20. The second danger sign is if you are getting into a habit of drinking unthinkingly on a regular basis. If someone at age 20 drinks one vodka every evening when getting home from work, there is a danger that will creep up to two vodkas, because once the habit has been established, most people become tolerant of alcohol and need more to achieve the same effect. This will gradually extend until the quantity drunk is likely to do physical harm in the long run. Of course, many people regularly enjoy one or two drinks a day for most of their lives. You do not *have* to decline into the danger zone, but you do need to be constantly on the lookout: in order to be able to enjoy the pleasure that alcohol can give, it is important to know that there is always potential danger, and to know how to calculate how dangerous your level of drinking really is.

Managing Your Drinking

CHANGING DRINKING PATTERNS

If you are concerned that you might be at risk because of the pattern of your drinking, there are four points to bear in mind.

1. Break any regular patterns, like having a drink every day after work. Find out how it feels to have at least one alcohol-free day each week.
2. Keep below the recommended maximum, using a drinking diary to assess accurately how much you really are having. It cannot be emphasized too much how easy it is to underestimate how much you drink, especially if you drink at home.
3. Make sure that you do not use alcohol as a "crutch" when you have other problems, such as feeling depressed, stressed, lonely, or anxious. There are other solutions to these problems. Drinking may

dull your feelings about them in the short term but in the long term it only compounds them.

4. Learn to be able to say *no* when you are offered a drink. It is easy to start drinking too much if you often go to social gatherings in which alcohol is not only freely available but almost pushed upon you. Fortunately, it is more socially acceptable to refuse an alcoholic drink now than it was a few years ago. Increased awareness of the dangers of driving after drinking has had a great effect. But whether it is socially acceptable or not, we each have the right to say *no* if we want to (see also pp. 141–142). If you find it difficult to refuse a drink, then practice doing so until you are making the decisions that you want to make.

REDUCING THE AMOUNT YOU DRINK

The physical harm that alcohol can cause depends on the amount you drink, not on whether you are dependent. The more you drink above the recommended maximum, the more likely you are to suffer one or more of the physical dangers of alcohol. If you are not dependent, cutting down will not be too difficult. It will be rather like breaking any other habit (see Chapter 28). In this chapter we show how the six steps described in Chapter 28 can be adapted for cutting down the amount you drink.

Step 1: Preparation: Making a positive decision to change. As with changing any habit, the most important step is the first: getting it clear in your mind that you want to change. Unless you really want to cut down, you will not succeed in doing so. Start by thinking about what is good about drinking for you. *What do you gain from it?* Take time to think about this, and ask yourself whether you really gain what you hope to gain (for example, peace of mind, a good night's sleep, a feeling of friendship, better communication). If you do, then before cutting down, you should think about how else you could get these things. Ask yourself how other people get them. Read those chapters in this book that deal with the things that concern you.

Go on to think about what makes you want to cut down. *What problems does drinking cause for you? Or for others around you?* Think about a whole range of problems like putting on weight, sleeping badly, sexual difficulties, hangovers, arguments, poor concentration, worry, loss of trust or self-respect, the expense, and so on. Think about problems that it *might* cause as well as problems that it *already has* caused. Alert yourself to as many risks as you can.

Your next task is to weigh up the balance between the two lists and to decide whether you really want to cut down. It can be very helpful to talk to someone else at this stage, since many of the advantages of drinking are immediate and relatively easy to remember, while the disadvantages are often delayed and not so easy to keep in mind. If you make a positive decision to cut down, summarize your reasons for doing so. Keep your summary and read it frequently while you are changing your drinking habits.

Step 2: Keep track of how much you drink. Assess your current drinking carefully before you make any changes. Keep a detailed drinking diary for at least a week (maybe two), even though your pattern of drinking may be regular. Remember to count more for the (larger) drinks poured at home, and for refills. Examine your diary to see if there are any times or situations when you tend to drink more than you want—or risky situations for you. These are the times for which you need special preparation so as to be forearmed and on your guard. Continue to keep an accurate diary while you make the effort to change, and at the end of each week, work out how well you have done.

Step 3: Devise your personal strategy. Plan your week ahead in detail in order keep within the recommended number of units. Decide exactly how much you are going to drink and when. If you are uncertain what you will be doing, then make out a simple plan for yourself, like drinking only on three days, and drinking not more than four units on any one day. If you drink at home, it may help to remove the alcohol, or put it out of sight, and to explain what you want to do to others. If you go out with friends on Thursdays and drink a great deal, losing track of how much you have, devise a strategy to help yourself keep within limits. You could have one drink only and then switch to soft drinks, or you could alternate soft drinks and alcoholic ones. And you could drink slowly. But if you find it difficult to refuse a drink, then read Chapter 13 on assertiveness. If you cannot readily say *no*, then either you have difficulty asserting yourself, or you have a problem with alcohol dependency which should be tackled if you are not to damage your health.

Step 4: Think about what you could do instead. If you replace the drinking with another activity, your task will be much easier—especially if going without leaves a void to fill. It is even helpful to *combine* drinking with another activity, such as eating a meal or talking to friends. The other activities divert your attention from the drink and help you to drink less. If having a drink has become a way of not thinking about problems—of sweeping them under the carpet—the problems may well reemerge to trouble you when you go without. Problems rarely go away when you look the other way. It would be more useful to face them instead (see Chapter 6) and to revise your problem-solving skills (Chapter 8).

Step 5: Persistence and tracking your progress. At regular intervals, a week is probably best, use your diary to work out whether what you actually did matched with your plan. There are two possibilities: either you did well or you drank more than you planned. If you did well, you should reward yourself before going on to plan the next week. You are trying to break a habit and that always takes persistence. If you drank more than you planned, you need to look carefully at why before you make a plan for the next week. If things did not go according to plan, remember that the carrot works better than the stick. Think again about what you want to gain by drinking less. Think about any gains you have already made, however small. If you keep trying, you will be able to make the changes you wish to make.

Step 6: Managing lapses. Do not be hard on yourself when you break your resolve and have a lapse—just try not to let the lapse turn into a relapse. If you have failed, it may reveal that you are more dependent on alcohol, physically or psychologically, than you realized, and that is very useful to know. This does not mean that you will not be able to overcome the problem, but it does mean that there is a significant problem that you need to solve. At least you have discovered the size of the problem and have had the courage to face it; the next section describes strategies you can use to help you overcome the problem of physical dependence on alcohol.

Overcoming Dependence on Alcohol

Many people who have a problem with dependence on alcohol do not acknowledge this even to themselves, and therefore they cannot work to overcome it. If you have a dependency problem, and have acknowledged this to yourself, you are halfway there.

It is very easy to chastise yourself, even to despise yourself. Dependency on alcohol can make you do things which you do not really approve of, like breaking promises, or causing hurt and pain to those you love. Other people might be suffering because of the time you spend drinking and away from home; because you are irritable and unable to show affection when you feel it; because you are violent; because your marked changes in mood make it difficult for those around you to know where they stand; or because you are unreliable. Alcohol is expensive, so that the money you spend may be causing problems for you and others also. Alcohol dependence may cause problems at work, although some people who are dependent are able to carry on effectively at work without others even suspecting there is a problem. It may be your family rather than your work that suffers.

It is important, therefore, clearly to distinguish the "real" you from the things that you sometimes do, and from the way you behave because of the alcohol. You may be doing things you do not approve of. Instead of using this as a stick to beat yourself with, recognize that it means that the "real" you does have standards and ideals, and that is why you can recognize the difference between what you are doing and what you would like to be doing. It is important to recognize the self within, whom you respect, because if you cannot find this inner self-respect, it will be much harder to overcome the dependence. Overcoming dependence requires you to value yourself (Chapter 3) and enables you to see yourself beyond the alcohol dependence.

SEEK MEDICAL HELP

If you are dependent on alcohol, we advise you to see your doctor and to discuss the problem. Your doctor will know what help and support is available, and there is no doubt that overcoming your problem will be much easier with support. But there is also another important reason for seeing your doctor, and that is the question of withdrawal. If you have been drinking quite heavily for a long time, you might get withdrawal symptoms when you stop drinking, and these are potentially dangerous. You may need your doctor's help through this withdrawal phase, which may need to be done in a hospital or clinic.

DO YOU REALLY WANT TO OVERCOME YOUR DEPENDENCE?

Unless you are sure that you want to overcome your dependence, you will not be able to do so. The first step is the same one described on page 392: think through all the advantages and disadvantages of overcoming it. Are you happy with the way things are at the moment—with your family or other close relationships? With your work? If you are not, then think what you have to gain by overcoming your dependence. There are tremendous rewards for giving up alcohol: two things that you will have more of will be time and money; and all your positive features, all those parts of your personality which you like, will still be there. One of the myths that those dependent on alcohol often believe is that they will be less fun, or less amusing, without drinking—or less able to cope. But quite the opposite is true. If you decide that you want to overcome your dependence, then list all the things which you have to gain and keep the list in a place where you can frequently look at it.

REDUCED DRINKING OR ABSTINENCE?

If you have a problem with alcohol, should you reduce your drinking or give it up entirely? The traditional answer to this question used to be that you should aim for abstinence, not simply reduce the amount you drink. Then in the 1960s and 1970s there were a number of reports which suggested that some people formerly dependent on alcohol were able successfully to return to "social drinking." However, later evidence suggests that the majority of those who return to social drinking relapse, and start to drink too much again. It appears that so few people dependent on alcohol are able to return to social drinking without relapsing that the only good advice is to *become abstinent*. If your aim is simply to cut down, it is unlikely to work.

HELPING YOURSELF TO BECOME ABSTINENT

If you really want to give up alcohol, you can; but you must give yourself as much help as possible because it is going to be difficult. Think as often as you can, daily if possible, about what you have to gain in the way of a better life.

Get help. It is going to be much easier if you have help and support from people who understand your situation. There are several sources of help and it is worth approaching them all. First, there is Alcoholics Anonymous, or "AA." There are branches in almost every locality, and the number and address should be in the telephone directory, and available from your library, or your doctor. AA runs "self-help" groups where you will meet others in the same situation. Their work has a distinct religious aspect which some do not like, but the main focus is on helping each other to remain abstinent from alcohol. There are also many medical services now available for dealing with substance abuse. Your doctor can put you in touch with special services to help you abstain from alcohol, some of which are hospital based and some community based. The advantage of these services is that people who know the position you are in will be able to help and support you through the most difficult times.

Exercise. Spending less time drinking gives you more time for other things. Use some of this to get physically fitter. This will help you to feel good about your body and make it easier to abstain.

Look after your appearance. If you have let your appearance slip, and have extra money available because you are not spending it on alcohol, you could buy new clothes. As with exercise, this will help you to feel better about yourself. The better you feel, the easier it is to abstain.

Take one day at a time. Do not look far into the distance, but concentrate on remaining abstinent for today. There are two aspects to this injunction. The first is not to be too ambitious, not to say to yourself: "I won't ever drink again." Focus just on today. The second aspect is that you need constantly, every day, to renew your resolve not to drink. Once you have been dependent on alcohol, you are always at risk of drinking excessively again. Even when you have been abstinent for ten years, you cannot take for granted that you will not start drinking to excess again. You should renew your vow not to drink every single day.

Recognize the voice of the tempter. There will be times, frequent at first, less frequent later on, but never gone forever, when you are tempted to have a drink. The voice inside you will make it sound so plausible and attractive: "One drink can't do any harm." But it can—it will take you straight back to excess. "Everybody has the occasional drink; don't be such a fool." Not everybody has a problem with alcohol dependence— and that makes all the difference; but many of those who have an occasional drink have a great deal more than the occasional drink, and are doing themselves a great deal of harm. "No one will know." How is that relevant? You are returning to the way of life which you know you want to leave behind. "Don't believe that silly book you read—really, how can one drink harm anyone?" Do not believe this voice. There is no end to its thirst for alcohol.

This time is different. You may have tried to give up alcohol before and failed, so why, you may be thinking, should this time be different? The answer is that this time can be different if you are better prepared, have taken more precautions, have thought it through more, and have found yourself more help.

Do not be hard on yourself. You need all the positive encouragement you can get, and you particularly need it from yourself. You cannot afford to undermine yourself. Be prepared to forgive yourself for what you have done because of the dependence on alcohol. Value yourself and be positive about yourself.

Avoid drinking companions. Look back at your drinking diary. What were the situations in which the drinking occurred? Think about this carefully and then do all you can to avoid those situations which were particularly dangerous, or try to change them. One of the most dangerous for many people is being with others who drink. The voices of your companions add to your own inner voice: "Go on, have a drink." This is not the time to test your assertiveness skills to their full. It is better to avoid these situations instead. If you can only see these friends when they are drinking, it is better not to see them. Good friends will be prepared to see you on other occasions too. Surround yourself, as much as possible, with people who support your abstinence, not with people who undermine your resolve.

Understand that those close to you may be skeptical. Those close to you, your family, for example—may be skeptical that this time you will abstain. "I'll believe it when I see it" may be their attitude. Their attitude may well be reasonable in the light of past experience. How are they to know that this time will be different? Do not be angry with them. It will take some time to regain their trust in you. Accept this fact and you will not waste your energy fighting against their beliefs.

If you relapse. Take stock. Why did it happen? Go through the steps you took carefully. Did you miss out some of the ways of helping yourself? Did you prepare yourself fully? Did you try doing it on your own without any help or support? Prepare yourself again, only this time with more care, and if you find that there are other problems in your life that tempt you into drinking, like social anxiety, boredom, loneliness, depression, or lack of confidence, think about how to tackle these problems as well. There are many ideas in this book, and your doctor will also be able to tell you what other help is available.

Chapter Summary

Alcohol is a source of pleasure in life, but it can be dangerous.
　　Assess your drinking using the assessment tree:

- Are you dependent on alcohol?
- Are you drinking too much?
- Is your drinking pattern potentially dangerous?

A drinking diary will help you work out how much alcohol you drink.
　　You can change your drinking pattern using six steps:

1. Make a positive decision to change.
2. Keep track of how much you drink.
3. Devise your personal strategy.
4. Think about what you could do instead.
5. Persist.
6. Manage lapses.

Be honest with yourself about your drinking: you can overcome problems although you may need a helping hand.

30

Overcoming Sleep Problems

Why we need sleep remains a mystery. Yet about one in five people think they have a sleep problem and sleeping badly can make you feel miserable, irritable, and unable to cope. There are three main kinds of problems: difficulty falling asleep, wakefulness during the night, and waking too early in the morning. In each case there seems to be a shortage of sleep: however, it is notoriously difficult to estimate how much sleep you really get. For many people the problem is not that they sleep too little, but rather that they *think* they are not getting enough sleep. If this becomes a worry, then the problem tends to get worse. Worrying both interferes with sleep and leaves you feeling exhausted the next day.

Two key questions can help you decide if you have a sleep problem:

1. *Do you regularly feel tired throughout the day?*
2. *Does sleepiness interfere with your daily activities?*

If the answer to one or both of these questions is *yes*, then you may have a sleep problem. Luckily, for nine out of ten people the problem is easily solved.

SOLVING THE SLEEP PROBLEM

It is always helpful to know your enemy. The first step is to learn some facts about sleep, so you can settle your worries about not getting enough. The next step is to learn four simple but effective solutions:

1. *Tackle physical problems.*
2. *Establish regular routines.*
3. *Control your thoughts.*
4. *Use sophisticated sheep counting.*

We recommend that you read the whole chapter first, and then work through the solutions in order, because most people are likely to need only the first two. However, it is always worth experimenting, to build on these methods in your own way, and to find out whether the other ones may also be helpful.

Some Facts about Sleep

1. On average, adults sleep 7½ hours each night. Two-thirds of the population sleep between 6½ and 8½ hours. A few people feel fine on 4 hours a night and a few need as much as 10 hours.
2. The amount of sleep a person needs may well be inherited, and determined in the same way as their height. So you are not lazy if you need more than average, as Albert Einstein did, nor virtuous if you need less than average, as did Winston Churchill.
3. You need less sleep as you grow older.
4. The depth of your sleep varies throughout the night, and cycles of deep and light sleep are continuously repeated in waves. It is normal occasionally to wake at the "top" of one of these cycles, when you are in the lightest phase of sleep, and to fall into deeper sleep quite soon as the cycle continues.
5. A number of rather "odd" experiences may occur as you are falling asleep or as you are waking. For example, your muscles may twitch, or you may feel as if you are falling, or paralyzed and unable to move. You may also think you hear voices, such as people calling your name. These experiences are all normal.
6. One hour of sleep before midnight is worth just one hour of sleep—neither more nor less. Maybe this old wives' tale was designed to persuade people to get to bed earlier!

7. Experiments on sleep deprivation show that the occasional night of poor sleep may make you feel tired the next day, but has little effect on your performance. Just two hours of sleep, as long as this occurs on occasional nights only, seems adequate to prevent noticeable effects on thinking tasks. So there is no need to worry about sleeping badly the night before an exam. However, you cannot make a drastic cut in your sleep on a regular basis (e.g., from eight to two hours a night) without suffering bad effects. A reduction of one hour may not be harmful, but reducing by more than this may have a bad effect on your mood, concentration, memory, and on the more creative aspects of your thinking. Experiments also show that everybody has dreams, but some people do not remember them. If you deprive someone of their dream sleep, they automatically make it up. In fact, it is very hard to prevent people from dreaming.

8. Sleep is affected by many things: exercise, food, medications, alcohol, illness, mood, stresses, worries, among other things. You may be able to solve your sleep problem by changing any of these.

9. Sleep patterns tend to change slowly. It usually takes a few weeks to establish a new pattern.

SOME FACTS ABOUT SLEEPING PILLS

Sleeping pills are addictive, and may also make you feel drowsy during the day. If you are not already taking them, then do not let yourself develop a new habit. An occasional sleeping pill, taken on your doctor's advice, might be useful in the short term, but you should not take them regularly and frequently, and should not let yourself rely on them.

Four Solutions to Your Sleep Problem

1 TACKLE PHYSICAL PROBLEMS

Pain. Ensure that physical problems such as arthritis are adequately treated. Tell your doctor if pain interferes with your sleep—there will usually be a solution, and your doctor may not have realized your difficulty.

Breathlessness. If you regularly wake short of breath—needing to sit up or even get up, see your doctor. This could be caused by an accumulation of fluid in the lungs, or by narrowing of the airways (asthma). In either case, you may benefit from medication.

Waking to pass urine. The need to urinate often disturbs sleep, particularly for older people and pregnant women. If this disturbs you, the suggestions about how to change your drinking habits in the following box might help. We are not recommending that you drink less fluid overall, only that you redistribute the timing of when you drink. If you suffer from *diabetes* and have problems waking to pass urine, see your doctor. Since dehydration (lack of fluid) is a danger with diabetes, it is important that, in your attempt to solve the sleep problem, you do not drink too little fluid.

How to Reduce the Frequency of Waking to Pass Urine

1. Redistribute your drinking. Keep your overall drinking to between 2 and 3 liters or U.S. quarts a day, and limit yourself to about a quarter of a liter after 4 P.M. Drink the rest before then. It will help to calculate how much you drink in an average day before making changes.
2. Drink nothing for two hours before going to bed.
3. Urinate just before retiring.
4. If you normally take diuretic medication ("water tablets"):
   a. Check with your doctor that you still need them.
   b. Do not take them in the evening—discuss when to take them with your doctor.
5. Drink no alcohol or coffee within three hours of going to bed. These are both diuretics—that is, they make you urinate more than the amount of liquid they contain.

Alcohol. Alcoholic drinks interfere with sleep in two ways. First, they are diuretics (see box above). If you drink alcohol in the evening, you may wake several times in the night to pass urine or because you feel thirsty. Second, it is a sedative drug. It will send you to sleep at first, but tends to wake you as the effect wears off. For those who regularly drink more alcohol than is healthy, a poor night's sleep can be the normal state of affairs, and often reflects a vicious cycle. The poor sleep makes it hard to cope, which makes reliance on alcohol more attractive. But alcohol makes the sleep problem worse. In this case the reliance on alcohol should be tackled (see Chapte 29).

Your bed. Is your bed lumpy, or does it sag? If it is uncomfortable, then think of buying a new one. You will spend so much time in it that it is worth getting the best you can afford, and it is important to choose the kind of bed that makes you feel comfortable and not be unduly influenced by sales talk or labels. Calling a bed "orthopedic" or extolling the virtues of waterbeds is not enough to make those beds good for you, or to make them comfortable for both you and your partner together, particularly if you are very different sizes and shapes or if one of you is more restless and easily disturbed than the other.

Ask to lie on a bed before you decide to buy, and refuse to be hurried. Take your partner with you if possible. Remember that if you both lie quite still, flat on your backs staring up at the ceiling, you will certainly have no way of telling what will happen to one of you when the other stretches out or turns over suddenly.

Also, ask yourself whether you are too hot in bed. It is surprising how many people complain they wake up hot and sweating in the night only because their bedclothes are too warm. Using cooler bedclothes, opening the window, or turning the heat down might help.

Stimulants. Coffee, tea, and tobacco are the main culprits, although chocolate, cocoa, and cola drinks also contain caffeine. Different people are affected differently, so you may have to experiment to find out whether they affect you and try out alternatives like herbal tea, chamomile, or decaffeinated drinks. If you sleep badly, then consider all caffeine drinks guilty until proved innocent. People vary as to how close to bedtime they can take caffeine. For some people even a cup of coffee after lunch can interfere with sleep.

Many stimulants are hard to stop taking because they are addictive. If you are addicted, you may go through a phase of feeling worse before you feel better after stopping them. Once you have got through this "withdrawal" phase, however, your sleep should improve.

When your partner snores. Snoring is likely to cause sleeplessness not for those who snore, but for their partners. The noise of snoring can be extremely irritating, and it is difficult not to get upset or angry if repeatedly woken just as one is falling to sleep. It is usually caused by vibration of the soft palate—the upper, back part of the mouth, and happens most often when people breathe through the mouth or if they have an unusually floppy soft palate.

Some people snore when they have a blocked nose. This can be caused by colds and allergies—for example, to house dust mites. These mites are present in all houses and common in pillows and mattresses, as they flourish in warm conditions. Allergic responses to dust mites are therefore likely to be worse at night and to be present all the year round. Your doctor may be able to advise you on how to deal with the allergy.

Others snore only in some positions. Sleeping propped up may help, but pillows may not work as it is easy to slip off them. A bolster is better, or you could consider raising the head of the bed. If your partner snores only when lying on his back, it may help gently to persuade him to turn over, or to sew a ping pong ball into the back of his pajamas to prompt him to turn over of his own accord whenever he moves onto his back.

Some people snore only at some stages of the sleep cycle—for instance, they might snore for a while as they are falling asleep but become quiet as they settle into deeper sleep. If you can be patient the snoring may stop, but if you wake these people up as they start to snore you will only have to go through the process all over again.

Sedatives (including sleeping pills) tend to make the soft palate more floppy and to increase the chance of snoring, and the most common sedative is alcohol. Try cutting out all alcohol, both during the day and in the evenings, for *at least a week* to find out if this is the cause of the problem. A one-day trial is not enough.

For reasons which are not clear, obesity is associated with snoring, in which case it is worth considering losing some weight—without being too quick or ambitious about it (see Chapter 31). Pregnancy, too, can bring on snoring which usually disappears after the pregnancy is over.

If the snoring continues to disturb you, it might be worth buying earplugs, or talking to your partner about sleeping in separate rooms (if you have the space)—occasionally, for part of the night, or regularly. Sleeping well may be better for the relationship than *sleeping* together. The decision to sleep apart because one person snores need have no profound repercussions on a relationship if both of you understand what you are doing and why.

Finally, if snoring is a major problem, and the measures already discussed fail, see your doctor. Some people have a particularly floppy soft palate, or polyps at the back of the nose, for which surgery is effective.

2 ESTABLISH REGULAR ROUTINES

If you have dealt with the physical problems and still sleep badly, then try to establish regular routines.

An evening routine. A relaxing bedtime routine gives your mind time to settle for the night, and helps you leave behind all the worries and excitements of the day. Your last meal should not be too large nor too late, and we recommend that you start the evening routine 1½ hours before you aim to be asleep. You can shorten the routine later if you want to.

Here is an example: from 9:30 to 10:15 do something calm and enjoyable, like knitting, watching TV, playing with the computer, or reading. At 10:15 wash and get ready for bed. Make a warm drink to take to bed with you (warm milky drinks reduce the chances of waking once you are asleep, or you could try herbal tea), and read for 15 minutes before you settle down at 11.

If you have chores to do in the evenings, like making packed lunches or sorting out clothes, then do them before you start the routine (or make them the first step in the routine). You will only worry if they are not done. The routine should be a way of closing down the old day, not a way of getting ahead on the new one.

Give your routine a high priority, even though you will not always be able to stick to it. Explain what you are doing to others so that they understand and respect it, and remember how much better you will feel if you can overcome the irritability, weariness, and other problems caused by sleeping badly. You may have to unplug the telephone or ask people not to call you after 9:30.

A morning routine. Sometimes a sleep problem continues even after you have established an evening routine. This is the stage to think about what you do in the mornings as well. No amount of willpower will send you to sleep at the right time, but you can force yourself to get up in the morning. We suggest that you give yourself a *short sharp shock* to make sure that you are tired in the evenings and to find out more about how much sleep you really need.

Here is an example. If you normally start the day around 7:30 A.M., then for one week set your alarm earlier than this—for instance, at 7 A.M. Get up immediately. Do not even wait until 7:05. Make yourself a getting up routine that you can go through without thinking—washing, making coffee, dressing—and only think about the day ahead when the routine is done. Do *not* snooze during the day or in front of the TV at night, and for the moment do not allow yourself to sleep late on weekends.

After one week (or perhaps two) you should notice yourself becoming sleepy in the evenings, and find it easier to fall asleep. If you are getting sleepy around 11 P.M. and getting up at 7 A.M. then you need about eight hours sleep. You may then want to shift back to your normal wake up time, but remember to shift bedtime correspondingly.

3 ATTEND TO YOUR THOUGHTS

If you have dealt adequately with physical problems and established regular routines but still lie awake worrying, then you need to consider those two great enemies of good mood: *anxiety* and *depression* (see Part Four of this book).

Lying awake worrying: Sheep in wolves' clothing. Are you kept awake by your worries? Or do they simply fill the time you are awake? Lying awake worrying may be a bad habit that can be broken by establishing a firm rule with yourself. When you catch yourself worrying say to yourself: *this is not the time.* Once you have settled down it is time to sleep, not to think about problems. You have probably noticed that at 3 A.M. problems loom large, and worry spreads rapidly from topic to topic. The problems seem overwhelming or insoluble, and get alarmingly out of proportion. They are far better tackled during the day rather than when you should be sleeping. So tell yourself *this is not the time* and think them through properly later. You could use the techniques of problem-solving (pp. 62–68), or learn the decision tree technique for dealing with worry (p. 226).

You may worry that by the morning you will have forgotten something important. Two simple methods can help. First, spend five minutes, before you settle down, making a note of the things that you think you might worry about. Get them out of your head and onto the paper, ready to deal with later. Second, keep a notepad by the bed and jot down anything that seems important whenever it occurs to you. Then if you start worrying instead of sleeping, you can say *this is not the time*, feeling safe that these things will not be forgotten.

Some couples make a habit of discussing important issues at bedtime, such as work, the children, or troubles between themselves—no wonder they sleep badly. Such discussions should be vetoed. *This is not the time* should be sufficient for one partner to veto the discussion. Make a time to discuss the issue properly—but not within 1½ hours of bedtime!

Waking early if you are depressed. Waking *at least* an hour before your usual time without being able to get back to sleep, *and* feeling very miserable—worse than at any other time—can be a sign of severe depression. If this describes you, then read Chapters 22 to 24 on depression and think about whether it is time to consult your doctor.

4 USE SOPHISTICATED SHEEP COUNTING

The fourth solution combines relaxation techniques with counting "games." This is the solution to try last. It is not a substitute for the others, but a supplement.

Relaxation. Learn how to relax, then you can use the method to help you sleep. Instructions are given in Chapter 11. When lying in bed, it may be easiest to use the "relax only" method rather than tensing muscles up before you let them go, but try anything that you think might be helpful such as the mindfulness form of meditation (see *Further Reading*, p. 515).

You could relax first, and then start the counting games. When you are as relaxed as you can get, focus your attention on your breathing. Keep your attention entirely in the present, thinking about exactly how it feels as you breathe in and out.

Counting games. Three games are described here, and you could probably invent some more of your own. You could even try counting the proverbial sheep. If so, it helps greatly to imagine them passing through a gate or walking single file along a path. In other words, fix your attention on one spot and visualize the sheep moving endlessly past it. Counting is helpful because it is monotonous and takes little effort. Just like a boring television program, it holds your attention sufficiently to prevent you from thinking of other things. Of course, as you get sleepier, your attention wanders; you will lose count, and may then start worrying again. When this happens, calmly return to the counting game, starting wherever you like and trying to focus only on that.

Counting backward. Count steadily backward from a high number like 400, or 232. Count backward slowly, lying comfortably with your eyes closed if possible. Continue counting down, one number at a time, roughly for each full breath. See how far you can get. Reset yourself calmly when you lose count, or go on from wherever you next choose. It is the monotony of counting, and not the actual numbers, that matters.

Counting breaths. Count each full breath. Breathe in, count one. Breathe out steadily. Breathe in, count two. Continue up to six, hold your breath and count six of your heart beats then breathe out. Allow yourself to take, naturally, a deep breath in, then as you breathe out pass into an even deeper state of relaxation. Breathe naturally for a few minutes and repeat the exercise of you need to.

The count down. For this you need to imagine a place of "serene tranquillity," or somewhere you have been calm and relaxed, like sitting in your favorite armchair, lying in the sun, or sitting by a stream. Think of somewhere you have been and try to imagine it clearly. You will visit this place by descending to it down a soft staircase of ten steps. In your imagination stand at the top of your staircase. On each count down, you will take one step and sink slightly into the softness of the stair. Count down about one step a second, and as you say the last one, "zero," imagine arriving in your calm and tranquil place. Feel all the sensations that go with it. Stay there and enjoy it. Don't worry if it fades, and don't try to will yourself to sleep. Just stay in your place.

A note of caution. Exercise during the day can make you tired enough to sleep at night, but exercise late in the evening can keep you awake because it is stimulating and arousing mentally, even if it tires you out physically.

Waking in the middle of the night. If you wake during the night and toss and turn restlessly, settle yourself down with a simple routine. For example:

1. Tell yourself not to worry. Losing some sleep is not harmful.
2. *This is not the time to think about problems.* Write them down to think about later.
3. Think about your physical state. Are you thirsty? Or too hot? Or too cold? Is the room stuffy?
4. Do something to break the pattern, and to trigger off another sleep cycle. You could read for a bit, or go to the bathroom and have sip of water, then settle down again as if for the first time.
5. Use relaxation or meditation exercise, or counting games.

NIGHTMARES AND DREAMS

Nightmares are more common in children than in adults and also when people are upset, worried, or distressed. They can be especially alarming or distressing following severe stresses or traumatic events, such as a car accident or assault (see also pp. 377–378). Often they disappear of their own accord, as if the mind had completed its natural reprocessing of daily happenings, made sense of what happened, and been able to lay the matter to rest. When they persist, it can be helpful to talk to a sympathetic listener about the nightmares, and especially about the feelings they arouse in you. Some people find that nightmares become much less frequent if they make a habit of thinking in the early evening about anything that might have troubled or upset them during the day and try to deal with the problem, or talk about it calmly, before starting their bedtime routine.

Some of the images in nightmares and bad dreams may well have symbolic meaning. For example, at a choice point in life you may dream of crossing a river, or of leaving someone or something important behind. Your sense of being powerless to help someone you love may appear in a nightmare scene of watching them sink into quicksand. Dreaming that you are being chased and are unable to run away may reflect your feelings of being trapped or threatened in some way.

But symbolic elements of nightmares and dreams may also combine with some completely random and unrelated elements, as if (as some psychologists suggest) brain cells need to keep firing just for them to keep functioning well, and different ones will do so at different times. Images associated with recent events, and their meanings, may also be reprocessed during sleep and only some of them break through to consciousness, producing bizarre and incomprehensible associations that we then try to make sense of when we wake.

When frightening dreams or nightmares happen repeatedly, their frequency may increase if going to bed makes you anxious about having them. Then, just as when overcoming a phobia (see Chapter 19), it is helpful to face the fear: to relate the dream, or write it down, several times, describing *all* of its alarming and disturbing aspects; and reminding yourself repeatedly that it is "only a dream" and not really harmful.

Chapter Summary

Almost everyone with a sleep problem can overcome it by taking simple steps. There are four simple but effective solutions.

1. Tackle physical problems first. Make sure you can get comfortable, avoid diuretics and too much alcohol in the evening, and cut down on stimulants such as coffee, tea, hot chocolate, and tobacco.
2. Establish regular routines for the evening, and possibly for the morning as well.
3. Control your thoughts. *This is not the time* to think about problems.
4. Relax and use counting games to help you switch off.

31

Good Eating Habits

Habits That Last a Lifetime

Eating should be a source of health and of pleasure, but for many, it is a source of neither. A bad diet can cause heart disease, obesity, tooth decay, ulcers, and other disorders of the digestive system, and excessive concerns about shape and weight engendered in modern society can turn eating from a pleasure into a burden. Dieting has become a way of life for a very large number of people, especially women; and in its wake follow bulimia and anorexia.

There are two basic elements of good eating, and of the habits that can last a lifetime: *what* to eat, and *how* to eat.

WHAT TO EAT: FIVE PRINCIPLES FOR A HEALTHY DIET

Over the last thirty years, a great deal of scientific research has been carried out on the relationship between diet and disease. The practical lessons can be summarized as *five* principles.

1. *There are no good or bad foods, only good or bad diets.* No single food is "evil." A crème brûlée contains a great deal of fat including cholesterol. But the occasional crème brûlée is not harmful, nor is

the occasional "junk food." But the key is that it is only occasional. The important issue is how much fat there is in the total diet, not in individual foods. The first principle, therefore, is to think in terms of your whole diet. Whatever your favorite foods are, you can eat them, at least occasionally.

2. *Reduce fats.* In Western society we eat too much fat, and in particular too many saturated fats. The practical ways of reducing the intake of saturated fats are summarized in the accompanying table.

Ways of Reducing Intake of Saturated Fats

Grill rather than fry.

Use lean meats—and cut off excess fat.

Eat fish, beans, legumes, or nuts.

Choose low-fat cheeses.

Use unsaturated oils for cooking: olive, grape-seed, or sunflower oils.

Avoid large quantities of high-fat foods: e.g., pastries, cakes, biscuits, chips, chocolate.

Eat no more than four eggs a week.

Eat oily fish: e.g., mackerel, herring, salmon, and tuna.

---

3. *Reduce total sugar.* Use fruit rather than sugar to add sweetness. Choose low sugar drinks and avoid adding sugar to drinks and cereals.

4. *Increase dietary fiber.* The word "fiber" is going out of fashion to be replaced by *non-starch polysaccharides* or *(NSP)*, but the principle is the same. A good diet contains a lot of NSP, which is to be found in fresh fruit, preferably with skins, lightly cooked vegetables, whole-meal bread, potatoes (with skins), pasta, rice, porridge oats, and high-fiber breakfast cereals.

5. *Reduce salt.* Use spices (and herbs) to add variety to life.

OBESITY REACHES EPIDEMIC PROPORTIONS

Obesity, especially in young people, is reaching epidemic proportions in America and in some European countries including the UK, with major implications for health and for education. Two of the main contributing factors are: (1) the ready availability of attractive junk foods and drinks, packaged in ever-increasing sizes, and (2) taking less exercise. Poor diet in children is linked with poor concentration and disruptive behavior, both of which interfere with learning. The life expectancy of obese young people is also significantly reduced. So obesity has serious consequences, and learning what and how to eat is therefore increasingly important. This chapter focuses on ways of developing eating habits that can last a lifetime, and it also explains some of the facts about dieting.

HOW TO EAT

The main problem about eating is the *way* we eat, and the culprit is the extreme views which our culture engenders about shape and weight, especially in women. Obesity is one problem, but excessive dieting can be even more of a problem. Extreme ideas about diets may result in either a cycle of binge-eating followed by starvation (bulimia) or to extreme losses in weight (anorexia).

If the way you eat or your concerns about your shape and weight are a problem for you, then read the rest of this chapter.

BODY AND MIND

Research has found that about 80% of American women and almost 50% of men have tried to diet at some time in their lives and many of these have never been obese or even at a weight associated with an increased risk of ill health. Indeed, if you look at an active group of men and women in sports, such as tennis or football players, they will be of quite widely differing shapes and weights, many of which do not conform to the fashionable norm.

Dieting seems to be rather like a cultural disease, or even another epidemic. Fashion dictates, and fashion at the moment favors slimness—for men as well as for women, but especially for women. Therefore to look good it is important to be slim, and if you are not slim, you will be pressured by the media, by the diet industry, and by the people around you to do something about it. Regardless of whether nature intended you to be that way, regardless of the number of curves or muscles you were born to develop, it is hard to resist the many influences on you to slim down.

IMPLICATIONS FOR SELF-ESTEEM AND SELF-CONFIDENCE

The message beamed at us in Western societies is that we should be slim; and that if we do the right things we will be slim. This has little to do with health and a lot to do with commercial interests.

When this cultural message is swallowed hook, line, and sinker, it has wide-ranging effects on the way that people feel about themselves, particularly on their self-esteem and self-confidence. As dieters are only too aware, losing weight is supposed to be a way of making you feel good about yourself. It is as if losing weight is a way of solving all of life's problems at once. In this cultural climate it can feel devastating to be the "wrong" shape.

Six Determinants of Weight and Shape

There are two things wrong with this cultural message. The first is that slimness, to the degree envisaged, is *not* especially healthy. The second is that, contrary to the impression given, it is not easy to lose weight. And this is because weight and shape are not determined only by what we eat: many other factors make their contribution as well.

1. *Genetics.* There is a strong genetic influence on body shape, size, and weight. In an interesting research study carried out in Denmark, a large group of adults who had been adopted as young children were weighed. Their weights were compared with the weights of both their natural (biological) parents and their adoptive parents. The result showed that their weight was similar to that of their biological parents, but not to their adoptive parents. It seems that what we inherit goes a long way to determining our shape and weight: we are likely to look like our parents and grandparents.
2. *The set point and metabolism.* The body acts, possibly for genetic reasons but also according to your age and activity levels, as if it was seeking its own weight level. It seems as though each of us has a weight "set point"—which works rather like the thermostat in a house. If we try to lose weight so as to fall below our set point, physiological forces act to try and prevent the loss in weight. Our body makes better use of the food we eat. In other words the way that our bodies use food is not fixed and static. It changes according to how we treat it, and tends to protect itself from the effects of dieting.
3. *Age.* Young adults, both women and men, continue to change in weight and shape, or to "fill out," after they have gained their full height. Older people in general are heavier than they were when they were younger, and many women gain weight rather suddenly

around the time of menopause. However, elderly people may lose both weight and height toward the end of their lives.

4. *Exercise, fitness, and posture.* Certain types of exercise build up certain muscle groups, so swimmers develop big, strong shoulders and runners develop their calf and thigh muscles. People may look different when fit because their posture changes and they move more flexibly. At the same time exercise uses up energy. Although regular exercise increases appetite, its overall effect tends to be a reduction in weight although only if the output of energy is greater than the input (through food and drink).

5. *Drinking habits.* Alcohol, because it is high in calories, is not only fattening, it also fills you up without providing you with the nourishment you need.

6. *Eating patterns and habits.* Eating a large quantity of fatty foods, despite the genetic and physiological factors described above, will lead to weight gain. "Junk" foods and drinks which are high in fats or sugars are potent causes of obesity, and should be taken, if at all, only occasionally and in small quantities. If you gain weight when you eat a small amount of fatty food, then you may be trying to hold your weight below that demanded by your genetic constitution and your "set point."

The Dangers of Diets

Dieting is deprivation. It is going without. The body is a well-adapted mechanism designed to help you survive, and it resists attempts at severe dieting with physiological means. The more often you have tried to diet, the more efficient these means become and the less effective your diet will be. Your body will find ways of compensating for the way you treat it, so the weight you lose by dieting will not be equivalent to the energy reduction you make. You will be fighting a never-ending or losing battle. At the same time, dieting poses some serious dangers.

- *Cycles of starving and overeating.* The more you deprive yourself of food, the more you will crave it. The stronger the cravings, the more likely you will give in. Once you give in it is tempting to overeat: "I've blown it now; I might as well give up, and start again tomorrow." Because you gave in, you then try to impose greater control and the cycle begins again. Many people on diets swing between the extremes of restricting and overeating. The net result is not a loss of weight, but a feeling of being out of control.

- *Upsetting the appetite controls.* Frequent dieting can upset the natural feelings of hunger and fullness. The hunger is never satisfied, and therefore it never leaves you, but at the same time, you get used to it and cease to notice it. When the diet is stopped, this appetite control system no longer functions adequately: it becomes hard to recognize whether you are "really" hungry, even when you are full. The natural control system can be reestablished by eating regular meals over a period of a few weeks.
- *Preoccupation with food.* The natural reaction to deprivation, to severe dieting, is to think more about food. Food can become a serious preoccupation, and ruminating about it starts to interfere with other activities. The preoccupation is counterproductive because it makes the diet harder to bear and binging more likely.
- *Pseudo-success.* It can be tempting to confuse successful dieting with other kinds of success. Dieting can feel good because it helps to achieve a socially desired goal. It takes effort, and so demonstrates a certain kind of strength. These successes make people feel better about themselves, as if being slightly smaller made them better people. It is easy to forget that you are the same person, with the same personality, strengths, and weaknesses, whatever size you happen to be.
- *Mood swings.* Happiness may go with a successful dieting plan and misery with an unsuccessful one. Self-esteem can be higher when you are able to restrict your food, but lower (sometimes extremely low) when you overeat. Mood swings start to feel out of control, and dieters may learn to control their moods by eating. Eating improves mood, but only temporarily. It brings relief from hunger and from preoccupations with food, and after eating, while the food is being digested, other bad feelings are dampened down. Eating is often followed by a period of relative calmness. In the long run this has two undesirable consequences: food intake is controlled by mood rather than by physiological requirements; and both mood and eating swing violently. It becomes progressively harder to stick to a diet, and easier to blame oneself for failing to stick to it. The result is more unhappiness, not less.
- *Fatigue, stress, and strain.* This is a direct consequence of deprivation, and can be exacerbated by the emotional roller coaster that goes with dieting.

Eating Disorders Associated with Dieting

The two problems associated with dieting and with excessive concern with weight and shape are anorexia and bulimia nervosa. These are both potentially serious and dangerous conditions that usually start in adolescence and affect many more women than men. For many people, these problems begin following attempts to control weight by dieting. It is important to seek professional help for either of these conditions, even if they are at an early stage.

ANOREXIA NERVOSA

Anorexia involves excessive dieting and loss of weight that can sometimes be so extreme that it threatens life. People with anorexia will go to enormous lengths to lose weight, often eating tiny, calorie-controlled meals in secret and exercising excessively. Some take large quantities of laxatives after eating, with the mistaken idea that this will prevent them from gaining weight. They may overestimate their body size, even when emaciated, and remain convinced that they are too fat. Being "fat" is associated, in the minds of people with anorexia, with being bad, and putting on weight feels terrifying. Most women with anorexia stop menstruating, feel exhausted, and find it hard to keep warm. They also lose contact with their contemporaries and suffer from low self-esteem and lack of confidence.

BULIMIA NERVOSA

Bulimia is also associated with a fear of gaining weight, with fears of losing control, and with low self-esteem. People who suffer from bulimia, however, are usually of normal weight. They are subject to an extreme eating cycle and alternate between complete starvation and enormous binges, usually carried out in secret. In an effort to control possible weight gain after binging, they may also induce vomiting or take laxatives. They often feel that their eating is out of control. Those with bulimia may eat carefully controlled, reduced-calorie foods between binges and binge on large quantities of "banned" foods, such as chocolate, cakes, pies, bread, and soft drinks. They usually feel distressed and upset by the binge eating and less upset if they succeed in following a strict diet. Binge eating, like anorexia, may disturb menstruation.

DANGEROUS BEHAVIOR

Some of the things that anorexics and bulimics do are dangerous, and can cause serious harm. These are listed in the box below.

The Dangers of Anorexia and Bulimia

The dangers of low weight

Biochemical abnormalities in blood (especially low potassium) leading to dangerous heart arrhythmias and seizures

Low blood glucose leading to loss of consciousness and death

Heart failure

Dangerously low blood pressure

Weak bones leading to fractures

Dehydration

The dangers of using laxatives

Laxatives do not help to overcome the fattening effects of food. Loss of weight following laxative use is due to loss of fluid. This is dangerous. It leads to biochemical abnormalities in blood—including low potassium—which may cause dangerous heart arrhythmias.

The dangers of self-induced vomiting

Dental erosion and cavities

Biochemical abnormalities in blood (including low potassium) leading to dangerous heart arrhythmias

---

Sensible Weight Control

Because of the dangers of anorexia and bulimia, it is important if you want to diet to do it in a safe and sensible way. It is certainly possible to diet while using habits that can last a lifetime, and this is the safest way to work at it, provided that you are absolutely certain that you both want and need to lose weight.

First, set yourself a broad, not a narrow, target. Consider the determinants of weight already discussed and think about what is likely to be a healthy, natural weight for you at your age. This is like asking you to decide what your "set point" is at the moment—something that you will only be able to guess. Then, define a weight to aim at, within for example, a range of four to six pounds (two or three pounds either side of a precise target). The reason for this is that weight is always subject to minor variations, depending on factors such as water retention, so you will never be able to keep yourself exactly at one weight.

Next, set up a routine that can help you establish a lifetime habit. Plan regular eating times. The traditional pattern of three meals a day is a good one, but it does not suit all people. It is important, however, that you do not try to go for long periods during the day without food—if you do you are in danger of pushing yourself into a binging-starvation cycle. Small snacks between meals and right before bedtime help to prevent hunger-induced binges. Having established regular eating *times*, the next question is what, and how much, to eat. The key to safe dieting is to eat a well-balanced diet but slightly less of it, and since the aim is to establish eating patterns to last a lifetime, there is no hurry. So, at this stage, having decided on a pattern of eating times, simply keep to these times and eat a balanced diet. Do not ban any foods (this might be counterproductive because you might develop cravings for them), and do not restrict what you eat (this might trap you into thinking more about food). At this stage you are trying to find out how much to eat in order to keep your weight stable: neither gaining nor losing, but remaining within your chosen range. You are also ensuring that your appetite control system is in good working order: telling you when you are hungry, but leaving you alone in between meal times. This stage should last at least three weeks (a month if you can manage it).

If you have eaten in this way without gaining weight for at least three weeks, and your weight is above your target range, make a *small* reduction in the overall amount you eat, but retain a balanced diet and regular meal times. The best way is slightly to reduce your intake at each meal. Fatty foods contain more calories than other foods, so reducing the amount of fat is particularly effective. It is essential to make small changes only. Your body will react dramatically to drastic changes, and will undergo physiological alterations that resist weight reduction. Alcohol contains many calories. One good way of reducing overall intake is to reduce alcohol.

One "trick" to help you reduce food intake is to eat slowly. The feeling of being satisfied comes partly from the level of sugar in your blood, and this rises with a short delay when you eat a normal meal. If you eat slowly, you will be less likely to go on eating beyond the point of satisfaction.

Losing weight cannot be done both quickly and safely. There are real dangers involved, and it is far better for your health and well-being to adapt a sensible, lifetime habit through making small changes so that you lose weight steadily but slowly.

Some people find that weighing themselves is discouraging as they are easily misled by normal day-to-day fluctuations or become increasingly preoccupied with their weight. For others, daily weighings help maintain motivation. We recommend that you find your own way of keeping track of your weight, but that you ignore minor fluctuations. Your size, weight, and shape are reflections of only one, relatively unimportant, aspect of yourself. To keep them in perspective, think also about the many other aspects: your work and daily occupation, family and relationships, pleasures and relaxations, skills and talents, and about your involvement in activities of all kinds, physical, social, and political. You are not your weight.

Establishing Good Eating Habits

Experiments done with golden hamsters showed that these animals naturally controlled the types of food they ate. The precise way in which they did it remained mysterious, but the effect was to provide them with a balanced diet containing all the elements that they needed. If they were deprived for some time of one kind of food, they appeared not to suffer, but when it was offered they then chose to eat it in preference to other things.

Children are obviously not like golden hamsters. But the principle may still be important. If a child is being offered a varied and nutritionally healthy diet, then there is no need to worry about which of the foods offered will be eaten. Too much of one thing will eventually give way to something else. It is far more important, once out of babyhood, to establish regular meal times. Children will have likes and dislikes, and parents may feel it is important to encourage them to try new things, but the child itself is likely to be the best judge of how much it wants to eat. If it is important to you that a child finishes up what it is given, then give it very little to start with, and as the child gets older, allow it to help itself on condition that it eats what it takes. It takes quite a long time to learn how to make this judgment, so the sooner you start the better. Nobody can learn to get it right without making literally hundreds of mistakes on the way.

The message is that small children can control their eating very well, and they will do so better if their appetite controls are set by regular meal times, if they are offered a well-balanced variety of foods, and if they are allowed to make their own choices. Eating then becomes a pleasure rather than a pain.

One of the difficulties of establishing lifelong eating habits in the family is that food is so readily available. Walk into the kitchen or open the fridge, and you can find it any time. So another useful strategy, both for families and for people trying to lose weight slowly by sensible methods, is to use "stimulus control" procedures.

STIMULUS CONTROL

Being controlled by a stimulus means that whenever you see it you react to it. Whenever you see food you eat some. If this is a problem for you, if you tend to nibble at, or binge on, food which is lying around, then the solution is to control the stimulus. There are three steps to stimulus control. The first is to make sure that food is out of sight and out of reach except at meal times. The second is to develop the habit of eating only when you are sitting down to a meal at a table. And the third is to concentrate on eating and enjoying your food whenever you do eat. That means not swallowing it down as you read the paper or spooning it in automatically in front of the TV. In brief, outlaw the casual consumption of food. You can use the method of stimulus control in other ways too. For example, avoid walking past the bakery just as the bread comes out of the oven or past the fast food outlet. Shop from a list, and at a time when you are not ravenously hungry. Buy foods that need preparation, so that you cannot nibble whenever you feel tempted. Limit the amount of food you store at home. Drink water or eat some carrots rather than dipping your finger into the cake mix if you have to cook when you are unbearably hungry.

It is precisely because food is good, because it gives pleasure, that it is so tempting to eat too much, and at the wrong time. But if it were not so enjoyable, our ancestors might not have bothered to search for it and might not have survived. This "searching" behavior dies hard. New and tempting foods and recipes are constantly set before us. Once the lifetime habits are securely in place, there is nothing to be lost from enjoying eating in all sorts of ways, including meals with friends, visits to restaurants, and the occasional feast.

MISUSES OF EATING

Because food is such a potent source of pleasure, it can be used as a substitute for something else. Using food to show love can lead to bad habits: for example, eating for comfort or when feeling sad, eating to control mood, and eating as a cure for boredom or loneliness. Eating is not a way of solving other problems. The danger of using it in this way is that it will become a problem in itself, leading to obesity, bulimia, or anorexia.

People with anorexia and bulimia suffer from an extreme form of the problem that also besets dieters: they feel good about themselves when they succeed in restricting their eating, and bad about themselves when they fail. In many cases self-esteem is strongly based on their opinion about their shape and weight. If you are suffering from anorexia or bulimia, then we recommend that you read one of the books mentioned at the end of the book and also seek medical or psychological help. If, in attempting to diet, you are starting to lose control of your eating— by sometimes binging, or being tempted to use laxatives, or making yourself vomit, read this chapter carefully (and also Chapter 10) and start by focusing on regular meals with snacks: breakfast, snack, lunch, snack, evening meal, bedtime snack. The snacks can be as little as one small apple and should not be junk food. The meals need not be large, but should be well-balanced. By carefully planning three meals and three snacks each day, you will find it easier to regain control of your eating.

HELPING SOMEONE WITH AN EATING PROBLEM

It can be very difficult if someone close to you is suffering with anorexia or bulimia. People with these difficulties often reject help. They may be secretive, easily upset, and angry, and often do not tell others honestly what they are doing. This can be because they feel bad both about their behavior (which may include such things as lying and stealing) and about hurting people they love. Or they might be terrified of trying to change because they feel they will not be able to control the weight gain. For some people their entire sense of self-esteem depends on their success in controlling their eating and weight. For them, being encouraged to change is especially frightening. It may seem to threaten what has become an essential support system. They can become angry when others try to help.

One of the most difficult things for those close to people with eating disorders is to find a way of showing that they care, without either becoming overanxious and overinvolved, or angry and overdetached. The middle road is best, although difficult to maintain. It is helpful if close friends acknowledge openly that there is a problem. But it is usually more fruitful to try and help sufferers to develop as independent people than to try and solve the eating problem for them. The aim for friends and family is to remain emotionally close—available when needed—without becoming intrusive. These eating problems are common in teenage girls and young women, at a time when relationships within the family are changing. It is likely to be a time of turbulence and distress. The best way of helping may be to remain the stable point within an unstable world.

Chapter Summary

Good eating habits ensure that eating remains a source of health and of pleasure. They involve limiting, rather than banning, those foods that are fattening or unhealthy, and developing a regular eating pattern: *what you eat* and *how you eat* are both important. Obesity, resulting from eating an excess of "junk" foods (high in fats and sugars), is an increasing problem in Western cultures. Excessive dieting is also a problem.

Cultural pressures to diet can spoil the pleasure and undermine self-esteem rather than make you feel good about yourself, because the amount you eat is not the only thing that determines your weight and shape. *Dieting can lead to serious problems:*

- Cycles of starving and overeating
- Upsetting the appetite controls
- Preoccupation with food
- Pseudo-success
- Mood swings
- Fatigue, stress, and strain

Two disorders associated with dieting—anorexia and buiilmia—have dangerous consequences.

It is possible to control your weight both safely and sensibly by establishing regular meal times and avoiding cycles of either undereating or overeating. Keeping food out of sight (and out of mind) in between meal times—stimulus control—is helpful, and it is important not to use eating as an (ineffective) way of solving other problems, such as feeling lonely or bored.

PART SEVEN

THE WORKING MIND

This final part of the book is about your mind as a tool for thinking. Just as a degree of physical fitness contributes to pleasure from physical activity, so a degree of "mental fitness" enables you to gain pleasure from the use of your mind.

The first two chapters in this part on study are not for students only. They are for anyone who wishes to learn or to develop a hobby or interest.

Our memories often let us down. We devote two chapters to showing how you can make sure that your memory works for you.

The last two chapters, on making decisions and thinking straight, bring together many of the themes of this book, and take them a step further.

Your mind is a powerful tool. "The Working Mind" shows how you can use it to enjoy your life to the fullest.

32

The Fundamentals of Effective Study

The Pleasures of Study

Study is not only for students: good study methods are useful to us all. A little regular study is analogous to a little regular exercise: it strengthens habits and develops skills that are useful for a lifetime. The principles explained in this chapter are appropriate to a wide range of situations: to high school or university students studying full-time; to part-time students, attending evening classes or studying alone; to people who wish to improve their vocational qualifications; and to people who want to pursue a hobby or learn a new language. This chapter is relevant whether you want to study a topic, learn a musical instrument, or write a novel, because the ideas in it can be applied to any task which requires you to make use of your mind in a systematic way.

A little regular study can provide you with one of the great pleasures in life; your learning will accumulate and you will enjoy knowing more about the things that interest you. Such knowledge will also build your confidence and help you to feel proud of your achievements. If you are a student, then studying efficiently will be a bonus, giving you more free time as well as better results. Good study techniques are not difficult to master, and it is surprising how few students make use of them. Do not be put off by their apparent simplicity; often the simple and straightforward methods are the most effective.

The Law of Mass Effect

There is one central law about study: the law of mass effect. This states that the amount of work you do (the amount you learn or the amount you write, for instance) is strongly correlated with the amount of time you spend doing it. Certainly, many students study in an inefficient way, so that long hours of hard work achieve much less than they could. But it is important not to believe the myth that by studying incredibly efficiently you can achieve a lot by doing remarkably little. What you can do is achieve a great deal by combining work and recreation in moderate amounts. Any worthwhile study will therefore take some time. The main reason why people who study often achieve less than they want to is that they do not put in the hours. Therefore, if you want to study, you need to set aside time to work. So why not make it easy to start, and fun to do?

Making It Easy to Start

Most people find it difficult to get down to work. You might promise yourself that you will sit down and write for an hour at eight o'clock in the evening. At eight o'clock you think it would be nice to have a cup of tea. At a quarter past eight you make a quick phone call. At half past eight there is a program on the radio or TV. At nine o'clock you listen to the news. At 20 past nine a friend phones. At half past nine. . . .

All this is common experience and there must be few people who do not waste time or use their time in this way. But the single most important difference between good and bad students is in the ability to get down to work.

The problem with not getting down to work is twofold: first, it results in too little work being done; and second, it results in an unsatisfactory use of the time when you are trying to get down to work, because so much of the time not working is spent in a kind of no man's land, which is neither work nor recreation but being about to work, worrying about work, not quite relaxing but not quite working either.

In order to get down to work, you need to make it as easy for yourself as possible. Just as it takes time for an engine, starting from cold, to run smoothly, so it is with ourselves. Sometimes we need a kick-start to get going; but once in the swing of it, it is usually much easier to keep going and can be a real pleasure too.

FOUR WAYS OF HELPING YOURSELF TO GET DOWN TO WORK

1. *Create a good work environment.* There is nothing more dispiriting than looking at the place where you are going to study and finding that it fills you with gloom. Try and keep a particular place, a room or part of a room, for work. Make this place attractive in your own particular way. Decorate it with pictures, or flowers, or whatever it is that you enjoy. Make yourself an inviting tabletop, for example, by getting rid of unnecessary clutter.

2. *List the tasks beforehand.* We tend to use any excuse not to get down to work, and one is uncertainty over where to begin: "Shall I do this, or that?" And the uncertainty becomes an excuse for doing something else. Plan in advance what it is you are going to work on. The simple expedient of writing a list of the various things to do and the order in which you are going to do them can save hours of wasted time. Try not to be too ambitious when you make your plan. You can always do something extra at the end if there is still time.

3. *Keep the benefits of study clearly in mind.* However easy you make it for yourself to start the work, there will still be a small hump to get over. You need to keep before you the benefits to be gained from doing the work. With large tasks this is particularly important; otherwise, an initial enthusiasm might wane and you may never find the energy to start. Write down all the things you could gain from doing the work, and read the list when you are due to start, to give yourself a boost. This is particularly useful if you are going through one of those phases when you feel discouraged, or have lost heart.

4. *Leave your work environment inviting for the next time.* Most people tidy up, and find the things they need in order to get started, at the beginning of the study session. When they stop the session, they leave everything in a disorganized mess. The problem with this is that the mess becomes a barrier to starting the next work session. The solution is simple. Spend the last few minutes of the study period tidying up and getting ready for the next session so that it will be easy to start. This is also one of the best times to plan in advance what to do next.

Making It Fun to Do

MAKE USE OF YOUR BEST TIME OF DAY

You may have little choice when to study, or it may not matter for you anyway. But some people work better, or more easily, at some times of day than at others. Some people are morning workers; others work best in the evenings. If you have preferences, try and accommodate them.

STUDY IN SHORT PERIODS

Many people fail to study because they believe that once they get down to it they should keep at it for hours. This is so daunting that they do nothing at all. It is much better to have more modest goals and actually do the work. We recommend that you work in fairly short, "bite-sized pieces," the size of the bite depending to some extent on you and to some extent on the subject matter. If you are studying in the evenings, after work, then we recommend keeping the bites small; otherwise, you are likely to turn on the TV instead.

VARIETY—THE CHOCOLATE BOX APPROACH

An enormous slab of chocolate would be difficult to eat all at once, but in a box of assorted chocolates each chocolate is small, and there is a great deal of variety. Whatever it is you want to study, break up the study into short periods with frequent breaks, and give yourself variety. If you do this you will find it much easier to "eat" your way through the box, and you will find that you have completed a great deal of work.

A student came to us for help because he was finding it very difficult to carry on with his studies. Each morning he faced several hours of sitting in the library "studying," feeling bored and tired. We asked him to tell us about his study. "It's just the same each day. I go to the library and read." "Do you never write anything?" "Of course, I have to write essays." We carried on asking him exactly what he did. It turned out that what he saw as the one task of "studying" was a myriad different tasks. He would order books from the librarian; some he would read as reference books, selecting material and taking notes. Sometimes he would read novels, as part of his study, reading all the way through. Before writing an essay he would return to his notes, and condense them. He would plan his essay and play around with some of the ideas. Then he would write, and then edit what he had written. At any stage he might talk to other students or discuss topics with a tutor.

In fact, he was not just doing the same task all the time but doing a wide variety of tasks. We suggested that he plan out his next morning's study, identifying the different tasks and ensuring that he only did each one for a relatively short period—for example, about 45 minutes at a time. We also asked him to schedule in breaks. The plan for his next morning looked like a chocolate box. It was made up of a variety of small, more or less, appetizing chunks. A week later he was a transformed student: keener on his work and more satisfied than he had been before.

This transformation had been achieved by the simple process of breaking the study period up into a variety of tasks, and showing him that what he had seen as one boring activity was in reality a number of different activities, any of which might become boring if you did them for too long. When study becomes boring and repetitive, like an assembly line, it loses its variety and hence its attractiveness.

Planning and Organization

STUDY WITH A PURPOSE IN MIND

Why do you want to study? Whatever the reason, keep it in mind. Keep it in mind in order to: decide what information you want, decide on your priorities, and choose what to do with the information you collect. You do not have to have a very erudite or scholarly purpose; you could just be curious.

Suppose you want to learn Portuguese because you want to be able to speak a little when you go to Portugal on vacation. The words and phrases that you learn—the tapes and books which you might use to learn from—all these should be chosen bearing in mind that it is for a vacation that you wish to use the language. If you were learning Portuguese for business purposes, then you would need a different vocabulary. Your purpose helps you decide what and how to learn. Perhaps you want to learn Portuguese in order to read business reports but do not need to speak the language. So your purpose also helps you to decide what to practice. If you want to learn the language in order principally to read it, then practice reading it. If you want to learn it principally to speak, then practice speaking it. If you want to be able to understand, then practice listening to it. The purpose helps you to decide how much you need to do. Your aim, in learning Portuguese, might be to be able to order a meal and ask directions. You may not need to be fluent.

Most people read books from cover to cover in a linear fashion even though, for most study purposes, this is not the best thing to do (pp.

457–459). It is unfocused, and wastes a lot of time. When studying, think more of the way in which you might read a newspaper—browsing, selecting, reading some articles right through, dipping into some, and ignoring others altogether. Select what you read and select how much you read. In making the selection keep the purpose in mind. What are you aiming to get from this bit of reading, this bit of study?

The same is true when taking notes (pp. 459–462). Keep the purpose in mind. Do you want these notes to replace having to read the book again? Or to remind you what is in the book and where to find it? Do you want to remember the contents in detail, or to bring away some main ideas? Is the material such that once you have remembered the main headings you can remember the rest, or does it demand that you remember a great deal of specific information? It is not only the ultimate purpose (ordering a Portuguese meal) that you need to bear in mind, but also the more immediate one. Reasons for note-taking can vary from improving concentration to making you feel productive; notes can provide a memory aid or a sense of achievement. Exactly what form your notes will take depends on what you are making them for.

SALAMI—CUTTING BIG PROJECTS INTO SLICES

Big projects often pose particular difficulties. They can be daunting at the beginning because they are so big. And they can be dispiriting in the middle when the initial blush of enthusiasm has paled and the end is still out of sight.

No project is too large, or large projects would never get done, but large ones do need to be tackled systematically—for example, by using the *salami* principle: cut big projects into slices. If you "eat" the slices one by one, you will eventually consume the whole "salami." In other words, set yourself small manageable tasks so that by progressing through them you will eventually accomplish the large task. Most people grossly underestimate how long it takes them to do something they have set for themselves, and often have to double their original estimates. Focusing on the demands made by each "slice" makes these estimates much more accurate, as well as making each slice more appetizing.

AN ATTITUDE OF PROJECT COMPLETION

The *salami* approach can enable you to organize and begin a large project, but there may be other, new projects you are keen to get on with as well, and this is where the danger lies. It can be tempting to abandon the current project and start a new, more exciting one instead, so that over time you accumulate a number of half-finished projects. If you want to complete them, you need to adopt the kind of attitude that helps to ensure that starting new projects does not prevent you from finishing old ones. Be prepared to delay the onset of new projects. Keep them in the planning stage until the old ones have been completed.

Finishing the Study Period

FILE YOUR WORK FOR EASY ACCESS

At the end of your study period, sort and file your materials. "I know I've made some notes on this somewhere. . . ." The best notes in the world are of little help if you cannot find them at the right time. When studying, one of the things you need not be wasting your time doing is looking for information, looking for notes you put somewhere, or looking for the right file. You need a simple and effective system for filing your notes and material whether your notes are on paper, or on the computer. The system does not need to be elaborate. It can make use of shoe boxes or those well-tried methods which efficient offices find effective: envelopes, files, storage boxes, filing cabinets, or a series of notebooks. If you do not know how to file your notes, then it may be sufficient simply to file them in the order in which you write them. We tend to be good at remembering roughly when we did things and which things we did before others. If you use a loose-leafed file, and take a separate piece of paper for each new study time, then you can always re-sort later if you want to and such re-sorting is even easier if your notes are in electronic form.

The other key to not wasting time trying to find things is to have a specific place, or computer file, in which you keep your notes. When you finish a piece of work, always put it back in its place. Do not leave it out where it might get mixed up with other things, or incorporated into the newspapers or your children's play.

REWARD YOURSELF FOR EACH STUDY PERIOD

Animal trainers know the importance of reward. The principle is simple: you will enjoy doing things more if they are rewarding and then you will be more likely to want to do them again. In order to boost your chance of studying, you can build in extra and immediate rewards. For example, you might decide that if you spend three hours studying on Saturday afternoon you will then go out to the movies. If you are studying in smaller chunks, then a token system might help. For example, for each hour of study you might give yourself a token. You can then "spend" the tokens on "luxuries"—things that you would not allow yourself to do or buy without the tokens, but that you very much enjoy (make yourself some pancakes; soak in the bath; buy a plant or new pen). In this way studying becomes associated with pleasures that you can think of if you are finding it difficult to get down to work. The key to success is to keep the rewards simple and fairly immediate. Giving yourself something good to look forward to helps you to work, whereas giving yourself the pleasure before you work makes working that much harder.

Chapter Summary

1. Regular study can be fun and rewarding.
2. The principles of effective study are simple, but often ignored even by experienced students.
3. The *law of mass effect* is central to study: even if you study efficiently, you still need to put in the hours.
4. *Four ways of making it easy to start study:*

   - Make yourself an inviting work environment.
   - List the tasks to do beforehand.
   - Keep the benefits of study clearly in mind.
   - Leave your desk inviting for the next time.

5. *Make study fun:*

   - Use your best time of day.
   - Use the *chocolate box approach* by keeping study periods to bite-sized chunks, and by giving yourself variety.

6. *Study with your main purpose in mind.*
7. Use the *salami* principle: regular small slices of study will add up to big achievements.
8. *Complete* your projects.
9. *File and tidy up* at the end of your study periods.
10. *Reward yourself* for each completed study period.

33

Key Study Skills: Reading, Taking Notes, and Using the Material

Reading

One of the most valuable skills students need to master is the ability to learn from reading. The method most people use is to read from cover to cover—the method most of us learned in childhood. This is an excellent method for some purposes—for example, if you are reading a novel or a biography, or if you want to follow an author's train of thought through an interesting or complex field. It may also satisfy curiosity, and be a relaxing way of reading, but nevertheless it is not the only method, nor is it the best method for some purposes. You would not read the Sunday papers in that way (or you would do nothing else all Sunday), nor is it the best way to get the most out of reading for study purposes. The four-pronged approach which follows provides you with another option.

THE FIRST PRONG: PREPARATION

Read to extend your knowledge, not for learning. The kernel of truth that lies in this remark is that we learn better if we can relate what we read to what we already know, and if we can fit what we read into categories that are meaningful to us. Using a period of preparation enables you to prepare your mind for the new knowledge. First, spend three minutes thinking about what you already know about the subject. Then browse through the book or chapter. *Browsing* is a skill which many people have but which has often been knocked out of them by attitudes to reading picked up at school. When you go into a bookstore looking for something to read, such as a guide to your next vacation destination or a novel, you probably browse through a few books to help to decide which to choose. Such browsing, far from being an inferior kind of reading, is a key reading skill, and it is useful not only in bookstores and libraries. It is an excellent preparation for serious study. It gives you an overview of the material and helps to prepare your mind which, subconsciously, is laying down the structure that will help you to learn.

When you browse you let your attention be caught by whatever attracts it: think of the way you glance through a newspaper or magazine. Do not read a great deal of continuous text. You may go through the book or chapter backward, or forward, or skipping around. Browsing should feel more like play than hard work. It will set your subconscious mind to work. You will be learning about the organization of the text; you will be taking in its use of diagrams, footnotes, and headings. You will be seeing what topics it covers and getting an idea about the style. You will also be relating the new information to what you already know.

THE SECOND PRONG: OVERVIEW

Having quickly browsed through the chapter or book, concentrate next on obtaining an overview. Read any summaries. Look through the headings and the index. Read the conclusion. Go back through the material, and for each main section, look at any diagrams or tables. Then skim through the sections looking for the main points: these are often presented at the beginning and ends of sections.

By the end of the overview you will know what the chapter or book is about and have taken in its main messages. For many purposes you will have done as much reading as you require. But if you need to study the material in detail, you may need to carry out a closer reading. Try this method out on the other chapters in this book.

THE THIRD PRONG: THE CLOSER READING

Even for this closer reading you should not, normally, read the chapter or book through, word by word, from beginning to end; nor should you reread those parts which you have already read. After the overview you will be in a position to decide which parts you already know and do not need to study, which parts you do not wish to study, and which parts you do not already know, and therefore wish to study. Only those parts which are of this third kind should be studied in detail.

Understanding difficult passages. Everyone when reading comes across parts they do not understand. This may be because the material is inherently difficult, or it may be because the author has not written clearly. Do not spend hours trying to understand a difficult passage before reading beyond it for two reasons: first, if you leave the difficulty on one side, your subconscious will set to work on it; and second, what comes after the difficult passage may help you to understand it.

THE FOURTH PRONG: REVIEW

An early review of what you have read and learned is a key step both in organizing the material and in remembering it in the long term. The 35-minute study period (pp. 483–485) incorporates this early review within its structure.

This four-pronged approach, far from taking longer than the normal method of reading from cover to cover, will take much less time and will also help you to learn and remember the material. It takes less time because for most material you only need to read a portion of what has been written. Reading all parts of the chapter, regardless of whether you already know the material and regardless of whether you want to know it, wastes time and can also be boring and discouraging.

Taking Notes

Most people try to make use of notes. Notes are a way of recording information, but they are not passive recording. Note-taking involves actively organizing the material and putting your own stamp on it. There is no one right way of doing it: that depends on your preferences, on the purpose for which you are taking notes, and on the material. When you are taking notes you are writing for yourself. As long as you can understand your notes when you reread them, they will have achieved their purpose.

Notes can take many forms. You can rewrite notes and condense them (see p. 460), and each rewriting will help you with remembering and processing the information. Notes might take the form of pictures as well as words.

WHY ARE YOU TAKING NOTES?

When considering whether and how to take notes, think first of how you wish to use them. For example, if you are taking notes from a book, do you intend never to look at the book again? In this case the notes may need to be fairly detailed. Or are they intended to serve as a summary or reminder only?

What are you studying for? Whatever the reason, tailor your notes to this purpose. Do not spend a lot of time making detailed notes when this is not appropriate—for example, when you can refer back to the book for the details.

At different times in your study you might use notes for different purposes. Notes can help in understanding; they can be used as an external memory; or they can be used in helping to prepare an essay or other piece of writing. Note-taking while reading (or listening) can also help you to concentrate.

NOTE-TAKING AS AN ACTIVE PROCESS

Working with the material you read, rather than just absorbing it, makes it easier to remember. It puts a stamp on it, and makes it yours. So your notes should be your way of organizing the material, and not just a brief copy of what you are reading. Try to pick out what you think are the key points, and organize the material in your own way. Your organization may reflect the structure of what you are reading, but it need not do so. In making notes you are choosing what you consider important in the light of your understanding of the material, your interests, your purposes, and what you already know. It is always easier to remember material that you have worked with than material that you have just allowed to sink in.

TYPES OF NOTES

If you own the book you are reading, you might underline or highlight key points, make comments in the margins, and put a query by those passages you find puzzling or with which you disagree. If you read with a pencil in your hand and not too reverent an attitude in your mind, then you will be reading actively—processing the information as you read it. Your pencil marks can form the basis for your notes.

The most common form of notes are those written in a linear, but *hierarchical* fashion. The hierarchy is provided by headings and subheadings. The summary to this chapter (p. 468) is an example of such a structure. In

The Spider Diagram.

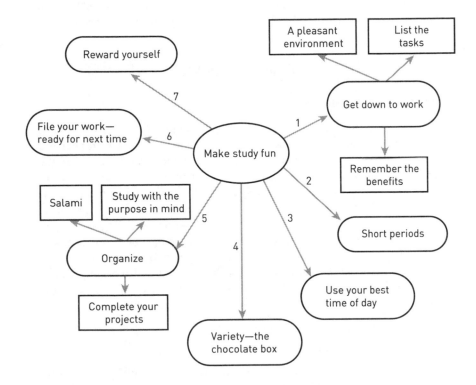

deciding how much to write under each subheading, the guiding principle should be the least that will ensure that you can recall what you want to recall when you make use of your notes later.

Spider diagrams. Spider diagrams are another form in which notes can be made, and an example is given in the box above. The hierarchical structure is readily represented. One advantage of such notes over linear ones is that relationships between elements which are not in the form of a hierarchy can be more readily indicated by drawing lines that connect the elements. Another advantage is that it is easier to add elements.

There are two situations in which spider diagrams are particularly valuable. One is in condensing notes. For detailed initial notes an ordinary linear set may be best—but just before taking an exam, for example, it can be very helpful to condense all the relevant points onto a spider diagram drawn on a single sheet of paper. The visual memory of this sheet of paper can work as a cue for remembering more details and help in organizing answers to questions. Their second main value is in making notes prior to writing something. Tony Buzan is an enthusiast for spider diagrams; he calls them "mind maps," and further details are given in his book *Use Your Head.*

Using the Material

CONDENSING THE NOTES

One technique which many people find useful when working toward exams is that of condensing notes. The process is like that of making a stronger and stronger liqueur: the notes are boiled down until only the essence is left, the vital part. At each time of revising, a new set of notes is made—notes of notes. In making the notes of notes, you will do some reorganization—as you notice similarities between what were disparate elements. In reducing the notes, you also make use of your increasing understanding—what you once needed full notes to remember you can now remember using only one or two keywords, and these keywords can cue you in to all the rest. The *process* of condensing also involves using the material and working with it, which makes it easier to recall when you need it. It helps you to rehearse the process of retrieving it, and makes it more readily accessible.

WORKING WITH THE INFORMATION

There is no point in storing information if it is not useful. The more ways we think about something new, and the more ways we use new information, the better we learn and the better use we make of it. So, do not just learn information; work, and play, with it. For example, you could draw a diagram to represent some of the information. Or you could tell someone about what you have read and try and explain what it is that you found most interesting. You could try to apply what you have learned to something else you know about—to shed new light on old knowledge.

THE MULTIMEDIA TECHNIQUE

The more "modalities" you make use of in your study, the better you will remember and the more creative your work will be. Write, read, and speak about your subject. Listen to what others have to say about it. The use of different color pens, and of pictures and drawings, can help in making notes. They can serve as useful aids to memory; they can force you to clarify the relationships between the different elements of your notes, and they can help in processing and manipulating information. An attitude of playfulness in making notes stimulates creativity. If you are bored with your notes, you will be bored and uncreative with the material. Think of ways of making your study *fun*. Are there audiotapes of your subject, or video recordings? You could dictate audiotapes of your notes and listen to them in the car, or in the evenings at home. In this way you are not only making use of different *modalities* for learning but also using time which would otherwise not be used for such learning.

BOOSTING

In Chapter 35 we stress the value of "a little and often" (p. 485). If the kind of studying which you are doing involves a significant amount of learning, it will be helpful to boost your learning with short periods of review. This might be done by carrying a notebook which you can read at odd moments—when waiting for a friend to show up or when traveling on a bus. Portable and car cassette machines can be valuable aids to learning. You can record on cassette the facts you need to learn, and play back when you are driving. You can also make use of odd times in the day to run through what you have learned in your head.

A Review Strategy for Exams

If you are studying for exams, then it is best to plan your review well in advance (see also pp. 481–485). Do not panic, however, if your exam is already looming and you have only just picked up this book. There are still some things you can do to help.

First, we will consider the situation in which the exam is still some way off and you can plan a review strategy. The elements of such a strategy are as follows:

1. Start with an overview: What are your strong points? Where are your gaps in knowledge? Where should you devote your energies? It is never possible to know everything. Think more about how to make use of what you do know than about how to learn a large number of new things.
2. When learning, use the rehearsal method outlined on page 481.
3. Plan a timetable for your review. Do not be too ambitious. Make the amount of time you can spend reviewing realistic, and don't expect to review too much in any given time.

4. Plan a review of the review. In other words, plan to cover your material in review once, and then to review everything again in about a quarter the time it originally took to review. You might even review a third time—in an even shorter time.
5. You will always cover less in a given time than you originally estimated. Make sure that there is some slack in your timetable. End your review some time before the exam (as much as two weeks before if possible) so that there is time to read just when you fall behind schedule (this happens to everyone). If one part of the review is taking a lot longer than you thought it would, cut your losses and move on to the next topic. Use the "slack" in your timetable to return to the problematic topic.
6. Condense your notes at each review so that you end up with brief notes you can review just before each examination.
7. If possible practice answering examination questions, and under conditions as close to those of the exam as you can devise. For multiple-choice examinations, practice answering relevant multiple-choice questions. For essay papers, practice writing and giving yourself the same time allowed during the exam.

Every exam is to some extent a game, and you will improve by practicing playing the game. Once you have a basic knowledge of the subject, then how well you do in the exam will depend more on your examination technique than on your extra knowledge. Indeed, too much knowledge causes its own problems because extra knowledge may enable you to see complexities in the questions which the examiners do not intend. If your teachers cannot provide opportunities to practice then form a group with your fellow students, or do it on your own. Answer some questions under examination conditions, and then discuss your answers with others if you are part of a group. This provides examination practice as well as extra learning and review.

If the exam is imminent and you have not previously planned a review strategy, the key is to use your remaining review time well. The danger is that you will feel so anxious about the exam that you will waste the time you do have. Work out the number of hours you still have for review. Decide on the best use of these. Would it be best to use the time practicing exam questions, or reviewing your notes? Do you have time to browse through your notes? Or to highlight important parts? Could you write a series of condensed notes, perhaps using spider diagrams? Do not forget the fundamentals of good study (see Chapter 32), such as getting down to work and rewarding yourself, and, however the exam goes, give yourself a treat after it.

Examination Nerves

It is normal to worry before an exam—the problem is how to manage the worry so that it works for you rather than against you, so that it helps you to focus your attention rather than allowing it to wander over alarming possibilities, to keep your nose to the grindstone rather than escape into endless distractions, to think quickly and coherently rather than become muddled and confused. Anxiety, even in quite high degrees, can be extremely useful both when you are preparing for an exam and during the exam itself, so anxiety in itself is nothing to worry about. Thinking of it as "arousal" instead of anxiety may make it more understandable and acceptable, and learning how to keep it within the "effective" range for you may well be useful (see also Chapter 20). This is something that can be learned, and that improves with practice.

First, it helps to know what to expect. Anxiety may make it hard to sleep, filling your mind with thoughts about all the things that could go wrong (none of the topics you studied come up; your mind goes blank; you answer the wrong questions; you misunderstand what the examiners want of you; you forget everything you ever knew). Thinking these things does not make them true—they are just reflections of the pressure you are putting yourself under to do well, so do not be tempted to believe that they are likely to happen just because they are in your mind. Thinking you are stupid does not make you stupid—it makes you miserable or angry. For more on how to deal with upsetting, or catastrophic, thoughts, see Chapter 9.

Anxiety about exams also increases the chances of making unrealistic predictions: that you will fail completely, that your career will be ruined, that your family will never forgive and forget. Research studies have shown that these unrealistic predictions increase the nearer the exam comes and decrease dramatically the moment the examination is over. Just before an exam, it is common to predict not only that the exam will go wrong for you, but that everything else in life will also go wrong: your relationships, your finances, your health, and even events in the outside world—airplanes seem more likely to crash, earthquakes more likely to happen, and so on. One reason for this is that the heightened level of anxiety produced by the impending exam has "primed" other information in your mind concerning things that could go wrong, as if they were all stored in the same box, and facing the examination has taken the lid off. The most important message you can give yourself is this: these predictions are exaggerated and unrealistic. They are another sign of anxiety, and you do not need to believe them but rather should ignore them.

Anxiety about exams also tends to polarize the difference between students and their teachers, sometimes to the extent that it feels like a battle between the two—as if *they*, the examiners, are against *us*, the students. Teachers once they have turned into examiners are suddenly supposed to be on the lookout for your mistakes and errors, to be lying in wait to catch you, to have an eye only for your shortcomings and not for your strengths. This is another "distorted" way of thinking that is common when anxiety is high, and it ignores the important fact that teachers and examiners are basically pleased and proud when their students do well. The better the students do, the better it reflects on their teaching. They actually remain on the same side as the student throughout, and can probably also remember just how it felt to be taking exams, and how easy it is to suppose that such an assessment reflects one's qualities *as a person* and not just one's performance in an exam on a particular subject.

Some of the strategies for dealing with exam nerves are outlined in the box on page 467.

The post-examination blues. Some people can bask in relief the moment the exam is over, but others feel let down and rudderless. An exam is rather like a hurdle that you cannot see beyond, as if life stopped at that point, which is of course absurd. But the purposefulness provided by preparing for an exam can feel good. So losing it can leave you feeling purposeless and lost. At the same time the result of the exam is unknown, leaving you in limbo, in a state of uncertainty. The more exclusively your life before the exam is focused around the exam, the worse the post-examination blues are likely to be. One solution is to make sure that you keep time beforehand for the pleasures you usually enjoy: talking with friends, going to the movies, listening to music, and so on. These pleasures will remain with you afterward. If they feel somewhat blunted, then do not withdraw from them, but recognize that you may be tired—even exhausted—and that until you have had some rest, and some recreation, they may not be so enjoyable as they once were. You will find more ideas on how to deal with uncertainty in Chapter 18 (pp. 230–232).

Finally: What if you fail the exam? This is where it helps to apply the 100-year rule (p. 221). Who will remember in 100 years? Or even in two years? What do other people do who fail exams? What other sources of pleasure and success do you have? Seeing the exam as a hurdle does not mean that you are running a race after which those who do not get a prize are chucked. Are people who always pass exams any happier than those who do not? These are the questions to ask yourself, in order to see the failure for what it is: a temporary setback but not a judgment on you as a person.

Some Strategies for Keeping Exam Nerves Under Control

Overall strategy: The long-term view

Answer these questions:

- Which topics do you know?
- What is essential or optional?
- Where are the gaps for me?

Make a detailed plan for what to do when. Write it down.

Daily technique: The short-term view

Close your eyes to the longer term, and:

- Take one topic at a time.
- Stop when your time is up, and move on to the next one.
- Take frequent, but brief, breaks (e.g., every 1½ hours).
- Do *not* stay up all night, or overdose on coffee.
- Eat, sleep, and take exercise regularly.
- Do *not* revise your plan daily but, for example, weekly.
- Take a whole day off each week.
- Rehearse your exam technique (writing to time, etc.).
- Condense your notes and ideas at each stage.

On the day

Prepare yourself in advance: your clothes, how to travel, etc.

- Look at your condensed notes, not at new material.
- Arrive in good time.
- Do not listen to scaremongering from others.
- Give yourself time to settle down.
- Read the instructions on the paper first.
- Read the questions carefully.
- Plan your timing, and write it down.
- Adapt what you know to the questions if they seem hard.
- If stuck, start to write notes. You will find that one thing leads to another and you will trigger your memory quite easily. You have not really "forgotten," so much as lost the way in.
- Do not try to write everything you know. Answering the question is enough.
- Do not try to be a genius, just answers the questions.

Note: **Given the brief time, your answers may have to be superficial. They can still be good, and well put together.**

Chapter Summary

1. Reading is a key study skill. Use the four-pronged approach:

   Preparation (browsing)
   Overview
   The closer reading
   Review

2. Make notes. These are personal and should be as short as is needed by you for your purpose.

   Why are you making notes?
      Note-making is an active process
   There are several types of notes:
      Underlining and highlighting of text in the book
      Linear and hierarchical lists (like this summary)
      Spider diagrams

3. Many find it helpful to condense notes at repeated reviews.

4. Work with the information.

   Practice skills (such as drawing, doing calculations, or speaking German)
   Draw a diagram to represent the information
   Explain your subject to someone else
   Relate what you have learned to other things you know

5. The multimedia approach: make use of several "modalities."

   Write
   Speak
   Dictate audiotapes
   Listen to tapes or radio
   Watch video or TV
   Use color in your diagrams

6. Give yourself a boost: a little and often

   Carry a notebook and look at it at odd moments
   Listen to a cassette in your car

7. Use a review strategy if studying for an exam:

   Rehearsal
   Timetable

Include a review of the review
Build in slack
Practice
Reward yourself after the exam

8. Examination nerves are normal. Learn how to manage them.

Prepare yourself for whatever the future brings.

34

How to Improve Your Memory
Part 1: The Palest Ink and Other
External Memory Aids

Since Greek times, people have been fascinated by memory. Before the widespread availability of portable writing materials, a good memory was vital for many activities. A politician in ancient Athens could not rely on the projected text, which for television newscasters and U.S. presidents has become routine. Carefully prepared speeches had to be memorized. The memory methods developed to help in such circumstances provide the basis for modern techniques used by entertainers and described in many books on memory. However, such methods play a relatively minor role in improving memory. Pencil and paper were not invented for nothing, and are still our most valuable external memory aids.

In order to improve your memory, you should consider making use of both external and internal memory aids. Internal aids are strategies for improving your mind's ability to retain the material you want. They are dealt with in the next chapter. External aids are techniques to relieve your mind of the need to remember. They are the subject of this chapter.

Your Mind Is Not a Computer

The computer on which this sentence is being typed has a magnificent memory, but a poor mind. You have only to write a sentence once, and it has remembered it, word perfect, forever more. You could give it a meaningless jumble of letters—wlklkk geio gui—and it still remembers accurately.

It is a mistake to believe that our memory works like a computer. How many times have you thought: "I'm bound to remember that," and then forgotten it the very next moment? We can rarely write on our minds just once and expect to remember the information forever.

Developing Your Memory Is about Using Appropriate Strategies

Memory techniques will enormously improve your memory, but using them will not be like changing your mind into a computer. Change will come through learning *strategies* which make the best use of your mind as it is. It is probably just as well that we do not remember most of what we experience. The Argentinean writer Jorge Luis Borges tells the fictional story of a man who remembered in the minutest detail almost everything which he had ever experienced.[1] But this ability was not a blessing. He could scarcely think because his mind was completely clogged up with disorganized memories. Twenty years after Borges wrote his story, the Russian psychologist A. R. Luria wrote about a real man who possessed an extraordinary memory, and again this ability interfered with his thinking.[2] In contrast, the techniques and strategies we describe here will enhance *thinking* as well as memory.

Eight Reasons Why You Might Want to Improve Your Memory

In order to make best use of this and the subsequent chapter, decide why it is that you want to improve your memory. In what circumstances does your memory let you down? Read both chapters and then focus on learning those strategies which seem best suited to your particular situation.

Here are eight reasons why you might want to improve your memory:

1. To remember future events: appointments, meetings with friends, invitations, etc.
2. Because you keep losing things—your eyeglasses, for example.
3. To remember your bank PIN number, or important phone numbers.
4. Because you keep forgetting to do things.
5. To remember people's names.
6. To help you to learn a new subject at school or in evening classes more efficiently.
7. To enable you to pursue a hobby more thoroughly.
8. To remember how to do something you need occasionally to do, like putting the roof rack on the car, or changing the vacuum bags, or using "mail merge" on your computer.

Even the Palest Ink Is More Reliable Than the Strongest Memory

Why do you need a good memory? In order to have access to the right information at the right time. This goal of having access at the right time is often better met by writing the information down in the right place than it is by searching your memory. A pocket diary is a good example of a written memory aid. An address book is another commonly used memory aid: common because effective. These aids sometimes fail in their desired use because they are not available at the right time (or because you forget to use them, or forget where you put them). The key to using written information effectively is to choose a few specific places in which to write your notes, and a few specific places in which to keep them.

Three Rules for Making Your Diary or Personal Organizer Effective

A reputation for poor memory is often made by forgetting appointments, or forgetting to do things which were promised. The solution lies in keeping an effective diary. There are three "rules" for making your diary effective:

Rule 1: Write *all* future engagements in the diary.
Rule 2: Look at the diary frequently, and at least every day.
Rule 3: Have only one master diary.

All three rules are easy to follow if the master diary is readily available. A small diary or personal organizer that you can keep in a pocket or purse is best. Never make a firm appointment without checking your master diary or without writing it into the diary. If these guidelines are followed, then the master diary will be a faithful record of your plans and engagements. Rule 1, by itself, is not sufficient, because if you fail to look at your diary you may miss an appointment. To prevent this, look through the day's appointments at the beginning of the day, and at the next day's appointments at the end of the day. It is also wise to look ahead once a day to ensure that you adequately prepare for each appointment. Rules 1 and 2 are not sufficient if you use more than one diary because you may look in the wrong one, and end up with two clashing appointments.

USING THE DIARY FOR FORWARD PLANNING

A diary is a valuable tool not only for appointments but also for forward planning. For example, you may be going on vacation in July. Perhaps three weeks before this, you need to pay the balance on the vacation and the week before, you should arrange to cancel newspaper deliveries or for someone to feed the cat. These things are easy to forget, or to leave until they are inconveniently late. The diary can be used to put these instructions to yourself on the appropriate days.

Alarms

Simple alarm devices can solve some memory problems. Suppose that you need to remember to put the casserole in the oven at 10:30, or to phone a friend at 11:00. It is easy to forget these things, but an alarm, such as is readily available on electronic wristwatches or on kitchen timers, solves the problem.

A Portable Notebook

Our memories often let us down because we do not jot down a note at the right time. Either we do not have a paper, or electronic, notebook handy at the right time, or we tell ourselves the old lie: "I can't forget that." Buy yourself a portable notebook. Then if you come across any information that you wish to remember, you can write it down at once—or as soon as convenient. At the end of the week, go through your notebook;

transfer any notes which need to be placed in a more permanent place; and get rid of the others so that your notebook does not become cluttered.

A portable notebook is one good way of helping with that almost universal problem of forgetting people's names, but in this case it is also extremely useful to combine external with internal memory aids, which are described in detail in the next chapter. Suppose that you are at a party and meet several people whose names you wish to remember. First, make sure that you take in what their names are. Then, use their names in a natural way when talking to them; and say good-bye to them by name when you leave: "See you next week, Barry." As soon as you possibly can after meeting them, write down their names together with a reminder, such as a one-sentence note about each of them. Back at home you could also describe them to someone else, and you can transfer your notes to a permanent place so that you can record the people's names before going to an event where you are likely to meet them again. If you want to be in a position to remember them at the drop of a hat, then it will help to notice any striking characteristics and to associate them with the name (Barry was the one with red-rimmed spectacles). You will also need to revise your notes often, and could use the review strategy given on pages 481 to 485.

Remembering Vital Pieces of Information, Like Your PIN Number

Because of the reliability of even the palest ink, the best thing to do with vital information is to write it down. But two problems arise: you may not have the information on you when you need it; and others may be able to read your secret information. The best solution to the first problem is always to have something on you in which you can store such information, such as your wallet or purse. If you have no such thing, then it may be worth buying a very small notebook and keeping it with you. The problem with secret information is that it is harder to deal with. One way to ensure that others cannot read it or use it is to "hide" the information. For example, your PIN number might be "hidden" in a list of telephone numbers as a phony phone number. The use of "internal" memory devices for remembering long and rarely used numbers is explained on page 486. This has the advantages both of secrecy, and of the information being with you in your head. The disadvantage is that you need to practice such devices, and to use them regularly, if they are to be reliable.

How to Put on Your Roof Rack

Even quite simple tasks, if we only do them occasionally, can be difficult to remember. The temptation is to put off doing the task because you know that you are going to waste a lot of time trying to relearn it. The root of the problem, again, is that old myth: when you first learn the task, you think, "I will never forget how to do this." The solution is therefore simple: write down instructions for yourself when you first learn the task, and keep these instructions in a convenient place. The best place might be with the relevant object—for example, the instructions for putting on the roof rack could be placed in an envelope and stuck to the roof rack with tape. Alternatively, you could file all such instructions in one place.

The Knot in the Handkerchief

The proverbial knot in the handkerchief reminds you that there is something you should remember, and it works well provided that you can remember what that is. One simple way of eliminating most of those irritating things we forget to do is to place an object or note to yourself in the right place. Suppose that you have written a letter and want to mail it in the morning. Place it where you will see it as you leave the house. Perhaps you need to check your tire pressures before leaving for work. Put the reminder on your car's steering wheel so that you cannot miss it. The two keys to success are: think carefully about the best place to put the reminder; and put the reminder there *now*—that is, when you are thinking about it. It also helps to have a standard place where you look for notes and messages—for instance, by the telephone, or on the kitchen table—and always to keep pencil and paper in those places. Then all the miscellaneous things you need to remember—to get some coffee, to go to the bank, to return the garden hose you borrowed, to give someone a message—will naturally draw themselves to your attention. Remember to throw away outdated reminders.

Where Did I Put My Keys?

Are there any things you often misplace—your keys or eyeglasses, for example? If there are, then the solution lies in creating a habit. Car keys are a good example. If there is no one routine place to put them, they get left on any convenient flat surface: the top of the fridge or by the phone, and later you have no idea where they are. This problem is solved by creating a routine place, such as a hook on the wall near the front door, and then establishing the routine of putting them on the hook immediately on coming into the house. The more automatic routines you can devise for yourself, like automatically putting the bottle opener in the lefthand drawer, the less time you will waste hunting for things that are lost.

Beware of Safe Places

One way of avoiding misplacing objects is to have a "place for everything." Obviously, you need to remember where that place is. A final warning before we leave the subject of external memory aids: whenever you find yourself thinking, "This is important; I will put it in a safe place," think again. The problem with safe places is that they are likely to be out of sight and out of mind too. If you forget where the "safe place" is you are unlikely to find the object until months after you need it. Wherever you do put important things, tell someone else, so that if you forget there is at least one other person who might remember.

Chapter Summary

1. Your mind is not a computer: you are likely to forget things which you learn only once.
2. Many of your memory problems can be solved by making good use of pencil and paper.
3. Develop habits that work to your advantage.

35

How to Improve Your Memory
Part 2: Internal Memory Aids

In the last chapter we stressed the use of external memory aids because they are simple and effective for many purposes, and often ignored in books on memory. But they are only half the picture. The other half of the picture is provided by using your mind efficiently, by using internal memory aids.

The law of mass effect (p. 450) is as important to remembering as it is to studying. It states that the amount you remember is strongly correlated with the amount of time you spend learning, and the strategies described in this chapter will enable you to make good use of the time you spend learning. Just as with studying, you cannot expect to learn and remember unless you put in time. The use of efficient strategies makes the time you spend learning both more effective and more fun.

The amount you remember is also affected by your mood, and in particular by your level of anxiety. If your head is full of worries, it is very difficult to learn. In order to learn most efficiently you need to be able to concentrate but without being anxious: *attention without tension* is what you need.

Organization

Four aspects of organization can help you to improve your memory: *chunking, using cues, relating,* and *making sense.*

CHUNKING

In order to remember a great deal of information, it is best to break it into mind-sized chunks of about *seven items.* You probably already use *chunking* when doing the weekly shopping. Suppose that you have 50 items to buy. It would be very difficult reliably to remember a list of 50 items, but the items are automatically classified into smaller chunks by the type of shop or section of the supermarket in which they are found: fruit, vegetables, meat, fish, dairy products, household items, drinks, toiletries, etc. This method of chunking used by supermarkets as well as by shoppers can be applied to a wide range of situations, such as preparing for the new school year or for reorganizing the accounts department.

USING CUES

The weekly shopping also demonstrates the value of using cues. We look around the shop, at the different kinds of fruit, for example, using them as cues to remind us what we want to buy. We can provide internal cues for ourselves as well. If we know that we want five things for packed lunches and we have only bought four, we must look around for the fifth. Remembering that there should be *five* things serves as a cue.

RELATING

Relate new bits of information to other things you already know, or to each other. In this way you can structure the material to be learned in a way that will make it easier to remember later. For example, you might remember that the Spanish word for cheese is like the English word, but not like the French one; or that Romanesque arches are like the ones at your local church; or that Patricia is the person who came to the party with Tom. What you already know can be used as a basis, or structure, to build on. The more you know, the more building blocks you have on which you can add new knowledge, and the more rapidly you will learn. As you consolidate what you learn, you are setting up an exciting learning spiral which will increase more and more rapidly.

MAKING SENSE

It is much easier to learn and to remember something that is meaningful than it is to learn something that makes little sense to you. Meaning can be given in many ways: for example, by relating what is to be learned to your previous experience and knowledge—"The gear shift is the same except that reverse is up not down"; "Setting the timer overrides the on-off button"—and by understanding the relationships between the different elements of what you are learning—"You have to open up the valve before you switch on the gas"; "Saving the work you have done onto the old file makes a new copy, so the old one is lost."

THE CASE OF ITALIAN WINES—AN EXAMPLE OF ORGANIZATION

Let us see how these methods of organization can work in practice. Suppose that you want to learn about *Italian wines* and you have bought a relevant book. In the section on *taking notes* (p. 459) we discuss the value of thinking about the subject matter before you start to read, to start the process of organizing. You might draw these initial thoughts in the form of a *spider diagram* (p. 461). The figure on page 461 shows what such a spider diagram could look like.

You are now ready to look quickly through the wine book to get an *overview* of the subject (p. 458). This overview will enable you to improve on your initial organization. For example, after browsing through the book, you might restructure the category types, as shown in the following box.

This restructuring illustrates several features that aid your learning. First of all, there are only three main categories (color, sugar, and fizz), and these are easy to remember because they relate to the experience of drinking wine. Thus these categories are meaningful. Second, the hierarchy of categories provides a *relationship* between different items to be learned. It is easy to remember the four possible colors of wine when you know that you are looking for colors, and give yourself the *cue* that there are four colors. Similarly for the other categories. Third, the principle of chunking has been used: it comes naturally out of the hierarchical organization. There are ten categories of wine listed, which would be a large number to learn as one chunk. But by organizing them under three categories, each *chunk* has only three or four pieces of information.

A spider diagram for learning about Italian wines.

Types of Italian Wines

Color
  Red
  White
  Rosé
  Amber

Sugar
  Sweet
  Semi-sweet
  Dry

Fizz
  Sparkling
  Frizzante (lightly bubbly)
  Still

A Review Strategy

Unlike a computer, we rarely remember something we have learned just once. We tend to forget what we have just learned (as illustrated in the graph on p. 481) unless we rehearse and use the material or revise our learning. Adopting an efficient review strategy is one of the best ways of improving your memory. Review shortly before exams is discussed on page 463.

WHAT IS AN EFFICIENT REVIEW STRATEGY?

It turns out that the most efficient review strategy, when you are learning facts or want to remember a large number of details, is to *review very soon after the original learning and then to space out additional review periods further and further apart.* This applies whether you are a student or whether you are learning bus routes in a new town, a complicated recipe, or how to set the video recorder. In plain language, if you recite to yourself, or go over in your mind's eye, something you want to remember as soon as possible after learning it, you will find it easier to remember later, and the more often you rehearse something, the better it will withstand the

Graph of how quickly we forget material we have just read.

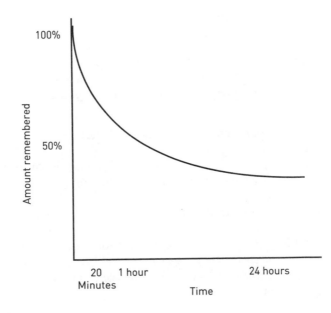

test of time. Your rehearsals can then be spaced at ever-increasing intervals. An efficient review strategy for everyone is one which leads to your remembering most after spending the least possible amount of time learning. Although the theory behind a good review strategy is somewhat complicated, the practice is simple, and can be illustrated using the *day-week-month* strategy that applies most obviously to students.

THE DAY-WEEK-MONTH (DWM) REVIEW STRATEGY

The *DWM* system is simple. We will explain it in some detail so that you can see how to design an efficient review strategy. But do feel free to design your own strategy to suit your own needs. Some flexibility is needed because few of us can keep to a rigid timetable.

Suppose that you wish to learn some Portuguese before going on vacation to the Algarve. You learn 20 words today. The *first review* could take place at the end of the session in which you first learn the words. The *35-minute study period* explained on page 483 is one way of doing this. Your *second review* could be one *day* later; your *third revision* could be one *week* after the second review; and the *fourth review* could be one *month* after the third review. Each review will take only a fraction of the original learning time. If it takes 20 minutes to learn in the first place, each revision will take about 2 minutes.

VARYING THE DWM SYSTEM

The *DWM* system is simple and effective. Like most of the skills presented in this book, you should feel free to adapt it to your needs. But there are a number of principles which will help you to make your own adaptations.

1. If you do not review, your memories will fade away like a line drawn in the sand.
2. The most effective time to review is as you are about to forget, but can just remember. Review when the line on the sand is faint but can still be seen.
3. You forget more slowly (and remember for longer) after each review. This is why review periods can be spaced further and further apart.
4. Two things should alert you to the need to adapt your review strategy:
   - If when you come to review, you find that you have forgotten most of what you learned. In this case you need to review sooner than you are doing.

- If when you come to review, you find that you remember it all clearly. In this case you are reviewing sooner than you need to and may be wasting time.

To take, again, the example of learning Portuguese. Suppose that you learn 20 new words. If when you review them a day later, you can only remember 10 words, and these with difficulty, you need to review sooner. If, on the other hand, you can remember 19 words without much trouble, you can probably shift your review to two days after the first learning.

MICROREVIEW

One of the keys to good memory is *review*. A structured review process ensures that you learn *effectively* and *efficiently*. This is the purpose of the DWM method. Structured review can usefully be enhanced by unstructured review. Even brief periods of review can have a very powerful effect on memory. Review for a few minutes whenever you can: while waiting for a bus or for a friend to show up. The effect is like polishing silver. *A little and often* will keep your memory shining. Remember reviewing is not just reciting, but making the material yours in some way, so you need to work with it, to remold it, and to use it during review in as many ways as you can think of.

Going through things in your head is extremely helpful. It makes you more sure of the things you can remember and also pinpoints the gaps. These tell you where to focus your energies next time. If you can use your notebook at the same time, you will be even better able to take advantage of opportunities for microreview.

THE 35-MINUTE STUDY PERIOD—AN EFFICIENT LEARNING TOOL

The 35-minute daily study period is an efficient way of learning a new subject. This is an ideal strategy if you wish to learn or study and can only devote a small amount of daily time to it. For example, you may wish to learn a new language, or study a new subject, such as history or botany. The 35-minute study period is relevant if the principal task is learning— acquiring knowledge or information. It makes use of three central principles of learning and memory:

1. The length of time we can maintain high-quality concentration
2. The optimum revision strategy
3. A little and often

The great value of the 35-minute study plan is that it is a very efficient way of working and it has, built into it, an effective review strategy, so your learning accumulates. The problem with the way in which most people learn is that they do not think about review until the last minute, and unless you review as you go, you forget most of what you learn.

The 35-minute study period is a flexible learning unit. You can use it once a day or less; or if you are a student, you can divide your daily learning into a number of 35-minute units. Think of this period as a building block.

Why 35 minutes? This is a period for which most people can concentrate well. If you study without a break for as long as an hour, the last 20 to 30 minutes is likely to be less efficient, your concentration less good than in the first 35 minutes, and it is also much easier to get down to work knowing that it is for a 35-minute stretch than it is if you have set aside an hour or more.

The general principle of the study period is that you spend about 60% of the time in new learning. The rest of the time is for reviewing—reviewing things you learned recently, and things you learned a month ago. The figure below illustrates one efficient way of using the 35 minutes. Use this as a guide for your own study.

The first 20 minutes are spent in new learning. A short break allows your subconscious to consolidate this new learning. You can then spend a couple of minutes reviewing what you learned new in *yesterday's* 35-minute study period, a couple of minutes reviewing what you learned new in the study period *one week ago,* and a couple of minutes reviewing what you learned new in the study period *one month ago.*

In the last 5 minutes, review what you learned in the first 20 minutes of the study period. Thus the first review occurs about 10 minutes after the end of the learning period. This is *not* too soon to review. On the contrary, it will prevent that first rapid phase of forgetting.

A 35-minute study guide.

We wish to emphasize that only about 60% of the study period is spent in new learning. The rest of the time is used for structured review—including a consolidating rest period. Most people are tempted to use up all the time on new learning. Indeed, it can feel silly to stop the new learning almost as soon as you have started. But this is just the ineffective method which most people use. At first it seems fine, but then it becomes clear that you are forgetting most of what you have previously learned and getting progressively more muddled. You will end up, at the end of the year, having wasted most of the study time. These frequent but short review periods work, both because they reinforce the memory and because they help you to consolidate what you have learned. This prepares you for absorbing what you next want to learn.

Practicing a Skill—A Little and Often

What is the most efficient way of learning a skill—learning to type, for example? *The answer is to practice frequently for short periods.* This has been elegantly shown by Alan Baddeley and his colleagues. To reach the same standard in typing, they found that it took, on average, 80 hours for those who practiced 4 hours each day, and only 55 hours for those who practiced 1 hour each day. Furthermore, those who practiced 1 hour a day retained their skills better than those who practiced for 4 hours a day. Of course, if you want to learn how to type in as few *days* as possible, it is better to practice for many hours each day. Those practicing for 4 hours each day took 20 days to reach the standard that those practicing for 1 hour a day reached in 55 days. But such concentrated practice is inefficient in terms of the total number of hours spent learning to type.

Recall—The Sherlock Holmes Approach

This is a common experience: you have lost your watch, or a bunch of keys, or a letter. You had them the day before yesterday but cannot find them now. You have looked in the obvious places. The temptation is to go on looking. The solution, however, is to *think*—the Sherlock Holmes approach. When Sherlock Holmes was puzzled by a problem, he would take to his armchair. A really difficult problem was "a three-pipe problem." Four times out of five you will find the object by thinking, if you think hard and persist. When can you last remember seeing the item? What were you wearing then? What were you carrying? Who was with you? What did you do then? Go through the time since you last saw the object in meticulous detail. If you are lucky, you will suddenly realize where it must be. If you are less lucky, you will have narrowed down the possibilities: there can only be two or three places where you could have lost it. Of course, you might realize that one explanation is that you left it in the train and that it is gone for good. The method of recall cannot magically restore all items, but it will often result in your finding it if it can still be found, or realizing what must have happened if it cannot, without wasting a lot of time.

This method of recalling in detail has other uses. You may have been introduced to someone and cannot now remember his name, or you know somebody asked you to do something, but you have no idea what it was. Think back to the situation in which you learned the name or the time when the request was made. Think about the details of the conversation. Who else was present? What did they say? If the conversation was not too long ago, you may remember something that happened or was said which can trigger the memory you need, or you could just think about the person who asked you to do something and allow your mind to wander around aspects of this person, and things associated with her. What sorts of things has she asked of you before? Is it to do with work or something else? Did it feel urgent? Or not very important? Give your mind a chance to "come at it sideways" by opening up all the relevant boxes in which the lost information might be stored.

Mnemonics

"Roy of York gained battles in vain" is a mnemonic device which some of us learned as children to remember the order of the colors of the rainbow (*red, orange, yellow, green, blue, indigo, violet*). Similar devices, some too rude to print, are used in medical schools to help in learning human anatomy. Although they are no substitute for review and organization, they can be particularly useful in helping to memorize lists or sequences of things. The method of connecting two visual images can help when learning foreign languages. Using them can also be entertaining, and with some persistence you could master a technique for memorizing the order of a pack of cards, but this would not help you to do much else.

The most frequently used mnemonic devices are simple rhymes, such as "thirty days hath September . . . ," and sentences such as "Roy of York. . . ." However, we also know that it is much easier to remember information that might not otherwise hang together if we apply the rules that we already know. It is much easier to remember how to say "super-califragilisticexpialidocius"—especially after hearing it sung, which gives it both a tune and a rhythm—than it is to remember Aunt Susan's address if she lives in Llanfairynghornwy. Not only do few of us know the rules of Welsh pronunciation, we also do not know how to understand the parts from which the word is made up. Nonsense can be memorable if it takes a form that we can make sense of.

And this is a rule we can make use of as a memory aid. If something you have to remember seems like nonsense to you, or comes in a string of disconnected bits, like a list of facts, names, or numbers, the best thing to do is to try and turn it into sense any way you can: sing it, make up rhymes, apply grammatical rules, transform the material into visual images, or use it to tell yourself a story, and it will instantaneously become more memorable.

Putting It All Together

We all depend on our memories all the time, whether we are students or not, and memory can let us down when we are tired, stressed, or distressed. That is when we are likely to rush out of the house leaving the keys behind, wander into another room only to wonder why we are there, or put the frozen peas in the bread bin and the bread in the freezer. Memory is both robust and also vulnerable. It is robust in the sense that most information which we find useful remains in our memory. It is vulnerable in the sense that sometimes it is hard to retrieve or recall it. Marthe, whose first language was French, but who spoke only English from the age of 18, reverted to speaking in French when she was 82 (and still in England), although until then, she had to search her memory for French words whenever she needed them. So we need as many strategies as we can devise, both to lay down the traces for the future and to help us get on the right tracks when we want to.

FOUR GENERAL STRATEGIES FOR LAYING DOWN THE TRACES

1. *Important things are easier to remember than unimportant ones.* Things that stand out in some way (your first kiss, the time you stood on a sea urchin, or the time you said something acutely embarrassing) will stick in your memory. Unimportant things can become more memorable if we attach to them some of the "signs" of importance—for example, by making them more *vivid* or by giving

them a personal *meaning.* The bright yellow folder will be harder to leave behind than the beige one, and writing your name on the outside of it will be more likely to draw it to your attention than writing something of no personal importance to you—like "memos" or "minutes."

2. *It is important to forget things as well as to remember them.* Although our memories seem to have an almost unlimited capacity, there is a bottleneck on the way in. Things can get lost in transit. So when you are in a confusing situation (meeting lots of new people, starting a new job, finding your way around a new place), *tell yourself what to forget.* You will remember best those things you pay attention to, but if everything grabs your attention, your memory will be overloaded. You can reduce the load by concentrating on what is most important to you (the job your boss wants done first, how to find your way home again), and try not to get distracted by too many other things.

3. *You need time for digestion.* The memory traces are not laid down, in permanent form, all at once. So if you cram in too much, or try to learn too many new Portuguese words without giving yourself some review time, you will feel as if your brain is full. Notice when you get to the stage of diminishing returns—when it no longer feels as if you can take in any more, both when learning how to use a new computer or when walking around an exhibition. Ideally, you should stop before this point. Continuing beyond it will not help you to lay down good traces, while stopping may enable you to observe a rather peculiar phenomenon. At first, when suffering this form of mental indigestion, you may feel confused or muddled. However, after a pause and a rest, you may be able to make *more,* not *less,* sense, and remember some of the material better. This is most obvious when learning a physical skill or a skill that involves coordinating mind and body, like typing or playing a new computer game. If you push yourself too far at one go, after an initial period of improvement you will start to make mistakes and your performance will deteriorate. If you stop practicing at this stage, instead of pushing on in an effort to overcome the problem, you will find that your performance improves apparently of its own accord—as you can see if you try again after an interval. It is as if your mind continues laying down the traces after you have stopped practicing.

4. *Ideas are sometimes more useful than facts.* Facts may not hang together, and will therefore be hard to remember. Ideas, and meanings, may help the facts to hang together, or give you a set of pigeonholes

in which to file the facts. It is sometimes worth thinking of yourself as a filing system, and working out how to label the separate storage places so that you know what to find in them—in personal as well as in other ways. For example, use labels such as "Things I did with Marion" and "Feeling the way I felt in my first job," as well as "Letters to be answered" and "Things to tell so and so."

FOUR GENERAL STRATEGIES FOR IMPROVING YOUR MEMORY

1. *The more you make use of information, the more readily available it becomes.* If you are finding it hard to remember something you normally remember well, think of things associated with it, or "prime the related categories." Imagine you have a thousand and one things to do at work, and at the same time are trying to plan a talk for the next day. If you give yourself some of the main headings or topics for your talk early on, you will prime the right categories in your mind, which may almost literally continue ticking, warming up the machinery for the bits that you need to use, so that when you do get time to think about the talk, you will more readily remember the things you need. This works even better if you write down the title for the talk and jot down briefly any ideas that come to you whenever you can.

2. *Give your mind space to work in.* A similar phenomenon occurs when one is focusing on a major project, whether that is working out how to decorate the kitchen and continue to use it, or how to put together an entirely new sales policy. First, immerse yourself in the project totally so that your mind can get to work on it, and then focus on particular aspects of it, but remember that the closer in you get, the harder it is to see the whole picture. At this point your memory can surprise you, and enable you to see entirely new possibilities: after working hard on one part of the project you drop it to do something else, or collapse because you are tired, and then at an unexpected moment—for example, lying in bed, shopping, or in the shower the next morning—you have a new idea. It is as if you were only able to put the information in your memory together in a new way after standing back from the front line. In order to make the most of your memory, you need to give your mind space to work in— give yourself both focused work on a project and time away from it.

3. *It is easier to recognize things than to recall them.* Even if you cannot tell someone else the way to Aunt Susan's house, you may be able to find it quite easily if you have been there before. If you

cannot remember which brand of pasta was the good one, a glance at the supermarket shelves may do the trick. If you cannot recall what was in the document being discussed, a brief glance at it will tell you whether you have read it, and that can start you moving along the right track until you find the information associated with it in your memory.

4. *Association works wonders.* It is not just that one thing leads to another, so that you can eventually find the word you want by thinking of others related to it, but also that the circumstances surrounding an event provide a wealth of information to cue you in. Deep-sea divers can remember the things they learned at the bottom of the sea better during their next dive than they can on dry land. This (partly) explains why so many people forget, once they reach the office, to do things related to their home lives, and remember them again as soon as they get back home. One of the added advantages of going away for a vacation is that it helps you forget the concerns associated with home. There is no need to worry that you will lose the thread completely on vacation, because the associations aroused by coming home again will trigger your memory efficiently on your return—and the new perspective provided by getting away may also lay some unnecessary concerns to rest.

In summary, for your memory to work well, you need to be able to forget things as well as remember them. The art of remembering well lies first in *selecting* what it is that you need to remember for your purposes, and then *deciding* what needs to "be in your head" or what can more usefully be stored in an "external" memory, in a diary, for example.

Chapter Summary

You can improve your memory through developing good strategies rather than through mental muscle-building exercises.

The law of mass effect: The amount you remember is strongly correlated with the amount of time you spend learning.

To learn most efficiently, you need to concentrate without being anxious: *attention without tension.*

Organize your thinking using four methods:

- *chunking* to break the information into chunks of a maximum of seven items

- *using cues* to remind you of what you want to remember
- *relating* the new information to what you already know
- *making sense* of the new information

Use an efficient *review strategy.* Review soon after the original learning, and then space out additional review periods further and further apart.

36

Making Decisions

In both our domestic life and at work, we need to make decisions, and in order to make good decisions, we need to be able to think clearly and weigh up evidence effectively. In the long term the decisions we make greatly affect our lives, so it is important to be able to make good decisions as often as possible. This chapter highlights the pitfalls in decision-making and provides a strategy for helping to make decisions that feel right.

Myths about Decisions

There are many myths about decision-making. One of them is that everything hangs on making the right choice. Open the right door and you will find yourself in the enchanted garden, open the wrong one and you will fall into the dungeon from which there is no escape. A second myth is that people are either decisive or indecisive. The decisive prince is determined, resolute in the face of uncertainty, knows at a glance what is right, and his good judgment is rewarded with lasting peace and prosperity (and possibly a princess). The hesitant fool wavers and deliberates, seeks advice which he ignores or forgets, selects inconclusive solutions to irrelevant problems, and suffers the agonies of indecision apparently in perpetuity. He who hesitates is lost.

Most people fall between these extremes, and can sometimes make up their minds quite easily and at other times are paralyzed: stuck on the horns of a dilemma. We seem to be able to play the part both of the prince and of the fool, for the most part, without attaining mythical levels of perfection or suffering, but also without knowing how to take control of the process.

These myths have interesting parallels today. Successful and hardworking people in many walks of life appear to make complex, quick, well-informed, and accurate decisions at a speed that defies the less experienced. When something goes wrong, then we hear how the weight of unremitting choice and responsibility leads to exhaustion, ulcers, disagreements, and loss of good judgment.

The general health and well-being of elderly people who are cared for by others show substantial improvement if they are encouraged to continue to make decisions, even about small things, such as which clothes to wear and when to have their tea. People working in emergency settings and those involved in the aftermath of distressing events of many kinds have lesser degrees of subsequent suffering if they were involved in making decisions at the time (for example, by directing the traffic around the crash, or comforting those in distress). The opportunity to make decisions, whether in daily life or in unusual, difficult situations, appears to protect people from suffering. Decision-making seems to be good for you.

But the demands can be too great. The responsibility of having too many, too weighty decisions to make quickly provokes high degrees of stress (see Chapter 20). It can produce quite uncharacteristic changes in someone's ability to function, leading to poor physical health, stomach ulcers, irritability, increased use of alcohol or caffeine, and eventually to "burnout." When the decision-making processes are overloaded, or impaired as they can be by fatigue, illness, worry, or other forms of distress, they become inefficient.

This was demonstrated in a simulated experiment made during attempts to develop safe and reliable systems for air traffic controllers. Air traffic controllers (at the time) used many different channels of communication. They watched movements on a video screen, listened to and provided information over earphones, received and sent messages using computer terminals and a notepad, and sat in a room surrounded by other noisy people doing the same thing. The methods they were using worked efficiently and safely—if one channel were to become faulty another was ready to back it up—provided the level of air traffic was within reasonable limits and everyone was functioning well. When these limits were surpassed, for whatever reason, communication and decision-making first slowed down and then, if the disruptive conditions persisted, fell apart.

Some surprising things happened. Controllers shouted messages to each other and thumped the table. They stood up, gesticulating and pointing, while trying to communicate with pilots thousands of feet up in the sky. Under these conditions they were able to understand the problem, but no longer able to make effective decisions. The demands made by unremitting decision-making can stretch people to their limits.

Six Strategies to Help You in Making Decisions

It is rarely possible to make the "perfect decision." Every course of action will lead to more choices and will throw up some unexpected difficulties. The following strategies should help you in making difficult decisions, but if you become too worried in the pursuit of the perfect decision, you will be more likely to become painfully indecisive.

1 THE BALANCE SHEET

Use a balance sheet to apply the "problem-solving method" (Chapter 8), to weigh up the advantages and the disadvantages of different choices. Divide a large sheet of paper down the middle into two sections, one for advantages and the other for disadvantages. Write the specific question you are thinking about at the top: Shall I expand the business now? Shall I book a summer vacation? Shall I take the computing course next term? Then fill in the columns, considering the decision from all its aspects: how it affects others as well as yourself, including its implications and consequences. Think of factors that are important in the long term as well as in the short term. This exercise is best done on paper since it is difficult to hold all the ideas in one's mind at once. Now look through the list and weigh up the balance. Some items will count much more than others. It can be helpful to give points out of 100 to each advantage and disadvantage, according to how important they are, and then to add the columns separately: 67 "for" and 38 "against." Or it might help, if there are many advantages and disadvantages, to decide on the two most significant in each column, and weigh them against each other without being distracted by relatively unimportant considerations.

2 TRIAL RUNS AND TIME PROJECTION

If you are having difficulty in making a choice—whether or not to move, for example—pretend that you have made one choice (to move) and then imagine, as fully as possible, what it would be like had that choice been made. Does it feel right? With important decisions which are not urgent, imagine "living" that choice for several days, and then imagine the other choice. This exercise gives you the opportunity to take yourself through a trial run and to make contact with your "gut reaction." You may then know what to do, but if not, you can go back to your balance sheet and think whether other points need adding.

Another way of doing this is to make use of "time projection." This is a simple strategy that involves imagining yourself at some future date, six months, five years, ten years ahead (see also Chapter 9, p. 86) having made the decision that you are now finding difficult. From your new vantage point, look back at the present, and at the decision you are trying to make. You may immediately find it easier to make up your mind, or you may wish to imagine taking different options in turn until you find the one that you like best.

You could also test out your reactions by tossing a coin, or thinking about what would happen if you made no decision at all.

3 A SOUNDING BOARD

Other people can provide a useful sounding board, and may reflect back to you their understanding of your problem and of your inclinations. Consulting too many people, however, can be a mistake because you may end up with too many opinions. "Ask three people whom you trust, and then make up your mind" is a useful guiding principle to prevent endless rumination. It is tempting to consult only those people with whom you expect to agree, but this will narrow down the possibilities. If you are searching for a completely new line of thinking, it may be more sensible to choose someone with a rather different, or more objective, opinion, such as the accountant rather than the sales manager, or the teacher who understands your talents and strengths rather than the parent who desperately wants you to become a doctor. If you were deciding whether or not to convert your house to make room for your elderly in-laws, you would probably talk it over with your partner and with other involved members of the family. It may also be sensible to consult a specialist in the care of the elderly, or to search in the library for other relevant information.

4 INFORMATION GATHERING AND SIFTING

Information is critical to making many decisions. If you are choosing a car, and safety is an important consideration, you need information about the safety features of the different cars. Before making such decisions, it is important to clarify those factors which are significant to you, but about which you need more information. Once you know what these factors are you can think about how to find the necessary information.

It also helps to learn how to evaluate the accuracy and reliability of the information available to you. Research tells us that decision-making improves with practice. It is a skill that can be acquired through experience, and more skilled decision-makers are less likely to forget important factors or misinterpret ambiguous information than inexperienced ones. In order to make effective decisions in some business settings, for example, inexperienced people need both to be trained in the use of relevant information systems, and given practice in making decisions. Otherwise, they will be more likely to make mistakes.

5 DEALING WITH CHAIN REACTIONS

Often decisions hang together. Larry wanted a new job, but his wife Emily was happy in the one she had. They discussed the options first, and made the decision that Larry would try to get a new job nearby, but that if he failed, then Emily would think about making changes herself. As things transpired, Larry found an exciting new opportunity, but it was a four-hour drive away—an impossible commute. A chain reaction of decisions was then set in motion. Major decisions were demanded of them thick and fast. They concentrated on making these decisions in the most sensible order for them. First, they discussed whether to work in different places, and decided they wanted to continue living together. Then, Emily decided to look for a new job. She was uncertain how to proceed, so she consulted a colleague, and with her advice in mind, spoke to her boss before starting the search for new jobs. She found a choice of jobs. One, less interesting to her, started immediately; the other could not begin for six months. Together she and Larry now had to decide when to sell their house, and when and where to look for another one. Every possible option seemed to involve them in financial strain (renting temporary accommodation in one place or two, storing their belongings, etc.), and every decision seemed important. For each aspect of the problem they could specify, they balanced up the relative advantages. They then made the best decisions they could. Having first given their attention to the series of big changes in their lives, they were then able to tackle the host of minor ones that followed—whether to sell the old sofa, how to transport their belongings, and so on.

6 KEEPING UP THE ENERGY RESERVE

Theoretically, you should spend more time and energy on big decisions than on little ones. Deliberating whether to wear the brown socks or the green ones, or whether to buy the giant size pack of laundry detergent, or which traffic line to join makes little sense. However, this is harder in practice than in theory. The first interfering factor is fatigue. Being tired can make it difficult to make even the simplest of decisions.

Preoccupation is the second interfering factor. People whose energies are necessarily devoted to important and worrying decisions, like whether to close the business or to have major surgery or to get divorced, frequently find the smaller decisions especially difficult and intrusive, as if their reserves are already depleted, and they have little attention for anything else. It helps then to ask yourself, "How much does this really matter?" Next, turn as many small decisions into routines as you possibly can, and leave the less important ones for later or for others.

False Dictators and Unsettling Gremlins

Many pitfalls beset the decision-maker, so it is important to know how to recognize them, and where to look out for these false dictators and unsettling gremlins that can put one off one's stride.

1. *Biased thinking* (for more on this see Chapter 37). The opinion of the last person you spoke to often seems the most convincing. Or the more weighty the authority behind a pronouncement that affects your decision, the more likely it is to influence you. Our decisions are easily swayed by minor or irrelevant factors, like whether the person you are interviewing for a job arrives soaking wet, having been caught in a storm.
2. *Categorical thinking*. This is the error of supposing that there is only one right choice. Completely "right," or indeed completely "wrong," choices are extremely rare. One might even go so far as to say that there is no such thing as a right choice. It is, therefore, more important to ask yourself how you could live with the choice you have made, what adaptations it will demand of you, whether it is a permanent choice, and whether it could be changed if things work out differently from the way you expected, than to bother about whether you have got it right. How could you ever know?

3. *Not thinking beyond the decision.* It is a mistake to assume that your decision will fix things for good, as if the process of change will stop as soon as the decision is made. Change never stops, and it constantly demands adaptation from us. It is an illusion to think any decision will fix a particular state of affairs in a static grip.

4. *Conservatism.* We have a tendency to think that whatever happened last time is bound to happen next time. It is easier to decide to do the same thing this time as you did last time, but that way you may miss new discoveries. Keep an eye open for new choices.

5. *Confusing problem-solving with worrying.* Some people, especially those of whom many decisions are demanded on a regular basis, expect themselves to be able to make decisions quickly. They may then find it worrying when a decision takes longer than usual. They may accuse themselves of worrying and fail to recognize that sometimes the process of problem-solving is difficult and takes time. Recognize that some decisions are more difficult to make than others and allow them more time.

6. *Information tangles.* Forgetting and misinterpreting information are two of the most misleading gremlins. Control them by keeping a notebook, using information sources efficiently, and asking others to keep you up-to-date. Most decisions can wait until you have the information you need.

7. *Expecting the feeling to come first, and the decision to follow.* Waiting until you feel "right," or feel "strong enough," to make a difficult decision may keep you waiting forever. The more difficult the decision the more tempting, and disrupting, this can be. You may have to decide whether to fire someone, or how to allocate unemployment payments, or tell an employee clearly that his carping criticisms are having a counterproductive effect on the whole department. In these cases you will be more likely to feel better *after* than *before* the decision is made (and the action taken).

8. *Fears and worries.* Fears and worries of all sorts can interfere with the process of making decisions. The decision may plunge you into a situation that you find frightening (accepting a promotion that involves speaking in front of large groups of people), or it may give pain to others (breaking up a relationship, telling relatives about your homosexuality). Remember that the harder the decision the more likely it is that two heads will be better than one. Find someone to share the problem with if you can, and think through the consequences of making your decision.

9. *Other "bad" feelings.* Almost any kind of distress interferes with the ability to make decisions, including fatigue, stress, depression, illness, and problems with relationships. One definition of the process of deciding explains that it involves "giving overt expression to one aspect of behavior while others are temporarily suppressed." Expressed in the language of a dictionary, this sounds like jargon. Expressed in other words, it means that making a decision occupies a fair amount of your attention, so other things have to be ignored or "put on hold" while you do it. Even experienced and speedy decision-makers have to think about the decisions they make, although they may hardly notice that they do so. If you are preoccupied, or your attention is demanded by other things, including distressing feelings, then this will be much harder to do. Decision-making then becomes unexpectedly burdensome. There are many solutions. You could allow yourself to take longer, and decide things more slowly. You could deal with the distressing feelings first, and then return to the decisions. If the decisions keep pressing, you could fall back on "conservatism" (less adventurous, but also less risky), delegate, or ask others to share some of the responsibility for the time being. Or you could plan a well-timed vacation and give yourself a break.

SOME DIFFERENT DECISION-MAKING STYLES

People vary in the way they make decisions and in the speed at which they make them. But our decision-making patterns are not fixed: they are more like tendencies that can be more or less influential depending on how they are used. Each style of decision-making has advantages as well as disadvantages, and different styles are useful in different situations.

Risk takers may tolerate a high degree of uncertainty with equanimity or they may enjoy the brush with excitement and danger. Their decisions may seriously alarm their more cautious friends if the costs of failure are high, but they may also earn our respect. They may need to learn to count the costs of their mistakes with accuracy. They need steady nerves.

Impulsive people tend to jump from one decision to another without due consideration. Their decisions can feel intuitively right (giving a compliment at exactly the right moment), but they can also be ill-considered and regretted later. If they focus on delaying the decision, and on weighing up advantages and disadvantages, they may feel happier with the choices they make.

Cautious people can provide a valuable check to risk takers, and often enjoy working in settings where safety is an important consideration. Overcautious people may hesitate before crossing the road, signing the insurance policy, or agreeing to take on an additional task at work. It may be helpful for them to practice making small decisions quickly, to tune in to what fits with their ultimate goals and values, and to cut down on the deliberation.

Clashing styles. Brendan made decisions quickly, and once the decision was made, he would say, "So that's settled," putting any doubts and deliberations out of his mind and getting on with the next thing. His wife Claire wanted to talk things through thoroughly, and in doing so she wanted to tune in to how it would feel to jump one way or another. This kind of clash can easily turn into an argument, but one thing it is pointless to argue about is which decision-making style is the best one. People go through different processes before they feel settled about a decision. Rather than accusing each other of jumping to premature conclusions or of wanting to rake over old ground, it would be more helpful to recognize the different styles and use negotiating skills (see pp. 162–166) to settle the difference.

Age differences in decision-making styles. Decision-making styles, generally speaking, change over the life span. When involved in the decisions of others, or asked for advice, it can be helpful to bear in mind these differences and to adapt accordingly. Younger people are more influenced by immediate and short-term considerations, pay little attention to longer-term consequences, and worry relatively little about making mistakes. Elderly people find adaptation to changes harder to cope with, and each adjustment a little more unsettling than the last. They may need longer to make decisions, and find decision-making about major issues progressively harder.

A rest from making decisions. For many people, one of the pleasures of being on vacation is having to decide nothing more important than what to eat or where to swim. Like anything else that is effortful, having an occasional rest from decision-making is beneficial. It is sometimes even essential—for example, when someone is ill. Then hearing someone say, "Leave that to me. I'll take care of that until you are well again," can bring great relief. Being unable to drop the reins temporarily when one is ill can also delay the process of recovery.

And to console those of you who are indecisive, let us quote Coleridge, who wrote to a friend in 1837: "Indecisiveness of character . . . is almost always associated with benevolence."

Related Chapters in This Book

Chapter 5   *Managing Yourself and Your Time*
Chapter 8   *Problem-Solving: A Strategy for Change*
Chapter 37   *Thinking Straight*

Chapter Summary

Decision-making is a skill that improves with practice.
Six strategies that help when making decisions:

- The balance sheet
- Trial runs and time projection
- A sounding board
- Information gathering and sifting
- Dealing with chain reactions
- Keeping up the energy reserve

Nine pitfalls to avoid:

- Biased thinking
- Categorical thinking
- Not thinking beyond the decision
- Conservatism
- Confusing problem-solving with worrying
- Information tangles
- Expecting the feeling to come first, and the decision to follow
- Fears and worries
- Other "bad" feelings

There may be no such thing as the "right" decision, and there is certainly no one decision-making style that fits all people and all circumstances.

37

Thinking Straight

A central theme running through this book is that psychology is useful. If you understand the psychological aspects of everyday life, you will be better able to face problems, to treat yourself right, to keep things in perspective, and to build up self-confidence (Part 2). You will be able to do this when dealing with difficulties in relationships, and when dealing with anxiety and depression (Parts 3 and 4). You will also be better able to keep moving along the road to recovery following more seriously distressing or traumatic experiences (Part 5). Knowing a little psychology can be essential when tackling problems that affect sleeping, eating, and drinking (Part 6). Furthermore, knowing how the mind works will help you develop your ability in learning, remembering, and making decisions (Part 7).

In Chapter 1, we wrote about the "two book shelves," one devoted to psychology and the other to management skills. Deeply ingrained in our culture is this false dichotomy between the skills needed for work and the skills needed for home. Many of the same skills are needed in both places: for example, the three keys of good relationships are just as important to the manager as they are to the parent, and time management is an organizational skill that is as important in running a home as it is in running a business. This book is about the organizational and psychological skills that will enable you to make changes in your life—in all aspects of your life—to make improvements both for yourself and for those around you.

In this final chapter, we bring together some of the themes of this book by focusing on straight thinking.

Thinking straight is not always easy: it is harder to think logically, and to avoid being led astray by illogical pitfalls, than it would seem. Even those of us who pride ourselves on our rational approach to life still make judgments on the basis of inadequate information—for example, when we jump to conclusions and think "I'll never get out of this mess," or try mind-reading and conclude "They think I'm stupid." Far more frequently than we realize we use thinking strategies that are based only loosely on fact, or we make one of a number of the standard mistakes studied and analyzed by psychologists. In Chapter 9 we explained how thoughts and feelings are related, and how it helps, when you feel bad, to look for another way of seeing things. This chapter describes some of the standard mistakes that bias our thinking, and explains how we can try to avoid making them in order to make better use of our minds for solving the problems and dealing with the impediments which we face.

Four Common Mistakes in Thinking

1 BEING MISLED BY THEORIES, BELIEFS, AND ASSUMPTIONS

We need theories of all kinds. They enable us to operate efficiently in a constantly changing world, and define for us those things we can take for granted: for example, that aspirin will relieve headaches, that friends will listen when we talk to them, and that suntan lotion is harmless. But opinions once formed are remarkably resistant to change, even in the face of contradictory evidence. As Francis Bacon once said, "The human understanding when it has once adopted an opinion draws all things else to support and agree with it."[1]

Opinions can easily slip into prejudices. Prejudices, such as beliefs about ethnic characteristics or about the differences between the sexes, are good examples of theories that may bias our judgments and be hard to change, and by looking at them in more detail we can unravel some of the ways in which beliefs are maintained in the face of disconfirming evidence. Imagine believing that children who take a long time to learn to read are less intelligent than others. Many processes combine to make it hard to change this belief. These can be demonstrated by illustrating what happens when you come across information that does not fit, such as hearing that your exceptionally clever friend, Max, was a slow reader.

First, information that does not fit is *discounted.* You decide your clever but slow-to-read friend is the "exception that proves the rule." One clever person who was a slow reader just does not count. Evidence about him impinges not at all on the belief: it is not even worth noticing.

Second, information that does not fit is *distorted.* You might argue that Max misremembers how long he took to learn to read. It felt hard because everything else came easy to him, or because his class was full of exceptionally able children and he was one of the slower ones. It is as if your mind argues like this: slow readers are not very intelligent; Max is intelligent; therefore he cannot have been a slow reader. In other words, we select facts that fit with our beliefs, theories, and assumptions and forget or dismiss the rest. We also confuse preferences with facts: it may be preferable to think that the criticism one receives from others is unwarranted, and a product of someone else's short temper, than to accept that it is justified or well deserved. It feels better to attribute the failure to achieve a target at work, such as an increase in turnover or greater client satisfaction, to the economic climate or to the behavior of one's competitors than to one's own mistakes and failings.

Third, information that does not fit is *deflected.* You recognize the challenge to the belief, but pay no attention to it, and forget it so it does not get stored. It is just as if the mind had no "pigeonhole" ready to accept discrepant information about clever people who were slow to learn to read. When you try to recall such information later, none comes to mind, because none has been committed to memory. Maybe you remember that Max is one of the cleverest people you know and assume that his cleverness must have been apparent from the start, whatever he says about it now.

What we see, notice, attend to, and remember is in many ways determined by the beliefs, frameworks, and theories that we already have, rather than the other way around. Our daily observations hardly ever change our preconceptions. This is relevant because distressing beliefs—such as "I'm not as good as others"; or "Everyone else copes better than I do"; or "The world is a dangerous place"—will be just as resistant to change, and just as likely to be inaccurate, as other sorts of beliefs. They are prejudices about yourself, about other people, or about the world. One of the reasons why these "prejudices" are hard to change is because we also *discount, distort,* and *deflect* information that does not fit with them (see also Chapter 10 and Chapter 26).

Ensuring Against the Bias

1. Look for evidence that could disconfirm your belief rather than for evidence that confirms it. If you believe that all swans are white,

then your belief can only change, and fit with reality, if you look out for swans that are not white. Finding more white swans only endorses the belief you already have without helping you to verify it. Looking for non-white swans (or for clever people who learned to read slowly instead of quickly) can tell you when an old belief needs changing.

2. When you come across instances that do not fit with your preconceptions, make sure you think about them, remember them, and ask yourself whether old beliefs need modifying (do not discount or deflect your successes or the compliments you receive).

3. Keep your preferences and inclinations out of it. This means both knowing what they are, and becoming aware of how they might bias your powers of reasoning. If you know what you "want to think" then it is easier to check out whether the facts really fit the case, or whether you are just shaping them up that way.

4. Do not worry about modifying beliefs as you go along. It can feel unsettling to have to change your mind—for example, about the benevolence of a certain teacher in your children's school, or the belief that hard work will ultimately be rewarded and recognized. Beliefs, theories, and assumptions can shift gradually over time, or change suddenly. In both cases the ability to adapt and change with circumstances is more likely to keep you thinking rationally and clearly than hanging onto the safe but unsupported beliefs.

2 BEING MISLED BY WHAT SPRINGS TO MIND

The information that most readily comes to mind has a disproportionate effect on opinions and reasoning in general. In 1946, Solomon Asch demonstrated this point in an experiment in which people were asked to form an opinion about a person who was described as "intelligent-industrious-impulsive-critical-stubborn-envious." If the adjectives were presented in that order, the opinions were more positive than if they were presented in the reverse order (starting with "envious-stubborn-critical . . ."). The adjectives presented first created a favorable or an unfavorable impression, and these first impressions then influenced the final judgment. All of us tend to give undue weight to things that spring to mind. The trouble is that what springs to mind at a particular time is often determined by extraneous factors like the order in which things were said during a work appraisal, or by whether you were feeling anxious or depressed.

There are many sources of this particular bias. The more recent an event, the more likely it is to influence your judgment. If you have a "near miss" when driving a car you will tend to be more careful the more recent this event. Unfortunately, in this case, the effect of recency soon wears off, and you quickly revert to your usual, less careful, behavior. But this may not happen if a recent argument has biased your view of someone you love and makes it hard to make peace once more.

Vivid, or emotionally salient, events also have undue influence on the way we think. This is a fact exploited by advertising, and it also affects our daily lives. Feeling good about something you did will make you think it is worth doing again; feeling bad about it will put you off. In summary, if something is important to you, arouses strong feelings, happened recently, or attracts your attention in an unusual way (for instance, because it is a novelty or rarity), then you are more likely to remember it and doing so is more likely to influence, and to bias, your judgment.

Ensuring Against the Bias

1. Take your time when thinking something through. Snap judgments are more likely to be unduly influenced by irrelevancies than considered ones.
2. Try to stand back from the heat. If your feelings are strongly engaged, your thinking may change when the feelings change. It helps to label your feelings, to identify the thoughts that go with them, and to check out whether these make sense and fit with reality (see Chapter 9).
3. Check out your thoughts on others. See how they react. Because everyone's experience and interests are different, using two minds rather than one is a good way of reducing this form of bias.

3 BEING MISLED BY THE INFLUENCE OF OTHERS

Thinking straight is often easier, and more likely to be logical and helpful, if you can use others as a sounding board. But there are nevertheless some pitfalls to avoid when listening to the opinions of others.

The halo effect. We tend to believe people we admire, even when their opinions may not be especially well informed. Athletes and pop stars are asked to endorse brands of laundry detergent or to give their opinions on world affairs, regardless of their expertise, because their fame alone carries a weight that influences our judgment. If you love French food, you may be more inclined to think that all things French are wonderful.

When people are influenced by the weight of authority, they run the risk of being misled by the halo effect. For example, people may listen to their doctor's pronouncements about career decisions, and to what their lawyers have to say about personal relationships. Or they may borrow authority to lend weight to an argument of their own: "Mr. Stein, a leading researcher and university professor, says that he has found a new method of weight control that really works." Or they quote from articles they have read in newspapers or journals as if the printing of the word lent it immediate credibility.

The presentation effect. If a salesclerk holds your interest by speaking well, by making you laugh, and by using apt illustrations, you will be more likely to believe what he or she says. The same is true at work, at home, and in social settings. The more boringly someone talks, irrespective of what they say, the less influence they will have. If you learn to express yourself assertively (Chapter 13), you will be more likely to be listened to.

Scientific reality. We live in times which set great store by the objectivity and "reality" of scientific observations. These are indeed responsible for much of the progress from which we benefit daily. The opposite side of the coin is that appealing to the scientific evidence, regardless of whether this is justified, is an unduly persuasive form of argument. As most of us are not experts, we are easily led astray. We may buy a new type of tire for our car, or stop buying cholesterol-rich foods, without knowing whether these decisions are really reasonable. Perhaps the best we can do is to keep an open mind, learn more about how to evaluate the information with which we are presented, and guard against false prophets.

Most branches of science develop their own technical language, or jargon. Jargon, or obscurantism, can easily mislead, especially if it is being used to impress or lend weight to a particular point of view. Asking people to explain in language you can understand is an excellent protection. Explanations may be hard to make, and understanding them may involve learning some new terms (the meaning of the word "software" is now understood by many more people than it would have been 25 years ago), but it is nearly always possible, and if it is not possible, then you may be justified in suspending judgment for the time being. This is not to say that you need to understand how the computer works in order to be able to use it, but that you would be justified in asking for a clear, intelligible explanation of the advantages of the new model if you were considering replacing your old one. The same goes for evaluating the psychological advice you are given.

The fundamental attribution error. Dick is a social worker. He enjoys the contact with clients most of all, and is a committed, hard-working member of the local childcare team. His colleagues think of him as reliable, communicative, level-headed, calm, and responsible. Dick is 29 years old, married to Clara, who works part-time in a residential home for elderly people, and they have two young children. Dick comes home from work exhausted and his marriage is suffering. Clara describes him to a friend as silent, detached from the family, forgetful when it comes to the chores, irritable, and irresponsible in that he leaves the vast majority of the parenting to her. The two views of Dick are almost diametrically opposed, and both of them are expressed as if they described his personality: in terms of stable or fundamental characteristics likely to endure. This is the fundamental attribution error: behavior is attributed to enduring qualities of people rather than to the situations, circumstances, and events that surround them.

In fact, people vary enormously in different situations. They adapt according to the demands made, and change as circumstances (and times) change. So we should beware of labeling others, or ourselves, as if our reactions and behaviors were fixed. The potential for change can be increased by changing circumstances rather than trying to change people. It is not that you cannot "teach an old dog new tricks" but rather that "all work and no play makes Jack a dull boy." In other words, changing the situation is extremely likely to change the person. The disaffected, lazy employee can become motivated and energetic if circumstances change.

4 BEING MISLED BY ASSOCIATIONS

Jim has a bad cold which has left him with a headache. He meets someone who complains of a headache and they start talking about the kind of cold they both have, about how to fend off its worst effects, and about how much it interferes with the ability to think straight. They are both making a fundamental thinking error which involves being misled by similarities. Because their problems are associated—they both have headaches—they assume the problems have the same cause. But the friend may be suffering from a totally different ailment—an allergy, sinusitis, an infection from a different source, and so on. The same argument would apply if they had been stressed, anxious, or had a tendency to drink too much.

You see a politician being interviewed on television. He has been caught unawares, wearing a crumpled shirt with his hair unbrushed. His appearance is more like that of an absent-minded professor than of a reputable politician, and your judgment about him follows suit. You will be likely to judge him as forgetful, a theoretician, with his head in the air rather than his feet on the ground. No wonder politicians take such pains to polish their appearance—and to get their hair cut at the right time.

A smart middle-aged man in a suit, carrying a briefcase, comes to your door and offers you his business card. He says he is opening an antique shop nearby, is interested in buying antiques from local people, and is offering free evaluations to those who are interested. He is very polite, apologizes for interrupting if you are busy, and offers to come back at a more convenient time if you wish. You invite him in, make a cup of coffee, fetch your grandmother's picture to ask him about, and when he leaves you find your purse has gone with him. His behavior was similar to someone more respectable, and he has capitalized on the general tendency to think that superficial similarities tell you about underlying ones.

Ensuring Against the Bias

1. When you notice that two things are similar, ask yourself also how they differ. See if you can find out whether they have different causes. My depression, or eating problem, might or might not have the same cause as yours.
2. Check out your expectations. Ask what you are basing them on, and whether that makes good sense. Are appearances a good indicator of the facts? They usually are, and this is why people can exploit them to their advantage, but they can also mislead. Taking them at face value, especially if the circumstances are unusual, may be misleading.

Four Statistical Rules

Statistics, the science of numerical facts and data, is complex and technical, but the ordinary thinker need not be a statistician in order to think rationally. A number of common errors in thinking can be reduced by knowing about basic statistical rules.

1 THE LAW OF LARGE NUMBERS

The larger the sample the more likely it is to reflect the characteristics of the population from which it is drawn. You may hear from a friend that the type of car you are thinking of buying is wonderful—entirely reliable, easy to park, and comfortable to ride in. You could check out its comfort and the ease with which it can be parked by taking it out for a test drive. But experience of just one car can tell you little about the reliability of the model. In order to judge whether this type of car is reliable, you need information from many cars. Arguing from other people's experience, or from your own, is often unsound. The larger the numbers on which the information is based, and the more random the sampling involved, the more valid your judgment is likely to be. Some features of the problems or difficulties you have will be like those of other people, but others will be unique to you. The same applies to the solutions you find. Using this book as a source of ideas that others have found helpful should not put you off trying out others for yourself.

2 COMPARISON, OR CONTROL, GROUPS

It is easy to be impressed with statistics such as the large number of people killed on the roads, or the small percentage of babies who die within the first year of life. In the absence both of comparison groups and of a knowledge of the total population at risk (the total number of car drivers, or of babies), most of these figures are of limited value. They may shock us, but they do not provide an adequate basis for value judgments or for decision-making, unless they are put into the context of comparison groups. Do the figures represent an improvement on previous years? How do they compare with other similar countries? What is the rate of change? Most statistics need to be placed in the context of comparison or control groups if they are to be meaningfully interpreted.

3 MAKING PREDICTIONS

It has been argued that boys are better at math than girls. Indeed, a difference between the mathematical skills of boys and girls has been found in various studies and at various stages of development. But this does not make it possible to predict how easily any individual boy or girl will learn mathematical skills. This is for two reasons. First, the behavior of the group does not tell us anything about the actual behavior of an individual. Second, the overlap between the groups may be far greater than the differences between them. In the case of mathematical abilities, there is an enormous range of ability present in both boys and girls. The similarities between boys and girls in mathematical abilities are far greater than the differences between them—and the similarities between people who have problems and difficulties in their lives also are far greater than the differences between them, as the vast majority of people experience difficulties at some stage in their lives.

4 CORRELATION AND CAUSE

It is often mistakenly assumed that because two things go together that the one causes the other. People with red hair often have pale skin, but the one does not cause the other. To take a different kind of example, Matthew gradually became more confident and more skilled as he settled down in his new job. During the same period his manager met briefly with him weekly to check out how he was getting on. The two events are correlated, because they happened over the same time period. But gradual change is far more likely to be independent of particular, intermittent events than to be caused by them. Taking an aspirin or two as you recover from the flu may make you feel temporarily better but is most unlikely to influence your rate of recovery.

It is harder to be certain about causes when thinking about social issues than about scientific ones. We are more certain that an icy wind in spring will wither the daffodils in its path, and less certain that family disruption will "cause" delinquent behavior in adolescents. We tend to assume that the one variable that we have identified (family disruption in this case) is the only relevant one, and to ignore the people from disrupted homes who never became delinquent. Indeed, these are so easy to ignore, especially when counting troublemakers, that in most societies we do not even know how many of them there are. Maybe this is like ignoring the things that go right in your life, or that you have done well, when you have a problem or things are going badly. Then it is easy to assume that the things you did wrong are the cause of the problem—which they may not be.

Persuasion, Manipulation, and Group Pressure

The pressure to conform to the group is surprisingly strong. If no one adopts a policy for dealing with harassment in the workplace (racial or sexual), then those who suffer from harassment may find little support. But as soon as most people have such a policy, then the group pressure to conform and adopt appropriate policies in the workplace increases. Groups can influence decision-making and individual thinking in many ways, but they can be wrong as well as right. So it may take strength of mind, and assertiveness, to maintain your opinion when everyone else disagrees with you.

Parting Words

Becoming aware of the sources of error in thinking is the main resource we can draw upon to improve our thinking. The clearer we think, the better we will be at making decisions, at problem-solving, and also at keeping things in perspective: (see pp. 78–80 for some more examples of crooked thinking).

Related Chapters in This Book

Chapter 6   *Facing the Problem*
Chapter 9   *Keeping Things in Perspective: Help from Cognitive Therapy*
Chapter 26   *Dealing with the Past*
Chapter 36   *Making Decisions*

Chapter Summary

The skills described in this book, whether they are drawn from the field of management or of psychology, are equally relevant to your work life and to your home life. They will help you to make the changes that you wish to make in any aspect of your life.

Many of these skills can be seen as various ways of thinking straight. There are four *common mistakes* in thinking:

- Being misled by false assumptions
- Being misled by what springs to mind
- Being misled by others
- Being misled by false associations

Many common errors in thinking can be avoided by knowing four statistical rules:

- The law of large numbers tells us that anecdotes are unreliable.
- Comparison groups are needed to provide a context for new information.
- Individual predictions may be impossible from group generalizations.
- Two things may go together without either being the cause of the other.

Pressure to conform to the group is surprisingly strong. Use all of your skills and strategies to resist when you need to. If you keep thinking straight, you will be better able to keep things in perspective, to make decisions, and to solve the problems that come your way.

Notes

Chapter 1   What to Expect from This Guide

1. L. P. Hartley, in the prologue to *The Go-Between* (Harmondsworth, England: Penguin, 1990).

Chapter 6   Facing the Problem

1. Konrad Lorenz, *Man Meets Dog* (Harmondsworth, England: Penguin, 1964).

Chapter 7   Treating Yourself Right

1. Charles Dickens, *The Life and Adventures of Nicholas Nickleby* (Oxford: Oxford University Press, 1987), p. 93.

Chapter 9   Keeping Things in Perspective: Help from Cognitive Therapy

1. Several books by Albert Ellis and Aaron Beck are available (see *Further Reading*).
2. Viktor E. Franke, *Man's Search for Meaning* (London: Hodder and Stoughton, 1964). (First published in German in 1946.)
3. D. M. Clark and J. D. Teasdale, Constraints on the Effects of Mood on Memory, *Journal of Personality and Social Psychology*, 48, (1985) 1595–1608.
4. D. M. Clark, P. M. Salkovskis, M. Gelder, C. Koehier, M. Martin, P. Anastasiades, A. Hackmann, H. Middleton, and A. Jeavons, "Tests of a Cognitive Theory of Panic," in I. Hand and H. U. Wittchen (eds.), *Panic and Phobias-Tests . . . Panic,"* 2 (Berlin: Springer-Verlag, 1988).

Chapter 10   Building Self-Confidence and Self-Esteem

1. Alice Walker, *The Color Purple* (New York: The Women's Press, 1983).

Chapter 14   The Second Key to Good Relationships: Recognizing Voices From the Past

1. Amy and Thomas Harris, *Staying OK* (London: Pan Books Ltd., 1986).

Chapter 18   Getting the Better of Anxiety and Worry, or Defeating the Alarmist

1. A. A. Milne, *The House at Pooh Corner* (London: Methuen, 1928), Chapter 8.
2. Philip Wakeham, "Living Target," in R. Hope (ed.), *Seamen and the Sea* (London: George Harrap & Co. Ltd., 1965).
3. Letter to Madame de Grignan, 26 April 1671. In *Madame de Sévigné, Selected Letters,* translated by Leonard Tancock (Harmondsworth, England: Penguin Books, 1982).

Chapter 23   Digging Yourself Out of Depression

1. A. T. Beck, A. J. Rush, B. F. Shaw, and G. Emery, *Cognitive Therapy of Depression* (New York: Guilford Press, 1985).
2. G. W. Brown and T. W. Harris, *Social Origins of Depression: A Study of Psychiatric Disorder in Women* (London: Tavistock Publications, 1978).

Chapter 34   How to Improve Your Memory: Part 1

1. J. L. Borges, *"Funes the Memorious,"* in *Fictions* (London: Calder, 1965) pp. 97–105.
2. A. R. Luria, *The Mind of the Mnemonist* (Cambridge, MA: Harvard University Press, 1987).

Chapter 37   Thinking Straight

1. Francis Bacon, *The New Organon and Related Writings* (New York: Liberal Arts Press, 1960). Originally published in 1620.

Further Reading

There are many good self-help books covering an enormous range of issues from varying perspectives. Different books appeal to different people and the best way to find the right books for you might be to browse through your local bookstore, or to get recommendations from friends you trust. We have our own favorites and we list some of them here.

The "Overcoming" series published by Robinson: London (www.overcoming .co.uk) are generally excellent, all with a cognitive behavior therapy perspective. They include:

Butler, G., *Overcoming social anxiety and shyness*, 1999.
Crowe, M., *Overcoming relationship problems*, 2005.
Espie, C., *Overcoming insomnia and sleep problems*, 2006.
Fennell, M., *Overcoming low self esteem*, 1999.
Ford, V., *Overcoming sexual problems*, 2005.
Freeman, C., *Overcoming anorexia*, 2002.
Gauntlett-Gilbert, J. and C. Grace, *Overcoming weight problems*, 2005.
Gilbert, P., *Overcoming depression* (revised edition), 2000.
Kennerley, H., *Overcoming anxiety*, 1997.
Kennerley, H., *Overcoming childhood trauma*, 2000.
Marks, M., *Overcoming your smoking habit*, 2005.
Scott, J., *Overcoming mood swings*, 2001.
Veale, D. and R. Wilson, *Overcoming obsessive-compulsive disorder*, 2005.

A Selection of Books that We Know Others Have Found Helpful:

Abrams, R., *When parents die* (London: Routledge) 1999.
Ainscough, C., and K. Toon, *Breaking Free* (London: Sheldon Press) 2000.
Antony, M.M., and R.P. Swinson, *When Perfect Isn't Good Enough* (New Harbinger Publications) 1998.
Baddeley, A., *Your memory: a user's guide* (London: Carlton Books) 2004.

Baer, L., *The Imp of Your Mind: Exploring the Silent Epidemic of Obsessive Bad Thoughts* (Plume Books) 2002.

Batchelor, M., *Meditation for life* (London: Frances Lincoln) 2001.

Beck, A.T., *Love is never enough* (London and New York: Penguin) 1989.

Bourne, E.J., *The Anxiety and Phobia Workbook*, 4th ed. (New Harbinger Publications) 2000.

Burns, D., *Feeling Good: the new mood therapy* (New York: William Morrow) 1981.

Burns, D., *The feeling good handbook: using the new mood therapy in everyday life* (New York: Harper & Row) 1990.

Buzan, T., *Use your head* (Essex: BBC Active) 2003.

Claiborn, J., and C. Pedrick, *The Habit Change Workbook* (New Harbinger Publications) 2001.

Cole, J., *After the affair: How to build trust and love again* (Vermilion) 2000.

Collin, R., *Travels with Rima: A memoir* (Baton Rouge: Louisiana State University Press) 2002.

Cooper, M., G. Todd, and A. Wells, *Bulimia Nervosa: A Cognitive Therapy Programme for Clients* (Jessica Kingsley Publishers) 2000.

Cottrell, S., *The Study Skills Handbook*, 2nd edition (New York: Palgrave, McMillan) 2003.

Covey, S., *The seven habits of highly effective people* (New York: Simon & Schuster) 1989.

Davis, M., E.R. Eshelman, and M. McKay, *The relaxation and stress reduction workbook*, 5th edition (Oakland: New Harbinger) 2000.

Dryden, W., *Overcoming Jealous* (Sheldon Press) 2005.

Ellis, T.E., and C.F. Newman, *Choosing to Live: How to Defeat Suicide through Cognitive Therapy* (New Harbinger Publications) 1996.

Feldman, C., *The Buddhist Path to Simplicity* (London: Thorsons, HarperCollins) 2004.

Forward, S., *Toxic Parents* (Bantam Books) 1990.

Frankl, V., *Man's search for meaning* (Boston: Beacon Press) 1962.

Gil, E., *Outgrowing the pain* (New York: Dell Publishing) 1988.

Gray, J., *Men are from Mars; women are from Venus* (London: Element, HarperCollins) 2002.

Greenberger, D., and C. Padesky, *Mind over mood* (New York: Guilford Press) 1995.

Goldhor-Lerner, H., *The dance of anger* (New York: Harper Row) 1990.

Hanh, T.N., *The Miracle of Mindfulness* (London: Ebury Press) 1999.

Hanh, T.N., *Anger* (London: Rider) 2001.

Hemmings, J., *Be your own dating coach* (Chichester: Capstone) 2005.

Horvath, T., *Sex, Drugs, Gambling and Chocolate* (San Luis Obispo: Impact Publishers) 1998.

James, J.W., and R. Friedman, *The Grief Recovery Handbook: The Action Program for Moving Beyond Death, Divorce, and Other Losses,* revised edition (HarperPerennial) 1998.

Johnson, S., *Who Moved my Cheese* (London: Vermilion) 2002.

Kabat-Zinn, J., *Full catastrophe living* (London: Piatkus) 2001.

Kinchin, D., *Post-traumatic stress disorder: The invisible injury* (Success Unlimited online) 2005.

Litrinoff, S., *Sex in loving relationships* (London: Vermilion) 2001.

McIlwraith, H., *Coping with bereavement* (Oxford: Oneworld) 2001.

McKay, M., P. Rogers, and J. McKay, *When anger hurts* (Oakland: New Harbinger) 1989.

McKay, M., and P. Fanning, *Self-esteem* (Oakland: New Harbinger) 2001.

Milsten, R., and J. Slowinski, *The sexual male: problems and solutions* (W.W. Norton & Company Ltd.) 2000.

Neeld, E.H., *Seven Choices: Finding Daylight After Loss Shatters Your World* (Warner Books) 2003.

Paymar, M., *Violent no more: helping men end domestic abuse* (Alameda, CA: Hunter House) 1999.

Quilliam, S., *Stop arguing start talking* (Vermilion Rand) 1998.

Rando, T.A., *How to go on Living When Someone You Love Dies* (New York: Bantam Books) 1991.

Rowe, Dorothy, *Depression: the way out of your prison*, 3rd edition (Hove, New York: Routledge) 2003.

Russianoff, P., *When am I going to be happy?* (New York: Bantam) 1988.

Schmidt, U., and J. Treasure, *Getting better bit(e) by bit(e): a survival guide for sufferers from bulimia nervosa and binge eating disorder* (Hove, New York: Laurence Erlbaum) 1993.

Schmidt, U., and K. Davidson, *Life after self harm: a guide to the future* (Hove, New York: Brunner-Routledge) 2004.

Schwartz, J.M., *Brain Lock* (Regan Books/HarperCollins) 1996.

Seligman, M., *Authentic Happiness* (London: Nicholas Brealey) 2003.

Stallard, P., *Thinking Good, Feeling Good* (Wiley) 2002.

Steketee, G., and K. White, *When once is not enough: help for obsessive compulsives* (Oakland: Harbinger) 1990.

Tannen, D., *You just don't understand: women and men in conversation* (New York: Ballantine Books) 1990.

Tannen, D., *"I only say this because I love you": How the Way we Talk Can Make or Break Relationships Throughout Our Lives* (Virago) 2001.

Tavris, C., *Anger: the misunderstood emotion* (New York: Touchstone books) 1989.

Walmsley, B., *Teach Yourself Good Study Skills* (London: Hodder Headline) 2006.

Wolfelt, A.D., *Understanding Your Grief: Ten Essential Touchstones for Finding Hope and Healing Your Heart* (Companion Press) 2003.

Wright, J.H., and M.J. Basco, *Getting Your Life Back: The Complete Guide to Recovery from Depression* (Touchstone) 2002.

Young, J., and J. Klosko, *Reinventing your life: how to break free from negative life patterns* (New York: Plume) 1994.

Zilbergeld, B., *The new male sexuality*, revised edition (New York: Bantam Books) 1999.

A Selection of Web Sites

www.fearfighter.com

www.livinglifetothefull.com (An interactive web-based course for depression and anxiety.)

Beating the Blues: www.ultrasis.com/products/btb/btb.html
www.ocdyouth
www.moodgym.anu.edu.au
www.ru.ok.com
www.phobics-society.org.uk
www.bullyingonline.org
www.smartrecovery.org
www.moderation.org
www.drinkerscheckup.com
www.mentalhelp.net/psyhelp
www.chronicpain.org.uk

Index

AA. *See* Alcoholics Anonymous
Abrams, Rebecca, 328, 329
Actions, 8
  alcohol and, 411
  fears/phobias and strategies plans for, 239–46, 251–52
  panic and related, 273
  worries and, 219, 224
  worries/triggers and, 219
Activities
  time management and classifying, 37–38
  time management and important/non-important, 39
Addiction
  alcohol, 417–21
  habits and other, 391, 404
  smoking, 403–4
  will to overcome alcohol, 418–19
Adult, voice, 145–46, 157
Age
  decision-making styles and differences with, 500
  eating habits and, 10, 437–38
  normal sexuality and, 199–200
Aggression, 128
  assertiveness, passivity and, 130–31
  depression and, 287–88
Agoraphobia, 237
Alarms, memory, 473
Alcohol
  actions and, 411
  addiction and will to overcome, 417–21
  alternative actions to, 416–17
  anger and, 180–81
  assessing drinking/consumption of, 406–14
  assessment tree and, 406, 407f
  becoming abstinent and, 419–21
  common problems caused by, 411t
  dangers of dependence on, 408–9
  deciding to change patterns of drinking, 414–15
  dependence questionnaire for, 408t
  dependency, 54, 407–9
  devising personal strategies to limit intake of, 416
  drinking diary, 412, 413t
  drinking patterns, 414–15
  drinks: content of, 412t

feelings and, 411
  health dangers of, 410t
  keeping track of intake of, 416
  managing intake of, 414–17
  managing lapses with, 417
  medical help with, 418
  mind/body and averting problems with, 406–22
  overcoming dependence on, 417–21
  persistence/tracking progress with, 417
  quantity of consumption of, 409–13
  reduced drinking or abstinence with, 419
  safe quantities of, 410–12
  sleep and, 316, 426
  summary, 421–22
  traumatic experience, overuse of street drugs and, 384
Alcoholics Anonymous, 419
Alexander technique, 106
American Lung Association, 404
Anger
  accepting responsibility for, 177–78
  alcohol and, 180–81
  applying skills of assertiveness to, 185–86t
  blindness caused by, 171–72
  characteristics of constructive, 187t
  dangerous double messages with, 173
  dealing better with own, 176–78
  escalating, 172
  factors triggering, 181t
  gender-difference myth of, 175–76
  green/skillful-expression of, 185–86
  identifying personal triggers and, 180–81
  instinctive impulse myth of, 175
  key facts about, 171–73
  loss/traumatic experience and, 331–32
  main effects of, 173, 174t
  making constructive use of, 187–88
  myths about managing, 174–76
  never-get-angry-again myth of, 176
  orange/thinking-things-through skills for, 180–85
  painful, 172–73, 181–82
  power of apology against, 188
  questioning rules and, 184t
  receiving end of, 186–87
  red/heat-of-moment skills for, 178–80

Anger (*continued*)
relationships and, 170–89
revenge myth of, 176
seeing things differently and, 182–83
sharing myth of, 175
summary, 189
techniques for improving red skills for, 179t
trauma and, 331–32, 383
understanding underlying pain of, 181–82
ventilation myth of, 174–75
working on assumptions/rules and, 183–85
Anorexia nervosa
dangers of bulimia and, 440t, 444–45
eating habits and, 440, 441
Anxiety
cycles of, 75f
dealing with panic and, 270–82
defeating worries and, 217–34
living with right amount of stress and, 254–69
mood and, 217–82
overcoming fears/phobias and, 235–53
panic and anticipatory, 279
panic and lowering general level of, 280–81
trauma, fear, panic and, 382
Apology, anger and power of, 188
Appetite controls, diets and upsetting, 439
Arguments, 161
Arrogance, undervaluing yourself and, 18
Arthritis, 110, 425
Assertiveness
aggression/passivity balancing act and, 130–31
alternatives to, 128
anger and applying skills of, 185–86t
balancing act of, 130–32
building strength with, 132–33
claiming rights toward, 129t
flexibility and, 133
meaning of, 128–29
reflecting/reacting balancing act and, 132
relationships and, 127, 128–33
self/others balancing act and, 131–32
sexuality and communicating with, 206–9
Associations
memory and, 490
thinking and being misled by, 508–9
Assumptions, theories, beliefs, misled thinking and, 503–4
Attitudes, depression: beliefs and, 305–6
Avoidance
creating new problems with, 46–47
interfering with life using, 47
making problems worse with, 46
panic, 279–80
phobias and, 242
traumatic experience, numbing and, 369, 370

Baddeley, Alan, 485
Balance sheets, decision-making and, 494
Basic skills
building self-confidence/self-esteem as, 89–103
cognitive therapy: keeping things in perspective as, 71–88
facing problems as, 48–51
learning how to relax as, 104–16

managing yourself/time as, 31–44
mental fitness and, 29–116
problem-solving: strategies for change as, 61–70
treating yourself right as, 52–60
Beck, Aaron, 71, 296, 300
Behavioral therapy, phobias and, 10
Behaviors
avoiding difficulties and observing, 49
safety, 241
stress and, 258–59
Beliefs
depression: attitudes and, 305–6
feeling out of control and changing, 361–65
theories, assumptions, misled thinking and, 503–4
trust and changing, 355–57
worthlessness and changing, 357–61
Bereavement. *See* Loss; Traumatic experiences
Blame
crooked thinking and taking, 79
limiting self, 95
Bodily changes, depression and, 286
Body
averting problems with alcohol using mind and, 406–22
breaking habits, stopping smoking and, 389–405
depression and thoughts of harming, 308–9
eating habits using mind and, 434–46
lifetime habits and, 434–46
mind and, 387–446
overcoming sleeping problems and, 423–33
Boosting, study skills and, 463
Boswell, James, 221
Brains, depression and biochemical changes in, 289
Breathing, relaxation and, 108, 109, 110, 111, 112, 115
Breathlessness, sleep and, 425
Brown, George, 307
Browsing, reading and, 458
Bulimia
dangers of anorexia nervosa and, 440t, 444–45
eating habits and, 440, 441
Buzan, Tony, 462

Caffeine, stress and, 261
Caricatures
change and, 22–26
The Conductor of the Orchestra, 25–26
The Drifter, 24–25
The Ostrich, 25
The Sage, 23
The Traveler, 23–24
Carnegie, Dale, 217
Catastrophizing, crooked thinking and, 78
Chain reactions, decision-making and, 496
Change
accepting future uncertainty and, 27–28
alcohol intake and patterns for, 414–15
breaking habits and making, 392–93
caricatures of, 22–26
climate/terrain and, 21–22
conditions for fruitful, 26–28
The Conductor of the Orchestra and, 25–26
depression and biochemical brain, 289
depression and bodily, 286

depression and two-part strategy for, 292
The Drifter and, 24–25
external forces for, 22
feelings/problems and, 362–63
frameworks and, 346–51, 352–53
internal forces for, 21–22
lighting one candle/cursing darkness and, 28
mental fitness and recognizing ability for, 20–28
The Ostrich and, 25
pitfalls of, 365–66
problematic past and strategy for, 343t
problem-solving and strategies for, 61–70
recognizing ability to, 20–28
relationships and assessing, 212
relationships and noticing how others respond to, 123–24
relationships and taking time for, 125
The Sage and, 23
signs of stress through, 258–59t
smoking and, 401
stepping lightly from past events and, 27
stress and major, 260
stress and thinking about personal, 259
stress and thinking about recent life, 259
stress signs and, 258–59t
summary, 28
thinking/behavioral patterns and, 154–56
The Traveler and, 23–24
understanding present conditions and, 27
Chewing gum, smoking, nicotine skin patches and, 404
Child
attention-seeking voice of, 147–48
common voices of, 146–48
comparing voice of, 146–47
complaint voice of, 148
dissatisfied/jealous voice of, 147
unfair voice of, 147
Chunking, organization and, 478, 479
Clinical experience, 5–6
Cognitive therapy
alternative diary: how to look for other perspectives and, 80, 81t, 82t
breaking patterns of negative thinking with, 301–3
crooked thinking and, 78–80, 182
depression and applying, 301–7
extremist words to watch out for and, 80
fundamentals of, 71–72
keeping open-minded in, 73–74
keeping perspective/help from, 71–88
link between feelings/thoughts in, 74, 75f
looking for evidence and, 82–83
looking for other points of view and, 83–84
meaning of situations and, 85–86
new wave of, 11
practical workings of, 82–86
pressurizing words to watch out for and, 80
reminder about perspective in, 87–88
rules of perspective and, 86–87
thought record: identifying problematic thoughts in, 76, 77t, 78t
viewpoint's vital importance in, 72–74
working on thoughts/beliefs in, 76–82
worst possible outcome and, 84
Collin, Richard, 330
Collin, Rima, 330

Comparisons, thinking, control groups and, 510
Compatibility, relationships and areas of, 210t
Complaints, fairness, managing criticisms and, 139–40
The Conductor of the Orchestra, caricatures, 25–26
Confidence. See Self-confidence
Conservatism, decision-making and, 498
Control groups, thinking, comparisons and, 510
Coping
depression and, 304
loss/traumatic experience, expressing feelings and, 331–32
panic attacks and, 281
traumatic experience and strategies for, 375, 376–77
worries and, 219
Coping with Bereavement (McIlwraith), 336
Criticisms
fairness, managing complaints and, 139–40
stifling, 98–99
Crooked thinking
catastrophizing and, 78
cognitive therapy and, 78–80, 182
discounting positives and, 79
emotional reasoning and, 79, 182
exaggerating and, 79
fortune-telling and, 79
mind-reading and, 79, 182
name-calling and, 79
overgeneralizing and, 79
perspective and, 78–80
scare-mongering and, 79
taking blame and, 79
Cues, organization and using, 478

Day-Week-Month (DWM)
memory and varying, 482–83
memory review strategy, 482
Debriefing, traumatic experience and, 371
Decisions
age differences with styles of making, 500
bad feelings about, 499
balance sheet and, 494
biased thinking and, 497
categorical thinking and, 497
chain reactions and, 496
clashing styles of making, 500
conservatism and, 498
different styles of making, 499–500
energy reserves and, 497
expecting feelings followed by, 498
false dictators/unsettling gremlins and, 497–500
fears/worries and, 498
information tangles and, 498
information-gathering, sifting and, 495–96
loss and making, 333
mind and making, 492–501
myths about, 492–94
not thinking beyond, 498
problem-solving/worrying and, 498
rests from making, 500
sounding board and, 495
strategies to help make, 494–97
summary, 501
trial runs/time projection and, 494–95

Delirium Tremens (DTs), 408
Dependence. *See* Addiction
Depression
　aggression and, 287–88
　applying cognitive therapy to, 301–7
　basics of sleep, diet, exercise to alleviate, 316
　becoming less vulnerable to, 315–21
　beliefs/attitudes about, 305–6
　biochemical brain changes and, 289
　black dog of, 306
　bodily changes and, 286
　breaking patterns of negative thinking with,
　　301–3
　building supportive relationships to alleviate,
　　318–19
　clarifying values/goals to alleviate, 316–17
　coping with, 304
　cycles of, 75*f*
　daily functioning influenced by, 285
　daily-activity diary and, 296–99
　dark filter of, 288
　deep, 310–11
　digging out of, 294–314
　distraction as first line of defense with, 301–3
　experience of, 284
　feelings and, 286
　guilt and, 286
　identifying problematic thoughts caused by, 303
　key questions about, 304*t*
　labeling, 306
　long-term strategies for, 315–20
　looking for alternative perspectives with, 303–5
　loss and, 287
　mind's common cold of, 283–93
　mood and, 283–321
　not putting eggs all in one basket and, 318
　payoffs for, 289–91
　planning and, 298–99
　pleasures in life to alleviate, 317–18
　rating activities for mastery/pleasure, 297–98
　reality and, 304
　recognizing danger signs of, 320
　related chapters about, 313
　relationship between thoughts/feelings and,
　　300*f*
　SAD and, 289
　setting simple tasks with, 295–96
　short-term strategies: episodes of, 295
　signs/symptoms of, 286*t*
　spending time and, 297*t*
　summary, 292–93, 313–14, 320–21
　support systems for, 307–8
　supporting friends suffering from, 311–13
　swatting NATs caused by, 303–5
　thinking and, 286
　thoughts of bodily harm with, 308–9
　time course of, 291–92
　trauma, loss and, 382
　troubleshooting, 298
　two-part strategy for change, 292
　understanding, 287–89
　when to visit doctors for, 309–10
　working on activities with, 295–99
　working on thoughts with, 299–301
Diary
　alcohol and drinking, 412, 413*t*
　cognitive therapy and alternative, 80, 81*t*, 82*t*

　depression and daily-activity, 296–99
　memory, personal organizer and, 472–73
　perspective and alternative, 80–81, 82*t*
Diet
　depression and basics of sleep, exercise and,
　　316
　eating habits and healthy principles of, 434–35
　menstruation and, 440
　stress managed through exercise and, 265
Diets
　cycles of starving/overeating, 438–39
　eating habits and dangers of, 438–39
　eating habits and disorders associated with,
　　440–41
　fatigue/stress/strain and, 439
　mood swings influenced by, 439
　preoccupation with food and, 439
　pseudo-success, 439
　upsetting appetite controls and, 439
Difficulties
　adopting attitude of approach with, 50
　catching problems early during, 49–50
　clarifying avoidance of, 48
　consulting feelings about, 49
　moving past avoidance and facing, 47–51
　observing behavior with, 49
　past voices and marital, 152–53
　recognizing existence of, 47–48
　signs of avoiding, 49
　tackling, 50–51
　tuning into thoughts with, 49
　unwritten messages tied to, 48–49
Digestion time, memory, 488
Discounting positives, crooked thinking and, 79
Discussion, 161
Disorders, eating habits and dieting associated
　　with, 440–41
"Distant elephants" rule, 7
　time management and, 40–41
Doctors, depression and when to visit, 309–10
Domestic violence, 186
"Don't Just Do Something, Listen" (Storr), 340
Double standards, undervaluing yourself and, 17
Dreams
　sleep, nightmares and, 432–33
　summary, 433
The Drifter, caricatures, 24–25
Drinking. *See also* Alcohol
　eating habits and, 438
Drugs, traumatic experience, overuse of alcohol
　　and street, 384
DTs. *See* Delirium Tremens
DWM. *See* Day-Week-Month

Eating habits
　age and, 10, 437–38
　anorexia nervosa and, 440, 441
　bulimia nervosa and, 440, 441
　dangers of anorexia/bulimia and, 440*t*
　diet dangers and, 438–39
　disorders associated with dieting and, 440–41
　drinking and, 438
　establishing good, 443–46
　exercise/fitness/posture and, 438
　genetics and, 437
　healthy diet principles and, 434–35
　helping others with problems, 445

how to, 436
implications for self-esteem/self-confidence
    and, 436–37
lifetime of, 434–37
mind/body and good, 434–46
misuses of, 444–45
obesity and, 435–36
patterns and, 438
saturated fats, ways to reduce and, 435t
set point/metabolism and, 437
stimulus control and, 444
summary, 443–46
weight control and sensible, 441–43
weight/shape determinants and, 437–38
Ellis, Albert, 71
"Emotional baggage," 97
Emotions
    "baggage" and, 97
    panic and, 273
Energy reserves, decision-making and, 497
Epictetus, 71
Errors. See Mistakes
Exaggerating, crooked thinking and, 79
Examinations
    feeling blue after, 466
    review strategy for, 463–64
    study skills, nerves and, 465–67
Exercise
    depression and basics of sleep, diet and, 316
    eating habits, fitness, posture and, 438
    stress managed through diet and, 265

Facing problems. See also Problems
    avoidance, storing up trouble and, 46–47
    crumbs beneath skin and, 45–46
    facing difficulties and, 47–50
    related chapters about, 50–51
    tackling difficulties and, 50–51
Facts, ideas, memories and, 488–89
Fairness
    agreeing/apologizing to critic in interest of, 140
    asking for clarification in interest of, 140
    assertiveness and, 127–33
    building framework for, 134–36
    child's voice of un-, 147
    claiming rights and, 135–36
    clarifying priorities in interest of, 141–42
    clarifying wants and, 135
    exercise for sticking to important points for,
        139t
    guide to good listening for, 136–37t
    listening to others and, 136
    managing criticism/complains for, 139–40
    naming problems in interest of, 140
    refuse to be labeled for, 139
    in relationships, 127–43
    saying "no" nicely in interest of, 142
    saying "no" with assurance in interest of, 141
    self-confidence/self-esteem and, 134–35
    skills, 136–42
    sleep-on-it rule and, 142
    specifying needs in interest of, 140
    stating feelings/opinions in interest of, 140
    steps toward, 134–42
    sticking to important points for, 138–39
    summary for, 142–43
    treating self with, 134t

using body as indicator of, 140–41
using unselfish "I" for, 137–38
Fantasies, sexuality and abnormal, 196
Fears
    adapting strategies to different phobias and,
        248–50
    answers about experiments with, 245–46
    avoiding, 242
    carrying out experiments with, 243–44
    clarifying roles with, 251
    creating props and, 241–42
    decision-making, worries and, 498
    developing "ever-ready" attitude with, 248
    fainting-induced, 248–49
    giving support without overprotection with, 251
    hard-to-practice, 248
    helping others to overcome phobias and,
        250–52
    hiding feelings about, 241
    investigating facts: overcoming, 246–47
    keeping busy and, 241
    loss/traumatic experience and, 332
    making predictions about, 242–43
    most common phobias and, 237t
    no danger, but real, 236
    normal setbacks with, 247
    overcoming anxiety, phobias and, 235–53
    overcoming feelings and, 363
    panic and fear of, 280
    panic triggered by reaction to, 272–76
    planning rewards with, 252
    planning strategies for action with,
        251–52
    progress with, 247–48
    props/hiding behind others and, 241–42
    putting things off and, 241
    real and palpable, 250
    safety behaviors with, 241
    safety nearby with, 241
    social, 249–50
    strategic plan for action: overcoming, 239–46
    summary, 252–53
    thinking about experiment's outcome and,
        244–45
    trauma, anxiety, panic and, 382
    vicious circles perpetuating problem of, 237–38,
        239f
    working out plan of protection against, 240–42
Feelings, 8
    alcohol and, 411
    avoiding difficulties and consulting, 49
    "blue," 466
    changing problems and, 362–63
    decision-making and bad, 499
    decision-making preceded by expecting, 498
    depression and, 286
    depression and relationship between thoughts
        and, 300
    expressing, 362–63
    hiding, 241
    loss/traumatic experience and coping
        with/expressing, 331–32
    overcoming fear of, 363
    stress and, 258
    trauma and difficult, 382–83
    understanding, 362
    understanding and responding to, 362

Fitness, eating habits, exercise, posture and, 438
Flew, Anthony, 138
Flexibility
  assertiveness and, 133
  self-confidence and, 94
Food, diets and preoccupation with, 439
Forgetting
  memory, remembering and, 488
  memory and, 481*f*
Fortune-telling, crooked thinking and, 79
Frameworks
  case examples of past and changing, 355–57,
    358–61, 362–65
  changing problematic, 354–66
  creating context for change within, 352–53
  developing world, 344–66
  disadvantages of living with outdated, 351–52
  feeling out of control and, 361–65
  laying foundations for change with, 346–53
  meaning of painful experiences within, 347–51
  naming painful experiences within, 347
  nontrust, 355–57
  problematic past and changing, 343*t*, 354–66,
    355*t*, 356*t*
  recognizing patterns within, 350*t*
  summary, 366
  traumatic experience and recovery, 371–75
  understanding, 346–51
  worthlessness, 357–61
Frankl, Viktor, 73
Freud, Sigmund, 9, 287
Friendships, developing feel-good, 100–101
Future
  change and accepting uncertainty of, 27–28
  decision-making without thinking of, 498
  worries and clarifying uncertainties about,
    229–30

Gaskell, Elizabeth Cleghorn, 73
The Gender Trust, 202
Genetics, eating habits and, 437
Goals
  time management and being led by values and,
    34
  time management and clarifying values and,
    32–45
Gourville, 224
Grief, loss and journeys through, 328–30
Group pressure, thinking, persuasion
    manipulation and, 511
Guilt
  depression and, 286
  loss/traumatic experience and, 331
  trauma, shame and, 383

Habits
  addictions and, 391, 404
  alternate behaviors replacing, 396–97
  awareness training and breaking, 393–95
  characteristics of, 390
  consistency and tracking progress with, 397–98
  deciding to change and breaking, 392–93
  describing, 393
  developing early-warning system for stopping,
    395–96
  developing stop strategies for, 396
  devising strategies for stopping, 395–96

eating, 10, 434–46
example of monitoring record for
    nail-biting, 394, 395*t*
how to break, 391–98
how to stop smoking, 401–3
interpersonal roles and, 390–91
key facts about smoking, 398–401
managing lapses with, 398
mind/body, stopping smoking and breaking,
    389–405
monitoring, 394
note of caution while monitoring, 394, 396
preparation for stopping, 395
reasons for breaking, 391–92
rewards for stopping, 396
routines of daily living as, 390
so-called "bad," 390
steps for breaking, 392*t*
studying record of, 394
summary, 405
support from others to stop, 396
varieties of, 390–91
Halo effect, thinking and, 506–7
Hamilton, Richard, 15
Harris, Amy, 148
Harris, Thomas, 148
Harris, Tirrel, 307
Health Education Council, 412
Help
  alcohol and medical, 418
  eating habits, problems and others needing, 445
  keeping perspective and cognitive therapy,
    71–88
  past, transactional analysis and, 145
  patterns and recognizing past, 350*t*
  seeking professional, 339, 376
  stop-smoking, 404
  strategies and decision, 494–97
  stress and, 267
  worries and turning to others for,
    232–33
Helplessness, loss/traumatic experience and, 332
Hollywood conspiracy, 195–96
Homeostasis, relationship systems and principles
    of, 160–61
How to Stop Worrying and Start Living
    (Carnegie), 217
Hypervigilance, panic, self-monitoring and, 280

Ideas, memory, facts and, 488–89
Information
  decision-making, sifting and gathering, 495–96
  decision-making and tangled, 498
Injury, traumatic experience and, 384

Jealousy, sexuality, trust and, 208–9
Judgment, burying, 99–100

Leisure, time management and, 38–39
Life
  inner game of, 5
  loss of control in, 34–35
Loss
  anger and, 331–32
  building self-confidence in times of, 334
  coping with/expressing feelings, 331–32
  decision-making and, 333

depression and, 287
dilemmas encountered during times of, 338–39
essentials impacted by, 328t
fear and, 332
guilt and, 331
helping others suffering from, 339–40
helplessness and, 332
journeys through grief and, 328–30
life, control and, 34–35
making new relationships in times of, 335–36
meeting basic needs and, 333–34
rebuilding social life in times of, 334–35
remembering, 330
sources of support in times of, 336–37
starting to adjust to, 333–36
stress and, 259
summary, 340–41
trauma, depression and, 382
traumatic experience, bereavement and, 325–41
types of, 326t
understanding experience of, 327–28
when to seek professional help in times of, 339

Management
myths and anger, 174–76
psychology and, 4
scientific background and applications of
    psychological science in, 12
time, 32, 33–36, 37–38, 37f, 39, 40–41, 42–45,
    43t
Manipulation, thinking, group pressure and
    persuasion, 511
Mass effect, study and law of, 450, 477
Materials
study skills and using, 462–63
study skills: reading, note-taking, and using,
    457–69
Mattresses, sound sleep and quality of, 426–27
McIlwraith, Hamish, 336
Meaning, traumatic experience and searching for,
    380–81
Medication, panic and value of, 281
Medicine, scientific background and research in
    physiology and physical, 12
Meditation, 233
relaxation and, 109–10
Memory
alarms, 473
appropriate strategies to develop, 471
association and, 490
beware of safe places and, 476
chunking and, 478
diary/personal organizer and, 472–73
digestion time and, 488
DWM and, 482–83
efficient review strategies and, 481–82
forgetting/remembering and, 488
forgotten, 481f
frequency of use and availability of, 489
ideas/facts and, 488–89
important/unimportant things and, 487–88
internal aids for, 477
making sense and, 479
micro review strategy and, 483
mind and how to improve, 470–76,
    477–91
mind space and, 489

misplaced objects and, 475–76
mnemonics and, 486–87
organization and, 478–81
organization example: Italian wines and, 479,
    480f
palest ink and other external aids for, 470–76
palest ink more reliable than strongest, 472
portable notebook and, 473–74
practicing skills and, 485
reasons to improve, 471–72
recognizing/recalling with, 485–86, 489–90
relating and, 478
relearning simple tasks and, 475
remembering vital information with, 474
reminders and, 475
review strategies and, 481–85
strategies for improving, 489–90
strategies for laying down traces with,
    487–89
summary, 476, 490–91
35-minute study period and, 483, 484f, 485
traumatic experience and facing, 379
traumatic experience and making sense of,
    374–75
using cues with, 478
using tools and, 487–90
Menstruation, diet and, 440
Mental fitness
basic skills for, 29–116
principles underlying, 13–28
recognizing ability for change and, 20–28
unconditional positive regard and, 16
valuing yourself and, 15–19
Metabolism, eating habits/set point and, 437
Microreview strategy, memory and, 483
Mind
averting problems with alcohol using mind and,
    406–22
body and, 387–446
breaking habits, stopping smoking and,
    389–405
depression: common cold of, 283–93
eating habits using body and, 434–46
fitness guide to, 4
fundamentals of effective study using, 449–56
how to improve memory and, 470–76, 477–91
internal memory aids for, 477–91
lifetime habits and, 434–46
making decisions with, 492–501
overcoming sleeping problems and, 423–33
palest ink and other external memory aids for,
    470–76
reading, taking notes, using material and,
    457–69
thinking and being misled by what springs to,
    505–6
thinking straight with, 502–11
working, 447–512
Mind-reading, crooked thinking and, 79, 182
Mistakes, learning from/ignoring, 94–95
Mnemonics, memory and, 486–87
Mood
anxiety and, 217–82
depression, 283–321
diet and swings in, 439
twin enemies of good, 215–321
Multimedia technique, study skills and, 462–63

Myths
 anger and gender-difference, 175–76
 anger-management, 174–76
 decision-making, 492–94
 instinctive-impulse, 175
 never-get-angry-again, 176
 revenge, 176
 sharing, 175
 ventilation, 174–75

Name-calling, crooked thinking and, 79
NATs. *See* Negative Automatic Thoughts
Nausea, panic and, 273
Needs, loss and meeting basic, 333–34
Negative Automatic Thoughts (NATs), depression
   and swatting, 303–5
Negotiation
 bottling up insults during, 166
 broadening basis of, 165, 205
 building on other's input during, 165
 clarifying during, 165
 cooperation game and, 162–63
 cooperation pointers for, 163
 cutting out blame during, 165–66
 discovering other's wants and, 164, 204–5
 looking for common ground and, 164–65, 205
 looking for trade opportunities during, 165,
   205–6
 lose-lose patterns and, 164
 no-deal possibility in, 164
 plenty-for-all patterns and, 163–64
 preparation for skillful, 164–65
 relationship patterns and, 163–64
 relationship systems and principles of, 161–62
 sexuality and broadening basis of, 205
 sexuality and practicing, 203–6
 skills, 162–66
 strategies for practicing, 165–66
 watching for escalation during, 166
 win-lose/lose-win patterns and, 164
Nerves
 strategies for controlling exam, 467*t*
 study skills, examinations and, 465–67
Nightmares
 sleep, dreams and, 432–33
 traumatic experience and dealing with, 377–78
No
 fairness and saying, 141, 142
 saying yes means saying, 40
 sexuality and saying, 206–7
 time-management: saying yes and, 40
Non-starch polysaccharides (NSP), 435
Normality
 age, sexuality and, 199–200
 interest in sexuality and degrees of, 197–98
 loss of interest in sexuality and, 198–99
 sexuality
  transsexual feelings and reactions of, 201–2
  understanding range of normal variations
    and, 194–95
 sexuality and acts of, 196
 sexuality and finding out about, 194–202
 sexuality and Hollywood conspiracy of
    body/physical, 195–96
Note-taking
 active process of, 460
 condensing, 462

 hierarchical, 460
 reason for, 460
 study skills and, 459–62
 study skills: reading, using materials and,
   457–69
 types of, 460–61
NSP. *See* Non-starch polysaccharides

Obesity, eating habits and, 435–36
Organization
 chunking and, 478, 479
 making sense and, 479
 memory and, 478–81
 memory and example of, 479, 480*f*
 relating and, 478
 using cues with, 478
The Ostrich, caricatures, 25
Others
 assertiveness, self and, 131–32
 change, relationships and noticing response
   from, 123–34
 changing self in relationships and not, 125
 discovering wants of, 164, 204–5
 eating habits, problems and helping, 445
 fairness and listening to, 136
 fears, props and hiding behind, 241–42
 habits and support from, 396
 loss and helping, 339–40
 negotiation and building on input from, 165
 overcoming phobias/fears and helping, 250–52
 perspective and viewpoints from, 80–81, 82*t*,
   83–84
 relationships and talking to, 167*t*
 sexuality and discovering wants of, 204–5
 thinking and being misled by, 506–8
 traumatic experience and helping, 339–40
 worries and help from, 232–33
Overgeneralizing, crooked thinking and, 79

Pain
 anger and, 172–73, 181–82
 frameworks and meaning of experiences with,
   347–51
 frameworks and naming experiences with, 347
 naming past experiences of, 347
 recognizing meaning of past experiences of,
   347–51
 relaxation, tension and, 105
 relaxing out of, 115
 sleep and, 425
Panic
 actions related to, 273
 alarm bells setting off, 270–76
 anticipatory anxiety and, 279
 avoidance of, 279–80
 breath control and, 278–79
 calm breathing and, 278–79
 clarifying thinking related to, 276–77
 coping with attacks of, 281
 dealing with anxiety and, 270–82
 dealing with responses to attacks of, 279–80
 emergency reminders about, 281–82
 emotions and, 273
 fear of fear with, 280
 fear reaction triggering, 272–76
 lowering general level of anxiety and, 280–81
 nausea and, 273

nocturnal, 276
paper-bag breathing and, 279
pinpointing misinterpretations about, 277–78
resetting alarm system related to, 276–81
self-monitoring and hypervigilance with, 280
sensations, 273, 278*t*
setting, 272–74
summary, 282
symptoms of, 273*t*
thoughts and, 273
trauma, anxiety, fear and, 382
triggers, 274–76
understanding, 272
value of medication with, 281
working on thoughts feeding, 276–78
Parent
argument with, 150–52
common voices of, 149–50
encouraging/not-good-enough voice of, 149
no-anger voice of, 150
no-fussing voice of, 149–50
voice of, 148–50, 151*t*
Passivity, 128
assertiveness, aggression and, 130–31
Past
adult's voice and relating to, 145–46
case examples of changing framework of,
355–57, 358–61, 362–65
change and problematic, 343*t*
changing framework of problematic, 343*t*,
354–66, 355*t*, 356*t*
changing patterns of, 154–55
child's voice and relating to, 146–48, 149*t*
comfort zone: creating context for change and,
352–53
common patterns related to, 155*t*, 156*t*
disadvantages of living with outdated
framework of, 351–52
feeling deserving of punishment for, 351
feeling stuck in, 351
framework for seeing the world and relation to,
344–66
help from transactional analysis and, 145
identifying strengths/resources with, 353
laying foundations for change with, 346–53
life now compared to, 346
naming painful experiences from, 347
parent's voice and relating to, 148–50
questions for unraveling meaning of, 156*t*
questions to help recognize patterns of, 350*t*
recognizing meaning of painful experiences
from, 347–51
related chapters about, 156–57
relationships and interfering voices from, 150,
151*t*, 152, 153–54
relationships and recognizing voices from,
144–57
repeated crises arising from, 351
summary, 366
summary of relationships and, 157
thinking badly of self in, 351
traumatic experience/loss and dealing with,
342–66
understanding framework of, 346–47
unsatisfactory relationships stemming from,
351–52
using humor/playfulness with, 353

Patterns
alcohol intake, 414–15
changing thinking/behavioral, 154–56
cognitive therapy and breaking negative
thinking, 301–3
common, 155*t*
eating habits and, 438
frameworks and recognizing, 350*t*
lose-lose, 164
past, 154–55, 155*t*, 156*t*, 350*t*
plenty-for-all, 163–64
questions for unraveling meaning of, 156
questions to help recognize past, 350*t*
relationship, 121, 153–56, 163–64
sexuality and submission, 207–8
win-lose/lose-win, 164
Pavlov, Ivan, 10
Perfectionism, time management and curse of, 41
Perspective
alternative diary: how to look for other, 80–81,
82*t*
cognitive therapy and keeping things in, 71–88
crooked thinking and, 78–80
importance of viewpoint and, 72–73
link between feelings/thoughts and, 74, 75*f*
looking for other points of view and, 83–84
open-minded, 73–74
reminder about, 87–88
rules of, 86–87
thought record: identifying problematic
thoughts and, 76, 77*t*, 78*t*
Phobias
about, 235–36
adapting strategies to different fears and,
248–50
answers about experiments with, 245–46
avoidance and, 242
avoiding, 242
behavioral therapies and, 10
carrying out experiments with, 243–44
clarifying roles with, 251
common types of, 237*t*
creating props and, 241–42
developing "ever-ready" attitude with,
248
fainting-induced fears and, 248–49
hard-to-practice fears and, 248
helping others to overcome fears and, 250–52
hiding feelings about, 241
investigating facts: overcoming, 246–47
keeping busy and, 241
making predictions about, 242–43
no danger/real fears and, 236
normal setbacks with, 247
overcoming anxiety, fears and, 235–53
planning rewards with, 252
planning strategies for action with,
251–52
progress with, 247–48
props/hiding behind others and, 241–42
putting things off and, 241
real/palpable fears and, 250
safety behaviors with, 241
safety nearby with, 241
social fears and, 249–50
strategic plan for action: overcoming, 239–246
summary, 252–53

Phobias (*continued*)
  thinking about experiment's outcome and, 244–45
  vicious circles perpetuating problem of, 237–38, 239*f*
  working out plan of protection against, 240–42
Physiology, scientific background and research in physical medicine and, 12
Pie charts, time-management, 36, 37*f*
Pitfalls, change and, 365–66
Positives, crooked thinking and discounting, 79
Post-Traumatic Stress Disorder (PTSD), traumatic experience and, 384–85
Posture, eating habits, exercise, fitness and, 438
Predictions, thinking and making, 510
Prejudice, 503
  attacking, 98
Present, change and conditions in, 27
Presentation effect, thinking and, 507
Principles, time management and central, 32
Problems. *See also* Difficulties
  adopting attitude of approach with, 50
  avoidance, interfering with life and, 47
  avoidance exacerbating/creating, 46–47
  avoidance of difficulties and, 49
  changing feelings and, 362–63
  changing roles in relationships and, 122–23
  clarifying avoidance of, 48
  consulting feelings about, 49
  crumbs under skin and, 45–46
  difficulties and, 47–50
  early catching of, 49–50
  facing, 45–51
  fairness and naming, 140
  observing behavior with, 49
  physical relaxation and occasional, 110
  recognizing difficulties and, 47–4
  relationships and dispute, 122
  relationships and loneliness, 122
  storing up trouble and, 46–47
  strategies for change and solving, 61–70
  summary, 50–51
  tackling difficulties and, 50
  tuning into thoughts with, 49
  unwritten messages and, 48–49
Problem-solving
  brainstorming during, 65
  guidelines for, 69
  identifying problems during, 63–64
  stages of, 63–68, 70*t*
  strategies for change and, 61–70
  strengths as weaknesses/weaknesses as strengths and, 62
  summary, 70
  taking steps and, 66–68
  technique of, 62–68
  thinking of as many solutions possible during, 64–65
  uses of, 68
  when to seek help during, 70
Prokofiev, Sergei, 74
Props, creating, 241–42
Psychology
  management and, 4
  scientific background and experimental research in, 8–9
PTSD. *See* Post-Traumatic Stress Disorder

Reacting, assertiveness, reflecting and, 131–32
Reading
  browsing and, 458
  closer, 458–59
  overview of, 458
  preparation for, 457–58
  review of, 459
  study skills and, 457–59
  study skills: taking notes, using materials and, 457–69
Reality, thinking and scientific, 507
Reasoning, crooked thinking and emotional, 79, 182
Recall, memory and, 485–86, 489–90
Recovery
  principles to guide, 374*t*
  traumatic experience and framework for, 371–75
Recreation, stress managed with, 266
Reflecting, assertiveness, reacting and, 131–32
Relating, organization and, 478–79
Relationship(s)
  anger in, 170–89
  assertiveness and, 127, 128–33
  assessing change in, 212
  case example, 120–24
  changing patterns in, 154–56
  changing yourself and not others in, 125
  changing-roles problems in, 122–23
  compatibility in, 210*t*
  depression and building supportive, 318–19
  dispute problems in, 122
  fairness in, 127–43
  false beliefs about, 167–68
  focusing on specific areas of difficulty in, 121–23
  guidelines for improving, 124–25
  how to improve, 117–89
  importance of, 119–26
  keys for good, 126, 127–43, 144–57, 158–69
  learning to take responsibility in, 123
  loneliness problems in, 122
  looking for patterns in, 121
  loss and making new relationships, 335–36
  noticing how others respond to change in, 123–24
  past's relation to unsatisfactory, 351–52
  patterns in, 121, 153–56, 163–64
  questions about direction of, 209–11
  recognizing patterns in, 153–54
  related chapters about, 156–57
  sexuality and intimate, 190–214
  sexual-performance anxiety in, 212–13
  solitude and, 124
  stress and, 266–68
  summary, 126, 168–69, 213–14
  systems, 158–69, 163*t*, 166*t*
  taking time for changes in, 125
  talking to others about, 167*t*
  therapies, 12
  trust in, 211–12
  uncertainties in, 209–13
  voices from past in, 144–57
  voices from past interfering with current, 150–54
  working with people in, 125
Relationship systems
  cooperation game in, 162–64
  false beliefs about, 167–68

how-to-cooperate pointers in, 163*t*
lose/lose patterns in, 164
negotiation skills and, 162–66
no deal in, 164
opinions asked in, 167
patterns in, 163–64
plenty-for-all patterns in, 163–64
preparation for skillful negotiation in, 164–65
principle of homeostasis in, 160–61
principle of joint responsibility in, 159–60
principle of negotiation in, 161–62
rules for fair fighting in, 166*t*
strategies for skillful negotiation in, 165–66
summary, 168–69
win-lose/lose-win patterns in, 164
Relaxation
Alexander technique and, 106
application of, 110–11
applying skills for, 114–15
basic exercise for, 108
breathing and, 108, 109, 110, 111, 112, 115
deep muscular, 109*t*
developing attitude of, 112
extension course, 115
how to, 106–12
learning how, 104–16
meditation and, 109–10
mental/physical, 109–10
muscle groups and, 108
occasional problems with physical, 110
other chapters about, 116
out of pain, 115
in practice, 113–15
practicing, 108–10, 111, 114
practicing in difficult situations, 111
preparing for, 106*t*, 107–8, 113–14
routine, 112*t*
skill of, 105–6, 114–15
summary, 116
tape, 110
tension/pain and, 105
why bother with, 105–6
yoga and, 106
Remembering, memory, forgetting and, 488
Reminders, memory and, 475
Responsibilities, relationship systems and joint, 159–60
Rest, stress managed with, 265–66
Rewards. *See also* Treats
fears and, 252
habits and, 396
phobias and, 252
self, 52–53, 57–59
study, 455–56
treats and ideas for, 58*t*
treats and turning routine pleasures into, 59
Rogers, Carl, 16
Routine
as servant, 40
stress and disruptions to, 259
Rowe, Dorothy, 290
The Royal College of Psychiatrists, Physicians, and General Practitioners, 412
Rules
anger and, 183–85, 184*t*
"Distant Elephants," 7
fairness and sleep-on-it, 142
measuring-rod, 86

middle-of-night, 86
100-year, 86, 221
perspective, 86–87
relationship system, 166*t*
self-esteem and, 101*t*
thinking and statistical and, 509–11
time management: tools and, 39–42, 43*t*
water-under-bridge, 86–87
"Russia under the Mongolian Yoke," 74

SAD. *See* Seasonal Affective Disorder
The Sage, caricatures, 23
Salami effect
study and, 454
time management and, 41
Saturated fats, eating habits and ways to reduce, 435*t*
Scare-mongering, crooked thinking and, 79
Scientific background
applications of psychological science in management and, 12
applications of psychological science to therapy and, 9–11
behavioral therapies and, 10
cognitive therapy and, 11
experimental research in psychology and, 8–9
new wave of cognitive therapies and, 11–12
research in physiology/physical medicine and, 12
therapies focusing on relationships and, 12
Scientific reality, thinking and, 507
Seasonal Affective Disorder (SAD), depression and, 289
Self
assertiveness, others and, 131–32
constructing personal reward system for, 57–59
creating right conditions for change and, 56–57
fairness with, 134*t*
limiting blame on, 95
parting thoughts on right treatment of, 59–60
reasons for rewarding your, 52–53
right treatment of, 52–60
time and management of, 31–44
treats: adding pleasure to life for, 53–56, 57–59
Self-confidence
basic insights about becoming more, 91–93, 102
behaving "as If" and, 93–94
being kind to self and, 95
building self-esteem and, 89–103, 134–35
doing things and building, 92
eating habits and implications for self-esteem and, 436–37
effects of low, 90*t*
fairness and, 134–35
flexibility and, 94
lacking, 89–90
learning from/ignoring mistakes for, 94–95
limiting self-blame and, 95
loss/traumatic experience and building, 334
misleading appearances and, 92
as more than just one thing, 91–92
practicing, 93
reflective, 92–93
related chapters on, 102
self-esteem and, 95–101
strategies for building, 93–94, 95*t*
summary, 102–3

Self-confidence (*continued*)
  traumatic experience and taking risks to build, 379–80
  zig-zag path and, 94
Self-esteem
  attacking prejudice inhibiting, 98
  best effort/perfection and, 100
  building self-confidence and, 89–103, 134–35
  burying judgment inhibiting, 99–100
  eating habits and implications for self-confidence and, 436–37
  effects of logical fallacy/past legacy on, 101
  fairness and, 134–35
  friendships and, 100–101
  related chapters on, 102
  rules perpetuating, 101t
  self-confidence and, 95–101
  sources of, 97
  stifling critical voice inhibiting, 98–99
  strategies for building, 99–101
  summary, 102–3
  value of, 97
Self-monitoring, panic, hypervigilance and, 280
Seligman, Martin, 283
Sensations, 8
  panic, 278t
  stress and, 259
Set point, eating habits/metabolism and, 437
Sexuality
  abnormal fantasies and, 196
  age and normal, 199–200
  assertive communication and, 206–9
  attitudes toward/principles of, 192–93
  breaking up kindly and, 206
  broadening basis of negotiation with, 205
  causes of loss of interest in, 198–99t
  considering principles/attitudes toward, 194
  dealing with difficulties and, 193–213
  discovering other's wants and, 204–5
  examples of difficulties arising from relationships with aspects of, 191t
  finding out about normality with, 194–202
  happiness-seeking principle and, 193
  Hollywood conspiracy, normal bodies and, 195–96
  identity and worries about orientation of, 200–202
  intimate relationships and, 190–214
  jealousy/trust and, 208–9
  living with uncertainties and, 209–13
  looking for common ground and, 205
  looking for trade opportunities and, 205–6
  negotiating in practice with, 203–6
  no-harm principle and, 193
  normal acts and, 196
  normal degrees of interest in, 197–98
  normal loss of interest in, 198–99
  patterns of submission and, 207–8
  relationships/performance anxiety and, 212–13
  saying no gently and, 206–7
  self-determination principle and, 193
  transsexual feelings, normal reactions and, 201–2
  understanding range of normality/normal variations with, 194–95

  using good communication skills and, 202–9
  varieties of expression with, 196–97t
Shame, trauma, guilt and, 383
Shape, eating habits and determinants of weight and, 437–38
Sibling rivalry, 150
Skills
  anger and assertiveness, 185–86t
  anger and orange/thinking-things-through, 180–85
  anger and red/heat-of-moment, 178–80
  basic, 31–44, 48–51, 71–88, 89–103, 104–16
  boosting study, 463
  examinations, nerves and study, 465–67
  fairness, 136–42
  materials and study, 462–63
  memory and practicing, 485
  mental fitness and basic, 29–116
  multimedia technique and study, 462–63
  negotiation, 162–66
  problem-solving: strategies for change as basic, 61–70
  reading, note-taking and using study, 457–69
  reading and study, 457–59
  relaxation, 105–6, 114–15
  sexuality and using good communication, 202–9
  spider diagram and study, 461f, 462, 479
  study, 457–69, 467f, 467t, 479
  techniques for improving red, 179t
Skin patches, smoking, nicotine chewing gum and, 404
Sleep
  alcohol and, 316, 426
  attending to thoughts and, 429–30
  breathlessness and, 425
  counting backward to, 431
  counting breaths to, 431
  counting down to, 431–32
  counting games and, 431–32
  counting sheep to, 430
  depression and basics of diet, exercise and, 316
  establishing morning/evening routines with, 428–29
  facts about, 424–25
  facts about pills used to induce, 425
  mattresses and, 426–27
  mind/body and overcoming problems with, 423–33
  nightmares/dreams and, 432–33
  note of caution and, 432
  pain and, 425
  reducing frequency of urination during, 426t
  relaxing to, 431
  snoring and, 427–28
  solutions for problems with, 425–33
  stimulants and, 427
  tackling physical problems inhibiting, 425–28
  waking in middle of night from, 432
  waking to urinate during, 426
Sleeping pills, facts about, 425
Smokenders International, 404
Smoking
  addiction to, 403–4
  applying steps to stop, 401–3
  being assertive with stopping, 403
  benefits of giving up, 400t

cravings, 403
deciding to change and stop, 401
devising strategies to stop, 401–2
disadvantages to stopping, 400–401
freshening up from, 403
how to stop, 401–3
key facts about, 398–401
major health problems exacerbated by, 399*t*
major reasons for, 401*t*
mind/body, breaking habits and stopping, 389–405
nicotine chewing gum/skin patches and, 404
obtaining help to stop, 404
using awareness training to stop, 401
using ciggy bank to stop, 402
why stop, 398–99
withdrawal symptoms, 403*t*
Snapdragon, 221
Snoring, sleep and, 427–28
Social life, loss and rebuilding, 334–35
Sounding boards, decision-making with, 495
Spider diagrams, study skills and, 461*f*, 462, 479
Starvation, diets and cycles of overeating and, 438–39
Statements, time management and personal, 34
Statistical rules, thinking and, 509–11
Stimulants, sleep and, 427
Stimulus control, eating habits and, 444
Storr, Anthony, 340
Strategies
memory-developing, 471
traumatic experience and coping, 375
Strength
assertiveness as builder of, 132–33
weaknesses and, 62
Stress
behaviors and, 258–59
caffeine and, 261
camel's back, reducing "outside" load and, 263–64
changes: signs of, 258–59*t*
changing attitudes, reducing "inside" load and, 263
dealing with, 260–68
diet/exercise and, 265
disruptions to routine and, 260
examples of events causing, 260*t*
facts about, 254–56
feelings and, 258
help during times of, 267
laying foundations to manage/prevent, 264–68
living with right amount of anxiety and, 254–69
losses and, 260
major changes and, 260
notes of caution about, 261
outside/inside, 255–56
performance influenced by, 255*f*
physical effects of, 256
recognizing, 257–60
recreation and, 266
relationships and, 266–68
rest and, 265–66
sensations and, 259
starting with end in mind with, 262–63
summary, 268–69
taking stock of situation and, 261–62
tell-tale signs of, 257

thinking about personal changes and, 259
thinking about recent life changes and, 259
thoughts and, 258
trouble/strife and, 259
upside/downside to, 254–55
weight/size of, 257–58
Strife, stress, trouble and, 259
Study
attitude of project completion with, 454–55
creating good work environment for, 451
easy start with, 450–51
easy ways to work and, 451
filing work for easy access with, 455
finishing period of, 455–56
having fun with, 452–53
law of mass effect and, 450, 477
leaving work environment inviting for, 451
listing tasks before, 451
mind and fundamentals of effective, 449–56
planning/organization and, 453–55
pleasures of, 449–50
purpose and, 453–54
remembering benefits of, 451
rewards for, 455–56
salami effect: cutting big projects into slices for, 454
skills, 457–69
summary, 456
using best time of day to, 452
using short increments of time to, 452
using variety of techniques to, 452–53
Study skills
boosting and, 463
closer reading and, 458–59
condensing notes and, 462
examination nerves and, 465–67
mind and reading, taking notes, using material as, 457–69
multimedia technique and, 462–63
note-taking as active process and, 460
overview of reading and, 458
post-examination blues and, 466
preparation for reading and, 457–58
reading and, 457–59
reason for taking notes and, 460
review of reading and, 459
review strategy for exams and, 463–64
spider diagram and, 461*f*, 462, 479
strategies for controlling exam nerves and, 467*t*
summary, 468–69
taking notes and, 459–62
types of notes and, 460–61
using materials and, 462–63
working with information and, 462
Submission, sexuality and patterns of, 207–8
Summaries
alcohol, 421–22
anger, 189
change, 28
decisions, 501
depression, 292–93, 313–14, 320–21
dreams, 433
eating habits, 443–46
fairness, 142–43
fears, 252–53
frameworks, 366
habits, 405

Summaries (*continued*)
  loss, 340–41
  memory, 476, 490–91
  panic, 282
  past relationships, 157
  problems, 50–51
  problem-solving, 70
  relationship systems, 168–69
  relationships, 126, 168–69, 213–14
  relaxation, 116
  self-confidence, 102–3
  self-esteem, 102–3
  stress, 268–69
  study, 456
  study skills, 468–69
  thinking, 512
  time-management, 43–44
  traumatic experience, 340–41, 385
  valuing yourself, 19
  worries, 234
Support systems, depression and, 307–8

Temper tantrums, past voices and, 152
Tenseness. *See* Relaxation
Theories, beliefs, assumptions, misled thinking
    and, 503–4
Therapies
  behavioral, 10
  cognitive, 11
  relationship, 12
  scientific background and applications of
    psychological science to, 9–11
  scientific background and new wave of
    cognitive, 11–12
Thinking
  being misled by associations when,
    508–9
  being misled by influence of others when, 506–8
  being misled by what springs to mind when,
    505–6
  black-and-white and crooked, 79, 182
  common mistakes in, 503–9
  comparison/control groups and, 510
  correlation/cause and, 510–11
  crooked, 78–80, 182
  decision-making and biased, 497
  decision-making and categorical, 497
  decision-making without future, 498
  ensuring against biased, 504–5, 506, 509
  fundamental attribution error and, 507–8
  halo effect and, 506–7
  law of large numbers and, 509–10
  making predictions and, 510
  mind and straight, 502–12
  parting words about, 511–12
  persuasion manipulation, group pressure and,
    511
  presentation effect and, 507
  related chapters about, 512
  scientific reality and, 507
  statistical rules for, 509–11
  summary, 512
  theories, beliefs, assumptions and misled, 503–4
  wishful and crooked, 79
Thoughts, 8
  avoiding difficulties and tuning into, 49
  breaking patterns of negative, 301–3

depression, bodily harm and, 308–9
depression and, 286
depression and identifying problematic, 303
depression and relationship between feelings
    and, 300
depression and swatting Negative Automatic,
    303–5
depression and working on, 299–301
inner, 5
panic and, 273
stress and, 258
thought records and identifying problematic, 76,
    77t, 78t
time management and experiments with, 33
Time management
  being led by goals/values and, 34
  central principle of, 32
  clarifying goals/values and, 32–34
  classifying activities and, 37, 38f
  designer week and, 36–37
  distant elephants and, 40–41
  end/start times for appointments with, 42
  important/nonurgent activities and, 39
  leisure and, 38–39
  making time to plan and, 43
  managing yourself and, 31–44
  once-past-desk method of, 42
  out-of-control lives and, 34–35
  perfectionist curse and, 41
  personal management as, 31–32
  personal statements and, 34
  pie charts and, 36, 37f
  salami and, 41
  saying yes/no and, 40
  summary, 43–44
  thought experiments and, 33
  tools/rules of, 39–42, 43t
  treating routine as servant in, 40
  using starter motor and, 39–40
Time projection, decision-making, trial runs and,
    494–95
Time-management trade
  appointment end/start times in, 42
  curse of perfection in, 41
  distant elephants in, 40–41
  making time to plan in, 43t
  once-past-desk rule in, 42
  routine as servant in, 40
  salami in, 41
  using starter motors in, 39–40
  yes equaling no to something else in, 40
Tools
  memory and using, 487–90
  time management: rules and, 39–42, 43t
Transactional analysis, 148
  past and help from, 145
Trauma
  anger and, 331–32, 383
  definition of, 367–68
  depression, loss and, 382
  difficult feelings associated with, 382–83
  fear, anxiety, panic and, 382
  feeling physically unwell and, 383
  guilt, shame and, 383
Traumatic experiences, 323
  aftermath of recent, 367–85
  anger and, 331–32, 383

avoidance/numbing of, 369, 370
building self-confidence in times of, 334
building self-confidence to take risks after, 379–80
common reactions following, 368, 369t, 370
coping strategies and, 375
coping with flashbacks from, 376–77
coping with/expressing feelings and, 331–32
dealing with nightmares from, 377–78
dealing with past and, 342–66
debriefing and, 371
decision-making and, 333
dilemmas encountered during times of, 338–39
duration of reaction from, 370
essentials impacted by, 328t
facing memories after, 379
fear and, 332
guilt and, 331
helping others suffering from, 339–40
helplessness and, 332
increased arousal after, 369, 370
injury and, 384
journeys through grief and, 328–30
loss/bereavement and, 325–41
making new relationships in times of, 335–36
making sense of memories surrounding, 374–75
meeting basic needs and, 333–34
overuse of alcohol/street drugs and, 384
PTSD and, 384–85
rebuilding social life in times of, 334–35
recognizing echoes of previous, 382
recovery framework with, 371–75
reexperiencing, 369–70
remembering, 330
rethinking first impressions after, 380–81
returning to site of, 379
searching for meaning after, 380–81
sources of support in times of, 336–37
starting to adjust to, 333–36
summary, 340–41, 385
understanding experience of, 327–28
varying reactions to, 371
when to seek professional help in times of, 339, 376
The Traveler, caricatures, 23–24
Travels with Rima (Collin), 330
Treats
adding pleasure to life with personal, 53–56, 57–59
avoiding punishment trap and, 59
breaks/rests as, 59
constructing personal reward system with, 57–59
frequency of, 57
ideas for rewards and, 58t
occasional big, 54–55
overcoming barriers using, 55–56
picking right, 57
saving up for/cashing in with, 58
timing of, 57
turning routine pleasures into rewards and, 59
unpleasant tasks softened with, 55
varieties of, 58–59
wrong kinds of, 53–54
Trial runs, decision-making, time projection and, 494–95

Triggers
anger, 181t
fear reaction and panic, 272–76
identifying personal, 180–81
panic, 274–76
range of, 275–76
worries and action, 219
Trouble
facing problems, avoidance, and storing up, 46–47
stress, strife and, 259
Trust
frameworks of non, 355–57
relationships and, 211–12
sexuality, jealousy and, 208–9

Uncertainties
change and accepting future, 27–28
relationships and living with, 209–13
worries and clarifying future, 229–30
worries and dealing with reactions to, 231–32
worries and living with, 230–33
worries and recognizing nature of, 231
Unconditional positive regard, 16
Undervaluing yourself. *See* Valuing yourself
Urine, sleep and reducing frequency of waking to pass, 426t
Use Your Head (Buzan), 462

Values
time management, goals and being led by, 34
time management and clarifying goals and, 32–34
Valuing yourself
arrogance and under-, 18
being bad and under-, 18
chef's tale about, 15–16
common reasons for under, 17–18
importance of, 17
mental fitness and, 15–19
no double standards with, 17
not being saint-like and under-, 17–18
summary, 19
unconditional positive regard and, 16
where to go from here and, 18–19
Vatel, François, 223–24
Voice
adult's, 145–46, 157
attention-seeking, 147–48
child's, 146–48
comparing, 146–47
complaint, 148
current relationships interfered with by past, 150–54
dissatisfied/jealous, 147
encouraging/not good-enough, 149
marital difficulties and past, 152–53
no-anger, 150
no-fussing, 149–50
parent's, 148–50, 151t
related chapters about past, 156–57
relationships and past, 144–57
temper tantrums and past, 152
unfair, 147

Wakeham, Philip, 221–22
The Way Out of Your Prison (Rowe), 290
Weaknesses, strength and, 62
Weight
  eating habits and determinants of shape and, 437–38
  eating habits and sensible control of, 441–43
When Parents Die (Abrams), 329
Work
  easy ways to study and, 451
  study and easy access by filing, 455
  study and inviting environment for, 451
Worries
  action trigger of, 219
  bad, 217–18
  banning nighttime, 226–27
  boxing, 227
  building walls around, 227
  calculator and, 222–23
  clarifying uncertainties about future and, 229–30
  continuing with pleasurable activities and, 231
  coping rehearsal of, 219
  crowding out, 225
  danger signal of, 219
  dealing with persistent, 224–30
  dealing with reactions to uncertainty about, 231–32
  decision tree and, 224–25, 226*f*
  decision-making
    fear and, 498
    problem-solving and, 498
  defeating anxiety and, 217–34
  doing what's available with, 231

how to rid ninety percent of, 220–24
influence of, 218*t*
keeping problems in perspective with, 232
lesser of two evils and, 219
limiting problems associated with, 231
living with uncertainty and, 230–33
looking for positive endings with, 232
measuring rod and, 221–22
normalizing life with, 231
100-year rule and, 221
questioning assumptions about, 230
reasonable selfishness and, 231
recognizing nature of uncertainty, 231
related chapters about, 233–34
removing pressures and, 232
self-perpetuating process of, 220
strategies for letting go of, 224–27
strategies for nebulous fears and, 227–30
summary, 234
talking out problems and, 231–32
turning mind elsewhere and, 232
turning to others for help with, 232–33
unimportant, 221–23
unlikely, 223
unpacking fears and, 228
unresolved, 223–24
uses of, 218–19
using action instead of, 224
worst outcome with, 228–29
Worthlessness, frameworks of, 357–61

Yes
  response of but and, 290
  time management: saying no and, 40
Yoga, 106